Administrative Office Management

Complete Course

PATTIE ODGERS, Ed.D.

Coconino Community College
Flagstaff, AZ

B. LEWIS KEELING

Former Professor Emeritus
Bucks County Community College
Newtown, PA

VISIT US ON THE INTERNET
www.swep.com
www.thomsonlearning.com

South-Western
EDUCATIONAL PUBLISHING
Thomson Learning™

Australia • Canada • Denmark • Japan • Mexico • New Zealand • Phillipines
Puerto Rico • Singapore • South Africa • Spain • United Kingdom • United States

Project Manager:	Dr. Inell Bolls
Production Coordinator:	Jane Congdon
Art/Design Coordinator:	Darren Wright
Manufacturing Coordinator:	Carol Chase
Marketing Manager:	Tim Gleim
Publishing Team Leader:	Karen Schmohe
Cover and Internal Design:	Imbue Design
Production Services:	Litten Editing and Production

Administrative Office Management

12TH EDITION

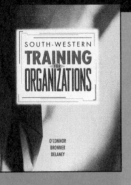

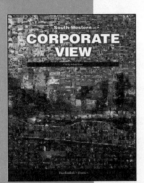

The 12th Edition of **Administrative Office Management** continues to reflect current management thinking with regard to managing office and business information systems and supervising staff. It covers management principles and concepts including organizational trends, technology, and global business ethics. This edition includes more technology-based end-of-chapter activities and focuses on key topics like Managers and Change, Managing Globally Aware Office Workers, Just-in-Time Hiring, The Virtual Organization, The Virtual Workplace and Virtual Workers, Retraining Needs for Existing Workforce, Women as Leaders, Group Think, Teamwork and Teambuilding Elements, Job Stress and Time Management, Designing and Writing Office Procedures, and Intercultural Communication and Diversity. Following the comprehensive textbook package list below is a list of other interesting office technology products for your review.

Administrative Office Management
- Textbook — 0-538-72220-7
- Activity Workbook w/Disk — 0-538-72234-7
- Instructor's Manual — 0-538-72237-1
- Presentation Software — 0-538-72236-3
- CD-ROM Test Bank — 0-538-72238-X
- Online Course Syllabus — 0-538-72239-8

Training for Organizations
- Text-Workbook — 0-538-71122-1
- Manual — 0-538-71123-X

Corporate View
- Text-Workbook w/ CD-ROM — 0-538-72285-1
- Testing Software on CD — 0-538-68868-8
- Instructor's Manual — 0-538-68476-3

E-Commerce
- Text-Workbook — 0-538-68918-8
- Electronic Instructor CD-ROM — 0-538-68918-8

Power Business Reading
- Text — 0-538-69222-7
- Instructor's Manual — 0-538-69223-5

Composing at the Computer
- Text — 0-538-68928-5
- Template Disk — 0-538-68930-7
- Instructor's Manual — 0-538-68931-5

CNN Video: Interacting in Today's Office — 0-538-72221-5

Part Opener
Offers a two-page spread of key topics and chapters to be covered at a glance

Internet

groupware

mobility

part 4

Managing the Office Environment and Systems

chapter 12   *Computer Systems and Related Equipment*

chapter 13   *Telecommunications and Office Network Systems*

chapter 14   *Internet Services, Distant Office Network Systems, and Other Computer Issues*

chapter 15   *Trends and Challenges in Administrative Office Management*

Quotations
Offered by historians and other people of fame to introduce chapter contents

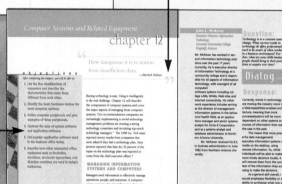

Objectives
Focus on expected outcomes from each chapter

Dialog from the Workplace
Offers profiles of managers who describe their jobs and explain methods of solving human and technical problems in the office

Two-Column Layout
Provides better readability by breaking up long lines of text and providing more white space

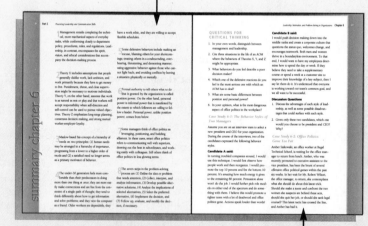

End-of-Chapter Activities
Include a summary, critical thinking cases, chapter projects, and technology-based activities involving Internet searches

What's New?

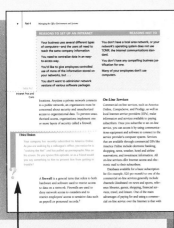

Internet Research Activities
Each presents an office scenario with questions for the student to research and analyze orally or in writing

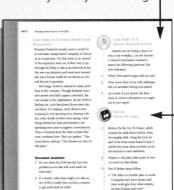

Debate the Issue

Feature at the end of each Part allows students to react to issues presented in several chapters and serves as a role-playing or mock in-class debate activity

Ethics/Choices
Examples of business ethical dilemmas throughout the text which allow students to exercise decision-making skills to determine the proper course of action

Management Tips
Practical suggestions from office managers in today's workplace

Message for AOMs
Concludes each chapter with a final thought and brings together the chapter contents

Other Features

Thomson World Class Learning Course Syllabus
Offers an online course syllabus for distance/distributed learning at www.worldclasslearning.com

CD-ROM Testing Software
Provides the instructor the ability to create printed tests, Internet tests, and computer-based tests

Presentation Software
Provides chapter-by-chapter PowerPoint slides on disk correlated to text

preface

Administrative Office Management, 12th Edition, is written in a practical, common-sense manner and reflects current management thinking based on extensive research in office systems, information management, technology, communications, and administrative procedures. This multidisciplinary textbook is designed to teach applied systems thinking to students pursuing both administrative support and information management careers.

To compete effectively, the United States needs competent technicians, humanistic supervisors, and highly skilled front-line workers. Our economy—one which is international, information-based, and technology driven—runs on their efforts. As competitors on the global front are thriving, the cultures of organizations in America are readapting to their environments on a daily basis. Still, incredibly and at the same time, businesses are being asked to do more with less. To confront these new, diverse, and multifaceted challenges, administrative office and business professionals need up-to-date knowledge, as well as techniques, to achieve innovative and speedy solutions to problems. Effectively managed administrative office information systems are critical to the success of all organizations and ultimately to the success of our country in the world marketplace. Those with a quality-oriented approach and with an eye to global competition must manage organizations—public or private, domestic or international.

OUR AUDIENCE

Administrative Office Management, 12th Edition, is appropriate for college and university students who have had no experience in an office environment (as an office-oriented supervision text), as well as for those currently on a career track leading toward managing an office. In addition, it can be used as a training tool for future business technology instructors. Moreover, users of this textbook will find it to be an excellent reference source for those in organizations whose responsibility it is to oversee information systems.

Not only does the 12th Edition cover current management principles, concepts, and organizational trends, but it also focuses on the reality concept that it is everyone's job to manage office information systems, from the top executive to the receptionist. The text provides a strong, management-based background using a humanistic approach for managing and supervising staff in an office environment. Technological changes in the workplace demand that each employee be computer-oriented with knowledge of efficiency techniques relative to office systems. It is ideal for training and enhancing the productivity of information systems workers at all levels—administrative, managerial, technical, and professional.

THE BOOK AT A GLANCE

Part I

In this opening section, we introduce students to the basic concepts and trends in administrative office management. These basics include a discussion of traditional office management practices, emerging elements of management and practices, administrative management resource areas, and restructured office systems and training needs.

Part II

This part stresses leadership and communication skills in business environments, including groups, teams, and conflict issues.

Part III

In this segment, we discuss managing human resources in the office. These resources include staffing and on-the-job employee practices, as well as work ethics and business etiquette issues.

Part IV

This part features managing computer, telecommunications, and office network systems. The whole concept of connectivity with Internet services and managing distant workers is discussed. Finally, the trends and challenges in administrative office management as a result of new technology are covered.

Part V

Part V covers additional office topics. These include other essential communication skills, employee recognition and compensation, health-related issues, office design, health and safety issues, and remaining office systems— such as, records, copying, telephone, mail, and accounting.

FEATURES NEW TO THIS EDITION

To update and further strengthen our coverage of the office management field, we provide these new features in the 12th Edition.

- **Extensively researched** by the authors, this edition includes new research in excess of 235 publications with 1997–1999 references.
- **Quotation** at the start of each chapter introduces the chapter contents with a familiar thought from a famous person or historian.
- **Management Tips** in each chapter provide practical suggestions from the practices of office managers today.
- **Ethics/Choices** sections throughout each chapter are examples of office and business ethical dilemmas that allow students to determine their own actions, then discuss them with the entire class.
- **Tables** have been expanded from earlier editions and feature "need to know" or "how to" topics that may require procedural steps

to follow, tips to remember when completing certain tasks, or a checklist to refer to at a later time.

- **Message for AOMs** (administrative office managers) feature concludes each chapter with a final thought that brings together the chapter content.
- **Debate the Issue**, at the end of each part, allows students to deal with issues presented in the part's chapters and react to each by expressing their points of agreement or disagreement. This feature can be used as either a role play or mock in-class debate activity.

FEATURES RETAINED FROM PREVIOUS EDITION

We have kept many features of the prior edition which have proven to be well received:

- The *personal, informal writing style* that effectively communicates with readers.
- Retention of *general management principles*.
- *Dialog from the Workplace* profiles of managers who describe their jobs, explain their methods of solving human and technical problems in the office, and provide personal information about their education and work experience. These profiles give students practical information from managers and supervisors currently on the "firing line."
- A *glossary* concludes the text and contains all definitions of key terms throughout the chapters.

END-OF-CHAPTER ACTIVITIES

At the end of each chapter, you will find more technology-based, Internet-research projects incorporating the following activities:

- **Questions for Critical Thinking:** Designed to stretch the reader's thinking, these questions interrelate the content to the reader's philosophy, value system, and work experience.
- **Case Studies:** The first two case problems are designed to improve the reader's problem-solving skills by requiring the student to think critically about the problems and develop workable solutions. The third case problem is an Internet Research Activity and is intended for students to surf the Web in order to supplement chapter material with the most recently published research about issues, products, or services.

SUPPLEMENTS FOR THIS EDITION

- **Activity Workbook** includes six applied projects per chapter. The workbook contains the following applied activities for each chapter: Decision Making at Work, On-Line Research and Communication Work Skills, Computer Activities that include word processing and spreadsheet projects, and a Chapter Case Study. Most projects in the workbook are based on a fictitious company, called International Business Services, located in Phoenix, Arizona.

- **Instructor's Manual** includes a chapter outline for each chapter, teaching suggestions, solutions to end-of-chapter activities, solutions to workbook activities, and chapter test questions.
- **Student Template Disk** contains word processing and spreadsheet files.
- **Electronic Testing Software** offers a test bank on CD-ROM. Through the testing software, the instructor has the ability to create a printed test, Internet tests, and computer-based tests.
- **Thomson World Class Learning Course** provides a Web-based course syllabus that contains course and PowerPoint slides information for distance/distributed learning.
- **Presentation Software** includes a minimum of four MS PowerPoint slides per chapter with animations, sound, and transitions. The slides are designed to provide an overview of key concepts presented in each chapter.

ACKNOWLEDGMENTS

The authors would like to recognize and thank South-Western Educational Publishing, a Thomson Learning Company, for providing strong editorial support through the project management of Dr. Inell Bolls and the production management of Jane Congdon. Special thanks to the Odgers children, Melissa and David, who have unquestionably understood the importance of this project. We are grateful to our reviewers, who offered helpful observations for improvements throughout the development process. The reviewers for this edition included:

Dr. Marguerite Shane Joyce
California State University
Los Angeles, CA

Anna Burford
Middle Tennessee State University
Murfreesboro, TN

Kathryn G. Woolard
Beaufort County Community College
Washington, NC

Pattie Odgers, Ed.D.
Flagstaff, Arizona

contents

virtual

empowerment

technology

Identifying Basic Concepts and Trends

1

Traditional Office Management Practices

> Important principles may and must be flexible.
>
> —*Abraham Lincoln*

objectives

After completing this chapter, you will be able to:

1. Identify the five schools of management thought.

2. Define the three broad categories of skills needed by administrative office managers.

3. List and describe the traditional management functions.

4. Explain the relationship among the terms *delegation, authority, responsibility,* and *accountability.*

5. Describe the four steps in the control process.

6. Define eight principles of management.

In general, Chapter 1 serves as an introductory overview of the essential elements contained in this textbook. Specifically, however, this chapter explains traditional elements of management and its functions, how traditional management is changing, and why change is working in today's business environment.

Effective information management is at the heart of what most businesses do. Information is recognized today as one of the most strategic resources that an organization possesses. Information must be carefully managed because it is not only the critical basis for sound decision making but also an essential element in achieving improved productivity over global competitors in business. The ways in which information is produced and office activities are managed are changing. Management is in a state of transition.

Lisbeth K. Green

Controller, Corporate Employee
Information Services
Intel Corporation
Santa Clara, California

With more than 17 years of experience in payroll and benefits, Ms. Lisbeth K. Green currently holds the position of controller, corporate employee information services, at Intel Corporation in Santa Clara, California. Intel has approximately 18,000 domestic employees working in more than 40 states as well as 10,000 international employees.

Ms. Green received her B.A. from the University of California at Santa Barbara in 1968 and her MBA from Golden State University in 1983. She was named president of the American Payroll Association (APA) in 1993. As a member of APA, Ms. Green has presented both year-end and effective payroll manager classes for the association, contributed articles to *PaytecH,* and served on the certification board for the Certified Payroll Professional and the board of advisors for the Bureau of National Affairs.

Active in her local APA chapter, Ms. Green has served as chapter president as well as participant in many workshops, such as the California Payroll Conference, for which she was the director in 1991.

QUESTION:

Think back, Ms. Green, about your rise to success. What skills and competencies have helped you most? What advice do you offer those starting their careers in management?

Dialog *from the* Workplace

RESPONSE:

Success is certainly a relative term, and I honestly don't know if I'm a "success," but I do feel confident and comfortable with my chosen profession. I have always had a love of learning. I was fortunate to attend excellent schools that stimulated young minds and made learning "fun," and luckily the "fun" of learning never left me.

I enjoy reading and currently subscribe to many technical publications. Even though the information may be duplicated, the nuances from several articles help me grasp the overall flavor of the information. In addition, there's a bit of stubbornness in me, too, for I want to make sure information is correct, and if I see it more than once, I feel better! I tend to take notes on my reading, which helps me in retaining the information.

Another aspect that I feel has helped me accomplish some of my objectives has been my ability to keep an open mind and try to stay flexible. It's obvious how true the cliche "the only constant we know is change" is! I feel comfortable with change and embrace it as a natural evolution.

I also make it a point to meet with all the different groups I interface with at work in order to establish effective business partnerships. I really believe honest, open communication is the number one ingredient in any successful relationship.

It's important to be able to stay focused and organized, and I do that by using a good planning and scheduling tool. Currently for planning I am using MBO (management by objectives) and for scheduling I use a Franklin Planner. I have my time scheduled for as much as a year in advance, and I schedule everything, including my personal strategic time. This approach really works very well for me.

As far as giving advice to someone just starting in management, I would encourage them to:

Listen well. Stay well informed. Keep an open mind. Take advantage of every training opportunity. Always ask "why." Choose a "successful" manager as a personal mentor. Develop a good network. Read, read, read!

TRADITIONAL MANAGEMENT

Management is the process of administering and coordinating resources in an effort to achieve the goals of the organization. Every organization needs managers. How does management work? Essentially, a manager combines human resources (people), material resources (buildings, furnishings, machinery, tools, equipment, materials, and supplies), and financial resources (money, financial capital, and credit) into a productive system in which organizational objectives are attained.

Managers use a multitude of skills when making organizational decisions. *©CORBIS*

When you step into the management arena, you will find many traditional schools of management thought and levels of management activities. In general, management activities vary at different organizational levels and with diverse organizations' functions.

SCHOOLS OF MANAGEMENT THOUGHT

Because of their diverse personal philosophies, administrative office managers (AOMs) follow different lines of thinking in managing the information function. For example, some AOMs view the management process primarily as the *science* of managing—knowing *what* the principles are and *how* they should work. Others look upon management mainly as an art—knowing *when, how,* and *why* to apply a given principle in a particular situation. Like the question, "Which came first—the chicken or the egg?" no precise answer is available for resolving the question of whether management is a science or an art.

Over the years, various functions in the management process have been identified, and attempts have been made to classify the approaches used by management theorists and practitioners. In this discussion, we have divided the divergent streams of management thought into five schools—*classical, behavioral, management science, quality management,* and *systems.* Each school of thought emphasizes a somewhat different approach to management and draws separate, though related, conclusions as to the most significant factors in the management process. Although as students of administrative office management, you may not find the specific answers you desire in the literature of these schools, you will discover principles that will serve as guidelines for any actions you take and as aids in better understanding the information management concept. In Chapter 6, we will expand on the leadership styles that grew from each of these schools of thought.

The Classical School

In the eighteenth and early nineteenth centuries, the Industrial Revolution brought about the mass production of goods and created the modern industrial organization. Hence, it is not surprising that the early approaches to the study of management emphasized the essential nature of management and its relationship to the production process. It was during this period that the early classicists developed the structure and promoted the formal relationships in business organizations. The classical management theory supported two views toward the management of work and of organizations—scientific management and total entity management.

The Behavioral School

Today there is a clear-cut recognition that, as workers, we are interested in more than making money. We have social, psychological, and physiological needs that are of great importance to us. Three noted theorists of this school, namely Maslow, McGregor and Herzberg, each viewed behaviors of workers differently relative to human needs, which will be discussed in Chapter 6. Two main approaches managers used to deal with worker behavior were the human relations approach and the behavioral science approach.

The Management Science School

Management science, also known as *quantitative business methods,* makes use of engineering and mathematical skills as well as computer technology to solve complex decision-making problems. Simply stated, **decision making** is consciously choosing between two or more alternative courses of action. While this definition is readily understandable, the selection of such courses of action—that is, how a decision is made—is more complex. We do know, however, that *sound* decision making depends on the accuracy and timeliness of relevant information upon which to base the decisions relative to numerous business problems. Some mathematical techniques used by managers to make decisions include work sampling, waiting-line theory, and forecasting.

The Quality Management School

Quality management, or *total quality management (TQM),* is both a philosophy and a set of principles used to guide the entire organization in *continuous improvement.* To achieve this goal, TQM uses quantitative methods along with the organization's human and capital resources to improve (1) all processes, (2) performance in every functional area, and (3) the degree to which the organization meets the needs of current and future customers and suppliers. A few of the quality management tools that we shall examine in later chapters include brainstorming, goal setting, quality circles, statistical measurement, work team techniques, and workflow analysis.

The Systems School

In most modern approaches to the study of the management process, the systems concept is used as a means of describing the total organization. A **system** is a group of parts that are interrelated, form a unified whole, and work together to attain a definite objective. Thus, a business firm—the total system—is made up of the following major systems: *marketing, finance, human resources, production, accounting, purchasing,* and *administrative office.* Each of these major systems, in turn, is made up of lower-level subsystems that are responsible for accomplishing specialized functions. For example, the administrative office system consists of subsystems such as communication, computer technology, records management, reprographics, micrographics, and administrative personnel management.

LEVELS AND SKILLS OF MANAGEMENT

Typically, larger organizations have three levels of management—top, middle, and supervisory (also known as *first-line management*). The traditional management model has required a type of organization that is shaped like a pyramid. The pyramid organizational chart demonstrates a clearly defined structure that spells out the chain of command. The **chain of command** shows the authority-responsibility relationships that link superiors and subordinates throughout the entire organization.

The skills required at each managerial level are different. Although the purpose of this text is to teach you *all* the skills that managers need to be successful, let's start with three broad categories of skills you will need: conceptual, human, and technical. Although every manager needs all three skills to some degree, middle managers, for example, prac-

tice human skills the most, whereas supervisors practice technical skills the most, as shown in Figure 1.1.

Conceptual Skill

For a manager, conceptual competence includes analyzing problems, devising solutions and action plans, and anticipating the consequences of decisions. One example of conceptual skill is the ability to view an entity as a whole and see how a change in one of its parts affects all other parts or functions. Thus, an AOM is using conceptual skill when evaluating the need to install a centralized automated system for storing major company records. In making a decision, the AOM displays conceptual skill by questioning, exploring, and probing to see how such a change will affect all other phases of the information cycle, especially the processing and retrieving of records.

Human Skill

Human skills, also known as *interpersonal, "soft,"* or *people skills,* are skills that allow you to work effectively with others. These skills include a manager's ability to communicate, coach, lead, resolve conflicts, achieve consensus, and motivate workers. The application of such knowledge enables the AOM to identify, comprehend, and solve human problems.

AOMs exhibit their human skills when leading and directing workers and interrelating with peers and top management. For example, assume that you are appointed to serve as head of a labor-management team that is investigating a change in work schedules. In this role, you exhibit your human skills by being sensitive to

TYPE AND AMOUNT OF MANAGERIAL SKILLS NEEDED AT THE THREE LEVELS

Figure 1.1

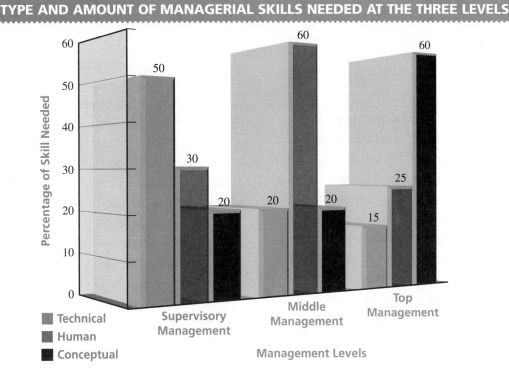

The ratio to which management levels need technical, human, and conceptual skills to perform their jobs effectively.

the feelings and needs of others and by creating an environment in which workers freely express themselves and offer meaningful suggestions for improvement.

Technical Skill

Technical skills are work-related skills that demonstrate the manager's ability to use the technology, tools, techniques, and procedures specific to a particular field. For example, administrative office managers need to understand and be able to perform such tasks as producing reports and minutes, ordering supplies and equipment, and streamlining document workflow. Of the three skills, technical skills are especially important to supervisors, because as

the first-line managers, they supervise workers on a one-to-one basis each day.

Regardless of the organization, managers with conceptual, human, and technical skills must be able to use those skills to perform the functions of planning, organizing, leading, and controlling human, financial, physical, and informational resources in order to achieve organizational goals.

FUNCTIONS OF MANAGEMENT

Suppose you are a traditional manager. What activities would you perform to accomplish the major functions of planning, organizing, leading, and controlling? Let's look at these functions in greater detail.

Planning Function

When a person spends little time and energy planning, this can lead to unforeseen obstacles, sudden problems, and missed deadlines. The result? Usually any time saved is spent "putting out fires." **Planning** is the management function of choosing or generating organizational objectives and then determining the courses of action needed to achieve those objectives. **Objectives** are the end results—the goals or targets that an organization, department, or individual seeks to attain.

Two examples of measurable objectives are:

- *By the third quarter, customer complaints at the reception area will decrease by 20 percent.*
- *By March 31, all new hires will be trained in the basics of the most current version of Microsoft Word for Windows as it applies to producing organizational documents.*

Some key points about planning that you'll want to remember are the following:

1. Planning precedes the other three management functions.

2. Planning is most closely related to the controlling function.

3. Effective managers are generally very good planners.

Planning Periods. Typically, managers make plans according to long-, intermediate-, and short-range time lines. Long-range plans usually cover a time span of three to five years or, in some cases, as many as twenty years. Intermedi-

ate-range plans cover one to three years, and short-range planning covers projects from one day to one year.

Planning at each of the three management levels typically goes like this. Top managers create strategic long-term and intermediate-range plans of one to five years or more. These types of plans usually include competitive strategies, new products, and/or capital investments. Middle managers, on the other hand, are concerned with intermediate- and short-range plans of one month to one year in length. This planning activity might deal with how to improve scheduling and coordination, for example.

Supervisors make short-range plans of one day, one week, or one to six months. These plans could be as simple as how to implement a new policy or work method or how to assign work. Table 1.1 describes some distinctive characteristics among the three levels of management by offering typical job titles, activities performed within time lines, and information needed by each to be successful.

In the past, traditional managers typically developed these plans with limited input from subordinates. However, in organizations that are using the strategic planning process, this trend has changed.

Strategic Planning Process. Many organizations—large and small alike—have undertaken the development of a "comprehensive strategic plan." An effective strategic plan seeks input from *all* members of the organization. The **strategic planning process** involves defining an organization's mission, setting its objectives, and developing strategies that will enable it to

Levels of Management	Typical Job Titles	Activities Performed	Information Needed by Manager
Top	Chief executive officer, president, vice president, superintendent, mayor	Long-range strategic decision making that sets the tone and vision for the future in terms of new products, new markets, new facilities, etc.	Concise synopsis of interrelated, departmental efficiencies; on-demand reports requested for immediate use
Middle	Department head, branch manager, principal, dean, administrative office manager	Intermediate-range tactical decision making that implements the strategies that have been determined by top management	Summary reports and graphs that show trends and exceptions to norms as related to resource usage spread over a weekly or monthly basis
Supervisory	Supervisor, foreman, department chair, lead secretary, registrar	Short-range operational decision making that ensures that specific jobs are performed which meet the objectives of the organization	Detailed, routine information needed to make immediate short-term decisions daily

Table 1.1

Distinctive Characteristics Among Levels of Management

operate successfully in its internal and external environment.

During this process, members of the organization envision its future and then develop the procedures and operations necessary to achieve that vision. The strategic planning process, in reality, creates the future for that organization. Long-term organizational effectiveness depends, in large part, on the strategic planning process. The strategic planning process, which is described in detail in Table 1.2, usually involves nine phases, beginning with planning and proceeding through implementation of the plan. Each of these phases, as you will note, builds on the previous ones.

At some point in your working future, either as an overseer of office information systems or as a team member in an organization, you may be asked to participate in a company-wide strategic planning process. If you are a manager, for example, you may be asked to formulate strategy as a member of the planning team. In another scenario, if you are a member of an administrative office staff, you may be requested to provide information needed for strategic planning purposes. In whatever capacity, your input and efforts will be beneficial, even essential, to the continued well being and growth of your organization.

Types of Plans. There are two general types of plans—standing plans and single-use plans. Standing plans are those that remain in effect within the organization. Examples of standing plans are policies, rules, and procedures.

Single-use plans are plans that are developed and used for a certain period of time. A budget is a type of single-use plan. It is a plan for a certain period of time—a fiscal year, an academic year, or calendar year, for example.

Another very popular single-use plan is a project. Organizations use a project planning process to achieve objectives. To better explain this process, imagine a group of people getting together to plan an "open house" activity for the company's customers, vendors, and distributors. The time frame for planning is short and the team's objective is very clear. How do they proceed? If the team follows a successful project planning process, they will probably answer the following seven questions and move to completion of the project in this manner:

1. Where are we now?

2. Where are we trying to go?

3. What are our goals and objectives and constraints?

4. What are the main steps that we must plan? What is their sequence?

5. When does each step need to be completed? Who is responsible? What will it cost? Will the benefits justify the cost?

6. Exactly what will things look like when we have done a good job?

7. Do we have approval to proceed?

Importance of Planning. Some managers feel that the most important step in getting any job done well is the planning step. The presence or absence of planning usually determines how much or how little time will be required to take the job to completion and to take any needed corrective actions. Planning is critical for managers and offers these benefits:

1. *Saves time.* When a plan is conscientiously prepared and then used, errors are significantly reduced, which results in time saved. Scheduling has been completed when the

1. Planning to plan	During this important first phase, the organization's leadership decides that planning is necessary. They then determine which organizational units are affected and, hence, who should be involved in the planning. From this information, a planning team is formed and decisions are made as to how long the process will take, what information is needed, and who will develop the data.
2. Conducting a values scan	The planning team examines their own, the organization's, and stakeholders' values to determine how those values affect the planning with which they, the planning team, have been tasked. The team also examines how conflicts among these values can be managed.
3. Forming a mission statement	The mission statement is written and describes why the organization exists, what functions it performs, how it performs these functions, and for whom they are done.
4. Developing strategic business modeling	The planning team conceptualizes specific alternative scenarios toward achieving its mission.
5. Conducting a performance audit	The planning team evaluates the organization's current performance in order to understand clearly and predict its capacity to achieve the future envisioned for it.
6. Preparing a gap analysis	As the audit reveals gaps between current and envisioned performance, the reasons for those gaps must be analyzed and understood. Armed with this information, the team can work and rework its modeling scenarios.
7. Integrating action plans	As certain scenarios take shape and show promise, the team integrates those scenarios and proposed complementary actions into a "grand strategy" or "master business plan."
8. Planning for contingencies	At this point, "what if" questions must be addressed, such as: "What if the organization loses an 'irreplaceable' staff member?" or "What if a key facility, like a computer room, is destroyed?" Actions are then proposed to deal with contingencies and still meet objectives.
9. Initiating implementation	All stakeholders are informed of the plan, and it becomes a part of everyday management decisions. At the same time, the organization continues to scan changes that affect it, and the strategic plan is institutionalized as an *ongoing* process.

Table 1.2

Phases in a Typical Strategic Planning Process

efforts of all parties involved are coordinated effectively to prevent materials and energy waste.

2. *Promotes flexibility.* Because managers have a plan and know basically what needs to be done and how to get there, adjustments are easier to make as the process moves toward completion. Task completion can be monitored and adjusted as group members participate in the implementation of the plan. Planning allows organizations to be highly responsive to change.

Organizing Function

Organizing is the multifaceted management function that gets things done. It includes (1) from the planning phase, determining the resources and activities required to achieve the organization's objectives, (2) combining these resources and activities into a formal structure, (3) assigning responsibility for achieving the activities, and (4) delegating authority (with commensurate responsibility and accountability) to carry out assignments. As such, organizing involves traditional management concepts such as delegation, authority, responsibility, and accountability.

Delegating Process. **Delegation** is the process by which managers distribute and entrust activities and related authority to subordinates in the organization. Effective delegating is more than just doling out responsibility. It is after you delegate that the challenge begins. It is then that you must strike a balance between letting go of a project and guiding it toward completion. Hanging on too tightly, or "micromanaging," can smother motivation and slow progress, whereas giving up all control could result in chaos.

The three aspects of the delegation process are (1) delegation of authority, (2) assignment of responsibility, and (3) accountability of results. How does the process work? In this process, authority is delegated downward while responsibility and accountability flow upward through organizations.

The manager delegates authority and assigns responsibility to perform certain duties or carry out special assignments, achieve given objectives, and meet stated standards to some person in the organization. That person is accountable to the manager for results, while the manager remains accountable to upper-level management, who in turn remains accountable to even higher levels of managers or owners.

Centralized and Decentralized Authority. **Authority** is the right to do something, to tell someone else to do it, or to make decisions that affect the reaching of organizational objectives. Authority in the workplace is a tricky matter. People who don't have it often want it, while people who have it frequently feel awkward using it. Consequently, those who have it frequently either underuse it or overuse it.[1] Still, authority is necessary because decisions must be made and difficult issues have to be dealt with. For example, employees need to be hired, coached, disciplined, and, occasionally, fired.

Authority in organizations is either centralized or decentralized. **Centralized authority** means that the concentration of power and authority is near the top of an organization. Centralized authority is, by its very nature, authoritarian. The upside of centralization is that decisions can be made quickly to react to changing needs. There are, after all, fewer layers of decision makers with whom to deal. The downside is that centralization of authority leads to a lessened sense of involvement by lower echelon workers, may lower morale, and certainly inhibits initiative.

Decentralized authority, on the other hand, is in effect when power and decision making are dispersed to successively lower levels of the organization. Though slower in its movements, decentralized authority usually creates a stronger organization. An added advantage is that customers often find that decentralization speeds up customer service and is more responsive to their complaints or concerns because decisions that affect them directly can be made at a lower level. Reengineered organizations today are based on the tenets of decentralized authority.

Responsibility and Accountability. Responsibility is the obligation that is created when an employee accepts a manager's delegation of authority. When a manager shares responsibility with subordinates, however, it does not mean he or she is abandoning responsibility. You as the manager still have the responsibility to:

Authority is necessary because business decisions must be made.
©*PhotoDisc, Inc.*

- know what's going on and how it affects your work environment or objectives,
- keep abreast of important decisions,
- track the progress of projects (or lack of it . . .),
- ensure that "derailed" projects get back on track,
- set the direction of subordinates,
- make the decisions employees can't,
- ensure that people are on course,
- offer a guiding hand by opening doors to clear the way, and
- measure performance.

Accountability involves judging the extent to which employees fulfill their responsibilities. When you delegate, you must also set up controls—controls to evaluate results and thereby ensure that responsibilities are met. Remember that you, even as a manager, are accountable to others for the results achieved by your subordinates. Such controls can be lumped together under the term *accountability*. The subordinate must be "held accountable" for all of his or her actions if the delegation of authority is to be effective.

Accountability tends to have a negative undertone to it, a perception that many workers would agree is well deserved. To say that you will be "held accountable" may not bring to mind that you will be praised and rewarded, but rather that you will suffer the consequences of any failures. Managers must strive to lessen the negative perceptions of "accountability" held by their subordinates, while at the same time ensuring that the job gets done!

When differences arise between actual performance and planned performance, corrective action can take the form of coaching, counseling, or correcting mistakes.

Consider the following eight tactics used by successful managers when delegating activities:

1. *Set goals that are measurable and specific.* Be clear on what you want to accomplish by giving clear, specific instructions. Example: Interview ten salespeople within the next two weeks about their needs for personal computer services from our office.

2. *Select the right person.* Before you choose someone, consider each candidate's interest in the assignment, as well as his or her training, ability, and availability.

3. *Schedule progress reviews.* The way to guide an employee is to establish, at the outset, a mutually acceptable schedule of meetings during which objectives are restated and specific steps taken to achieve them are dis-

cussed. In this way, problems can be detected and averted.

4. *Establish checkpoints or "milestones" for, and with, subordinates.* Whether taking a trip or completing a project, a large objective is best reached by completing a series of smaller steps and considering where you are at the end of each step.

5. *Be available as a resource.* If an employee asks for help between checkpoints or requests more frequent progress review meetings, don't turn him or her down.

6. *Delegate the entire project, whenever possible.* "Owning" a job—taking it from start to finish—is a great motivator. If an employee is excited about a project, less supervision is generally needed.

7. *Share responsibility and power.* Delegate not only the work but also the appropriate amount of authority over the project. Identifying the limits helps you keep ultimate control. If appropriate, rotate workers during phases of the project so that everyone involved learns the entire process.

8. *Keep your composure in the face of mistakes.* When the people to whom you delegate tasks make mistakes, offer to work with them, but leave with them the responsibility for solving the problems they have caused. Take care not to overreact.[2]

Leading Function

Leading is the management function of motivating individuals and influencing group activities to accomplish objectives. For a manager to lead effectively, he or she must access personal qualities, styles, and power combined with the leadership activities of communication, motivation, and discipline.

Given the volatility of organizations and the diversity of today's employees, lack of appropriate leadership abilities can lead to increased turnover among managers as well as employees. What works in an organization today might not work tomorrow. Because of their importance, leadership, supervisory, and motivational skills are discussed more fully in Chapter 6.

Controlling Function

Controlling is the management function of devising ways and means of ensuring that planned performance throughout the process is actually achieved. Frequently the terms *effectiveness* and *efficiency* are measurements used to gauge achievement. **Effectiveness** is the ability to get the "right things" accomplished by selecting the most suitable goals and the proper steps, people, and physical resources to achieve them. **Efficiency** is the ability to "get things right" in a reasonable and timely manner with a minimum expenditure of resources.

The Importance of Control. The function of control cannot be overemphasized if a company wants to stay in business. The consequences of poor quality control may result in irate customers, loss of business, and loss of reputation, as well as the costs of correcting damage resulting from poor control. Customers have a right to expect good quality in the products and services that they buy. The risk of not controlling processes effectively can be devastating.

The Control Process. The essence of the control process involves four steps: (1) setting performance standards, (2) measuring actual performance, (3) comparing actual performance with standards and analyzing deviation, and (4) responding to deviations by taking corrective action, when necessary. The budgetary process is one example of the control process that organizations use every day; the evaluation of employees is another.

The first step in the process, setting performance standards, requires several activities to have already occurred. In other words, you cannot set standards unless overall objectives and plans have been established and communicated first. Standards can be expressed in (1) numbers, such as numbers of items produced, (2) dollars and cents, such as payroll costs or maintenance costs, or (3) time standards, such as eight-hour document turnaround time.

The second step, measuring actual performance, requires that you decide such questions as *which* specific activities to measure (sales, costs, profits, orders), *when* the best time is to measure, and with *what* frequency in order to produce a fair and accurate result.

If, in the third step, actual performance is identical to the standard you initially established, no further control is necessary at the moment. However, step 4 would kick in if corrective action were needed. In other words, if actual results do not equal the stated standard for results or performance, then the manager must initiate corrective action.

What is the relationship among the four primary management functions? They are all necessary, related, and interrelated with each other as shown in Figure 1.2. But to be effective, the functions must be coordinated and controlled to

Figure 1.2

Management
functions are
interrelated.

RELATIONSHIP AMONG THE MANAGEMENT FUNCTIONS

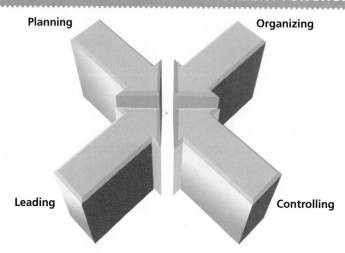

achieve the optimum level of performance as established by the vision of the organization. By way of review, Table 1.3 provides a formal and informal definition of the primary management functions and the key elements of each.

BASIC PRINCIPLES OF MANAGEMENT

Principles are broad, general statements that are considered to be true and that accurately reflect real-world conditions in all walks of life. Thus, you find principles of ethics, principles of sociology, and principles of accounting, to name a few. Over the years, new principles are developed. Old principles are questioned and, in some cases, changed or discarded if they no longer serve useful purposes.

When we group sets of principles into a general framework that explains the basic relationships among them, we have created a **theory.** Thus, the set of eight principles included in this chapter is classified and grouped into a managerial framework and can be thought of as management theory that has been practiced for

many decades. You will notice as you study these principles that many of their concepts have been introduced earlier in the chapter.

1. **PRINCIPLE 1—*Define Objectives.*** *The objectives of an organization and all of its divisions must be clearly defined and understood.* As previously cited, an objective is a desired goal—a target or an aim. A main objective of the administrative office management function is to coordinate and communicate the information activities of each of the organization's main divisions so that unit costs of production may be reduced and productivity increased by a specified annual percentage rate. Here, administrative office management provides a support service for all other functions.

2. **PRINCIPLE 2—*Accept Responsibility.*** *Responsibility for organizing work exists with managers at all levels, beginning with top-level managers and extending to first-line supervisors.* We've already discussed that responsibility is the obligation and accountability for prop-

Function	Formal/Informal Definition	Key Elements
Planning	The management function of choosing or generating organizational objectives and then determining the courses of action needed to achieve those objectives. *In other words,* it answers what to do, how to do it, and when to do it.	*Objectives:* end results, goals, targets. *Strategic planning process:* mission, objectives, strategies to operate successfully.
Organizing	The multifaceted management function that provides the formal structure through which work is defined, subdivided, and coordinated. *In other words,* it gets things done.	*Delegation:* distribute activities and authority to others. *Authority:* the right to make decisions. *Responsibility:* the obligation created when delegation of authority is accepted. *Accountability:* judging the extent to which responsibilities are fulfilled.
Leading	The management function of influencing individual and group activities to accomplish tasks. *In other words,* positive influences increase desired outcomes.	*Involves:* a leader's qualities, style, and power base and the leadership activities of communication, motivation, and discipline.
Controlling	The management function of devising ways and means of ensuring that planned performance is actually achieved. *In other words,* ensuring that what's planned actually gets done.	*Effectiveness:* getting the "right things" accomplished well. *Efficiency:* getting "things right" in a timely manner with minimum expenditure of excess resources.

Table 1.3

Management Functions and Key Elements

erly performing work that is assigned. At the top level, the CEO, or chief executive officer, determines the major work functions and formulates the company's long-range plans and objectives. Sound organization is necessary if these plans and objectives are to be achieved. Thus, top management must identify and accept the many responsibilities that accompany such high-level work. In the same way, each succeeding level of management in the organization (middle management and supervisors) must accept an appropriate amount of responsibility.

3. *PRINCIPLE 3—Unify Functions. All organizations are composed of various functions that must be effectively integrated so they can work together as a unit to achieve their major objectives.* The unity-of-functions principle has the following three requirements. (1) The various functions must be in *proper balance* in keeping with the importance of their contributions to meeting the firm's objectives. (2) A reasonable amount of *stability* in human resources must be maintained. (3) *Flexibility* must be ensured to meet seasonal or economic changes.

4. *PRINCIPLE 4—Utilize Specialization. An organization should utilize specialization to achieve efficiency. The more specialized the work assigned to individuals within the limits of human tolerance, the greater the opportunity for efficient performance.* A **specialist** is a person who masters or becomes expert at doing a certain type of work. Usually such expertise comes from extended periods of training, good work experience, or some combination

of the two. When people specialize, the quality of their work is higher, they are usually more accurate, they learn new tasks faster, and they can do more work in a given time period. Hence, such workers are more productive than those without specialized skills.

5. *PRINCIPLE 5—Delegate Authority. Authority must be delegated to individuals in the organization in keeping with the responsibility assigned them so that they can be held accountable for performing their duties properly.* As previously discussed, delegation is a three-part process that involves:

   1. *Assigning responsibility* to complete a task, which may range from preparing a report to participating actively on a committee.

   2. *Granting authority* to do the job, such as giving a department manager the power to hire and fire.

   3. *Creating accountability* to carry out the task assigned.

6. *PRINCIPLE 6—Report to One Supervisor. Each employee should receive orders from, and be responsible to, only one supervisor.* Reporting to one supervisor is often called the principle of **unity of command.** When employees receive orders from more than one supervisor, they often do not know from whom they should receive orders or what work should be done first. The result may be confusion among workers and a breakdown in morale and discipline.

7. *PRINCIPLE 7—Limit Span of Control. For effective supervision and leadership, the number of employees reporting to one supervisor should*

be limited to a manageable number. **Span of control** refers to the number of employees who are directly supervised by one person. Many large high-technology firms, such as the Ford Motor Company and the Xerox Corporation, have reduced their workforce through downsizing by layoffs, attrition, or other means. The resulting effect was to widen the senior managers' spans of control and thus provide "leaner" and "flatter" organizational structures.

8. *PRINCIPLE 8—Centralize or Decentralize Managerial Authority. Wherever possible, centralize managerial authority and responsibility for all highly complex or technical functions in one location and decentralize the responsibility for all simpler functions throughout the organization.* In organizations with centralized authority, similar functions are carried out in one place, and decisions tend to be made at or near the top of the organization. If, on the other hand, much authority is delegated to lower levels in the organization, decentralized authority exists. In a firm with decentralized authority, fewer levels of management exist, and the prevailing philosophy is that decisions should be made at the lowest levels possible.

THE CHANGING TRADITIONAL OFFICE

Traditionally, the administrative office management functions were limited to basic clerical services and to office personnel. However, the role of the traditional secretary and administrative assistant has changed significantly over the past

few decades due to corporate downsizing, the economy, and most importantly—technology.

The personal computer or PC, more than anything else, caused a fundamental shift in the traditional corporate pyramid. The computer allowed information to be transferred from the highest to lowest members of an organization with lightning speed, replacing the role of middle manager as supplier of information. It also blurred the traditional lines of distinction between line managers and their assistants. The reality is that the secretary, administrative assistant, office support paraprofessional, executive assistant, or whatever you may call this role has become increasingly more critical to businesses.[3]

Management is placing more reliance upon administrative office professionals and well-designed work systems as the new technology creates greater information-processing power. Administrative professionals will see their managerial responsibilities increase dramatically during the 2000 era and beyond. As more and more companies seek ways to increase productivity and decrease operational costs, management will rely more and more on office professionals to increase their knowledge base and take on more management responsibilities. For example, these new responsibilities will include more direct management of personnel, projects, and budgets, resulting in greater high-level decision-making responsibilities.

The "one-department office" concept has given way to a broader, company-wide information or *knowledge management* concept in which the administrative office manager, as well as high-level office support workers, has evolved into a *paraprofessional* who is responsible for an expanded area of work in the information age. To manage office information systems effectively in today's business environment, administrative professionals must approach the task as one that is multifaceted and interrelated.

As technology becomes more advanced, in many organizations, the "who, what, and how" of managing is pictured best by organizational charts that look like inverted pyramids, rather than the traditional upright pyramid as shown in Figure 1.3. Such charts picture a system that has been literally turned on its head! In other cases, management has become "horizontal." The change from a hierarchical to a horizontal organization can be represented by charts with fewer management levels and more emphasis on self-managing teams to accomplish an orga-

nization's mission. To some, emerging management practices are liberating; to others, these changes are simply frightening.

As the more traditional office scenery, cast, and settings are "reengineered," a natural question to raise is, "Who, then, is responsible for the management of office activities and information systems in organizations?" It may be simplistic, but in truth *everyone* in the organization has a stake in how information is processed and managed, as shown in Figure 1.4. We are seeing an increased "sharing" of responsibility for information management.

What students of administrative support and office management must recognize is that workers at *all* levels in an organization are becoming more responsible for decision making, for improving productivity, for making sure that the wants and needs of customers remain paramount, and for ensuring that the customer is well served. The survival of the organization and jobs in America depend on it.

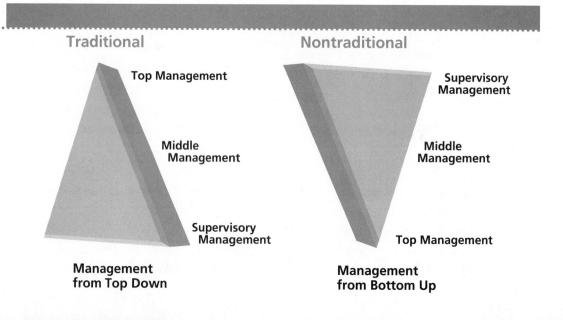

Figure 1.3

Organizational charts reflect the change from hierarchical (traditional) to horizontal (nontraditional) management.

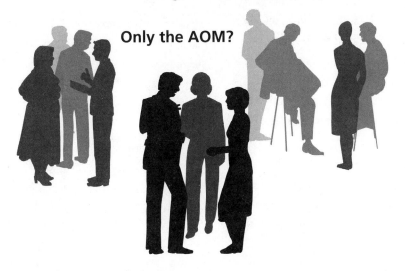

Who is responsible for the management of office activities and information systems in organizations?

Only the AOM?

Figure 1.4

Everyone in the organization has a stake in how information is processed and managed.

Message *for* AOMs

Those who support transforming management practices seem to be saying: Forget the pyramid, smash the hierarchy, break the company into its key processes, and create teams from different departments to run them. The future is about managing across, not up and down. The goal is to get everyone focused on the business as a "system" in which the functions are seamless.

How will administrative office managers of today be affected by these changes? How will AOMs go from functioning in traditional organizations to wading into the uncharted waters of a horizontal organization that thrives on totally undefined management roles and functions?

Part of the answer lies in the belief that managers will not walk alone. They will have help in managing change and in bal-

ancing organizational needs. Through empowering workers and working with and supporting cross-functional teams, tomorrow's managers will find that managing administrative and office information systems will be more interesting and rewarding—especially for those who are flexible and are challenged by managing change.

1 The five schools of management thought are classical, behavioral, management science, quality management, and systems.

2 The three broad categories of skills needed by AOMs are (1) conceptual skills, which include analyzing problems and devising solutions and action plans, (2) human skills, which allow a manager to identify, comprehend, and solve human problems, and (3) technical skills, which are work-related to a particular field.

3 Most managers perform the major functions of planning, organizing, leading, and controlling. Planning is choosing organizational objectives and the courses of action needed to achieve those objectives. Organizing involves traditional management concepts such as delegation, authority, responsibility, and accountability. Leading is a critical management function that includes motivating individuals and influencing group activities to accomplish objectives. Controlling means devising ways and means of ensuring that planned performance is actually achieved.

4 Organizing is the multifaceted management function that gets things done by combining resources and activities into a formal structure and then assigning responsibility for achieving the activities while delegating authority commensurate with responsibility and accountability to carry out assignments.

5 The control process involves four steps: (1) setting performance standards, (2) measuring actual performance, (3) comparing actual performance with standards and analyzing deviation, and (4) responding to deviations.

6 The eight principles of management are (1) The objectives of an organization and all of its divisions must be clearly defined and understood. (2) Responsibility for organizing work exists with managers at all levels. (3) All organizations are composed of various functions that must be effectively integrated to achieve their major objectives. (4) An organization should utilize specialization to achieve efficiency. (5) Authority must be delegated to individuals in keeping with the responsibility assigned them. (6) Each employee should receive orders from only one supervisor. (7) The number of employees reporting to one supervisor should be limited to a manageable number. (8) Centralize managerial authority and responsibility for complex functions, but decentralize for simpler functions.

QUESTIONS FOR CRITICAL THINKING

1. As you begin your study of office management, what in your opinion contributes to a change in traditional management thought?

2. Of the five schools of management thought, which two most nearly reflect your personal management style?

3. Describe a person you know who exemplifies good people or technical skills.

4. Reorder the four functions of management according to the most essential for (a) an AOM with two years of experience and (b) an AOM with ten years of experience. If they are reordered differently, explain.

5. Why is the strategic planning process described as comprehensive?

6. Describe five activities AOMs do that could be measured by either their effectiveness or efficiency.

Case Study 1-1: Not Making Waves

Francisco Grundy, an office worker in a large metropolitan police department, likes his job of ten years, but he isn't crazy about it. His basic attitude is "I'm just a cog in the wheel. I intend to keep my head down and not make waves. If something goes wrong, I play ignorant and say I don't know anything. It's gotten me by so far."

Discussion Questions

1. Does Francisco have an attitude problem? If so, what is it?

2. How does Francisco's attitude affect work within the department?

3. Given the fact that the police department Francisco works for is in the process of improving information management, what issues may Francisco have to deal with in a more horizontally structured organization?

Case Study 1-2: Developing a Problem-Solving Attitude

Barbara Kato heads up the customer services division of San Francisco Data Processing, a firm that processes the payrolls for hundreds of West Coast companies. One of the systems analysts who reports directly to Kato is Ralph Martens, who has been with the firm for ten years. During the past several months, Martens has become irritable and sometimes antagonizes customers. Kato realizes that she should speak to Martens about his relationship with the customers, but for some reason she has been reluctant to do so.

Today Kato gets wind of another "run-in" that Martens had with a customer. She sits back, sighs, and reflects: "I really must sit down and talk with Martens. But I am fearful that he may quit. He handles all this technical stuff so well, and I know that it would be difficult to find a replacement. But, yes, he is kind of touchy. I'll just put it off a little longer. Maybe he is having some personal problems at home."

Discussion Questions

1. What is the real problem involved in this case?

2. Can you identify clearly the specific nature of the problem?

3. Did Kato make the right decision to put off the discussion on the issue with Martens?

Case Study 1-3:
Internet Research Activity

Assume you are doing a report on *knowledge management in the new millenium.* Use the Internet to research information needed to answer the following questions. Key your responses.

1. Which search engine did you use (AltaVista, YAHOO!, Infoseek, Excite, etc.)? What other computerized search did you use?

2. List the keywords you used to do your search.

3. List three of the URL addresses that you accessed during your search. (Example: http://www.ibm.com)

4. As a result of your search, list three items of current information that you might use in your report.

Endnotes

[1]Andrew S. Grove, "Knowing When—and How—To Assert Your Authority," *Working Woman,* April 1993, p. 24.

[2]Tess Kirby, "Delegating: How to Let Go and Keep Control," *Working Woman,* February 1990, p. 32.

[3]Nancy Miller, "Administration 2000," *The Secretary,* February 1997, p. 19.

The Impact of Emerging Elements of Management

chapter 2

> " All things must change to something new, to something strange.
>
> —*Longfellow* "

objectives

After completing this chapter, you will be able to:

1. List five workplace trends that affect the ways in which offices function in 2000 and beyond.

2. Cite an example of a paradigm shift.

3. Relate the concepts of empowerment and cross-functional teams to business reengineering.

4. Name alternatives to the command and control hierarchy in organizations.

5. Describe a manager's role in a reengineered or high-performing organization.

6. Summarize the job outlook for office management and support positions, according to the Bureau of Labor Statistics.

In today's business climate, the operative word is *change*. Traditionally, dealing with changes at work was merely a matter of learning new skills, which were generally just added onto the existing ones. None of it was easy, but it did not require that we completely retool the most basic element in the workplace—ourselves. The new organizational roller-coaster ride can create confusion and disorientation at *all* levels of management and operations. There are no safe havens, no stable industries, and no occupational ranks in which "business as usual" can be counted upon. Workers of today and tomorrow need the ability to change with the changes and even to create change.[1]

EMERGING ELEMENTS OF MANAGEMENT

Most persons would agree that no single company could be best for every kind of employee. They would further agree that even if you are

John M. Carney

Director of Human Resources
Bancroft, Inc.
Haddonfield, New Jersey

John M. Carney manages the human resources function of Bancroft, Inc., a diverse, not-for-profit human services corporation of more than 600 employees. Now heading a team of five human resources professionals, Carney has had several years of previous experience as a director of human resources in the private, for-profit sector in both union and nonunion settings.

Carney received his B.A. in psychology from the University of Delaware. He did graduate work at Temple University in the field of vocational guidance. Carney is nationally certified as a senior professional in human resources (SPHR).

QUESTION:

What methods or techniques of motivation have you found most effective in working with your subordinates?

Dialog *from the* Workplace

RESPONSE:

My basic belief is that the vast majority of employees want to be productive and do a good job. Therefore, they bring a lot of self-motivation with them to the workplace. What happens once they get there to decrease motivation usually involves the effect of the working environment, in particular the supervisory management "climate" of the office.

While most situations are somewhat different, over the years I've tried to follow some basic management principles that seem to help maintain the basic self-motivation a person brings to the job. I try to establish clear job expectations for each individual on my team, taking into consideration their skills and abilities, and making sure we both understand what these expectations entail. By doing this, performance criteria are estab-lished up front. These expectations become the basis for regular candid feedback about performance, a way to recognize employees for good performance and to provide information if corrective action is needed. To me, setting clear job expectations and providing timely feedback form the basis of how employees feel about their jobs. It answers the two questions most employees are always asking in one way or another: What do you want me to do and how am I doing?

I believe that employees want to be a part of what's happening in their work environment. So, I place a great deal of emphasis on the "team" approach. I try to involve each employee in the planning and goal-setting process that affects our department. Listening to and responding to the ideas of employees makes them feel they are contributing and are an important part of the group.

Also, what has helped me to motivate employees is to review regularly the department's performance as a team. When we honestly look at how we are performing as members of a team and openly discuss what is working or not working, we can make the changes necessary to improve performance. However, the focus has to be on *performance* and not on personality or attitude differences. When this honest climate is developed, employees feel that support is available from their supervisor or from the other employees in the department.

I've also found it helpful for employees to understand how their work contributes to the end results by showing them the importance of their jobs to the department and the organization. Here I aim to explain how their jobs or projects fit into the "bigger" picture and why the assignment is being given. Just explaining to an employee the reason why something needs to be done is a positive motivator.

Finally, I believe that treating the people you supervise with dignity and respect is a great motivator. Showing a personal interest in how they are doing and where they want to go—their personal goals—sends a message that you as a supervisor are aware of them and have a general interest in them as human beings.

managing to get it right today, you can be sure your success will not last—at least, not as currently constructed. Things will change, and swiftly. Competitors will come and go; the economy will boom or bust; fortune will smile on you or frown. Employees—experiencing it all—will change their minds about what they need, want, or think they deserve.[2]

A reputation for being a great place to work must be earned anew every day—which requires that managers today must do a lot of juggling. Issues like job security, the work environment, the focus on collaboration and self-managed teams, the commitment that people have to a company's mission statement, and the compensation and benefits program are all part of the whole, and no single part dominates.

In reality, of course, one element sometimes will take over. Then you have to work to bring everything back into balance. That is what leadership is all about—continually managing that balance, not just ensuring greater productivity for the company and its stockholders.

Many of the faces of change have long been predicted: the paperless office, increased electronic communications, the increasingly diverse workforce, management by teams, and managing a different employee—the *knowledge worker*. But until expanding global competition made them a necessity for survival, most managers resisted these changes.

Managers and Changes in the Workplace

Changes in the workplace require managers to be prepared to manage *challenges* rather than to manage solutions. In addition to the technical, human, and conceptual skills as discussed previously, managers need to cultivate, in themselves and other workers, three different levels of *change skills.*

Level one is *flexibility.* Being flexible means that managers can react quickly and positively to sudden disruptions of routine processes. Level two is *efficiency* improvement. This skill requires that managers proactively make continuous improvements to current routine processes, products, and services. Finally, the level-three change skill is *adaptability.* Creative managers are also adaptable, meaning that they deliberately seize new changes in the environment surrounding the organization to create new products, services, and processes.[3]

The change experts agree on one thing: The positive attitude of resilient people is the most potent survival skill needed when facing change.[4] When screening employees' accomplishments, it is notable that managers generally retain the employees who make them "feel good." Employees who can adapt to change maintain an upbeat, energetic attitude while others are in a state of virtual collapse.

At all levels and in all types of enterprises, those who succeed in times of chaos are those who manage to turn the situation "inside out" and find some personal advantage in it. Those are the most sought-after employees for tomorrow's business success.

The Pros of Change. It is human nature to resist change. As a result, almost everyone feels afraid when asked to change. It's what you do with the fear that counts. The technique called "reframing" can be profoundly effective.

Reframing refers to looking for evidence of a more positive, less catastrophic, view of some change. By reframing the concern, issue, or problem, most of us can usually find the energy to take the next step. In other words, even though change usually involves some loss, the resilient worker views change as opening up new opportunities for gain.

The Cons of Change. To be complete, the opposing view of change must be stated. As changes (sometimes seen as inconvenient choices and disruptions at work) continue to mount, this constant state of "red alert" takes its toll on many workers. Workers begin to experience fatigue, apathy, and irritability. Poor decision making, reduced trust, decreased honesty, and a tendency to vent job frustrations at home are common side effects resulting from work-related stress.

As the stakes rise and confusion grows, these stress symptoms can include such severe dysfunctional reactions as malicious compliance (doing only what is absolutely necessary), chronic depression, addictive behaviors, and overt, as well as covert, undermining of the company. Change is indeed troublesome.

Table 2.1 recaps and compares the upsides and downsides of change on organizations and their people. Change and how it is approached, the possible physical and mental outcomes change manifests, and what effects those outcomes have on the organization are presented.

The Ability to Manage Change. Back on the plus side, participation in such transformations may be a more valuable part of your resumé in the future than any specific job skill

UPSIDE OF CHANGE	DOWNSIDE OF CHANGE
If change is approached as: A necessary survival skill that allows one to succeed in times of chaos	If change is approached as: Inconvenient choices or a disruption at work
Change results in the following physical and mental outcomes on workers: ■ Renewed energy and enthusiasm ■ New goals to reach for ■ Reason to stay on the job and be challenged	Change results in the following physical and mental outcomes on workers: ■ Fatigue ■ Apathy ■ Irritability
With the following effects on the organization: ■ New approaches to and resources for effective decision making ■ Better suited to challenges and future problem solving ■ Can manage change and meet the unknown with confidence	With the following effects on the organization: ■ Poor decision making ■ Reduced trust and possible sabotage ■ Decreased honesty and directness

Table 2.1

The Upside and Downside of Change on Organizations and Their Workers

has been in the past. Well-rounded people who can derive satisfaction from many areas and activities may be better suited to solving a company's problems. People who like to deal with ambiguity and those who do not need structure or a well-defined job will be in high demand. Organizations of the future will need people who can survive change and still enjoy their work. Managers and employees at companies who are embracing and managing change in a positive way can consider themselves fortunate.

The worth of future managers may well be determined by how well they manage change; that is, how well they coordinate the application of resources that facilitate subordinates' adaptation to change. Wonderful people placed in no-win situations generally make, at best, ineffective employees. Examples abound. One that comes to mind, in relation to the office environment, is that of equipping the office with all the latest in information processing hardware and software but not providing the necessary resources to train office staff how to use it.

Workers who are allowed to feel incompetent, ineffective, or "obsolete" will probably leave their employment. Managers may neglect adequate training because they feel confident

Management Tip

Learn to view change as an opportunity that will help you demonstrate your ability to be flexible and adaptable. When you "fight" change, you use up valuable energy that could be better spent celebrating the change or understanding its positive aspects.

that they can readily find replacement workers who are already trained. Those managers must remember, however, that with the current rate of change in technology, today's "whiz-kid" fresh out of a technical training course will also become tomorrow's obsolete worker unless his or her skills are constantly updated and expanded. Trying to glean new skills from a high rate of turnover is a self-defeating process. Managers who resort to this method are operating in a reactive, rather than a proactive, mode.

Paradigm Shifts. A **paradigm** is defined as a set of assumptions or a frame of reference. One definition of **paradigm shift** is a fundamental change in the assumptions we make about a certain body of knowledge. Simply put, this concept means that people will go for years believing one thing—for example, that the typewriter is necessary in any office, despite mounting evidence to the contrary. When all of a sudden they notice the conflicting evidence, change their minds, and wonder why they continued to believe otherwise, a paradigm shift occurred in this instance.

What is happening in this high-tech and networked business world is that many people and corporations are going through paradigm shifts, where the accepted "reality" of their

world is changing. Numerous examples exist of new realities some businesses are facing: some are losing their share of customers, while others are finding that workers' attitudes about authority and control are different from those of a few years earlier. Some businesses make the transition required of these paradigm shifts; others do not and are simply out of the race.

To further clarify a paradigm shift related to office information systems, suppose you are a business owner. As a business owner, you embrace the common belief that investing in technology will increase your business's productivity and reduce paper within the office. Unfortunately, researchers seeking relationships between office technology and productivity have uncovered some nasty surprises, which indicate that a hefty investment in such technology has not always yielded a comparable improvement on bottom lines. You are at first skeptical of this new information, but eventually realize it is valid.

The reason technology has failed to produce becomes painfully obvious: technology alone does not improve productivity. Using a personal computer to type letters, crunch numbers, or lay out pages certainly saves time, but automating a single task in a business process does just that—automates one small piece of a process that may include dozens of inefficient steps. The additional use of this technology is not an instant cure for paper-management problems. You realize that you must gear yourself to manage *all* operations of the system more effectively, not simply spend more money to find a "miracle cure."

Paradigm shifts, then, are not simply a matter of buying into the latest innovations. Businesses are beginning to recognize this shortsightedness. As a result, many are effecting gains in productivity by redesigning entire critical business processes and, when applicable, using technology to support that new design. Paradigm shifts, if recognized and embraced by management and workers alike, can keep organizations abreast of change and ahead of competition.

Managers in Changed Organizations

As previously discussed, the familiar management hierarchy depicted on organizational charts as a pyramid was a formal diagram that showed how work was divided and, most importantly, who reported to whom. But that mentality, which worked so beautifully a century ago, has become self-destructive these days.

Few business leaders really foresaw the changes that occurred in the early 1990s, such as the cutthroat competition, the emergence of a more skilled and educated workforce, and fancy technologies that do everything faster and smarter. A paradigm shift occurring in workplaces today involves reorganizing the organizational chart. The pyramid is passé; wheels, clusters, and inverted pyramids are increasing in popularity.

Business Reengineering, Empowerment, and Work Teams.

In 1993, Michael Hammer and James Champy's book entitled *Reengineering the Corporation* told businesses about the benefits of the new managerial idea called reengineering. This powerful concept professed that, when properly applied, reengineering allowed companies to do much more with far less—less investment, less time, fewer people. **Reengineering** is a name for the stem-to-stern redesign of the way a company works, from its organizational structure to its corporate culture.

Business reengineering is not about fixing anything. Business reengineering means starting all over, starting from scratch. Old job titles and old organizational arrangements—departments, divisions, groups, and so on—cease to matter. What matters is how best to organize work, given the demands of today's markets and the power of today's technologies.

Reengineering, then, is the fundamental rethinking and radical redesign of business processes to achieve dramatic improvements in measures of performance such as cost, quality, service, and speed. Reengineering is about making quantum leaps in performance, not marginal or incremental improvements.

Many would question in this era of the new millennium, just how effective reengineering attempts have been. We will discuss that very important issue shortly, but first, let's look at how reengineering works. Two principal concepts underlie the successfully reengineered company: the empowerment of employees and the use of cross-functional teams.

Empowerment means giving employees closest to the customer the authority and tools needed to make more decisions. Empowerment is founded on the belief that the person doing the job knows better than anyone else the best way to do the job and how to improve job performance. As a result, empowerment utilizes a worker's abilities and potential to a much greater extent, while cutting costs and serving customers better. This eliminates the need for customers to be shifted from one employee to another, speeds decision making, and decreases mistakes.

Does empowerment improve a company's bottom line by giving employees the freedom to make decisions and treating them as partners? According to Barbara Ettorre in a 1997 *HR Focus* article, she asserts that for employee empowerment to succeed, it must be measurable and directly linked to strategic goals and processes, as well as to individual accountability. Comprehensive measures for evaluating accountability and assessing strategy are therefore important. Other elements that have been found in successful empowerment programs are

Empowerment solves problems with customers when they occur.
©*PhotoDisc, Inc.*

stable leadership at the top, emphasis on innovation at all levels, few layoffs, profit sharing, and power sharing schemes.[5]

Another reengineering approach is to use **cross-functional teams** of disparate employees working together in a way that makes them aware of changes that may affect their jobs. These teams, based around task relevance, can propel organizations to new levels of success by increasing employee enthusiasm, involvement, cooperation, and commitment to success.[6]

For example, suppose the organization wanted to develop a new product line or new service. With cross-functional teams, workers from marketing, manufacturing, human resources, and administration would share information and ideas and follow this new idea from start to finish.

Do cross-functional teams work? In general, research suggests they do; however, there is one cautionary drawback. If team members work repeatedly with each other over a period of time, their problem-solving abilities appear to become limited. It is suggested, therefore, that companies reorganize periodically into new teams based on new task relevance.[7]

As with most new ideas, reengineering at first was thought to be the only way to improve the organization's productivity and resulting bottom line. Increasingly, however, there is controversy regarding its total effectiveness in delivering the results organizations want and need today.

In 1995, Champy, one of the original two authors who introduced reengineering to the business world, publicly stated that he felt reengineering was in trouble. He concluded that the key problem was not the concept or its application, but rather management. According to Champy, managers, by and large, are not changing the way they do their jobs in order for operational work to be reengineered.[8]

In a 1998 *Business Week* article, Aaron Bernstein recapped the difficulties of carrying out reengineering in an environment of competition, mergers, and profit-hungry investors.[9] As a sequel to these issues, the question has been asked, "Is downsizing in a reengineered organization bad for business?" Is there a relationship between a shortage of employees who have good work ethics and are loyal and reengineering and downsizing efforts? Some would argue that reengineering and downsizing have weakened the ties that spur employee commitment and productivity.[10]

Alternatives to the Command-and-Control Hierarchy.

As illustrated in Figure 2.1, some of the imaginative alternatives to the pyramid style of organization that are currently surfacing are as follows:

1. The *inverted pyramid,* created by the retailer Nordstrom's, literally turns the traditional organizational structure upside down. This organizational structure is relatively flat. There are only a few levels, with salespeople and sales support people on top, making the key decisions. There is, in fact, only one formal rule at Nordstrom's that employees are expected to honor: Use your own best judgment at all times. The company believes that salespeople should pay more attention to their customers' needs than to their bosses' needs.

Cross-functional teams allow workers to share information.   ©*CORBIS*

2. The *cluster* organization brings groups of people from different disciplines together to work on a semipermanent basis. In a cluster organization, groups are arranged like bunches of grapes on a corporate vine; the vine is the corporate vision that connects one group—a bunch of people working together—to another.[11]

3. The *wagon wheel* is another organizational chart redesign. This circular chart has three main parts—the hub of the wheel; a series of spokes, which radiate from the hub; and, finally, the outer rim. Customers are the center hub. The spokes could be the business functions such as finance, marketing, or engineering or they could be teams dedicated to working on new product development or customer satisfaction. Keeping it all together on the outer rim are the chief executive and board, who are placed there to make sure

Figure 2.1

Three alternatives to the command and control hierarchy.

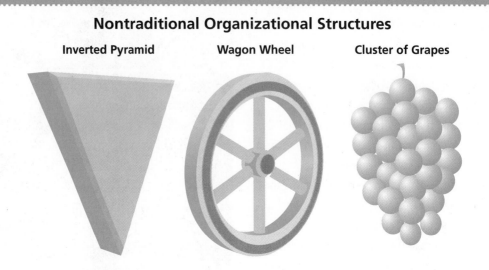

Nontraditional Organizational Structures

Inverted Pyramid   **Wagon Wheel**   **Cluster of Grapes**

everybody has, at his or her fingertips, everything needed to serve the customer. In this organizational design, managers are coaches and supporters, not authoritarian whip-crackers.

When wagon-wheel companies create new business lines, they sometimes sprout satellites from the original nucleus. W. L. Gore & Associates, makers of Gore-Tex fabrics, introduced this form of organization more than 30 years ago. Organized around opportunities, where teams evolve and leaders emerge, founders Bill and Vieve Gore empowered their associates in 1958 through freedom. To foster a creative and energizing work environment, Bill Gore proposed four principles to guide Gore Associates:

1. Everyone try to be fair.

2. Everyone encourage, help, and allow other associates to grow in knowledge, skill, and scope of activity and responsibility.

3. Everyone make his own commitments—and keep them.

4. Everyone consult with other associates before taking actions that may be "below the water line." (Interpretation: *a unique, but nontraditional, creative approach*)

Other characteristics of the "lattice" organization that the founders envisioned included:

1. no fixed or assigned authority (sponsors, not bosses),

2. natural leadership defined by natural followership,

3. objectives established by consensus,

4. person-to-person communication encouraged, and

5. tasks and functions organized by commitments.

The result is a culture that fosters innovation and business success. Today W. L. Gore &

Associates is as well known for its unique corporate culture as it is for its innovative products and has repeatedly been named one of the 100 Best Companies to Work For in America.[12]

Each of these newfangled organizational types has its cadre of supporters, those who claim that their pet design is the once-and-for-all cure for all that ails a company. Not true. Without the right mind-set, supporting measures, rewards, and management (and sometimes the absence of management), any type of organization is doomed.

But if you do it right, redesigning an organization can be hugely effective in harnessing the intelligence that resides within it. Reengineering is not the same as reorganizing, delayering, or flattening the organization, although reengineering may, in fact, produce a flatter organization.

The Horizontal Organization. Entrenched bureaucracy can be seen in the typical vertical organization, a company where staffers look up to bosses instead of out to customers. And even after these companies undergo all the cutting, downsizing, and delayering designed to streamline such a company's operations, too many layers of management still slow decision making and lead to high coordination costs.

In the quest for greater efficiency and productivity, corporate America's biggest names have redrawn their hierarchical organizational charts. The trend is toward flatter, **horizontal organizations** in which managing "across" has become more critical than managing "up and down" in a top-heavy hierarchy.

In its purest state, the horizontal organization might boast a skeleton group of senior executives at the top in such traditional support functions as finance and human resources. But virtually everyone else in the organization would work together in cross-functional teams that perform core processes, such as product development or sales generation. The upshot: The organization might have only three or four layers of management between the chairperson and the staffers in a given process.

As the concept of horizontal organizations has taken hold, aspects of organizational life, as we know it now, have been altered. Self-managing, quick performance teams have become the building blocks of the new organization. Performance objectives are linked to customer satisfaction rather than profitability or shareholder value. Moreover, many workers are now rewarded not only for individual performance but also for the development of their skills and for team performance.

Gaining quantum leaps in performance requires rethinking the way work gets done. To do that, some companies are risking flattening out. Presented in Table 2.2 are seven key elements that characterize horizontal corporations.

Given all the emerging elements so far discussed in Chapter 2, it may be a good idea to construct a description of a high-performing organization.

High-Performing Organizations

In a 1998 book entitled *Pathways to Performance,* Canadian author and organizational expert Jim Clemmer states that high-performing organizations are thriving in today's chaotic world as they adapt and pioneer a wide variety of highly decentralized structures. These organizations are

Element	How to Implement
1. Build around process, not task	Eliminate all activities that fail to add value or contribute to key objectives.
2. Flatten levels in the hierarchy	Reduce supervision and combine fragmented tasks. Use as few teams as possible to perform an entire process.
3. Use teams extensively to manage	Limit supervisory roles by making the team manage itself within a common purpose.
4. Allow customers to drive performance	Make customer satisfaction—not stock appreciation or profitability—the primary measure of performance. (The profits will come and stock will rise if the customers are satisfied.)
5. Recognize team performance	Encourage and reward team members who develop multiple skills rather than specialized know-how.
6. Optimize supplier and customer contact	Encourage employees to enter into direct, regular contact with suppliers and customers.
7. Inform and train all employees	Empower employees with authority and information to make decisions and achieve goals.

Table 2.2

Seven Key Elements of Horizontal Corporations

giving up control of people so that people can control their own and their organization's destiny. In addition to some of the structures mentioned in Chapter 1, like clusters and inverted pyramids, other organizational descriptors include network, shamrock, flat, modular, starburst, pancake, and virtual. Whatever the names given to define organizational structure, as top organizations grow, they will shed a variety of structures and models to suit their changing circumstances and be characterized as follows:

- *Intense customer and market focus.* Field people and hands-on senior managers drive the organization in daily contact with customers and partners.

- *Team-based.* A multitude of operational teams manage whole systems or self-contained subsystems such as regions, branches, processes, and complete business units.

- *Highly autonomous and decentralized.* For example, local teams take it upon themselves to adjust their company's product and service mix to suit their market and conditions.

- *Networks, partnerships, and alliances.* Learning how to partner with other teams or organizations is fast becoming a critical performance skill.

- *Fewer and more focused staff professionals.* Accountants, human resource professionals, purchasing managers, and the like are either on an operational team or they sell their services to a number of teams.

- *Fewer management levels.* Spans of control stretch into dozens and even hundreds of people (organized in self-managing teams) responsible to one manager.
- *One customer contact point.* Continuity with the customer is maintained by an unchanging small group of individuals.[13]

THE ROLE OF THE ADMINISTRATIVE OFFICE MANAGER

In addition to continuing to effectively organize and administer limited resources (such as capital, human, physical, and information), the office professional must also learn and apply new approaches to organizational efficiency and increased productivity. To help create and maintain world-class organizations in era 2000 and beyond, administrative office managers must be familiar with and be adept at putting into practice the following workplace approaches and trends:

- Teaming in a collaborative work environment which uses networks, groupware, and data communications technology
- Performing work tasks that are shifting in nature from clerical to paraprofessional
- Using more broad, general skills rather than skills which are narrow in scope
- Becoming a knowledge worker who is highly self-reliant instead of a worker who is dependent on others
- Developing into a worker who is capable of effectively tracking and measuring his or her own on-the-job quality, productivity, and performance

Though formidable, these trends neither negate nor minimize the importance of other current concepts that also greatly influence how office work is performed in today's workplace. These concepts include change, customer service first, cultural diversity issues, empowerment, total quality management with continuous improvement, and global competitiveness.

Figure 2.2 illustrates how complimentary, yet at times divergent, aspects of an office professional's job resemble one of refitting the puzzle pieces together in different ways.

Whereas a comprehensive discussion has been or will be given to each piece of the puzzle in the text, Chapter 2 attempts to synthesize the modern role of managing office information systems by connecting the many diverse functions of that job in an organizational framework that is ever-changing.

Organizational Framework for Administrative Support Occupations

The Vocational-Technical Education Consortium of States (V-TECS) and International Association of Administrative Professionals (IAAP) recently surveyed 1,000 secretaries by using an occupational inventory of skills to identify national skills and performance standards for the field. The findings, which identify the knowledge, behaviors, and skill areas that serve as an organizational framework for administrative support standards, follow.

- *Occupation-specific knowledge,* which includes the application of communication and mathematics skills in the performance of tasks.
- *Workplace behaviors,* which include
  1. Work ethics—such as dependability, confidentiality, initiative, and enthusiasm for

Figure 2.2

The management of money, people, facilities, and information is greatly influenced by emerging workplace concepts, approaches, and trends.

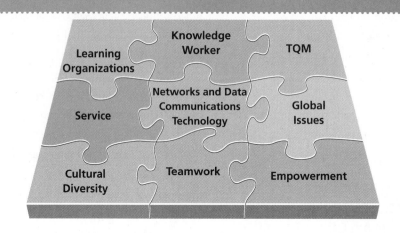

new tasks, ethical decision making, and continuing education.

2. Interpersonal relationships—such as respect for individual diversity, giving and responding to constructive criticism or praise, conflict resolution, and a positive attitude.

3. Teamwork—such as organizing workloads, setting priorities, evaluating options, and understanding interactive relationships for effective teamwork.

4. Problem solving and critical thinking skills.

- *Technical skills,* which are comprised of the following core skills and occupation-specific skills:

1. Core skills include organizing, planning, maintaining equipment/supplies, performing financial functions, managing records and files, communications, document pro-

duction using computers, information distribution, and desktop publishing.

2. Occupation-specific skills include supervising personnel and preparing legal and medical documents.[14]

Companies Transforming into Learning Organizations

As more organizations become knowledge-based, they realize how important continuous or lifelong learning can be to their overall success. It is, therefore, essential that organizations promote and capture learning at the individual, team, and organizational levels. That need has fueled considerable interest in the concept of the learning organization. How AOMs perform their roles is indirectly determined by the organization's commitment to the "learning organization" concept.

Within a **learning organization,** training is central to actual work. Learning is emerging as a *by-product* of work rather than something done in isolation. In a learning organization, learning is the daily responsibility of line managers and work teams; the work itself becomes the primary learning process. A learning organization includes these characteristics:

- A climate that encourages, rewards, and enhances individual and collective learning.
- A view that mistakes and failures are learning opportunities.
- A widely available and unlimited access to information and resources.
- A desire for continuous improvement and renewal.
- Learning which is integrated with and a part of everyday work.
- Opportunities for open dialogue and inquiry.[15]

Responsibilities of the AOM

The scope and responsibilities of the AOM are identified in this section, and each of the managerial functions is analyzed as it applies to office activities. The logical sequence of these functions and their related activities are shown in Table 2.3.

Although similarities exist in the job content, no two AOMs have exactly the same job responsibilities. For example, in a small- to medium-size firm, the AOM is often an accountant who works closely with one of the newest and crucial departments in most organizations today—the **information technology (IT) department.** An IT department has overall responsibility for the manner in which networked computers, information technology equipment, and software are used throughout the organization.

The differences in responsibilities assigned to AOMs are due to several factors, the most important of which is the size of the organization and how it is structured. In a medium- to large-size organization, an AOM directs the volume of services where the collection,

MANAGERIAL FUNCTION	OFFICE ACTIVITIES
Planning	Developing policies and objectives for the various information-processing services, such as communications, records management, etc.
Organizing	Applying basic principles of organization in determining the working relationships among employees.
Leading	Directing and supervising effectively the office activities and promoting static-free communication lines between employees and employer.
Controlling	Developing, installing, and improving administrative office systems and procedures to be followed when completing each major phase of office work.

Table 2.3

Managerial Functions and Related Office Activities

production, manipulation, and dissemination of
information are the main responsibilities of the
office staff.

Activities Performed by the AOM

Administrative activities are numerous but have
primarily included being responsible for (and
being given commensurate authority to ensure)
timely and efficient processing of documents,
preparing and administering budgets, monitoring policies and procedures, and maintaining
the stability of the administrative operations in
organizations.

If you were to ask what AOMs do, the
responses would probably be as varied as the
people you would ask. For example, some opinions might suggest that they

- have an ability to "juggle lots of projects,"
- can talk to customers about problems and
  assist in resolving them, or
- can handle crises while keeping everyone
  informed and calm.

Further, the traditional administrative office
manager is often characterized as one who has
"thick skin," maturity, sound judgment under
pressure, and a loyal interest and knowledge of
all aspects of the company's operations and
success.

Career planning is a necessity in today's dynamic
marketplace.   *PhotoDisc, Inc.*

JOB OUTLOOK

Changing times lead to changing employment,
keeping the world of work in constant flux. The
wide array of occupations in the American labor
market responds to societal, global, scientific,
commercial, and legislative developments.
These forces cause a decline in employment for
jobs that once offered solid careers while creating rapid growth in positions that were unheard
of not long ago. In today's dynamic marketplace, people must plan their careers carefully
and be aware of which occupations will be in
demand in the future. Employment projections
from the Bureau of Labor Statistics (BLS) provide important information for office support
professionals to use in formulating long-term
career plans.

Some changes in technology and business
practices have caused employment to decline or
at least to take on a different look. For example,
while the volume of paperwork is expected to

increase dramatically, the employment of typists and word processors, in the traditional sense, will probably fall. What will result will be the employment of AOMs who will bring a combination of administrative, technology, and teamwork skills to the business environment. This reflects the growing use of software programs and equipment that increases efficiency and allows other office personnel to do more of their own keying of documents.

According to the BLS using the ten clusters of occupations based on the federal government's Standard Occupational Classification (SOC) system, two trends of particular interest to office management show that through the year 2006:

- *Executive, administrative, and managerial occupations* are expected to grow about as fast as the average for all occupations. Because of the strong competition for these jobs, appli-

cants with previous work experience, specialized training, or graduate study have an advantage. Computer skills are now essential as managers rely on computerized information systems to assist with the routine functions of their organizations.

- *Administrative support occupations* will continue to employ large numbers of workers, although employment will grow more slowly than average. Despite the tremendous increase expected in the volume of document-processing tasks, increased automation and other technological changes will cause a decline in some occupations, including keyboardist, word processor, data-entry keyer, bookkeeping, accounting, and auditing clerk. A projected faster-than-average increase in employment of receptionists reflects rapid growth of the services industries in which they work.[16]

Message *for* AOMs

To manage office information systems effectively in today's business environment, administrative professionals must approach the task as one that is multifaceted and interrelated. What is emerging is a requirement that all office support professionals be visionaries. That is to say, they must regularly use their "change" skills more readily in customer-oriented, worker-empowered environments. It is almost as if office professionals today are painting new identities as they redefine their roles each day in the workplace.

Administrative professionals will see their managerial responsibilities increase dramatically in the year 2000 and beyond. As more and more companies seek ways to increase productivity and decrease operational costs, management will begin to rely more and more on their office professionals to increase their knowledge base and take on more management responsibilities: personnel management, project management, budget manage-

ment, and more high-level decision-making responsibilities.[17]

The challenge for tomorrow's managers of office information systems is to possess the mind-set to *evolve with the times*. As technology and communication tools become more sophisticated and easier to use, the monumental task of managing the abundance of data and turning it into useable and shareable information will describe an effective administrative office management professional.

summary chapter 2

1 Workplace trends that affect the ways in which offices function in 2000 and beyond are business reengineering, empowerment, work teams, alternatives to the pyramid structure, the knowledge worker, the horizontal organization, and high-performing organizations.

2 A paradigm shift means a fundamental change in the assumptions made about a certain body of knowledge (for example, that the typewriter will be an integral piece of office equipment, when its function is being replaced almost exclusively by computers). The paradigm shift would be the realization that computers are the integral piece of equipment.

3 Two principal concepts which underlie the successfully reengineered company are the empowerment of employees and the use of cross-functional teams.

4 Among the alternatives to the pyramid style of organization are the inverted pyramid, the wagon wheel, and the cluster organization.

5 The change from a hierarchical to a horizontal organization can be represented by charts with fewer management levels and more emphasis on self-managing teams to accomplish an organization's mission. As such, one skill managers must embrace is being able to change as their company's business changes toward more networks, teams, and critical customer focus with less centralization and fewer management levels.

6 Executive, administrative, and managerial occupations are expected to grow about as fast as the average for all occupations. Administrative support occupations will continue to employ the largest number of workers, although employment will grow more slowly than average.

QUESTIONS FOR CRITICAL THINKING

1. Cite an example of a paradigm shift you've experienced in your own life.

2. Contrast your understanding of the key elements of a pyramidal organization with a horizontal organization.

3. From any outside reading you may have done, describe a local or national company that, in your opinion, has undergone reengineering within the past three years.

4. In your opinion, do you think reengineering has run its course and will soon be replaced by another revolutionary managerial idea? Explain.

5. Evaluate your prospects in administrative management in light of the job outlook through 2006.

Case Study 2-1: Downsizing Operations

When recently downsizing its home-office operations, the Valeria Company laid off eight of its employees in the order processing and records management departments. One of the workers, Bob Azilla, brought the dismissed workers together and told them that they have a good case against the company. Azilla explained to them, "See? Right here in the policy manual it says that if there is a layoff, senior workers with acceptable work records will be given preferential treatment."

Maria Torres, age 45 with eight years' experience in order processing, replied, "Preferential treatment? Ha! They let us go and kept all the young ones. Let's show those big shots that they violated their own policy and we are going to nail 'em."

Spearheaded by Azilla, the workers met with Tim O'Connor, the human resources manager. O'Connor cautioned them, "Just forget it. We didn't violate any company policy. Read it again. The policy states that only senior workers with acceptable performance are covered. You people were dismissed because of your poor performance."

Azilla burst out, "Well, we'll see about this! This is the first time we've heard anything about our poor performance!" His coworkers applauded and yelled, "Right on, Bob!"

Discussion Questions

1. In a few words, what is the real problem in this case?

2. Did Azilla make any mistakes? If so, what is the nature of his mistakes?

3. Did O'Connor make any mistakes? If so, what is the nature of his mistakes?

Case Study 2-2: Mass Exodus of Good Employees

RAS and Company is two years old and supplies gifts and other items to smaller gift stores in the Midwest. Although RAS is a young company, the employees are paid very well and have enthusiastically "built the company from scratch." The founding president, Mr. Robin, has been affectionately called a "slave driver" but is known to work as hard as anyone else to see the company succeed.

Within the past three months, however, employees seem to be getting edgy and are not as enthusiastic compared to the first year in business. In addition, there appear to be several "hush-hush" conversations occurring between workers throughout the workday.

The RAS board of directors' annual meeting is next week. Yesterday, Ms. Alisa Stevens, the board chairperson, received an anonymous letter suggesting that she look into company personnel records and ask President Robin why ten of their 65 employees have quit within the past six months. Three of the ten were on the top management team reporting directly to Mr. Robin. Ms. Stevens has just placed a call to Mr. Robin.

Discussion Questions

1. Is there a management problem surfacing at RAS and Company that may prevent it from realizing its organizational objectives? Does it relate to the four management functions you've studied? If so, in what ways?

2. What issues other than rapid growth contribute to the predicament?

3. If you were Ms. Stevens, what would you say on the phone to Mr. Robin?

Case Study 2-3:
Internet Research Activity

Assume you are doing a report on *changing management practices.* Use the Internet to research information needed to answer the following questions. Key your responses.

1. Which Web search engine did you use?

2. List the keywords you used to do your search.

3. Write down three of the URL addresses that you accessed during your search.

4. As a result of your search, list three items of current information you might use in your report.

Endnotes

[1] Ronni Sandroff, "The Psychology of Change," *Working Woman,* July 1993, p. 52.

[2] "The Best Companies To Work For," *Inc.,* November 1992, p. 30.

[3] Min Basadur and Susan Robinson, "The New Creative Thinking Skills Needed for Total Quality Management to Become Fact, Not Just Philosophy," *American Behavioral Scientist,* September-October 1993, pp. 122–123.

[4] Ronni Sandroff, "The Psychology of Change," *Working Woman,* July 1993, p. 54.

[5] Barbara Ettorre, "The Empowerment Gap: Hype vs. Reality," *HR Focus,* July 1997, p. 10.

[6] Randy Ross, "The Real Trick to Reengineering," *PC World,* July 1993, p. 55.

[7] Roberta Maynard, "A Client-Centered Firm's Lesson in Teamwork," *Nation's Business,* March 1997, p. 32.

[8] John A. Byrne, "Reengineering: What Happened?" *Business Week,* January 30, 1995, p. 16.

[9] Aaron Bernstein, "Oops, That's Too Much Downsizing," *Business Week,* June 8, 1998, p. 38.

[10] James E. Challenger, "Downsizing Is Bad for Business," *USA Today Magazine,* January 1997, p. 67.

[11] Nancy K. Austin, "Reorganizing the Organization Chart," *Working Woman,* September 1993, p. 23.

[12] Adapted from a W.L. Gore organizational profile bulletin produced by the organization in 1998 at its headquarters in Flagstaff, Arizona.

[13] Jim Clemmer, *A Guide to Transforming Yourself, Your Team, and Your Organization* (Canada: MacMillan, 1998).

[14] Melissa Briscoe and Joyce Logan, "Hitting the Mark," *The Secretary,* April 1997, p. 21.

[15] Laurie J. Bassi, George Benson, and Scott Cheney, "The Top 10 Career Trends," *The Secretary,* May 1997, p. 22.

[16] Rick Melchionno and Michael Sean Steinman, "The 1996–2006 Job Outlook in Brief," *Occupational Outlook Quarterly,* Spring 1998, pp. 3–8.

[17] "From the Front Line," *The Secretary,* April 1997, pp. 8–10.

Resource Areas Influenced by Administrative Office Managers

chapter 3

> On Advancement—You can't steal second base and keep one foot on first.
>
> —*Unknown*

objectives

After completing this chapter, you will be able to:

1. Name the four resources that administrative office managers are called on to manage.

2. Describe effective guidelines to follow when developing administrative office budgets.

3. List the two areas of human resource management that office administrators most closely oversee.

4. Discuss the advantages of each of the following ways to acquire new equipment and furniture: purchase, lease, and rent.

5. Identify trends in office work patterns that are affecting furniture acquisition for the workplace.

6. Explain the relationship between quality and continuous improvement in organizations.

Up to this point, we have discussed the application of management practices in general. This chapter describes particular activities most AOMs are expected to oversee and manage. The chapter concludes with a discussion of new approaches to managing these office activities.

RESOURCE MANAGEMENT AREAS

On a day-to-day basis, office administrators must still apply the management functions of planning, organizing, leading, and controlling when managing crucial, yet limited, organizational resources. Typically, the four resource areas that office managers are called on to manage include

1. *capital* resources or money;

2. *human* or *people* resources, their time, and communication flow;

3. *physical* resources or facilities, equipment, and consumable supplies; and

4. *information* resources, in terms of space and office/document workflow.

Craig S. Mack

Building and Facilities Engineer
Bachelor of Architecture Degree,
University of Nebraska
Deere & Company
Moline, Illinois

Mr. Mack is responsible for all maintenance, security, safety, fire protection, janitorial services, and preparation of the design for the reconfiguration of the corporate headquarters at Deere & Company in Moline, Illinois. Mr. Mack has been with Deere & Company for 14 years and has held his current position for the past six years. Previously, he was one of the corporate architects in the facility engineering department.

Warren W. Power

Manager, Office Administration
B.S. Mechanical Engineering,
Iowa State University
MBA, University of Iowa
Deere & Company
Moline, Illinois

In his position at Deere & Company, Mr. Power is responsible for providing the services, equipment, and furniture that employees need to perform their daily jobs. Mr. Power has been with John Deere for 26 years and has held positions in manufacturing, engineering, corporate standards, and engineering systems and for the past 12 years has been in general office personnel and administration.

Question:

How does the accelerating rate of change in the office environment influence you in selecting, procuring, and maintaining office furniture and equipment?

Dialog *from the* Workplace

Response:

Since we've been in our current jobs, the rate at which new technologies are being introduced into the office has increased dramatically. Office equipment, such as typewriters and telephones, was previously purchased with the expectation of a useful life of 10 to 15 years. The advent of the microchip changed all of this. Today the primary office equipment consists of computers, printers, and facsimile machines, which are rapidly becoming smaller and less expensive. As a result, firms today are able to give their employees more tools to do their jobs than they ever have in the past. While this additional equipment improves efficiency and productivity, it also creates additional problems for the office manager.

The rapid changes that are occurring in the office environment significantly impact the design of our facilities, both old and new. All aspects of new facilities, including wiring, lighting, walls, windows, environmental requirements, and furniture, are designed or selected to enhance today's office technology and to ensure the ability to adapt to foreseeable changes. While this changing environment makes the facility designer's job more difficult for new construction, the real challenge lies in changing our existing facilities.

Large firms, such as Deere, have millions of dollars invested in office facilities and furniture. Most of these facilities were built and furnished prior to the microchip revolution. As a result, many of our existing buildings and furniture do not meet the needs of today's office environment. Our firm, like most firms, can't afford to replace all of our buildings and furniture to accommodate these emerging technologies, so it's up to the office manager to find alternatives. Fortunately, our problem is not unique, and businesses throughout the world have developed products and accessories to make existing furniture and facilities more compatible with new technologies. The facility manager's challenge is to select a set of products that provides employees with an ergonomically acceptable workstation that still provides an aesthetically acceptable office environment.

In addition to the activities performed by AOMs which were described earlier, other examples of office activities associated with managing each of these resources are more fully presented in Table 3.1.

Administrative Office Budgets

Budgets are statements of planned revenues and expenditures that are organized by category and period of time. They account for future use of money, time, personnel, space,

AREAS	TYPICAL ACTIVITIES PERFORMED
Administrative Office Budgets	1. Keeping track of costs and expenses such as telephone, mailing, photocopying, facsimile, messenger, and courier service expenses. 2. Preparing budgets. 3. Comparing budgeted office administrative amounts to current usage patterns and adjusting for deviations.
Manpower Utilization and Organizational Communication	1. Recognizing the signs of stress and helping others reduce its effect on the job. 2. Helping yourself and others manage time, priorities, and general work habits. 3. Communicating effectively in cross-cultural work settings to increase office productivity.
Facilities, Equipment, and Supplies Acquisition	1. Researching the benefits of buying or leasing office space, computers, and equipment. 2. Staying informed of emerging office software and other products that are efficient, ergonomically sound, and economical. 3. Buying quality office products from dealers who offer affordable prices and speedy delivery while keeping the price/value relationships of office products optimized.
Office Area Design and Document Workflow	1. Buying equipment and supplies while keeping trends, such as recycling and reductions in office space and staff, in mind. 2. Researching new trends in office design on a regular basis to keep office workflow running smoothly. 3. Investigating trends and new products in communication and software technology that are designed to improve office area design and document flow.

Table 3.1

Overview of Resource Management Areas

buildings, and equipment. Thus, budgets express the plans, objectives, and programs of the organization in numerical terms. Once the budget is set in motion, measures of actual expenditures are periodically taken and compared with projected, budgeted amounts. The progression of budgetary expenses may be "on target," or management may note deviations from the plan and, as a result, take corrective action.

Objectives of Budgeting. Throughout the process of budgeting, management tries to attain the following objectives:

1. *To establish procedures for planning and studying future revenues and expenses* so the organization's budget may be reviewed and modified when needed.

2. *To coordinate the activities of the various departments in the organization* so that individual department heads become more aware of the financial problems of others on the management team.

3. *To build a basis for administrative control* by providing managers with factual measures of performance that they helped to develop and for which they are held responsible.

4. *To communicate formally the plans that have been approved by management* and the actions that management wishes the organization to take during the budget period.

5. *To motivate all individuals by creating a climate of cost consciousness* in which they are stimulated to reach desired performance levels.

Methods of Budgeting. Initially, a method of budgeting must be determined which will provide the best opportunities for control at all management levels. In the following discussion, two of the many methods of budgeting are briefly described—incremental and zero-base budgeting. Because neither of these methods completely meets the needs of managers as they establish their programs of budgetary control, we shall conclude with a discussion of a form of compromise budgeting.

Incremental Budgeting. The traditional or conventional approach to budgeting is called **incremental budgeting.** This method involves the addition of a given percentage of increase (the *increment*) to the budgeted amounts of the preceding period to arrive at new figures. In other words, cost data from the prior period are revised upward under the assumption that a given percentage of increase in business activities will bring about a like increase in department expenditures. In a similar fashion, if it becomes necessary to reduce the budgeted amounts, all budget items are reduced by a stipulated percentage. Thus, under incremental budgeting, all departments, regardless of their cost effectiveness, share equally in increases or decreases.

One of the downsides of incremental budgeting is that it carries forward into each new budgeting period the inefficiencies and wastes of the prior period. Thus, the cost of such waste becomes part of an ever-growing budgeting base. With this type of budgeting, there is little opportunity or incentive for managers and supervisors to assess which projects or programs are deserving of special attention and additional funds.

Zero-Base Budgeting. The objective of any budgeting method is to allocate resources to those operations that contribute most to the goals of the organization. **Zero-base budgeting (ZBB)** is a resource-allocation method that requires budget makers to examine every expenditure anew each budget period and to *justify* the expenditure in light of *current* needs and developments. Thus, unlike incremental budgeting, the zero-base budget figures are not based upon a percentage of increase or decrease related to the previous budgetary period. Instead, each year the budget is reduced to zero. The budget maker starts from the base line (zero) each time an expenditure is examined and justifies the first as well as the last dollar to be spent.

Most of the data collected about a program are presented in a document called a *decision package*. This document describes the program broken down into the smallest decision units that can be defended. A *decision unit* represents the lowest operating level where meaningful cost data can be compiled. Each decision unit is summarized in terms of the reasons for its existence, the benefits the organization gains from the unit, and the consequences for the company if the unit were to be terminated. Also included in the decision package is the manager's evaluation of alternative ways of getting the job done.

The benefits realized from the use of ZBB include

- Managers focus their attention upon analysis and decision making, thus improving the planning process.
- Each budget request must be justified in relation to the costs and benefits of each program.
- Top-level managers are enabled to follow up and exercise control over costs and performance.

On the other hand, users of ZBB experience problems such as these:

- There is difficulty in evaluating and comparing different decision packages because departments differ in both structure and purpose and may use different performance measures.
- The method requires more time and effort from operating managers who may have had little training in ZBB.
- There is difficulty in ranking a large number of decision packages fairly.
- The required cost-performance information may not be available or may be difficult to obtain.

Compromise Budgeting. The incremental budgeting and ZBB methods are often modified in order to overcome the disadvantages described earlier and to realize the benefits to be gained from each method. Under a compromise budgeting approach, the budget maker does not start from zero but instead accepts the realities of business conditions as they exist and makes the needed adjustments or compromises. That is, the budget maker reduces the amount of funds allocated to those programs or activities that have been evaluated as less beneficial.

For example, under a compromise budgeting approach known as *modified ZBB,* the budget committee may undertake the preparation of the current budget by accepting 90 percent of last year's budget. Thus, operating managers are asked to submit ZBB decision packages only for the least essential 10 percent of their costs. As a result, operating managers prepare detailed justifications for only those parts of the budget where real decisions are likely to be made.

Master and Sub-Budgets. Once budgets have been determined, it's a good idea to assemble the information so it can be used effectively by members of the organization. Usually an organization assembles a master budget that summarizes and represents all departmental needs. It is not unusual, however, to find that an organization prepares and uses sub-budgets. These sub-budgets reflect major areas, such as capital, production, sales, and personnel, through their individually projected expenditures. As an AOM, the portion of an organization's budget that you

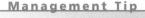

Management Tip

Knowing how to get things done is only part of the job; knowing how to get things done at a minimum cost and within budget is what is expected of all office support professionals.

will prepare, and subsequently work with, typically contains the following three categories:

1. *personnel budget,* which takes into account salaries and benefits paid to office employees,

2. *capital budget,* which reflects any proposed acquisition of equipment, computers, and possibly facilities used by the office staff, and

3. *expense budget,* which forecasts various general and administrative expenses such as office supplies, postage, computer software, paper, and telephone costs.

Since budget preparation requires additional information, answers to some typical questions you might have relative to preparing and using office budgets are shown in Table 3.2.

Budget Reminders. Here are a few "do's and don'ts" that apply to budgeting:

1. **Accountants should not prepare budgets.** Although accountants might compile budget information at an organizational level, budgets should be prepared by those in the organization who both control and depend on the expenditure of funds—especially those employees at the operative level. Budget preparation should flow upward within organizations.

2. **Budgets do not predict the future.** Each budget is instead a fiscal plan, expressed in dollars and cents, that is based on historical information showing the organization's cyclical variations. Budgets also incorporate projected new or unusual expenditures.

QUESTIONS	RESPONSES
Of what value are budgets to managers?	As a plan for receiving and spending money, budgets represent expectations from business operations.
How do managers go about setting up a budget?	1. Managers predict the sales and other income they expect to receive. 2. Then they identify the portions of the expected income for expenses that will be required to run the business.
How are budgets developed using computers?	1. Most managers today use computers to help prepare budgets with spreadsheet software like Excel or QuatroPro. 2. Unless a business is new, future budgets will be based on past budgets. 3. Typically, most managers are told, for example, that the economy will expand by 4 percent next year. With the computer, it is a simple matter to take the figures for the current year's operations and ask the computer to add 4 percent to all items.
How are budgets monitored?	1. As operations go forward on a day-to-day basis, information is collected on actual operating results. If actual results match the budget, there are no major problems. 2. However, if there are variances (differences between planned and actual results), action is required.
What three actions can a manager take to ensure the ultimate success of a business using budgets?	1. Prepare realistic income and expense budgets. 2. Monitor operating results closely. 3. Make adjustments on the basis of experience.

Table 3.2

Typical Questions About Preparing and Using Office Budgets

3. **Budgets must not be rigid.** They must be flexible enough to absorb changes that will occur when new regulations or unique circumstances come into play. No manager can plan for every contingency, since a company's operations are impacted by variables—many unexpected—both from inside and outside the organization. But again, flexibility in budgeting is critical to dealing successfully with any of these financial contingencies.

4. *Budgets are proactive rather than reactive documents.* A budget serves as an early warning to management when the organization, or a portion of it, is heading into financial difficulties; it is not supposed to be utilized after the fact. Yearly budgets work best when they are reduced to either monthly or quarterly working documents that are consistently reviewed for potential problems.

Manpower Utilization and Organizational Communication

Human resource management involves developing plans and practices that facilitate realizing the full potential of workers and using that potential to pursue the organization's quality and performance objectives. Though human resource management is practiced throughout an organization, the major areas of responsibility that AOMs assume include recruiting qualified people and advancing employee involvement by empowering workers.

Recruiting Qualified People. When recruiting and hiring, an office manager should look for applicants who possess both technical and "soft" or people skills. This is not as easy as it sounds. Such people are in high demand in all organizations. When recruiting, however, remember that a thorough review of a "good" interview, reference checks, and a neat, well-constructed resumé indicating appropriate training are critical to selecting the best candidate. Generally speaking, performance on previous jobs is still one of the best indicators of future performance, so carrying out reference checks is a must.

Recognizing and Empowering Employees. Employee involvement, recognition, and empowerment are successful because of sound communication practices in organizations that use them. Office communication cannot be managed per se. Through understanding its dynamics, however, a manager can facilitate the communication process and improve organizational communication. People, not organizations, communicate. An organization's communication system, therefore, reflects a variety of individuals with different backgrounds, education levels, beliefs, cultures, moods, and needs.

Recruiting can be achieved through effective newspaper ads. © *PhotoDisc, Inc.*

The merging of space-age telecommunications technologies with advanced computer techniques has led to improved communications within organizations and to innumerable ways of gathering, generating, using, and disseminating information. Examples of useful information-processing technologies that facilitate electronic office communication are (1) personal computers, (2) electronic mail, (3) teleconferencing, (4) videoconferencing, (5) telecommuting, and (6) computer networking. It is exciting (and at times a little scary) to realize that, as we blink, additional new technologies are being developed, tested, and rushed to the market!

Facilities, Equipment, and Supplies Acquisitions

Facility and office equipment acquisition is an important responsibility for an administrative office manager. Office equipment can include items from desktop copiers and telephones to fax machines and computer systems—in short, all are laborsaving machines and gadgets used in an office to process documents and information. Newly acquired machines and furniture must mesh with existing systems and fit into existing space, yet be able to adapt to future needs as an organization grows.

Deciding to Purchase, Rent, or Lease. An AOM can acquire office space, new equipment, and furniture in basically three ways. You can purchase, rent, or lease the items you need.

Purchase. When purchasing, of course, you will own the building or equipment outright. If your company decides not to purchase through budgeted funds (and that is often the case with office space), you can finance the purchase with a loan, repay it in installments, and take title to (full ownership of) the building or equipment once the loan is repaid. In this case, your budget would reflect the cost of installment payments.

Is it better to buy and own outright than to rent or lease? The most prudent response is "it depends."

- *It depends* on an organization's current cash flow and projected cash needs.
- *It depends* on the desired rate of change or "upgrading" within your office and the level of interest in warding off equipment obsolescence, especially where rapid advances in computer, copier, and communications technology are concerned
- *It depends* on how easily you can get rid of the obsolete equipment you have purchased.
- Finally, *it depends* on the costs associated with maintaining and insuring the equipment once it is purchased.

Cash flow, equipment obsolescence, and maintaining and insuring equipment are considerations that should be basic to every business purchase. To meet short-term needs, organizations often choose to rent or lease equipment.

Rent. When you rent, you do so on a simple month-to-month basis. Most sound businesses

Management Tip

As with any legal contract, if you do not understand the terms and conditions of a purchase, lease, or rental agreement, do not sign it until you have consulted an attorney.

do not choose simply to rent equipment, except in an emergency or on a stopgap basis. They prefer to lease.

Lease. When you lease, you make monthly payments over a stated period of time, but you do not own the equipment unless your lease agreement allows you to buy at a reduced cost at the end of the lease period. Leases have certain advantages. For example, they allow the organization rapid replacement with upgraded equipment, no loss of value or "depreciation" of equipment you owned, ease of disposal (return it to the owner!), and maintenance of the equipment by the owner. When evaluating the benefits of purchasing over leasing, study Table 3.3, which offers a comparison of six factors to consider.

Office settings often reflect the open design.   ©*CORBIS*

Selecting Office Furniture and Equipment. Traditionally, office furniture and equipment have been designed and used with the efficiency of space planning and cost consciousness in mind. While these factors are important to "living within the budget," they overlook a more critical consideration—the ergonomic needs of the modern office support worker. **Ergonomics** is a concept that furniture, equipment, and office products should fit people, not the reverse. In other words, by applying ergonomics to the work environment, employee efficiency and well-being increase as equipment, work routines, and work environments are adapted to meet employees' physical and psychological needs.

Therefore, in order to manage the furniture and equipment needs of the office, the AOM must understand

- the nature of the work being performed,
- the ergonomic needs of the workers, and
- the increasingly complex physical environment of the modern office, particularly in light of the "reengineering of business tasks" occurring in today's offices.

Because of the need for office furniture and equipment to meet ergonomic requirements as well as the trend toward open-space planning, AOMs recognize the value of using furniture that is adjustable, easy to move, and multipurpose. For these reasons, the use of modular rather than conventional furniture is preferred. **Modular furniture** (sometimes called *systems furniture*) is a collection of integrated, interdependent furniture components that can be quickly and easily assembled, disassembled,

	FACTORS THAT FAVOR PURCHASING	FACTORS THAT FAVOR LEASING
Cash Flow	If the company has an abundance of cash and desires owning equipment	If the company has limited but adequate cash flow on a monthly basis
Obsolescence	If the equipment can be used over a long period of time	If changes in technology outdate this equipment quickly
Maintenance	If the company wants to undertake maintaining and servicing the equipment after the warranty period has expired	If the company prefers to have maintenance expenses be a part of the monthly payment
Insurance	If the company prefers to be solely responsible for insuring the equipment against damage or loss	If the company prefers to have insurance expense be a part of the monthly payment
Lease Agreement		If the company prefers to make monthly payments over a stated period of time, realizing that it will not own the equipment unless the lease agreement allows the equipment to be purchased at a reduced cost at the end of the lease period
Tax Considerations	If the company prefers to lower taxes by depreciating the purchased equipment over a number of years	If the company desires to claim the monthly payments as a tax-deductible business expense

Table 3.3

Factors to Consider When Deciding to Purchase or Lease

and rearranged to meet employee and department needs. A module is one unit or component of office furniture that has a specific function, such as a desk, an acoustical partition, or a work surface with a pedestal containing several drawers. Functionally designed modular furniture has a panel-dependent workstation with detachable components that can be adjusted to fit a worker's individual needs. A modular workstation typically occupies less space than that required for conventional layouts.

For example, the traditional conference room is being transformed functionally by technological innovations, equipment improvements, and changes in the workplace. Because these rooms are increasingly used for various events, such as training, meetings, teamwork, and business presentations, they need to have furnishings that are flexible enough to support these different activities. This furniture must have the ability to store, secure, and facilitate easy access to equipment, provide support to the technology required by the activity, and satisfy the aesthetics and comfort of all those who will use the meeting area at the same time.[1]

Work Patterns and Furniture Trends. As office patterns change and telecommuting increases among workers, office furniture dealers have new opportunities to market unique types of products. Sales in ready-to-assemble (RTA) furniture and furniture which accommodates alternative officing are substantially on the rise.

Ready-to-Assemble Products. With more Americans spending at least part of their workdays at home, workers are faced with the problem of where to put their computers, printers, papers, and other supplies of the modern office. Their need for a manageable home workspace has led to a flurry of activity in home-office furniture, a market that is forecasted to grow by 10 percent annually.

Ready-to-assemble (RTA) products are pieces of furniture the consumer or home-office worker puts together at home. Home-office workers include not only the telecommuters and the self-employed who work out of their homes, but also those workers who finish work at home *after* working at the office. According to *American Demographics* magazine, the group of people who worked at home in 1998 accounted for 60 million workers.[2]

Alternative Officing. The latest movement in the $20 billion office furniture business is "alternative officing." Given the speed with which business operates, it makes sense that the traditional office environment must adapt. Here are some examples of space compression office environments:

- *Free-range teaming*—the freedom of movement and expression in open space that supports a collaborative work culture.
- *Hot-desking*—space is claimed on a first-come, first-served basis. In other words, employees arrive at the office, select from available wired workstations, plug in, and log on.
- *Hoteling*—employees book reservations for office space with a company concierge, who then assigns the employee to a workplace, switches the phone lines, wheels out employee's personal belongings (college diplomas and pictures of the kids), and places the right nametag on the door. Space is reserved by the day in the hotel model; by the hour in the motel model.[3]

When selecting office furniture or equipment, refer to the sound reminders, which are listed in Table 3.4.

Purchasing and Maintaining Supplies. When you manage office equipment, most of the time you must buy supplies used in the

1. The furniture should contribute to safe and comfortable working conditions.

2. The furniture should be attractive and harmonize with the office decor.

3. The furniture should be of good quality, solid construction, and suitable design to facilitate the work to be done.

4. The quantity of furniture should be sufficient for the number of employees and suitable for the types of tasks performed.

5. The furniture should be adaptable to multipurpose use wherever possible.

6. Specialized furniture should be purchased only if justified by cost savings, greater efficiency, improved productivity, and convenience.

7. The furniture should meet the preferences of the workers.

Table 3.4

Guidelines for Selecting Office Furniture

equipment's operation as well as other consumable supplies for general use within your office.

Purchasing Supplies. The purchasing of office supplies entails labor costs that equal the total cost of the products themselves. Ordering, receiving, distributing, and paying for office supplies create expenses arising from wages, payroll taxes, and employee benefits. Current and more economical trends in performing this ongoing office task include

- Eliminating the company stockroom by choosing office product distributors that offer immediate just-in-time delivery,
- Using technology to cut costs with easy order forms and electronic catalogs and paying the vendor by monthly invoice summary, rather than with each delivery.[4]

Quill Corporation, a leading office supplier, offered the following suggestions for establishing procedures to save valuable time and dollars when purchasing office supplies.

1. *Choose the right supplier.* When choosing a supplier, remember these four steps:

   - Determine your organization's needs by asking these questions: "What quantities are used? . . . . How often are orders sent in?" and "What inventory control methods are followed?"

Ethics/Choices

An office supply dealer delivers one "free" copy of a new software package to your residence after you, the AOM, placed an order for ten copies of that software. Do you keep the software?

- Evaluate potential suppliers according to prices that are clear, guaranteed, and competitive. Ask if volume discounts are available, and note whether delivery times, quality, prices, and response times are consistent.
- Test suppliers to see how they actually perform. Evaluate delivery time, accuracy, and condition of delivered goods; also check bills for accuracy.
- Monitor the supplier's performance. Good suppliers offer regular customers their best deals and inform them about new products and sale prices.

2. *Get the most for your organization's dollar.* Test and compare generic and brand-name products to see which ones meet your standards. Good suppliers guarantee quality standards for their private label products in addition to offering a lower price.

3. *Organize for efficiency.* Well-organized ordering procedures can save time and money. Designate one person to gather supply requests and place orders. Set a regular time to inventory supplies and place orders. Keep supplies in a central location. Label shelves with item names so you can see what is running low.[5]

Table 3.5 describes five typical activities performed by the person who manages office supplies for a large department or organization.

Maintaining Supplies. One of the most "uncontrollable" categories of office expenses, and one of the hardest to manage, has traditionally been consumable office supplies. Most companies would be hard-pressed to find an employee who has not occasionally slipped at least one or two yellow sticky pads into his or her briefcase. But what about those workers who have perpetually sticky fingers? Even though small and inexpensive as single units, items like ballpoint pens, paper clips, magnetic disks, postage, and paper collectively add up to a major expenditure for most offices.

Monitoring internal use of supplies without being a "scrooge" is a real balancing act and one which, to most AOMs, simply does not feel good. An office manager must keep in mind that waste and even theft of supplies and services compete with business needs for funds. Be sure there is a control system in place to minimize (you cannot eliminate) the following activities: taking office supplies for home use, making photocopies for personal use, placing personal long-distance telephone calls, and using postage to mail personal correspondence.

An office manager can effectively and "humanely" monitor office consumables by finding the best suppliers of office supplies, by developing an effective inventory control system, and by allocating supplies fairly, which will

STEPS	ACTIVITIES
1. Determine supply needs	One person should be in charge of the office supplies. This person should keep usage records of supplies used in order to determine "normal" needs per person or department.
2. Store supplies	Standard items used by most employees are maintained and locked in either a stockroom, a mailroom, or cabinet.
3. Distribute supplies	As soon as an order is received, deliver the supplies to appropriate persons, making sure that recipients initial receipts.
4. Reorder supplies	When a supply needs to be replenished or requires a special purchase, the appropriate person is notified and an order is placed showing a paper trail of the order—who, what, when, and where. Because poor-quality office supplies result in higher expenses, use care when selecting both suppliers and products. Select a supplier that knows your office supply needs, will be able to deliver products on time, and will give competitive prices or special offers.
5. Safeguard against pilfering	Expect any control system to only reduce, not eliminate, employee pilferage. An office supply stock area controlled by one person provides the most control, whereas an honor-system check sheet will provide some control over supplies.

Table 3.5

Managing Office Supplies —Typical Activities

help discourage employee pilferage. **Pilferage** is the taking (theft) of items or services without permission.

Office Area Design and Document Workflow

The administrative office manager's role in creating a functional office area design and effecting efficient office and document workflow is a major one. How well this task is accomplished affects productivity, organizational climate, and morale—the essence of what management is tasked to carry out.

When designing a functional office area, consider these factors to enhance office productivity:

1. Coordinate the use of space with environmental factors such as temperature, light, noise control, color, and safety.

2. Design workstations with at least a chair, a working surface, and some storage facilities nearby and accessible for easy reach.

3. Design areas with office workflow in mind— a workflow that will enhance the information processing cycle from one workstation to another. Keep workflow continuity paramount in your design; work should not zigzag among office staff.

4. Allocate sufficient space for each workstation and ensure that its use is maximized.

5. Continue to monitor, on a periodic basis, the current level of space usage and adjust, as necessary, for long-range space needs.

6. Research the advantages and feasibility of a modular, open-design office environment. This design may reduce costs and improve communications within your office.

7. Minimize office safety hazards by careful review of design plans before implementation.

8. Ask employees for their input on what will work best for them prior to making any final decisions.

Management Tip

Before beginning a task, visualize the end result. This step will eliminate nonproductive effort and excess time spent on completing the task.

NEW APPROACHES TO MANAGING

Managing with a new set of perspectives is becoming a mandate. As a result of today's global economy, new approaches to managing office productivity and efficiency are taking shape. Three of these approaches are creating a climate for quality and continuous improvement processes, managing within worker-empowered organizations, and recognizing change as positive and real.

Quality and Continuous Improvement

The quality movement has a tremendous impact on how organizations function today. **Total quality management (TQM),** when used to best advantage, is integrated into *all* functions of a business, including its administrative support activities. The measurement of success is customer satisfaction; the way to guarantee that satisfaction is through higher standards of quality as achieved through TQM and the **continuous improvement process (CIP).** These processes help employees and management alike accept change and continuous improvement as a necessary way of life.

Because of the quality movement, AOMs have no choice but to manage differently and better than before. To make a quality improvement process successful, managers must commit to new beliefs. The six TQM and continuous improvement beliefs are described in Table 3.6.

In reality, most customers are easy to please. They simply want us to do what we say we are going to do when we say we are going to do it. They are also pleased—and surprised—when we take the time to follow up and ask if they are satisfied with the product or service they received. The idea of calling to follow up with a customer is easy, but its implementation is rare in today's organizations. Imagine how many compliments

1. Acceptance of the customer as the most important part of the process.

2. Management's long-term commitment is to make the improvement process part of its management system by giving it management focus, leadership, and participation.

3. There is room to improve, and preventing problems is better than reacting to them.

4. Improvement must focus on the process, not the people.

5. Performance standards must be set to zero errors.

6. All employees must participate, with recognition for success given both to groups and individuals.

Table 3.6

Beliefs Held by Companies Seeking Quality and Continuous Improvement

and good ideas for improvement that an organization would receive if follow-up calls were viewed as *opportunities* rather than threats.

More and more, successful organizations will be the ones best able to apply the creative energy of individuals toward constant improvement. Yet, constant improvement is a value that cannot be imposed on people. It has to come from within the individual.

The only way to get people to adopt constant improvement as a way of life in doing daily business is by empowering them. When workers are not empowered, the following maladies manifest themselves in organizations: lack of trust, bureaucratic office politics, across-the-board rules and regulations, a boss's taking credit for others' ideas, and the belief that a worker cannot make a difference.

Worker-Empowered Organizations

In a world-class organization, everybody in the company has to be empowered to think every day about ways to make the business better in quality, output, costs, sales, and customer satisfaction. In government and other public service organizations, as well as in business, there are and will continue to be demands for high performance.

We need to get away from the old workplace adage that bosses think, managers manage, and workers work. Instead, we must commit to a new work style, which says that bosses, managers, and workers alike will think, manage, and work.

"Empowering" is the chief motivational tool used by the forward-thinking managers of today. To review, empowerment is a set of practices designed to authorize, drive, and enable day-to-day decision making at lower levels within an organization. In the past, engineers or professionals charged with that responsibility defined a "one best way." Employees were not expected or *allowed* to join in the search or decision-making process.

People are "empowered" when they are allowed and even encouraged to make decisions about the work they do. People are empowered when they feel confident about, in control of, and responsible for their decisions. In a political democracy, people empower leaders; in a business, leaders empower people. Empowerment is a powerful motivational tool. It can be characterized as an emotional and motivational "high" for workers who experience it.

Better workplaces and supportive work environments seem to promote more job satisfaction, commitment, loyalty, work, and initiative. Additionally, with a better work-family balance, companies will find there is an opportunity to better align workers' needs with workplace goals.

In research conducted to better understand workplace dynamics, what appears to be surfacing is simply that the same factors that help and encourage workers also seem to promote workforce productivity. Along with this newly recognized reality comes the requirement for a new resolve by AOMs to learn new techniques of managing employees—techniques that truly "empower" their subordinates.

People who feel they have a stake in an organization's success will have an enhanced sense of involvement in achieving the successful outcome. All employees—from top executive to receptionist—are stakeholders in a company's success. This sense of involvement and commitment must be encouraged from the top to the bottom of the company. For empowerment to truly work, managers must allow workers to make final decisions; otherwise, the concept is only words with no meaning.

Recognize Change as Positive and Real

Organizations need to consider the global effects of recent and future economic, political, and social realities when planning or considering a major change in the way they do business. We will see changes such as organizations restructured around new roles for information and technology. That is, new roles for information will affect the organization's structure, work procedures, and forms of management.

The Challenge of Change. Successful organizations, managers, and workers recognize the difficulties presented by change. Figure 3.1 presents several reasons each of us has given from time to time when resisting change. However, change is constant. There will always be emerging trends and ideas that will require each of us to alter our thinking and behavior. Upcoming challenges for the administrative office manager will be driven by agents of change—for example, alternative work systems and demographic trends.

Alternative Work Systems. We have already seen that, for example, because of changes in employees' work expectations, values, and "lifestyles," many organizations are responding with different types of alternative work systems. **Alternative work systems** are nontraditional working arrangements that include office sharing, job sharing, flextime, and telecommuting. These systems are more fully discussed in later chapters.

Demographics and Trends. What are some of those anticipated changes in the workforce?

Figure 3.1

In the past week, how many of these statements have you used when resisting an idea that required you to change?

For one, the entry-level jobs traditionally filled by younger workers will increasingly be performed by women and by older workers nearing retirement age.

Other trends will also affect the management of office activities. For example, workers are increasingly expecting organizations to develop initiatives that help employees with their personal/family lives. These initiatives include both traditional fringe benefits (health insurance and pension plans) and more contemporary forms of employer assistance such as flexible time and leave policies and dependent care programs.

Message *for* AOMs

When you accept a managerial position today, you are making the commitment to form a new professional identity. An AOM's first challenge is to adjust to the daily reality of managerial life, which is often pressured, hectic, and fragmented. It is critical for new managers to develop the ability to make careful judgments. For example, in managing individual performance, new managers have to learn to balance three sets of paradoxical forces:

1. Treat subordinates fairly, *but* as individuals.
2. Hold subordinates accountable, *yet* tolerate their mistakes and deficiencies.
3. Maintain control, *while* also allowing, and even fostering, autonomy.

summary chapter 3

1 Four resources that office managers administer are money through budgeting; people, their time, and communication flow; equipment and consumable supplies; and facilities, space, and office/document workflow.

2 Budgets are statements of planned revenues and expenditures that can be expressed by the incremental or zero-base method. Generally, master and sub-budgets are created to better control specific expenditures over the budgeting cycle. Employees at the operative level should provide input to the budgeting process.

3 Administrative office managers oversee the human resource management areas of recruiting qualified people and advancing employee involvement by empowering workers.

4 Decisions to purchase office furniture allow you to own the item outright. Leasing allows companies to more quickly acquire needed items with limited outflow of cash, whereas renting is a month-to-month pay commitment only and usually used by companies in emergency situations when a commitment to a leasing contract is not desired.

5 Office furniture trends are driven by a change in the way people work. Workers, for example, telecommute, take more work home to complete in the evening, and are self-employed and therefore need more ready-to-assemble furniture and modular furniture that can adapt to changing work patterns and styles.

6 Customer satisfaction is guaranteed through higher standards of quality as achieved through TQM and the continuous improvement process.

QUESTIONS FOR CRITICAL THINKING

1. Of the four resources that AOMs manage, in your opinion, which is the most critical?

2. What are budgets and how are they generally created, maintained, and reviewed?

3. If most organizations have a human resource department, why are office administrators involved in manpower utilization?

4. Why would you recommend purchasing instead of leasing a computer or fax machine?

5. Give two examples of ways employees pilfer consumable office supplies and what prevention tactics you might use.

6. In your opinion, will alternative work systems increase or decrease in usage during the next decade?

7. In your own words, describe what worker empowerment means.

Case Study 3-1: Selecting an Office Manager

Lucy Raynor is an office manager for Blake and Hall Law Office in downtown Los Angeles. Her friend, Althea, who is human resource manager for Silvers Professional Law Office (a firm that represents the movie industry), called and asked if Lucy would be available to serve on a screening and hiring committee for a new office manager. Silvers Professional Law Office is moving toward a more flattened organization, and special qualifications are needed in the new office manager. Althea trusts Lucy's opin-

ion about office administrative matters. Lucy said if it wouldn't take too long, she would be happy to help.

The next morning, Lucy received via delivery service a package that contained the following information on the top three candidates (some of the most significant data is given):

Candidate A

This candidate recently moved to Los Angeles from New York City. She does not drive a car but is taking driving lessons now. Having been an office manager for three years at an insurance company, she now wants to become a CPA— but she feels this is at least five years away. She wants to finish her bachelor's degree in business administration at the local university over the next three years.

Candidate B

Having been a top legal secretary in Beverly Hills for more than ten years, she states that she needs to leave her current position for personal reasons. In her most recent position, she coordinated facilities, equipment, and supplies acquisition and worked closely with the architect to design a state-of the-art office area.

Candidate C

As a legal secretary who currently is employed by the Silvers law firm, this candidate has consistently received very high performance appraisals in job evaluations during the past five years. She is well liked by almost everyone in the firm. At times, however, she tends to be a perfectionist and seldom solicits help from others in getting things done. Consequently, she ends up doing most jobs herself and has the most overtime pay of anyone in the firm.

Discussion Questions

1. Given the limited information provided, what criteria do you feel need to drive the selection of this office manager?

2. Of the three candidates, which one would you select and why?

Case Study 3-2: Planning with Demographics in Mind

Jerry Chambers, the human resource specialist for the Cap Company, which manufactures baseball caps in Des Moines, Iowa, just returned from a luncheon where a speaker from the university presented current data on demographic trends in his city.

Jerry is surprised and concerned about what he learned. The university professor said that the older worker would comprise 40 percent of the workforce in the new millennium. On the drive back to the office, Jerry is thinking of all the positives and negatives involved in future hiring decisions. He decides to talk to you, the administrative office manager, to get your ideas about how this might work.

Discussion Questions

1. As the AOM, in your opinion, what are some benefits of employing the older worker in the office?

2. What are some drawbacks to employing the older worker?

3. Do you feel companies need to plan in any special way for the older worker? If so, what type of planning should occur?

Case Study 3-3: Internet Research Activity

Assume that you are doing a report on *modular or RTA office furniture.* Use the Internet to research information needed to answer the following questions. Key your responses.

1. Which Web search engine did you use?

2. List the keywords you used to do your search.

3. Write down three of the URL addresses that you accessed during your search.

4. As a result of your search, list three items of current information you might use in your report.

Endnotes

[1]Tom Garrison, "New Trends in Corporate Presentation Furniture," *Managing Office Technology,* September 1995, p. 67.

[2]Marcia Mogelonsky, "A Desk at Home," *American Demographics,* June 1998.

[3]Leigh Gallagher, "Death to the Cubicle!" *Forbes,* September 7, 1998, p. 54.

[4]Al Toth, "Purchasing Office Suppliers: Make the Right Moves," *Managing Office Technology,* August 1995, p. 14.

[5]"Buying Right," *The Office Professional,* May 15, 1995, pp. 7-8. Reprinted from *The Office Professional* with permission from Professional Training Associates Inc., 210 Commerce Boulevard, Round Rock, TX 78664; 1-800-424-2112. Annual subscription rate is $48.

Forces That Influence Emerging Management Practices

chapter 4

66

It is not the employer who pays the wages. Employers only handle the money. It is the customer who pays the wages.

—*Henry Ford*

99

objectives

After completing this chapter, you will be able to:

1. **Identify the internal forces that are influencing emerging management practices.**

2. **Explain the difference between literacy and workplace literacy.**

3. **Identify the external forces that are influencing emerging management practices.**

4. **Describe the results of applying the continuous improvement process as a means of problem prevention.**

5. **Discuss the advantages to an organization that values diversity within its workforce.**

6. **Describe how the Americans with Disabilities Act affects management decisions.**

7. **Describe additional skills AOMs need to effectively manage globally aware office workers.**

An unprecedented interplay of technological, demographic, and global economic forces is reshaping the nature of work in America and redefining the American workplace and the role of its managers. The Old World before the 1990s relied on hierarchical, functionally oriented, command-and-control systems. Now we know these New World norms, although still forming, are heading towards flat, focused, flexible, and adaptive organizations capable of rapid responses to change.

Here are the ingredients for successful companies in the New World:

- They will be most adept at attracting, developing, assimilating, compensating, and retaining the talented people that they need.

Noel A. Kreicker

President and Founder
International Orientation
Resources (IOR)
Northbrook, Illinois

Noel A. Kreicker is president and founder of IOR, an international training and consulting company. IOR provides cross-cultural training, global business briefings language, and on-site, worldwide orientation services to over 100 *Fortune* 1,000 companies. Ms. Kreicker was a teacher in the Philippines as a Peace Corps volunteer from 1967 to 1969; an expatriate in Bogota, Colombia, in 1978; and travels overseas extensively. She writes and publishes articles on various aspects of cross-cultural training, communication, and leadership. In addition, she leads workshops for various international training associations.

QUESTION:

What are the most important skills for success as global managers, and what advice do these managers have for their successors?

Dialog *from the* Workplace

RESPONSE:

To determine what characteristics are necessary for overseas management in today's global economy, IOR surveyed 125 expatriate managers from around the world. The survey asked experienced international businesspeople about skills needed and challenges faced during assignments abroad.

Four *skills* were considered essential: flexibility, patience, the ability to listen well, and interest in learning foreign languages. One manager's comment is typical: "Patience, listening and learning skills, and the ability to adapt strategies to fit local circumstances are most important, as is having enthusiasm for local foods, drinks, and traditions."

Expatriates face *challenges* at home as well as at work. Common responses included loneliness and lack of established roots. This is exacerbated when expatriates work long hours and have little family time. Repatriation—fitting in back home professionally—was a concern of many.

Managers working overseas become aware of the value differences, which may impede *cultural understanding*. These include their own personal values, values of their native culture, and values of the host culture. Awareness of the first two helps in understanding the host culture.

U.S. citizens find that their inherent cultural assumptions, such as individualism, privacy, equality, and control over time, are not operative in most of the world. In Japan, for example, the welfare of the group comes before that of the individual. In China, there is no word for "privacy." Latin Americans believe that good interpersonal relationships are more important than arriving on time or adhering to a fixed schedule.

When asked what *demands* expatriates will face in the future, the global managers responded:

Learning to think on a global scale rather than on a U.S.-market scale.

Coping with a rapidly changing political environment, particularly in Eastern Europe and the Middle East.

Accepting that the age of American superiority is over.

Others included helping headquarters understand the reduced level of productivity that cultural differences can cause, finding qualified successors who possess the cross-cultural communication skills necessary to succeed in a foreign environment, and ensuring that expatriates are employed effectively upon repatriation.

While technical knowledge is important to success anywhere, cross-cultural understanding and communication skills are critical for success in a foreign environment. Future managers will no longer be able to operate effectively unless they understand other cultures.

- They will realize the importance of the soft stuff, like culture, change, motivation, and intellectual capital.
- And they will use self-managed teams and decentralize their decision making as the basic principle of their organization's design.[1]

Chapter 4 provides an in-depth discussion of the internal and external forces in the new millennium that are redefining management practices, organizational charts, and the manner in which people work.

INTERNAL FORCES

A number of forces are emanating from within organizations that are now shaping emerging management practices. Among those covered here are advanced information technology, workplace literacy, self-managed teams, knowledge workers, and just-in-time employment.

Advanced Information Technology

Technology is helping to shape the way workers work and managers manage. Rather than technology being a starting point in any strategic analysis, technology looks more like electricity as a resource that should be available *wherever* and *whenever* we need it. The ability to store, retrieve, analyze, and use this information can make the difference between a business that succeeds and a business that fails.[2]

Because of the significance proper use of information has to the success of all businesses, information technology (IT) departments are becoming critical entities in most organizations. Why? Information technology departments work with business issues as much as technologies, creating a need for technical professionals who are "business thinkers." Many businesses find that IT is now essentially a command center for customer contact due to the impact of the Web and **intranets,** which are the internal networks of particular company data that use Internet and Web technology.

Career-minded professionals will need a combination of technical knowledge and business savvy to advance; more and more companies fill IT management roles with generalists rather than specialists, emphasizing business skills. Experts say that interpersonal communication skills are among the most crucial because IT staff must communicate with co-workers in other areas of the business.[3] An opportunity for AOMs is to enhance the effectiveness and complement the IT department. Some might argue that in light of the aforementioned IT qualifications, an AOM has a whole new area on the career ladder now available.

Industries made lean and efficient by global competition coordinate resources by using computers to maximize productivity and ensure superior customer service. Chapters 12, 13, and 14 will cover in greater detail the degree of influence that advancing computer technology and information networks have on office information systems.

Workplace Literacy

A major concern for human resource managers today is the difficulty in locating and hiring a person who is literate; specifically, one who is able to function in a literate way while performing routine workplace activities. **Workplace literacy** is the aspect of functional literacy that is related to employability and skill requirements for particular jobs.

The foundation is literacy in a broad sense—that is, a combination of traditional literacy, which is the ability to read, write, and do basic math, and the ability to pull together the information obtained from reading and calculations and apply it in real-life situations. This application of knowledge requires information processing, logical reasoning, and critical-thinking capabilities together with basic reading, writing, and mathematics skills.

Because workplace literacy emphasizes combining knowledge gained in various facets of learning, it reflects closely the kind of proficiency required in the actual workplace—now and in the future, when the ability to grasp and process information will be increasingly in demand. The need for a high degree of workplace literacy is grounded in the reality that basic skill levels, which formerly were adequate, are now inadequate for employees faced with sophisticated quality control systems, team-based work, and global management practices. What degree of reading, writing, communication, and personal skills do AOMs seek in workers today?

Reading Skills. Today's office professional must be able to read well enough to understand correspondence, reports, records, equipment manuals, directories, charts, and graphs. Reading is the primary method used to locate information needed to make decisions or recommend courses of action. For example, when a new software package or upgrade version is purchased, employees are expected to have the reading and reasoning abilities to teach themselves the necessary information provided by the documentation or on-line help screens.

Writing Skills. Composition and grammar skills become more critical as more writing responsibilities are assumed by the office professional. Although word processing software can check spelling, word usage, and grammar, it cannot edit for content or completely proofread. Writers must be able to use a wide variety of reference books and software editing tools to fine-tune and professionalize their thoughts in writing.

Other Communication Skills. The authors of *Workforce 2000* assert that in the early part of the new millennium, 41 percent of new jobs will require high levels of communicating and

Solid writing skills are still needed in this age of software spell-checkers and thesauruses.   *©Digital Vision*

reasoning skills. The abilities to listen carefully to customers and co-workers and to speak well enough to convey one's point of view clearly and effectively are essential. The office professional must be able to communicate with customers both in person and by telephone, understand customer concerns, explain schedules and procedures, relay messages accurately, work as a team player, teach others, solve problems, and reason logically while probing for hidden meanings.

Clearly, the degree of preparedness expected of all workers is rising dramatically! To be competitive, organizations must either employ literate workers or upgrade the literacy levels of current workers. Table 4.1 compares the concepts of literacy and workplace literacy and gives examples of on-the-job workplace literacy skills needed for office-related reading, writing, and reasoning.

Self-Managed Teams

What appears to be happening today is the transformation of organizations into workplace communities with full gain- and pain-sharing for all; organizations where the fortunes of each member of the community—employee and investor—rise and fall with their performance in the marketplace. Self-managed teams are emerging as organizations view themselves as holistic and interconnected systems with each person accountable for the results of the organizations. For those companies that have successfully made the transition to team-oriented structures, the payoffs are noticeable.

These managing teams operate under democratic governance including a division of powers,

LITERACY VERSUS WORKPLACE LITERACY		
Literacy	In general, means the ability to read and understand a wide range of material, as well as the ability to write clearly and coherently.	
Workplace Literacy	The aspect of literacy related to employability and skill requirements for particular jobs. In general, workplace literacy requires information processing, logical reasoning, and critical-thinking capabilities, together with basic reading, writing, communication, and mathematics skills.	
Examples of on-the-job Workplace Literacy Skills		
Reading	*Writing*	*Reasoning*
Locates, understands, and interprets written information in documents well enough to perform tasks. These documents could be manuals, graphs, schedules, reports, or proposals.	Communicates thoughts, ideas, information, and messages in writing. Checks for complete and accurate information and edits for correct information, appropriate emphasis, form, grammar, punctuation, and spelling.	Discovers a rule or principle underlying the relationship between two or more items and applies it in solving a problem. Uses logic to draw appropriate conclusions from available information.

Table 4.1

Literacy Versus
Workplace
Literacy

accountability, and personal responsibility. Instead of the cumulative power of each level in the supervisory pyramid rising to a pinnacle where a chief executive officer retains ultimate control over the organization, a workplace with self-managed teams is transformed into a network of multiple power centers that exist based on task relevance.

What exactly is a team? Typically, a team consists of employees grouped together to complete a whole or distinct part of a product or service. Team members make decisions on a wide range of issues, often including such traditional management prerogatives as determining who will perform which tasks, solving quality problems, settling conflicts between members on the team, and selecting team leaders. The team approach seems to be more of an overall philosophy than a tightly defined set of rules.

Knowledge Workers

Knowledge is different from all other resources. It makes itself constantly obsolete, so today's advanced knowledge is tomorrow's ignorance. The productivity of knowledge and knowledge workers will not be the only competitive factor in the world economy. It is, however, likely to become a decisive factor for most industries.

Knowledge makes resources mobile. Knowledge workers, unlike manual workers in manufacturing, *own* the means of production: They are, in some cases, degreed specialists such as scientists, lawyers, and teachers. They are also office workers who are critical to organizations because of their daily interaction with company knowledge through creating, manipulating, and storing information. They carry that knowledge in their heads and can therefore take it with them. At the same time, the knowledge needs of organizations are likely to change continually even as an organization's employees move from job to job.

As a result, it is predicted that the workforce will consist of people who cannot be "managed" in the traditional sense of the word. They will not even be employees of the organizations for which they work, but rather contractors, experts, consultants, part-timers, and so on. An increasing number of these people will identify themselves by their own knowledge rather than by the organizations that pay them.[4]

The number one negative for knowledge workers is having much more information available to use than before. It is bad in the sense that it produces *infoglut*. Infoglut is not a static matter. It has been estimated in the *Encyclopedia of the Future* that scientific information doubles about every 12 years, and general information doubles about every two and a half years. The impacts of infoglut include the devaluing of information, as information overload leads to boredom. It also leads to stress and more work to keep up, with the loss of sleep as a consequence, leading in turn to lost productivity in the workplace and the classroom.

On the good side, however, information technology has given power to the people. These are fabulous tools of enormous power, which can flow to almost anybody who wants them. Information processed by human brainwork into knowledge and integrated and intuited into wisdom has quite suddenly become the world's most important resource. Why? Because information expands as it is used.[5]

Just-in-Time Employment

As permanent jobs become more and more temporary, temporary jobs are becoming more and more permanent. Becoming increasingly common, **just-in-time hiring** allows workers who are equipped with many different abilities to have an improved chance of finding employment in the future. Many companies recognize now that small numbers of versatile, sometimes temporary, workers can get jobs done as well or better than larger conventional workforces. Companies save money by using these temporary employees because there are no recruiting costs incurred or benefits provided. In addition, no company can afford to staff all the people for all of the things they need to do.

A multiskilled adaptable worker who can do two or more different types of jobs (e.g., desktop publishing and project management activities) has an edge on becoming and staying employed. Temporary employees bring with them knowledge and experience. They are usually self-starters and focus on completing the project. In addition, when they are no longer needed, they can be dismissed without emotional trauma.

Temporary Employment. What are some of the advantages of being employed by Manpower or Kelly Services? Many would suggest that temporary employment

- keeps work interesting.
- offers some flexibility with personal schedules.
- can be a bridge during a transition period in your career.
- can lead to a permanent job.

When considering a stint as a temporary employee, keep these things in mind:

- Choose the right staffing service.
- Communicate clearly with the staffing service and the contract employer.
- Use the staffing service as a resource to take advantage of as much training and as many assignments as you can.
- Be assertive, open minded, and responsive.
- Remember that you're a representative of the staffing service.[6]

Virtual Assistants. Another opportunity with a slight twist from temporary employment allows office support workers to perform administrative tasks in their own homes. They call themselves "virtual assistants." Essentially, virtual assistants are what were formerly known as home secretarial businesses, but they are connected to their clients electronically rather than, as before, by automobile. There are small businesses out there that need help with the little jobs so they can concentrate on what they want to do.[7]

EXTERNAL FORCES

Forces imposed on the organization from outside sources are many and varied. These external forces are discussed in the sections that follow: quality defined by customers, cultural diversity, Americans with Disabilities Act, managing globally aware office support workers, and external employment relationships.

Quality Defined by Customers

Quality is a judgment by customers or users of a product or service. A **customer** is an individual inside or outside an organization who depends on the output of an organization's efforts. A customer can be anyone who receives the work that you complete. For example, a customer may be your boss, a co-worker, another department, or someone who buys your company's products and services.

Quality is the extent to which the customers or users believe the product or service meets or, preferably, surpasses their needs and expectations. Quality improvement, therefore, is a lifetime commitment for organizations to make. There is no "quick fix." Given the current worldwide business arena, the product that was good enough yesterday barely squeaks by today and will be substandard tomorrow.

Quality is based on problem prevention, on the concept that we can prevent a problem only when we understand the *process* by which the product is produced or the service is rendered. A commitment to quality means stopping the process and fixing the problem before a customer becomes irate or before a critical stage is reached. Quality further means continuously searching for improved production processes and higher product or service standards.

Total Quality Management. Total quality management (TQM) applies quality principles to everything that a company does. Even the way an organization's departments work together on the inside—satisfying internal customers—is a hallmark of the TQM process. Living total quality means turning each employee into a problem solver for customers.

As a basis for understanding TQM, refer to Table 4.2. It explains the ideas and the current assumptions of each of W. Edwards Deming's fourteen points of management. Though it has taken many years, these ideas are practiced in many American companies today. As the table points out, Deming's way is more than just attention to quality control. It is a managerial philosophy for achieving lower costs and higher quality. The philosophy is universal. It works not only in the factory but also in hospitals, in service industries, and even in the office.

Why improve quality in the office? Because everything in an organization has to be done in the best way humanly possible. There is no room for "good enough." Applying quality to the service side of organizations includes look-ing at such issues as how promptly telephones get answered, how quickly callers get the information they need, and how accurate the information is that is given to customers. Quality improvement means changing the way business is done. The aim of quality improvement is to satisfy the customer *completely.*

Continuous Improvement Process and Prevention. The journey toward excellence is a never-ending road. Some people, because they see no end to the road, never take the first step. Others accept the challenge of the new day and continue down the road, forever improving and looking forward to tomorrow's challenges. These are the people who say "Good enough is not good enough. I can do better."

Managers need a map to help lead their companies down the quality road and keep them from running into dead ends. This road map, developed by Massaki Imai, is the *Kaizen* attitude, more commonly called the "continuous improvement process." The continuous improvement process (CIP) is an ongoing, continuous commitment to prevention of problems by focusing on the process. The basis for CIP is prevention as a means of improving quality. It makes sense that preventing problems is better than reacting to them!

Prevention implies that problems can be resolved before they occur. In other words, an organization's goal should be to do the job right the first time. Correcting a problem after it has occurred is always more expensive and frustrating than anticipating errors and taking preventive measures in the first place. Prevention

KEY POINT	HOW IT IS APPLIED
1. Create constancy of purpose for improvement of the product and service,	Rather than making money, the goal is to stay in business and provide jobs through innovative research, constant improvement, and maintenance.
2. Adopt a new philosophy about errors.	Make a change in accepting mistakes and negativism; they are unacceptable.
3. Cease dependence on mass.	Quality comes from improvement of the process, not inspection.
4. End the practice of awarding business on price tag alone.	Seek the best quality, and work to achieve a long-term relationship with that supplier.
5. Improve constantly and forever the system of production and service.	Improvement is not a one-time effort. Management must continually look for ways to reduce waste and improve quality.
6. Institute training.	All employees need to be trained—quality cannot be left to chance.
7. Institute leadership.	Leading consists of helping people do a better job and of learning (by objective methods) who is in need of individual help.
8. Drive out fear.	Encourage employees to ask questions or take a position on issues of concern to them.
9. Break down barriers between staff areas.	Employees need to work as a team so they can solve or foresee problems.
10. Eliminate slogans and targets for the workforce.	Let people put up their own slogans.
11. Eliminate numerical quotas.	Quotas take into account only numbers, not quality or methods.
12. Remove barriers to pride of workmanship.	People are eager to do a good job and distressed when they cannot.
13. Institute a vigorous program of education and retraining.	All people need to be educated in new methods, including teamwork and statistical techniques.
14. Take action to accomplish the transformation.	Workers cannot do it on their own, nor can managers. A special top-management team with a plan of action is needed.

Table 4.2

Deming's Fourteen Points Explained

Prevention is based on

1. Clearly understanding the requirements of the job/project.
2. Taking the requirements seriously and being vigilant.
3. Understanding all the functions of a job or process intimately.
4. Doing the job right the first time.
5. Working toward continual improvement.

Many advance the idea that there is a "10-1 payoff" if *PREVENTION* is used instead of *CORRECTION,* as shown in the following three office scenarios:

PREVENTION	CORRECTION
1. Prevention is spending time to record a message completely and fully so that you or someone else can respond properly.	1. Correction is spending ten times as many minutes to decipher, call back, and double check for the meaning of the original message.
2. Prevention is providing good office training and describing broad department goals so that all employees can see exactly how their work fits in and contributes.	2. Correction is spending ten times as many hours reprimanding, retraining, and doing the work yourself.
3. Prevention is spending one month learning the correct way to install and operate the office personal computer system for word processing, database management, and spreadsheets.	3. Correction is spending ten times as many months reinstalling software, losing data, and going back to the "old" way of doing things.

Table 4.3

"Prevention"—
The Basis of
Continuous
Improvement
Process

means having choices and being in control of your circumstances and environment. People prefer to change *by choice* rather than *by crisis.* Table 4.3 shows that prevention is based on five behaviors and attitudes of workers on the job.

Customer Call Center. What's a call center? A **call center** is an umbrella term that refers to reservation centers, help desks, information centers, or customer-service centers, regardless of how they are organized or what types of transactions they handle. They can incorporate multiple methods of customer communication—phone, fax, the Web, e-mail, and even interactive video kiosk. According to the Gartner Group, American companies spent an estimated $1.4 billion on call-center technology in

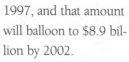

Management Tip

Customers deserve the most courteous and attentive treatment we can give them, and they are the lifeblood of every business. Without them, a business would have to close its doors.

1997, and that amount will balloon to $8.9 billion by 2002.

Because their technology can be leveraged to accomplish a variety of tasks, call centers are a major strategic factor for any type of business. The power that call centers have in capturing marketplace feedback, identifying customer expectations, and enabling companies to build products and services around those needs is astounding. Each contact with a prospective customer is a piece of the puzzle. The more pieces you have, the bigger the picture.[8] The end result is enough collected data to retain customer allegiance, thereby increasing revenue from products and services sold.

Here are some tips to help improve customer feedback and the way you use it:

- Develop a plan for collecting and analyzing customer feedback.
- Integrate all of the information and weigh it in terms of how it impacts your bottom line.

- Conduct follow-up telephone calls or mail letters to ascertain if problems have been resolved to your customers' satisfaction.
- Offer company-wide employee incentives to support the process.[9]

Cultural Diversity

New types of leaders are emerging—women entrepreneurs, people of color, techno-wizards and Generation Xers. By the year 2000, minorities will constitute 34 percent of the workforce, and by the year 2004, only 57 percent of people who enter America's workforce are going to be native-born White Americans.[10]

Cultural diversity can be defined as those human qualities that are different from our own and outside the groups to which we belong. Managing diversity requires valuing differences first and then creating structural or cultural changes that empower all members of the workforce to achieve meaning in their work and maximize their full potential in pursuit of organizational objectives. A difference does not indicate a deficiency.

Affirmative action legislation has spawned a multimillion-dollar business in the form of cultural diversity management. The concept of valuing differences is the cornerstone of the managing diversity movement.

Diversity includes differences such as physical and mental abilities, educational levels, gender, sexual orientation, age, and religion as well as cultural background. Diversity represents an enormous source of new ideas and vitality. Those organizations that learn to value employee diversity, and manage it as an asset, will be far more likely to flourish in the future. Those companies

Organizations experience greater rewards when they value diversity. © *PhotoDisc, Inc.*

that continue to view cultural diversity as a liability will be far more likely to fail.

Table 4.4 summarizes key elements surrounding the cultural diversity phenomena in organizations by defining and citing examples of primary and secondary issues that define cultural diversity. In addition, the table points out the benefits of valuing as well as the liabilities of not valuing diversity.

Americans with Disabilities Act

The employment provisions of the **Americans with Disabilities Act (ADA)** took effect in July 1990. Before the Act's passage, the majority of people with physical and mental disabilities—estimated to number in excess of 40 million Americans—had no legal recourse to redress disability discrimination. Managers and organizations need to conform with ADA's extensive rulings because it is the law. Further, ADA levies

hefty fines if an organization is challenged by an employee or potential employee and found guilty of noncompliance. Of most concern to office managers are Titles I and III of the ADA.

Title I. Title I covers the employment relationship. It prohibits employers with fifteen or more employees from discriminating against otherwise qualified job applicants and workers who have disabilities or become disabled. The job application process, the hiring decision, promotions, training, and wages all are covered by Title I. At issue are the conflicts—real and potential—with the reasonable accommodation requirement of the ADA.

Under ADA, **reasonable accommodation** means a modification or an adjustment to a job or the work environment that will enable a qualified applicant or employee with a disability to perform essential job functions. Reasonable accommodation also includes adjustments to ensure that a qualified individual with a disability has rights and privileges in employment equal to those of nondisabled employees.[11]

Examples of reasonable accommodation include making existing facilities used by employees readily accessible to and usable by an

What Issues Define Cultural Diversity?	Examples of Belittling Comments
Primary Issues	
Age	"Shouldn't you be retiring soon?"
Ethnicity	"Those people are too traditional to understand computers."
Gender	"Shouldn't she wait for a man to do that?"
Physical abilities	"Why don't we all get larger monitors?"
Sexual orientation	"Next he'll want health insurance for the guy he lives with."
Secondary Issues	
Education	"He couldn't even make it through high school."
Income	"I don't think she can afford good clothes."
Marital status	"What makes you think anyone could put up with him!"
Military experience	"He thinks he's still giving orders in the Army."
Parental status	"Poor thing, she grew up in a foster home."
Religious beliefs	"She's one of the 'born again' people."

Advantages of Valuing Diversity	Disadvantages of *Not* Valuing Diversity
1. Full utilization of human capital	1. High turnover among employees
2. Reduced interpersonal conflict	2. Low employee morale
3. Enhanced work relationships	3. Limited innovation
4. Shared organizational vision	4. Lagging productivity
5. Increased commitment among diverse employees	5. Increased inability to recruit the most talented new workers
6. Greater innovation and flexibility	

Table 4.4

Cultural Diversity

individual with a disability; restructuring a job; modifying work schedules; acquiring or modifying equipment; providing qualified readers or interpreters; or appropriately modifying examinations, training, or other programs. Employers are not required, however, to lower quality or quantity standards in order to make an accommodation, nor are employers obligated to provide personal use items such as glasses or hearing aids.

The decision as to the appropriate accommodation must be made on the particular facts of each case. In selecting which type of reasonable accommodation to provide, the principle test is that of effectiveness; in other words, whether the accommodation will enable the person with a disability to do the job in question.

Title III. Title III of the ADA requires that places of public accommodation and commercial facilities be accessible to people with disabilities. In essence, a business or establishment that is open to the public is considered a public accommodation. The law, under Title III, is concerned with barriers to building access, building corridors, restrooms, and offices so people with disabilities are able to move freely.[12]

Managing Globally Aware Office Professionals

Internationally speaking, the ability to transfer information electronically has made information itself a prime export candidate. Most countries do not have good information infrastructures and will buy information properly packaged from America.

To succeed as managers and employees in such a global environment, workers must

Businesses provide reasonable accommodation and access under the Americans with Disabilities Act.   © *PhotoDisc, Inc.*

acquire the tools that will make their organizations internationally competitive. American workers and managers specifically need an understanding of international business skills, cultural differences, global work teams, and transactional employment in order to help level the global playing field.

International Business Skills. There is nothing mysterious about what knowledge and types of skills today's workers need to become effective employees in international business. The key is not to wait but to develop the skills in an appropriate international context according to recognizable world standards. Some international business skills include the following:

1. *A basic understanding of international trade and economics.* Simply put, what a country produces efficiently, it can export; what it does not, it will likely import from

more efficient foreign suppliers. Organizations realize that improved trade opportunities happen when their employees demonstrate worldwide skills. These worldwide skills include knowing something about the religious beliefs, social customs, business philosophy, and family structure of the major trading nations.

2. *The ability to manage information.* One of the driving forces behind our global economy is the revolution in communications. To be competitive, businesses and their employees must be

   - Efficient users of electronic information and possess sound communication skills,
   - Familiar with the primary business documents used by nations as they conduct trade with one another, and
   - Familiar with the global network communications system that makes possible the instant transmission of business correspondence, news, and vast amounts of business data to virtually any point in the world.

3. *Knowledge of and sensitivity to political and cultural contexts.* Foreign government regulations must be understood and obeyed. Business culture can also vary dramatically from country to country. For example, in Muslim countries the workweek usually begins on Sunday.[13]

Cultural Differences. International business is fraught with unexpected events. Cultural differences are the most significant and troublesome variables encountered by a multinational company. Knowing what to do is as important as knowing what *not* to do. For example, gift-giving can create dilemmas. Sometimes gifts are expected and the failure to supply them is seen as an insult. Other times, however, the mere offer of such a token is considered offensive.

To avoid making blunders, a person must be educated to know the difference between what must be done, what must not be done, and what may or may not be done. Consider another example—many cultures have their own form of greeting. Often it is some variation of a handshake, but people also greet each other with hugs, nose rubs, kisses, and other gestures, depending on the culture. Failure to be aware of these customs has led to awkward and embarrassing encounters and to serious misunderstandings that could have been avoided.

In foreign countries, local people tend to be willing to overlook most of the mistakes tourists make; after all, they are just temporary visitors. But locals are much less tolerant of the mistakes of businesspeople, especially those who represent firms trying to project an impression of permanent interest in the local economy.

American corporations should think globally in the way they do business because they will surely gain a competitive advantage over other countries. American business should keep in mind that the French, Germans, British, Italians, and Spanish differ in how they conduct business, particularly in terms of names and greetings, appointments and punctuality, and socializing and gift-giving. Although it is impossible to detail every country's customs and etiquette, Table 4.5 recaps some business customs and tips to follow

COUNTRY	GREETINGS	APPOINTMENTS & PUNCTUALITY	SOCIAL & GIFTS
France	Prefer to be addressed by last name; shake hands at beginning and end of meeting	Make appointments in advance; punctuality is a sign of courtesy, but up to fifteen minutes late is still acceptable	Invitation to a home is rare; but, if invited, give flowers or chocolates to the host
Germany	Use titles and never refer to someone on first-name basis unless asked to do so	Make appointments in advance; punctuality is essential	If invited to a home, bring flowers and follow up with a thank-you note
Great Britain	Use first names upon introduction; shake hands only at first meeting	Make appointments in advance; arriving ten to twenty minutes late is expected	Invitation to a home, pub, or restaurant is normal
Italy	Refer to executives by their last names; hand-shaking and gesturing common	Make appointments in advance; if late, it requires an apology	If invited to a home, bring host a bottle of wine, flowers, or chocolates; exchanging business gifts is common
Spain	Use of first names occurs quickly; close friends greet with an embrace	Punctuality is not essential	If invited to a home, bring host flowers or chocolates; don't discuss business until after coffee is served

Table 4.5

Business Customs and Tips for European Business

Adapted from Karen Matthes, "Mind Your Manners When Doing Business in Europe," HR Focus, *January 1992, p. 19.*

when conducting business in the countries of France, Germany, Great Britain, Italy, and Spain.[14]

Global Work Teams. Global teams can make major contributions to multinational organizations, but they involve significant communications and cultural barriers that need to be overcome before success can be guaranteed. These teams help companies implement new projects, increase productivity, and facilitate cross-cultural influences.

Global teams come in various configurations. Generally, they fall into one of two categories: (1) intercultural teams, in which people from different cultures meet face-to-face to work on a project, and (2) virtual global teams, in which individuals remain in their separate locations around the world and conduct meetings via different forms of technology. Clear expectations, defined responsibilities, and an appreciation of cultural differences are among the basics to be accomplished by each team at the outset. Global teams concentrate on obtaining peak performance from solid use of the traditional methods of voice communication, e-mail, and teleconferencing.[15]

Transactional Employment. **Transactional employment** describes the work environment of today, where employees continuously develop their skills to allow them to constantly jump from one employer to another. This form of employment is already evident in multinational organizations that recruit individuals for positions in other countries.

Today, we see resumés that show people holding jobs for one or two years. And, depending on the industry and discipline, we frequently accept this when candidates explain this as tactical moves to obtain skill sets and enhance competencies. With the movement toward employees' owning their careers, it is a priority for employees to maintain their professional skills. This self-ownership leads us to terms like "free agency."[16]

External Employment Relationships

The company of the future will be a lean organization drawing on a network of external relationships. The trend toward outsourcing and partnerships will have an even broader impact in the future. Managing those relationships will be key. The job will be made easier when organizations truly understand their core competencies and then determine which noncore functions to outsource.

Core Competencies. A company must decide what its **core competencies** are—meaning the root business it is in and the primary functions of that business. These are often what the company handles internally; support systems are handled through outsourcing. Companies that once handled everything internally now find they must concentrate on their core competencies, so they outsource much more than they once did.[17]

Outsourcing. **Outsourcing** is a management strategy by which an organization utilizes specialized, efficient service providers to perform major, noncore functions. Total outsourcing activity will experience significant growth throughout the 2000 era, with revenues in the United States alone reaching 300 billion dollars. There are several reasons to consider outsourcing noncore business functions.

Outsourcing:

1. Gives access to world-class capabilities.

2. Accelerates reengineering benefits that aim for dramatic improvements in cost, quality, service, and speed.

3. Frees resources for other purposes; an organization can redirect its people and other resources to activities that serve the customer.

4. Eliminates difficult-to-manage functions.

5. Shifts company focus to the customer.

6. Frees up capital funds; outsourcing can reduce the need to invest capital funds in noncore business functions.

7. Reduces operating costs. Companies that try to do everything themselves often incur high research, development, and marketing expenses.

8. Provides access to resources not available internally.[18]

Outsourcing usually saves time and money—but sometimes it goes terribly wrong. Problems with outsourcing can include the inability of service providers to answer employee questions, provide correct information, or furnish service reports. The pitfalls of outsourcing can be avoided by implementing such measures as clearly articulating service delivery expectations, developing a vendor evaluation and selection process, and formulating performance outcomes.[19]

Once you've honed in on who you think is the best provider, interviewed for personal fit, and negotiated the best deal, the last step is to write a service agreement. In the service agreement, first specify service levels and costs. What do you expect? What are the timetables? Second, outline the methods you will use to measure effectiveness. Document all of this before you begin to work together.[20]

Rather than being a Band-Aid solution, outsourcing needs to be viewed as a long-term strategy, and partners need to be selected with the same diligence and calculation as in any other alliance. Because the company/vendor relationship is becoming increasingly long term, making the right selection becomes even more imperative. In light of this need, there are a number of factors to consider when choosing an outsourcing vendor:

- *Cultural Fit.* It is important that the culture of the vendor fit the culture of the organization so they can behave as partners.
- *Strong Client Base.* Look to see whether the vendor has long-term relationships or repeat clients.
- *Personal Integrity.* This may seem obvious, but one of the things a reliable outsource firm will quickly tell you is whether your company is *ready* for outsourcing.
- *Avoid Generic Solutions.* A firm worthy of assuming responsibility for your work must be flexible and skilled enough to provide innovative and customized approaches to problem solving.
- *Focus on Outcomes.* Collaborate in advance to identify specific outcomes and specific accountability for achieving them.[21]

In 1998, for example, U.S. companies spent more than $140 billion outsourcing information services, contracting out everything from installing PCs and software to developing new Internet-based commerce applications. And they plan to keep on spending—as much as $350 billion by 2002. As the cost of technology has come down, companies who need to inte-grate it are doing so, but they haven't the skills to do this in-house or the time to develop them.[22] Outsourcing is an opportunity most companies seize because it makes good eco-nomic and business sense given today's market conditions.

Message *for* AOMs

What are the driving forces shaping new leadership in the workplace? Many would argue that global telecommunications, corporate restructuring, and the extraordinary changes that we are going through have repealed every traditional law of leadership and management. The new leadership is one similar to a shifting mosaic that changes every day, and there is a powerful lineup of social, political, and economic forces that are systematically shattering these traditional notions of leadership.

The reality of modern business is that power is shifting and in many cases has already shifted *from* the system *to* the individual. Each person has to stand out today; we have entered the age of personal power, and that power comes from within, not from the system.

Successful companies do what unsuccessful companies are unwilling to do. Successful companies live outside of their comfort zone—they "think outside the box." Successful companies find opportunities. We can also say the same for successful people and leaders. Organizations and leaders that focus on fulfilling real human need and helping people to find meaningful and productive work are, without question, living outside their comfort zone, but they are positioning themselves to seize new opportunities and create a brave new world.[23]

1 A number of forces are emanating from within organizations that are now shaping emerging management practices. Among those covered here are advancing information technology, workplace literacy, self-managed teams, knowledge workers, and just-in-time employment.

2 Workplace literacy requires workers to have information processing, reasoning, and critical-thinking capabilities together with basic reading, writing, and mathematics skills that can be applied to work situations; functional literacy is not job related.

3 Forces imposed on the organization from outside sources are many and varied—specifically, quality defined by customers, cultural diversity, the Americans with Disabilities Act, managing globally aware office support workers, and external employment relationships.

4 The quality movement is based on problem prevention, which means stopping the process and fixing the problem before the customer becomes irate or before a critical stage of production is reached.

5 Those organizations that learn to value employee diversity and manage it as an asset will be far more likely to flourish in the future.

6 The Americans with Disabilities Act places heavy fines for noncompliance on organizations that practice discrimination toward people with physical or mental disabilities.

7 To be effective in international business, today's workers and managers need to develop skills in an appropriate international context according to recognizable world standards.

QUESTIONS FOR CRITICAL THINKING

1. Associate two of the internal forces with events that have affected your life in the past year and briefly describe the outcomes.

2. As a member of a self-managed team, what types of decisions would you make?

3. Describe one advantage of just-in-time hiring for the worker and one advantage for the organization.

4. In what ways is knowledge different from all other resources?

5. Associate two of the external forces with events that have affected your life in the past year and briefly describe the outcomes.

6. In your opinion, can cultural diversity really work in organizations?

Case Study 4-1: Workplace Literacy at Clean Sweep

Clean Sweep Janitorial Services is a good-size cleaning service in the Houston metropolitan area. Recently, cleaning supply sales representatives who have called on Clean Sweep's purchasing agent, Jim Sweeney, have told him how other janitorial companies are being sued because their workers have caused medical emergencies due to their inability to read and understand. Apparently, the workers cannot understand what the warnings on labels of chemically based cleaning products mean.

Given this information, Mr. Sweeney wonders if he should discuss the matter with the manager of the Safety Department, Mr. Jankowski.

Discussion Questions

1. Assume that Mr. Sweeney does contact Mr. Jankowski. What concerns should they discuss?

2. If you were Mr. Jankowski and were apprised of pending litigation for similar companies like Clean Sweep, what steps might you want to take to deal with the workplace literacy problem?

Case Study 4-2: Just-in-Time Hiring Policy

Mr. Larry Kuban, personnel director of a software accessories testing company, just got off the phone with an insurance representative who informed him the company's health and accident premiums would be going up 30 percent next year. This is alarming news to him, since top management is in a state of transition in the firm and decisions need to be made.

The president, his newly hired vice president for business services, Ms. Jerica Hatch, and Mr. Kuban meet, and it is clear that two decidedly different points of view are expressed. Ms. Hatch recommends laying off workers and implementing just-in-time hiring to meet the increase in benefits premiums. She said that is the action her previous company took and it makes good financial sense in the long run.

On the other hand, Mr. Kuban (who was a founding employee of the company ten years ago) promptly said, "We can't treat our employees that way—just calling them in when we need them, without any security or benefits. In my opinion, it's just not right or the fair thing to do."

Discussion Questions

1. If you were the president, which point of view would you support given the increase in premiums?

2. Describe any other options or compromises that might work.

Case Study 4-3: Internet Research Activity

Assume that you are doing a report on *temporary workers* or *just-in-time hiring.* Use the Internet to research information needed to answer the following questions. Key your responses.

1. List the keywords you used to do your search.

2. Write down three of the URL addresses that you accessed during your search.

3. As a result of your search, list three items of current information you might use in your report.

Endnotes:

[1]Ted Gautschi, "Developing Employees for the New World," *Design News,* May 18, 1998, p. 154.

[2]Dana H. Shultz, "Effective Information Management," The Law Office Technology Home Page, http://www/ds-a.com.

[3]Thomas York, "Business Specialists Needed," *InfoWorld,* April 6, 1998, p. 101.

[4]Peter Drucker, "The Future that Has Already Happened," *The Futurist,* November 1998, pp. 16–17.

[5]Ibid.

[6]Maureen Decola Harrison, "Permanently Temporary," *OFFICEPRO,* October 1997, pp. 24–25.

[7]Susan L. Fitzgerald, "Say Goodbye to 9 to 5," *The Secretary,* February 1997, p. 2.

[8]Alessandra Bianchi, "What's a Call Center?" *Inc.,* Tech 1998, No. 2, pp. 38–41.

[9]Carolyn M. Brown, "Customer Satisfaction: Turn Company Data into Company Profits," *Black Enterprise,* October 1998, p. 27.

[10]George Fraser, "The Slight Edge: Valuing and Managing Diversity," *Vital Speeches,* February 1, 1998, pp. 235–236.

[11]*ADA Compliance Highlights: A BNA Desk Reference* (Washington, DC: Bureau of National Affairs, 1992).

[12]Ibid.

[13]John McCaslin, "Preparing for Success in the World Economy: A Governmental Perspective," *The Balance Sheet,* January-February 1992, p. 23.

[14]Karen Mattes, "Mind Your Manners When Doing Business in Europe," *HR Focus,* January 1992, p. 19.

[15]Charlene Marmer Solomon, "Building Teams Across Borders," *Workforce,* November 1998, p. 32.

[16]Lance J. Richards, "Hiring Multicultural Vagabonds," *Workforce,* November 1998, p. 21.

[17]Jeffrey H. Epstein, "The Relationship Economy," *The Futurist,* November 1998, p. 8.

[18]JoAnn Davy, "Outsourcing Human Resources Headaches," *Managing Office Technology,* September 1998, pp. 6–7.

[19]Jennifer Laabs, "The Dark Side of Outsourcing," *Workforce,* September 1998, pp. 42–43.

[20]Charlene Marmer Solomon, "Protect Your Outsourcing Investment," *Workforce,* October 1998, p. 131.

[21]Rick Maurer and Nancy Mobley, "Outsourcing: Is it the HR Department of the Future?" *HR Focus,* November 1998, pp. 9–10.

[22]Julia King, "Managing Outside Help Is Latest IT Skill," *Computerworld,* October 26, 1998, p. 1.

[23]George Fraser, "The Slight Edge: Valuing and Managing Diversity," *Vital Speeches,* February 1, 1998, pp. 238–239.

Restructured Office Systems and Workplace Training Needs

> A teacher who is attempting to teach without inspiring the pupil with a desire to learn is hammering on cold iron.
>
> —*Horace Mann*

objectives

After completing this chapter, you will be able to:

1. **Describe a networked system in an office environment.**

2. **Explain how the office, as well as work, is going through restructuring.**

3. **Define the terms** *virtual organization,* *virtual workers,* **and** *virtual universities.*

4. **Explain how technology forces office professionals to develop new portable skills.**

5. **Discuss two reasons companies are investing time and money in retraining their existing employees.**

6. **Distinguish between the goals of corporate universities and that of universities and community colleges.**

Through computer networking, organizations benefit from time efficiencies and cost savings because files, devices, and programs are shared among employees. The trend is to develop networked systems in the office rather than to invest in individual computers, programs, and printers for each worker. Because of the sophistication of these network systems, new technologies and training in the workplace are changing and becoming recognized as critical to organizational success.

NETWORKED SYSTEMS IN THE OFFICE

Let's first learn some working definitions of what we mean when we refer to *systems* and *networks.*

Judy Norberg

Firm Administrator
Messerli & Kramer, P.A.
Attorneys at Law
Minneapolis, Minnesota

As firm administrator of a 32-attorney law firm located in Minneapolis, Judy Norberg is responsible for managing the business activities of the firm. Her responsibilities include general administration, human resources management, financial management, and facilities management. In addition, Judy is responsible for managing and coordinating all nonattorney personnel, space-lease negotiations, and expansion design. She has five staff reporting directly to her as well as all nonlawyer personnel. Judy has been in legal administration for over 10 years. She also has over 10 years of corporate management experience. Judy received her B.S. in business administration from the University of Minnesota.

Dialog *from the* Workplace

QUESTION:

How have enhancements in text/word processing changed the role of administrative personnel in the last three years? What efficiencies have been gained by the networking of microcomputers with text/word processing software?

RESPONSE:

When I think of how the computer has changed the role of administrative personnel over the last few years, thoughts come to mind like "ease of document preparation," "better and quicker communication," and "greater efficiencies."

Having been in the legal administration profession for over 10 years, I can reflect on how things were when I began. Secretaries had mag-card typewriters; word processing centers existed equipped with stand-alone word processors with screens. That equipment had a fraction of the flexibility and capability that microcomputers have today. There was no e-mail; there was no voice mail. Lengthy turnaround time for document production and seemingly endless telephone tag were ways of life. Today, many of our documents can be produced by calling up a short program (macro) and

completing it with variable information. Documents that used to take hours now take minutes.

Today, an administrative assistant or secretary needs to be a top-notch technician and administrative liaison. As a technician, he or she must be able to learn new software and hard-ware quickly and identify ways to streamline workload by its use. The role of administrative liaison is so important because as executives continue to move at a faster pace, the administrative assistant who can learn to think as they think and be willing to do more than is expected is truly invaluable. Employees with those traits are not easy to find, and when they are found, they must be valued!

The truly valuable administrative person is also adaptable. His or her natural way of thinking focuses on what *can* be done, rather than what *cannot* be done. Administrative personnel who exhibit this attitude energize themselves by constantly looking for a way to "build a better mousetrap." It is a win-win deal. The employee wins by growing; the employer wins because that individual is helping create a better organization.

Systems

A system implies the organization and order of a combination of elements or parts. Systems help us because we no longer enjoy the ease of using just one piece of equipment to complete an office task. Tasks are more complex, and various pieces of office equipment have the unique ability to blend with other equipment to become part of a system, connected by procedures, that have been developed to get things done. For example, some years ago a typewriter served as the input device, processor, and output device used to complete a three-page report. Today, a computer system can complete the activity with professional-quality results, error free, in a fraction of the time.

A **computer system,** such as that shown in Figure 5.1, is a group of computer devices that are connected, coordinated, and linked in such a way that they work as one to complete a task. With a computer system, the three-page report referred to earlier would be input using a computer keyboard, processed using the editing and other features of a word processing software program, and then output to a printer.

In addition to the computer and its related systems in the office, you will also find electronic telecommunications and mailing systems, accounting and records management systems, reprographic (copier) systems, distant office network systems, and office work flow and operational systems.

Networks

The development of communication channels and devices makes possible the widespread use of computer networks. A **computer network** is the linking together of central processing units (CPUs) and terminals via a communication system that allows users at different locations to share files, devices, and programs. Terminals and CPUs may be either geographically dispersed throughout a city, state, or country, or they may be situated within the physical constraints of a single office building.

With very few exceptions, most employers are networking personal computers (PCs) with other PCs instead of to a minicomputer or mainframe computer system. To be employable, future workers should have a working knowledge of the PC and of basic networking concepts. Employers need flexible, creative employees who are able to troubleshoot, solve problems, and find innovative ways to complete activities using networked technology and systems-oriented procedures.

OFFICE AND WORK RESTRUCTURING

Several network technologies will affect how office information systems are managed. For example, networked technologies are presenting a unique challenge that management has never faced before—the absent (from view), but working, employee. More and more, managers are working within a virtual organization with a staff of virtual workers and mobile workers.

The Virtual Organization and Virtual Workers

A new form of organization is evolving that uses information technologies to collapse time and space. Look around and you will see

Figure 5.1

Though comprised of many devices, a computer system works as one to complete office and business documents.
© *PhotoDisc, Inc.*

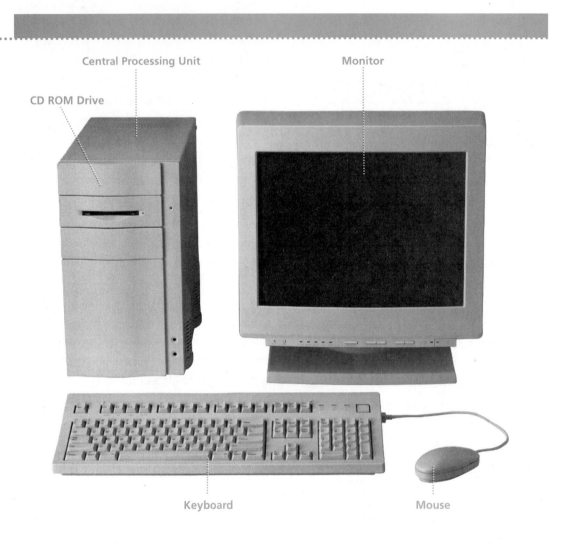

CD ROM Drive

Central Processing Unit

Monitor

Keyboard

Mouse

organizations on the business landscape that are changing rapidly in structure and function and will be, within a few decades, almost new entities. What is evolving are virtual organizations.

VeriFone Inc., which dominates the market in credit-card verification systems used by merchants, is a good example of a virtual organization. Everyone, from the chairman down to the most junior clerk, is issued a laptop computer and is expected to learn how to use it. Workers view their meeting place as the company's computer network. To maintain some human contact, executives, for example, meet face-to-face every six weeks. Internally, paper memos are banned, and secretaries—a rarity at the company's offices—are prohibited from handling executives' e-mail.[1] If an organization did not have a management culture that embraced computers for almost every task, then this long-distance operation would not work.

By using integrated computer and communications technologies, successful organizations will increasingly be defined not by concrete walls or physical space but by collaborative networks linking hundreds, thousands, or even tens of thousands of people.

Virtual organizations are collaborative networks that make it possible to draw on vital resources as needed, regardless of *where* they are located physically and regardless of *who* "owns" them—supplier or customer. Collaborative networks are able to deliver better products, higher quality, and higher returns to the bottom line. They leverage the strengths of each link in the value chain, improve efficiencies, reduce expenses, and focus on the coupling of processes and supporting systems.

These collaborative networks are becoming increasingly more popular because they allow businesses to form and dissolve relationships at an instant's notice and thus create new corporate economies. For example, instead of keeping fifty offices with fifty computers open all year long just to accommodate two months of rush business, it makes more sense to hire fifty virtual workers.

Virtual workers are people who work at home or away from the workplace and have their own computers and data communication devices. These workers can be physically located in Frankfurt, Germany, or Sedona, Arizona. It makes no difference. They dial into the company's database and become an extension of the company, connected by computers, fax machines, and other technologies.[2]

You may be asking how the customer is served by these new "virtual" concepts. One

scenario is that of a customer calling to place an order or get information about a product or service. When the call is received, all information about that customer flashes on the computer screen of the distant worker, wherever he or she is located. To customers, the process is

A virtual worker is an extension of an organization which is connected by computers, fax machines, and other technologies.   ©*CORBIS*

transparent, such that they are unaware of where, how, or by whom they are being served. Those widely scattered workers can operate as if they were all at company headquarters.

The main factor driving businesses toward virtual organizations is the pace of business operations. As Alvin Toffler predicted more than two decades ago, businesses now run at warp speeds, demanding immediate responses—anywhere, anytime. Today, it is survival of the fastest, not the fittest. Organizations are under pressure to cut drastically the time it takes to deliver a product from the engineer's workbench to the showroom floor. If they cannot deliver, organizations will lose millions of dollars in investments to a faster competitor who can deliver with an equal or better quality product.

Mobile Office Workers

Increasingly, the office is where the worker is—not the other way around. Millions of American workers today spend more of their time on the road instead of at their desks. This new mobile workforce demands new tools that both untether them from the workplace and, at the same time, allow them to stay in touch anytime, anyplace, and (very importantly) in any way—via phone, computer, fax, pager, videoconference, and so on.

Futurists predict that it is the dawn of a new era—the era of universal devices. For example, a pen-based "palm"-top PC will become your personal communicator, serving as your mailbox, your fax machine, your notebook, and even your electronic secretary.[3] What is unfolding is an office environment where all workers have a stake in and personal use for all types of office systems whenever and wherever they may be and at a moment's notice. The necessary technology is here. The driving force again is global competition and the pace at which businesses need to operate in order to compete successfully and survive.

We are an unwired society. It is the age of emancipation. Time and space have collapsed;

Mobile workers are connected by an invisible web of communication and intelligent technological devices.   © *PhotoDisc, Inc.*

the barriers to communication have fallen away. Workers are truly connected—linked to one another by an invisible web of communications networks and intelligent, integrated appliances.

Traditional offices have shrunk to mere "landing sites," where mobile workers dock for an hour or so at a communal electronic desk. Here, workers plug in their personal communicator and download all the data they have collected into a single electronic unit. This single electronic unit serves as an integrated, intelligent, document-processing, and management appliance combining fax, copier, printer, and scanner all in a machine no larger than a desktop laser printer.

Virtual organizations are becoming business ecosystems characterized by flexible relationships that are formed electronically within seconds. As a manager of office systems, how will you deal with these and other changes required of you in the future? Will there be a need for the type of employee we know today as "office manager"? Or will everybody, as a matter of routine, manage information systems as a member of the team in the flattened organization? There is mounting evidence that the latter option lies ahead.

TECHNOLOGY AND WORKPLACE TRAINING NEEDS

The impact of technology is evident in every aspect of society because it is a driving force in creating, using, and storing information. In a broad sense, **technology** can be viewed as an aid to making a task easier by using equipment and procedures to create, process, and output

Ethics/Choices

Suppose your friend Eddie told you in confidence that he is "getting over" on his boss by being an "absent, but working employee." Eddie said that the only time he really puts in a full day is when he comes to the office each Friday. Otherwise, instead of working an eight-to-ten-hour day, he puts in a maximum of five hours only and meets the requirements of the job well enough. What would be your reaction to Eddie?

information. Technology's impact is also evident in the changing job market. Employers will hire and pay good wages to employees who can demonstrate the ability to use technology effectively.

Therefore, all workers essentially must know how to use electronic information and communication technologies to manipulate data with computers and related equipment. These electronic information technologies manipulate text, numerics, graphics, voice, video, and sensory data.

Technology has lowered the skill levels of some jobs or eliminated them altogether, while raising the skill levels of other jobs. Technological advances also allow information and other resources to be transported faster. Today's workers most often need to locate, assess, and apply information as opposed to remembering things. The reason for this is because content changes

Management Tip

Seize every opportunity that comes along to be trained in new technology, equipment, and work methods. Workers who do this greatly improve their competitive edge in organizations.

and new information replaces old information at an alarming rate. What workers often lack today are skills for processing new information and integrating the new information with what they already know. Those processing and integrating skills are vital in a fast-changing business world.

As a result, employers need employees with new abilities. One is "how to learn" so employees can quickly apply strategies and tactics for learning new tasks. Another is to develop skills that are portable. To possess **portable skills** means you are able to transfer what you already know to slightly new situations. Workers need to recognize when a problem is enough like something they have done before that they can risk using skills and previous experience to solve the new problem.

As we discussed earlier, literacy at work, unlike in school, is seldom a matter of understanding or writing whole paragraphs. Rather, it involves sets of words that relate in a restrictive way to the organization and its particular work. Workplace literacy involves the ability to use words clearly and with brevity and accuracy in the context of a given job.

In similar fashion, the specialized language of the workplace is not academic in style; over time, workers tend to develop a highly specialized vocabulary, a language apart from the one learned in school. Though writing well is an important communication skill, researchers estimate that the typical U.S. worker spends only about 9 percent of the workday writing and about 13 percent of it reading. Another 23 percent of a worker's day is spent in speaking and a significant 55 percent in listening.

RETRAINING THE EXISTING WORKFORCE

In addition to employees who are entering the job market from school, there are many employees currently on the job who need retraining and skills upgrading to keep their jobs. Why are companies choosing to invest so much in workers with clearly deficient skills? Why not replace them with workers who have better skills? There are two reasons for this:

1. *Loyalty.* Companies realize that most of the people have been loyal employees for a number of years. In fact, they have performed their jobs competently, doing what organizations have asked them to do. For years, unfortunately, American industry has been intentionally modifying the structure of work to accommodate workers with diminishing levels of proficiency in the basic skills. Now, because companies are consciously changing the nature of that work, they feel responsible for providing workers with an opportunity to develop new skills.

2. *Few skilled workers.* The option of replacing these employees with ones who are more highly skilled is not possible. There simply are not enough skilled workers in the labor pool to meet the demand. Though companies cannot quantify the cumulative costs of all the instances where a lack of basic skills led to defects in products, productivity loss, or other problems, they have, to some extent, quantified the improvements in quality and productivity that result from having a workforce that has the basic skills.

Systematic Worker Education

The need for workforce training, retraining, and skill upgrading affects 80 percent of all workers who are currently in the workforce. In large sectors of the United States, unskilled work is being eliminated, but there is no formal system for worker learning. Current systems of mentoring, apprenticeship, and post-secondary education are seen as inadequate to meet this country's need for worker education. In light of this, for example, one state, New York, is taking the first steps toward systemic worker education. Thirty-four labor unions have formed the Consortium for Worker Education in New York City to develop a formal schooling system for workers that would provide continuous skills training and retraining programs.

The enterprise is uniting labor, business, education, and government. It has helped both blue- and white-collar workers as well as union members. The consortium currently provides programs to 35,000 people a year in workplace literacy, managerial skills, college preparatory, and computer literacy. Offering 650 classes in union halls, schools, and workplaces throughout the city, other boroughs—Brooklyn, Queens, the Bronx, and Staten Island—help 12,000 dislocated workers enroll in their programs annually. Fifty-nine percent of these workers are women; 84 percent, people of color; and 29 percent, unemployed.

Blue-collar workers and union members aren't the only beneficiaries of retraining. The unemployed professionals and managers cast aside by downsizing, mergers, restructuring, and new technologies are also helped. This type of relevant training is that which provides workers with the means of adapting to new technologies in a changing job market.[4] If systematic worker education programs pan out as expected, other states will probably follow suit.

Training Keeps Good Workers

Because employees are mobile, offering training or other career enhancements may be necessary to recruiting and retaining good workers. Assurances of long-term employment or defined career paths within the organization are far less important to employees in this new environment than career paths they can control and individual training that enhances their career potential.

That suggests a dual reality for employers: They must value their workers' knowledge and skills, at the same time acknowledging that today's employee may work for someone else

> **Management Tip**
>
> *One reason training is purposeful is because people often don't know exactly what they know and the application of that knowledge until training makes it clear.*

Corporate universities are one of the fastest expanding segments of higher education.

tomorrow. Japanese business culture, for example, tends to value personal relationships—and thereby the tacit knowledge in individuals—even more than Western culture does. As enterprises work more often through newly formed alliances than through their own internal organization, the ability to manage networks of people may be as key to future success as the core competencies of the partners involved.[5]

Corporate Training Programs

To meet the demands of a complex and fast-changing business world as described earlier, more and more corporations have taken a new approach to retooling their workforces. They've created their own universities to do the job.

Sears, Motorola, Saturn, Intel, and hundreds more have taken the plunge, making corporate universities perhaps the fastest-expanding segment of higher education. The number of these institutions has grown from 400 in 1988 and may well surpass 2,000 by the year 2000.

Corporate universities aren't a place, but a concept for organized learning that is designed to perpetuate the organization. By definition, a corporate university isn't a "university" at all because it does not grant a degree. It is instead a centralized, proactive organization that is responsible for all training and education at a given company. Its focus is far narrower than that of a traditional university. Ideally, the courses offered at a corporate university are in-depth, customized, and closely linked to the company's strategic mission.

Some corporate universities have their own bricks-and-mortar campuses, but many have no central location at all. They are virtual universities, which rely heavily on the Internet, intranets, satellite television, and other state-of-the-art technologies to transmit knowledge and skills. The faculty is often a blend of full-time employees of the corporate university, instructors borrowed from nearby community colleges or universities, and employees of various vendors or other companies.

Whatever form they take, corporate universities have the goal of producing highly skilled, knowledgeable, and adaptable workers who are invaluable in today's burgeoning "knowledge economy." The average corporate university translates into an investment of 2.3 percent of an organization's payroll, for an average annual operating budget in excess of $10 million.

For example, Motorola University, which began operations in 1981, has an annual operating budget of about $200 million. All Motorola employees worldwide must complete at least 40 hours of job-related training annually in such areas as technology education, software design, executive education, quality control, and competencies in marketing, sales and distribution.[6]

New Training Topics

Innovative organizations are teaming up with community colleges in particular to deliver much of the retraining needs to industry's workers. For example, certificates and degrees in customer service and quality processes are appearing in college catalogs. Similarly, new courses that include never-before-taught topics are being offered at postsecondary institutions. For example, you will hear topics such as these discussed:

- leadership for nonmanagers,
- global issues for the quality workplace,
- network training and certification
- project management skills,
- computer usage and network applications,
- microcomputer repair and troubleshooting,
- writing for results,
- teamwork dynamics,
- business ethics,

- total customer service,
- principles of total quality management, and
- leadership and empowerment strategies.

Successful companies are changing their attitudes and putting more people and financial resources into training at *all* levels, which is good. Organizations realize as never before that to improve the quality of the workforce, ongoing training and continuous learning are imperative. A trained and educated workforce that believes in learning as a lifelong process and continuing education as the key ingredient for individual success will become the cornerstone for successful companies dedicated to achieving company-wide continuous improvement.

> **Management Tip**
>
> *Periodically visit your local Chamber of Commerce and ask what training sessions it sponsors for its members. In most cases, you can get an up-to-date idea of new trends, procedures, and hot training topics in business in less than five minutes.*

Message *for* AOMs

If you step back and look at the big picture, there is a learning revolution at work. Organizations are valuing the brainpower and diversity of their workforce as never before. You see management structures changing, barriers coming down, and technology available to all workers through net-worked systems. Moreover, the AOM's job is in the process of *becoming.* Supervisors are becoming mentors and coaches—not taskmasters. As a result, workers are being asked to play roles as communicators, problem solvers, and decision makers—roles that are new to them but critical to your overall success as an AOM.

Basic skills within the context of worklife enable individuals to reach their fullest potential—whether that is measured by a healthy bottom line or a transformed attitude toward work and self. Don't fight the current—extract as much that is good and positive from this learning revolution as you can.

1 A computer network is created by linking CPUs and terminals via a communication system that allows users at different locations to share files, devices, and programs.

2 Using integrated computer and communications technologies, organizations will increasingly be defined not by concrete walls or physical space but by collaborative networks linking hundreds of people together.

3 Virtual organizations are collaborative networks that draw together vital resources as needed to deliver better products, higher quality, improved time to market, and higher returns to the bottom line. Virtual workers who work out of their homes with their own computers are doing work that is transparent to the customers being served. Virtual universities offer in-depth and customized courses that are closely linked to the company's strategic mission.

4 Portable skills allow workers to transfer what they already know to different situations. Workers, for example, need to know electronic information technologies that manipulate text, numerics, graphics, voice, video, and sensory data.

5 Employers invest in retraining their existing workforce because of loyalty to the workers and the recognition that there are few skilled workers in the supply pool.

6 The goal of corporate universities is to train their employees in line with their strategic plan; whereas the goal of a university or community college is to grant degrees and certificates.

QUESTIONS FOR CRITICAL THINKING

1. In your own words, describe your understanding of a computer networked system in an office environment.

2. Describe your understanding of a virtual organization.

3. What is the difference between a virtual worker and a mobile worker?

4. Discuss which new workplace skills are valued by employers and why.

5. In what ways are today's employees being retrained and by whom?

6. In your own words, describe why a learning revolution is occurring in the workplace.

Case Study 5-1: Volunteering at Innovative Products

David Sutton and Melissa Dodgers work together in the administrative services area at Innovative Products, Inc., in Seattle, Washington. Though Melissa respects David's work and regards him highly, lately she has been having some problems with his attitude. For starters, when Melissa was asked by the cooperative education coordinator at North Seattle Community College to mentor a graduating student in a 20-hour work internship project, David belittled Melissa and said she would get behind in her work. Further, he hinted that she was doing it just to "show off" and make points with the bosses. On another recent occasion, when Innovative Products networked the six PCs in their department, David volunteered Melissa to be the interim network administrator by saying "she has plenty of time."

Melissa normally would not have minded taking on this extra task because learning has always been important to her, but she thinks David's two actions are motivated by anger, jealousy, or both. As a result, Melissa is beginning to resent David and is starting to avoid him. He appears to be hurt.

Discussion Questions

1. Is there a perceived problem as far as Melissa is concerned? As far as David is concerned? If so, what is/are the precise problem(s)?

2. Evaluate David's behavior. Is Melissa overreacting?

3. Evaluate Melissa's reaction.

4. If this relationship continues as it is now, what do you think will be the possible immediate outcomes.

5. What recommendations would you make to resolve the apparent conflict?

Case Study 5-2: Workers Expect Free Training

Legal Advisors of Philadelphia employs approximately ten paralegals and fifteen administrative secretaries. It is the owners' belief that assistance with training costs should be available for any employee who seeks to improve skills. Therefore, the following policy was posted outside the human resource department on Friday around 4:00 P.M.

> Up to $150 in training allowance per fiscal year will be awarded to employees who choose to pursue training opportunities off the job. Reimbursement will require proof of registration and a final course grade of B or better.

Several employees were reading the new policy prior to 5:00 P.M. and they, in general, appear to be astonished that Legal Advisors would not pay for all expenses incurred in future training as long as a passing grade of C or better was awarded.

Discussion Questions

1. What do you feel the responsibility of a company is insofar as paying employees to upgrade their job skills?

2. If you were management, would you consider altering the policy? Defend your point of view.

Case Study 3:
Internet Research Activity

Assume you are doing a report on *corporate universities*. Use the Internet to research information needed to answer the following questions. Key your responses.

1. Which Web search engine did you use?

2. Write down three of the URL addresses that you accessed during your search.

3. As a result of your search, list three items of current information you might use in your report.

Part 1:
Debate the Issue

1. Retrieve the file Part 1—Debate, which contains the table shown below, from the template disk. Using the form for each of the six issues listed in step 3, quickly key some ideas you have as initial reactions to each statement.

2. Prepare to role play either point of view in a mock in-class debate.

3. Part 1 debate issues follow:

   a. "The integration of cultural diversity at this company has gone too far. There are people in jobs today because of what and who they are. Many do not have the best qualifications needed to do the job right. I know for a fact that better qualified applicants were passed over during the screening process."

   b. "A background check is your best tool against hiring a thief. You should be able to not hire someone if you know ahead of time that he or she has an arrest record."

   c. "My boss pays my salary. For all the talk about serving customers, the real objective is to keep the boss happy!"

   d. "If an administrative office system does not work well, it should be 'put on the computer' so that it will be better."

   e. "If a company installs a system, costs will always be reduced."

   f. "With a good administrative office system in operation, a firm does not need as many office workers."

POINTS OF AGREEMENT		POINTS OF DISAGREEMENT	
1.		1.	
2.		2.	
3.		3.	
4.		4.	

Endnotes

[1]Russell Mitchell, "Virtual Worker: Anyplace I Hang My Modem Is Home," *Business Week,* October 17, 1994, p. 96.

[2]Samuel E. Bleecker, "The Virtual Organization," *The Futurist,* March–April 1994, p. 9.

[3]Ibid., p. 12.

[4]Andy Humm, "Back to Work," *Social Policy,* Winter 1998, pp. 23–24.

[5]Jeffrey H. Epstein, "The Relationship Economy," *The Futurist,* November 1998, pp. 8–9.

[6]Richard Greenberg, "Corporate U. Takes the Job Training Field," *Techniques,* October 1998, pp. 36–38.

solutions

groupthink

motivation

Practicing Leadership and Communication Skills

Leadership, Motivation, and Problem Solving in Organizations

chapter 6

> "Work done with little effort is likely to yield little results."
>
> —B. C. Forbes

objectives

After completing this chapter, you will be able to:

1. **Distinguish among the characteristics of leaders and managers.**

2. **Contrast McGregor's Theories X and Y in relation to why people work and how Ouchi's Theory Z is different from Theories X and Y.**

3. **Describe the two principles behind Maslow's hierarchy of needs.**

4. **Identify the advantages to an organization of hiring a Generation Xer and an older worker.**

5. **Cite some common defensive reactions that allow people to maintain a positive self-image.**

6. **Distinguish between position power and personal power in organizations.**

7. **List some strategies managers can follow when dealing with power games and office politics.**

8. **List seven steps in the problem-solving process.**

Merely placing people together does not guarantee success in organizations that are comprised of individuals with diverse backgrounds and perceptions. The real challenge comes in effectively leading, motivating and solving problems as they are sure to arise.

EFFECTIVE LEADERSHIP

Effective leadership involves exerting influence in a way that achieves the organization's goals through enhancing the productivity and job satisfaction of the workforce. Successful leaders can increase their effectiveness by expecting the best from people, maintaining a positive self-regard, developing a desire for the entire team to achieve, and by simply saying "thank you."

The Nature of Leadership

When analyzing the dichotomy between leadership and management, management could be stated as "doing *things right*," whereas leadership could be described as "doing the *right thing*."

Brother David Nagel, SCJ

Director of Development
St. Joseph's Indian School
Chamberlain, South Dakota

Brother David Nagle, SCJ, is a member of the Congregation of the Priests of the Sacred Heart. Brother David received his associate of arts degree in foods and nutrition and bachelor of science degree in business administration from Cardinal Stritch College. After receiving his masters of theology studies at Catholic Theological Union in 1990, he assumed the position of director of development at St. Joseph's Indian School.

St. Joseph's employs 245 people in a variety of ministries, with its primary program being a residential child services facility. All funding for the school programs and its outreach programs comes from private donations. The development office provides a full line of services from its own printing shop and computer department to a mailing department.

QUESTION:

Think back, Brother David, about your success in managing the various technologies within St. Joseph's Indian School. What skills and competencies have helped the most? What advice do you offer to managers in an automated environment?

Dialog *from the* Workplace

RESPONSE:

First, you need to understand your business and how you meet the needs of your customers, both in house and outside the organization. Define the natural divisions of labor for your endeavor and choose managers for each of these divisions.

The team model works best. Set aside two days a week for team meetings; one day for policies, procedures, and learning; and the other day for production schedules and labor-related issues. Invite all the managers to share the issues of their operation. Educate all the managers about the other departments so everyone can see how their roles relate and interconnect.

Since managers are learning about other areas of the operations, see where employees can share related jobs. Cross-train employees within a department and between departments. This promotes an understanding of the job functions for all departments.

Periodically update managers in the progress they are making in their positions. Give them feedback on how the entire operation is doing. In a more general, less detailed way, explain the current situation to the entire staff. Let them know what is going on and how they can and do influence the final outcome.

The most important aspect of the operation is computer services, or information management. Let the organization direct the selection of the hardware and software. Bigger hardware is not always better in the area of information services. It is easy for an MIS manager to try to answer the organization's needs by putting in a larger computer or more hardware. If the software and skill levels of the staff are not there, the software and hardware are useless.

Be critical of proposed hardware and software changes. Let your MIS department demonstrate the value and ease of using all products. The user of the hardware and software should decide what is best for your organization. Involve managers and staff in the final selection and then pick the final product to purchase.

The key is team involvement. Ask questions of managers and staff to keep communications going. Praise good work; challenge when needed; give constructive feedback constantly. Together, as a team, the organization can fill its mission if everyone has a chance to be a part of the process through both the difficulties and rewards.

Management entails completing the technical, more mechanical, aspects of everyday tasks, while conforming closely to department policy, procedures, rules, and regulations. Leadership, in contrast, as shown in Figure 6.1, encompasses the spirit, vision, and ethical considerations that accompany the decision-making processing.

Morale can easily decline if companies have more managers than leaders. While a leader must possess certain inherent leadership qualities, raw charisma alone does not ensure success. Born or bred, leaders must not only successfully manage the day-to-day operations of their departments, but they must also determine the long-term goals of the company and enlist the wholehearted cooperation of their subordinates to accomplish these goals. The most effective way to motivate workers is to excite people with ideas and values—and then tie it all together with money. A good leader energizes an organization around a set of ideas.[1]

Leaders must determine their own strengths and weaknesses so that, in times of crisis, they can react with authority and calm. Leaders must first demand of themselves what they expect from others. When leaders show consistency, their subordinates trust them. True leaders do not make impulsive decisions, waver, or agonize over political outcomes, nor do they depart from convention merely for the sake of personal convenience. Instead, they possess character and a spirit of fairness that dictate each decision. Instilling ideas that inspire a sense of ownership, pride, and commitment that makes all subordinates eager to fulfill their duties is the job of a leader, not merely a manager.

Figure 6.1

Management is "doing things right," whereas leadership is "doing the right thing."

Does that mean being "just a manager" is not good? According to Craig R. Hickman, author of *Mind of a Manager, Soul of a Leader,* organizations need both leader qualities (visionary, empathetic, and flexible) and manager qualities (practical, reasonable, and decisive). He states that the ability to provide balanced managerial leadership is the essential skill. Further, the question is not "What approach works better?" but, rather, "What combination works best?"[2]

Leadership Habits, Attitudes, and Styles

Leaders have many unique facets that promote their overall effectiveness with people. A person's habits, attitudes, and leadership styles make him or her truly one of a kind.

Leadership Habits. Steven R. Covey wrote the popular book *The 7 Habits of Highly Effective People* in 1989 as a guide for businesspeople to recognize that our character is a component of our habits. Covey presents seven habits that, by becoming the basis of a person's character, will create an empowering center of correct maps from which an individual can effectively solve problems, maximize opportunities, and continually learn and integrate other principles in an upward spiral of growth. The seven habits he identifies and explains follow:

1. *Be proactive.* Being proactive means taking the responsibility to make things happen instead of sitting back and letting things happen to us.

2. *Begin with the end in mind.* Evaluate everything that matters most to us in the context of the whole.

3. *Put first things first.* Manage yourself by organizing your time and tying weekly goals into your principles and priorities.

4. *Think win-win.* Cooperation, not competition, is the key.

5. *Listen first—then express yourself.* Learn how to explain your ideas clearly and logically, in the context of the other person's viewpoint.

6. *Synergize.* All seven habits practiced together will unify and unleash new powers and create new, exciting alternatives.

7. *Sharpen the saw.* This means taking the time to renew the four sides of your nature: the physical, the mental, the spiritual, and the social/emotional sides.

Leadership Attitudes. Leadership attitudes often form out of a belief concerning why people work. Most notable of these notions are the ideas of Theory X and Theory Y as proffered by Douglas McGregor, author of the classic management book, *The Human Side of Enterprise.*

The idea that people work because they have to work is illustrated by the Theory X view of people. **Theory X** includes assumptions that people generally dislike work, lack ambition, and work primarily because they have to get money to live. Punishment, threat, and close supervision might be necessary to motivate individuals.

Theory Y, on the other hand, assumes that work is as natural as rest or play and that workers will accept responsibility when self-direction and self-control can be used to pursue valued objectives. Further, it can be argued with Theory Y that work can be inherently motivating in and of itself.

William Ouchi, who wrote the book *Theory Z,* in which he contrasted American and Japanese industry, concluded that Japanese industrial success and world-class productivity were results of better management, an approach he called Theory Z. **Theory Z** emphasizes long-range planning, consensus decision making, and strong mutual worker-employer loyalty. The

key to increased productivity, therefore, is to get employees involved by using such techniques as quality circles, developing interpersonal skills, and broadening career path opportunities and development.

Refer to Table 6.1 for a comparison of the X, Y, and Z theories.

Leadership Styles. Leaders can be categorized also by the attitudes and styles they use to get a job done. Leadership experience reveals that, in some situations, an autocratic approach might be best; in others, a participative approach; in some, a task-oriented approach; in still others, a people-oriented approach. This conclusion emphasizes that leadership is complex and that the most appropriate style depends on several interrelated

McGregor's Theory X	Assumes that people generally dislike work, lack ambition, and work because they have to get money to live. Punishment, threat, and close supervision might be necessary to motivate individuals.
McGregor's Theory Y	Assumes that people regard work to be as natural as rest or play and that workers will accept responsibility to direct and control their activities. Inherent in Theory Y is that work can be motivating in and of itself.
Ouchi's Theory Z	Emphasizes long-range planning, consensus decision making, and strong mutual worker-employer loyalty. The key to motivation and increased productivity is to get employees involved by using such techniques as quality circles, developing interpersonal skills, and broadening career path opportunities and development.

Table 6.1

McGregor's X and Y Theories and Ouchi's Z Theory

variables, such as a leader or follower's level of experience, task and environmental safety concerns, and the routine or unique nature of the task to be done.

Autocratic. An autocratic leader is one who makes most of the decisions alone instead of allowing followers to participate in the decision-making process. He or she feels that efficient operations result from arranging the work conditions in such a way that human elements minimally influence the task.

Participative. In sharp contrast, a participative leader involves followers heavily in the decision-making process by using group involvement to set basic objectives, establish strategies, and determine job assignments. With this management style, a cycle is established. The cycle begins with the employee participating in decision making. As decision making improves, worker satisfaction and morale improve, which then recycles back to the employee wanting to participate more often in the success of the organization.

Task-Oriented. A task-oriented leader is one who focuses on getting the job done with specific emphasis on planning, scheduling, and processing the work. These leaders exercise close control over quality and the process by continually dealing with issues, such as what tasks need to be done as well as when and how to do a particular task.

People-Oriented. A people-oriented leader focuses on the welfare and feeling of followers and has self-confidence and a strong need to develop and empower team members. In other

words, this approach gives power to the workers to accomplish the work because they have a commitment to the organization.

Women as Leaders

If women seem confused about what they want, society is even more confused about what it wants from women.[3] With each passing day, evidence is mounting on the unique skills and perspectives that women, as a group, bring to business. Most workers reject the stereotypes that describe female bosses as manipulative, wishy-washy, domineering, or less qualified than male bosses. As women rise in the ranks, the demands on their time and the breadth of their responsibilities increase along with their clout.

Regardless of gender, the goals and behaviors of many professional leaders are the same. However, the manner in which these goals and behaviors are achieved differ. The feminine approach tends to be holistic, process-oriented, inclusive, collaborative, emotional, and self-doubting; the masculine approach tends to be linear, result-oriented, hierarchical, territorial, and confident. Currently, the masculine traits are valued; however, women have learned to utilize the masculine style to be assertive, to summarize their viewpoints, and to make bottom-line decisions.[4]

Management Tip

The spotlight is not on managers when they are handling everyday office routines—it is when they are facing a crisis. Crises are inevitable. If one is going to happen, be ready for it. Conduct your own personal crisis-preparedness audit ahead of time.

Though, at times, rising in ranks in an organization can be bittersweet, many women say they are becoming increasingly optimistic about the prospects for change from the inside. Organizations are facing up to and acting in good faith on the realization that skilled managers are not determined by gender.

Today, many women find themselves at a crossroads. A taste of power has made many women desire it, while an awareness of its pitfalls and shortcomings has made others reevaluate its importance in their lives.

STAFF MOTIVATION

The major difference between most people and extremely successful people is the gap between what they *know* and what they *do*. Both groups have about the same knowledge base. Extremely successful people are just better at doing what they "should" be doing. Helping workers bridge

Effective leadership requires good communication skills.   © *CORBIS*

the gap between what they know and what they do is an important aspect of a manager's job. Some would call this *task motivation.*

Motivating Factors and Recognition

Promoting genuine and lasting employee motivation is not something management does; rather, it is a process that management fosters and allows to happen. Most employees are already motivated. Managers simply need to provide an environment that supports their motivation. Most employees want to do a good job. They want to excel and are naturally motivated to do so. The challenge is to release that motivation. This is easier said than done because the motivation to work is a complex drive influenced by both external and internal factors.

External Motivating Factors. External factors can be either positive or negative. Punishment, a negative factor, may include the threat of dismissal, a refusal to increase salary, or being "called on the carpet." Rewards, a positive factor, may include a salary increase or job promotion.

The problem most managers soon face when motivating exclusively with rewards is that they often run out. The problem with motivating by threat of punishment is that it breeds fear and resentment, which are likely to be expressed in behavior that interferes with achieving company goals. Common examples of this negative behavior are complaints, criticisms, absenteeism, wasted time, forgotten important details, communication of false information, rudeness to customers, and decisions that take the path of least resistance.

Internal Motivating Factors. Internal motivation most often occurs when an employee's qualities match the requirements of the job. Motivating supervisors compare employees to checking accounts: You can only make withdrawals after you build up a balance. Managers need to steer clear of sweeping statements such as "You're terrific" and focus instead on targeted praise, such as "Getting the report out on time last week was crucial; you really came through. Thanks." People remember this kind of constructive feedback.[5]

Staff Recognition. While the days of rewarding employees for long-term service aren't over, a growing number of organizations are bestowing specific rewards to workers who reach targeted business results and who demonstrate exacting goal-oriented behaviors. When employees don't meet corporate goals, they get limited or no extra rewards; but, when employees do, they get rewarded. And the new rewards are bonding an organization from top to bottom through a common purpose.[6]

Employee motivation is highly individualized. Recognition should be, too. Instead of highly structured motivation programs such as employee of the month designation, information recognition programs focus on spontaneous, sincere, and personal appreciation of employee efforts. Some examples of simple informal recognition techniques that companies use to improve employee morale and productivity include the following:

- Buy "Welcome to the team" flowers for an employee on his or her first day.

- Give "Time Off" certificates to employees.
- Hand out thank-you cards with candy or flowers.
- Give employees movie tickets for a job well done.
- Take an employee out to lunch.
- Wash an employee's car for him or her during lunch.[7]

Generally, entry-level office positions are classified as low-wage work. What research has determined is that major needs of low-wage workers are recognition for their good work and help with special problems, such as child care and immigration. When employees dislike their jobs or are indifferent toward them, their attitudes can lead to high turnover rates, theft, poor customer service, and low productivity. Managing low-wage workers successfully requires sensitivity, common sense, and a good measure of psychology.[8]

Some often-subtle signs of discontent within a nonmotivated workforce include:

- Staff members rarely participate actively in meetings.
- Workers display no creativity or innovation.
- Cliques form.
- Most people routinely are in a hurry to leave work exactly at closing time.
- Workers seldom smile—until it's time to leave.
- Workers don't feel comfortable coming to your office.
- You start to lose people.
- Employees shut you out of their personal lives.[9]

Motivation and Maslow's Need Theory

The relationship among motivation, ability, and performance would be simple if productivity were a function of ability alone. If it was, output would vary directly with increases in a worker's ability. However, because employees have their freedom of choice to perform either effectively, ineffectively, or not at all, motivation is necessary to increase output. On-the-job performance and success are related to the type and extent of motivation involved.

Although managers can certainly create a climate of positive motivation, in the final analysis, motivation comes from *within* each person. Theories of motivation, such as Maslow's need theory, focus on the question of what causes behavior to occur and to stop. The answers usually center on the needs, incentives, and perceptions that drive, pressure, spur, and force people to perform. The needs and perceptions are internal to the individual; the incentives are external factors that give value to the outcome of people's behavior.

For example, Maslow based his concept of a hierarchy of needs on two principles. First, human needs may be arranged in a hierarchy of importance, progressing from a lower to a higher order of needs. Second, a satisfied need no longer serves as a primary motivator of behavior. Examples of Maslow's needs' hierarchy and how they relate to worker motivation are shown in Table 6.2.

The five needs are briefly described next:

1. *Physiological or biological needs.* At the lowest level of the hierarchy of needs, but of primary importance when they are not met, are our physiological or biological needs, such as food, clothing, and shelter. Satisfaction of these needs is derived in part from money.

2. *Safety or security needs.* When the physiological needs are reasonably well satisfied, safety and security needs become important. For many people, this need involves the freedom from fear and anxiety that results in being able to plan ahead with confidence.

3. *Social or belonging needs.* Social needs include the need for belonging, association, acceptance by colleagues, and giving and receiving friendship and love. When people's social needs—as well as their safety needs—are not satisfied, they may behave in ways that tend to hinder motivation and, worse, defeat organizational objectives.

4. *Esteem or ego needs.* Above the social needs, esteem needs are of two kinds: those that relate to one's self-esteem (needs for self-confidence, independence, achievement, competence, and knowledge) and those that relate to one's reputation (need for status, recognition, appreciation, and the deserved respect of one's colleagues).

NEEDS	ON-THE-JOB EXAMPLES	IF NEED NOT MET, WORKER MAY FEEL:
Physiological	Pay	Anxious
	Rest	Physical pain
	Breaks	
Safety	Benefits plan	Frightened
	Fair treatment	Suspicious
	Safe and clean working environment	Distrustful
Social	Work groups	Hurt
	Company-sponsored events and activities	Withdrawn
		Alone
		Conspicuous
Esteem	Praise and recognition	Discouraged
	Promotion	Inferior
	Being asked for help or advice	Resentful
Self-Actualization	Learning new skills	Dampened enthusiasm
	Growing and developing	Nervous
	Feeling a sense of accomplishment	

Table 6.2

Maslow's Need Theory

5. *Self-actualization or self-fulfillment needs.* These needs include feeling self-fulfilled, realizing one's own potential, continued self-development, and being creative in the broadest sense of that term.

Motivating Generation X Workers

We have already begun to see the development of new business structures, ideas, and products that take into account under-30 employees' changes and preferences. The Generation X discussions have focused mainly on the youths' supposedly short attention spans and attention-deficit disorders, ignoring or underemphasizing what is perhaps the most crucial factor—that this under-30 generation thinks, and sees the world, in ways entirely different from their parents. Their developing minds learned to adapt to speed and thrive on it—they grew up on video games, MTV, and ultra-fast speed of action films. What are some work-related characteristics managers cannot ignore?

- *Parallel processing ability.* The under-30 generation feels more comfortable than their predecessors in doing more than one thing at once (e.g., doing homework while watching TV). This parallel-processing ability will allow workers to be better able to wear multiple hats and be part of many constituencies—what workers of tomorrow need.

- *Random-access thinking.* The Xers were the first to experience hypertext and "clicking around." Therefore, they can more easily make connections and are free from the constraint of a single path of thought.

- *Connected.* The previous generation was linked by telephone, a system that is synchronous (i.e., both people have to be there). In contrast, the under-30 generation has been raised with asynchronous worldwide communication of e-mail, broadcast messages, user groups, and Internet searches. As a result of this "connected" experience, young people tend to think differently about how to get information and solve problems.

- *Technology as friend, not foe.* To the older generation, technology is generally something to be feared, tolerated, or at best harnessed to one's purposes. To the younger generation, the computer is a friend. Being connected is a necessity. "What technology will I have?" is often the key factor in a young worker's decision about what job to accept.[10]

Rather than forcing the younger generation to use the methods of the past, managers should be offering them the resources to create their own approaches that will work in their

new mental/cognitive environment. Generation Xers are far more particular in the jobs they are accepting. Job candidates in their twenties are interested in working in a corporate culture where there are fun activities and camaraderie, as well as cutting-edge technology.

Working on multiple projects with little supervision comes naturally to this generation. Because many of them are latchkey kids and are used to taking care of themselves, they can work in an environment that allows them to be trusted in the job very quickly. They think in a very rapid-fire style (e.g., MTV, video games, action shows); they're used to multitasking as a way of life, so managers need to provide lots of opportunities. The Baby Boomers grew up under people who said you have to earn the right to benefits. Generation Xers just assume that's what they're due. For management, this conflict can cause frustration.[11]

Motivating Older Workers

For many, work doesn't need to end with retirement. As life spans lengthen and living costs increase, researchers say more older people will want and need jobs. Currently, 79 percent of workers begin collecting Social Security benefits at age 62. Wanting to work longer, and even being willing to be paid less for it and move into service jobs, may allow some people to get jobs. But businesses have incentives to encourage older workers to leave. They need people with different skills to operate the computer program that operates everything else.

When businesses do hire older workers, the results can be beneficial for everyone. Older workers are dependable, they have a work ethic, and they are willing to accept flexible schedules. In addition, employers also appreciate the value of seasoned judgment and a lifetime of experience.[12]

Motivational Problems and Behaviors

Managers must regularly deal with other motivational problems, specifically on-the-job personality disorders. **Personality disorders,** such as excessive absenteeism, tardiness, withdrawal, and personality conflicts, are defensive reactions and abnormal behaviors motivated by the need to survive. Self-preservation is an inherent, inborn instinct, and survival is the primary motivator for all of us. Because people with personality disorders know of no other way to survive, they are often defensive and exhibit abnormal behavior. These behaviors can negatively affect morale and restrict the performance of other motivated workers in the organization.

Motivated workers stay on top of situations by planning ahead. © *PhotoDisc, Inc.*

Defensive Behavior.

Nearly everyone has felt defensive at one time or another. For example, when someone is coming toward you with a raised fist or when you are being unfairly criticized, you are going to do whatever is necessary to protect yourself. You naturally put up a defense with actions or words. A **defensive reaction** is a way of thinking that cushions the blow resulting from an immediate inability to overcome an obstacle or barrier that has been placed in your path.

Defensive reactions allow you to maintain a positive self-image. In motivating workers, managers can expect workers to exhibit these common defensive reactions:

- *rationalization:* making an excuse;
- *projection:* blaming others for your shortcomings;
- *aggression:* treating others in a condescending, overbearing, threatening, and demeaning manner;
- *scapegoating:* using aggressive behavior against those who cannot fight back; and
- *withdrawal:* avoiding conflicts by leaving a situation physically or mentally.

Table 6.3 offers some examples of defensive reactions specific to the office environment.

Abnormal Behavior.

A second motivational problem is known as *abnormal behavior.*

> **Management Tip**
>
> *When making a decision or solving a problem, always try to seek out the best alternative rather than simply settling for the most convenient one.*

DEFENSIVE REACTION	EXAMPLES
Rationalization Making an excuse	▪ "The report is late because no one told me it was due today." ▪ "I'm late to work because my car ran out of gas."
Projection Blaming others for your shortcomings	▪ "I didn't get the work from Harriet soon enough to finish on time." ▪ "There are errors in this report because my secretary has been preoccupied with family matters."
Aggression Treating others in a condescending, overbearing, threatening, and demeaning manner	▪ "Let me explain it to you again!" ▪ "There's no excuse for your not being prepared."
Scapegoating Using aggressive behavior against those who cannot fight back	▪ "The new woman in the marketing department is the one who made the mistake, not me. But she will learn." ▪ "Jack must have forgotten to order copier paper before he left on vacation."
Withdrawal Avoiding conflicts by leaving a situation physically or mentally	▪ "I can't take her constant chatter any-more. I'm going to lunch early." ▪ "I've got another meeting to attend. Will you tell me who decided what?"

Table 6.3

Examples of Defensive Reactions by Office Workers

Abnormal behavior is the result of experiencing continual difficulties in adjusting to ordinary everyday situations. Being defensive and overly suspicious, using illogical thinking, and overcompensating for shortcomings are examples of these and other common unhealthy behaviors. For example, when an employee is counseled by his or her supervisor, should the employee establish the pattern to become defensive and continually blame someone else or some circumstance for his or her shortcomings, then that could be construed as abnormal behavior.

Job Satisfaction

In light of the preceding discussion, increasing an employee's job satisfaction cannot be left to chance. Two techniques used by successful managers are job enrichment and horizontal moves as a result of an organization's realignment of positions through a new process called *broadbanding.*

Job Enrichment. Close analyses of job histories reveal that the performance of workers starts to decline once they find themselves unchallenged in their positions. One way to ensure that employees do not lose interest in their jobs is to provide them with new challenges through such measures as job rotation and involvement in special projects, which often come under the term *job enrichment.* Job enrichment refers to an approach by organizations to lessen job monotony by redesigning the job. The usual ways of enriching a job are to build into it more planning and decision-making authority, increased autonomy and responsibility, and additional control over outcomes by employees.

Though job enrichment is used by major organizations to provide job satisfaction, it is not a cure-all for other problems such as dissatisfaction with pay or not getting along with the boss. In fact, if employees already feel they are overworked, underpaid, and unappreciated, job enrichment will most likely backfire. Employees will see it as being asked to do even more for the company without any apparent benefit to them.

Horizontal Moves and Broadbanding. A horizontal move can boost a career or stall it. Until recently, most advice on career development focused on how to move up the corporate ladder. The thinking was that only the inferior moved sideways—horizontal moves hinted at stagnation or failure.

However, as corporate America continues its cutbacks and layoffs that result in a broader,

flatter hierarchy, horizontal moves are no longer taboo; they are encouraged. Some companies use them as a way to keep valued employees challenged and motivated.

Today, career paths often take a zigzag pattern. Sometimes, careers follow a straight, vertical line; sometimes, they will move sideways. What is important to workers is to make sure that each move—vertical or horizontal—adds to their knowledge and prepares them for the next job.

In fact, one of the trends in the personnel business is a new horizontal structure called broadbanding. With **broadbanding,** as illustrated in Figure 6.2, employees are loosely organized into a few broad job categories, rather than the dozens of titles used in traditional systems. Such a system encourages employees to focus on developing particular skills instead of following the old-fashioned linear path of advancement.

POWER, OFFICE POLITICS, AND MOTIVATION

Information professionals need to understand power, office politics, and how they can positively or negatively influence a worker's motivation on the job.

Power and Motivation

The way managers and others use power in an organization can affect motivation. Power dynamics requires that individuals develop a personal power base in order to successfully accomplish their goals and tasks. Power is not an attempt to influence but the *ability* to influence others. Effective leaders know how and

Figure 6.2
. . . .

With broadbanding, the types of tasks are the basis for the few job categories into which employees fit.

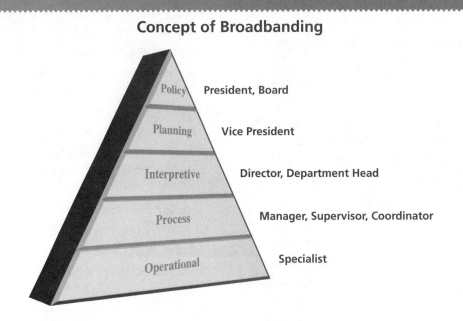

Concept of Broadbanding

Policy	**President, Board**
Planning	**Vice President**
Interpretive	**Director, Department Head**
Process	**Manager, Supervisor, Coordinator**
Operational	**Specialist**

when to use their power, whether that power is position or personal power.

Position Power. Formal authority to tell others what to do that is granted by the organization is called **position power.** Generally, the more position power held by the leader, the more favorable the leadership situation. For example, managers, supervisors, and military officers have strong position power.

The major benefit from position power is that leaders who have it can access needed resources in order to meet objectives. Position power also allows leaders to carry out their responsibilities with relative autonomy.

Personal Power. On the other hand, personal power is informal power that is manifested by the extent to which followers are *willing* to follow

a leader. **Personal power,** unlike position power, comes from below. Personal power is a day-to-day phenomenon. One day you might have it and the next day you might not. To be an effective motivator, leaders need to have both types of power, as shown in Figure 6.3.

Office Politics and Motivation

We would all like to claim that politics does not exist in organizations. However, human nature, being what it is, will always breed a certain amount of politics, intrigue, and alliances. Although it is not something you want to foster, organizational politics will continue to be widespread and is something that leaders should acknowledge as part of organizational culture, learn to live with, and, if possible, learn to use constructively.[13]

Some managers think of office politics as leveraging, positioning, and building alliances. In these cases, smart office politics refers to communicating well with superiors, drawing out the best in subordinates, and working easily with colleagues. Still, others think of office politics in less glowing terms. For example, in military lingo, it could be said that office politics is keeping your eye on the target, but remembering to watch your flank. Office politics is a complex issue.[14]

In dealing with power and game players, managers may want to consider these strategies:

1. *Avoid taking sides in power struggles.* Your goal is to be recognized as your own person and to gain a reputation for objectivity and

Ethics/Choices

Your intuition tells you that another manager of equal rank is pulling a "power play" on you by pointing out to your boss small errors you have made during the past few months. You would like to stop her behavior. How would you go about it?

fairness. You can be supportive of others, where appropriate, and still draw the line at fighting their battles for them.

2. *Keep social contacts constructive.* No matter at what level of the organization you might socialize, if you are part of a group that

POWER
Position   or   Personal

Figure 6.3

Is it better to have position power or personal power or both?

meets regularly for any reason, be aware of the presence of the "three P's":

- *Politics:* Is anyone using this group to build themselves up or tear others down?
- *Pretense:* Are you free to be yourself and say whatever is on your mind, or must you always be aware of what others will think?
- *Pettiness:* Are these get-togethers vicious, and are you afraid people would talk about you if you were not there?

DECISION MAKING AND PROBLEM SOLVING

Decision making is at the heart of management. Even so, many managers find decision making difficult. One thing is clear, however, and that is unless they can overcome their fear of decision making, their careers will stall.

The Decision-Making Responsibility

Poor decision makers may be smart and diligent, but when it comes to settling on a course of action, they resort to delaying tactics or they blame others to duck responsibility. At work, you aren't penalized nearly as harshly for making a poor decision as for not making a decision at all.[15] Avoiding this responsibility and failing to make a deadline are cardinal sins that few organizations will tolerate.

The Decision-Making Process. Decisions are based on facts, intuition, and past experience. On paper, decision making is a relatively simple process. The process starts with a need to make a decision. Then, at least two

alternative courses of action are determined, followed by a selection of the best choice from the alternatives. In practice, however, decision making is a very conscious process that involves the future.

Factors to Consider. Keep these factors in mind when making decisions:

1. The right person should make the decision.

2. Decisions should contribute to objectives and reflect the organization's vision.

3. Effective decision making takes time and effort but cannot be put off until later.

4. Though there is seldom only one acceptable choice, one usually surfaces as the best direction to take at the time given the particular circumstances.

5. Decision making improves with practice. The more you do it, the easier it becomes.

6. A decision may not please everyone. That is not its intent.

7. A decision begins the process for other activities to go forward.

Some questions follow that you can use to ease the task and guide effective business decision making. Managers should ask themselves:

1. What is the basic issue that must be addressed and resolved?

2. Is all the needed information available to make a timely and informed decision?

3. How have similar issues been handled in the past? Should anything be done differently this time?

ADVANTAGES	DISADVANTAGES
1. Provides the manager with a broad range of information.	1. Holds the manager accountable for the group's decision.
2. Lends a more "creative" approach to problem solving.	2. Takes the work group's time away from other aspects of their jobs.
3. Improves communication in the department.	3. May result in "choosing sides" and cause morale problems.
4. Creates high morale in the work group.	4. Allows for strong personalities to dominate the work group.
5. Stresses a stronger commitment to decisions made.	5. Requires more supervisory skill.
	6. Is difficult to use if the decision must be made quickly.

Table 6.4

Group Decision Making

4. If the stakes appear too high, is there a compromise that can be settled on as a safety net?

Should decisions be made by an individual or by a group? Clearly, the trend is toward empowerment and group decision making; however, to keep some perspective, Table 6.4 lists both the advantages and disadvantages of group decision making.

A systematic approach to decision making is another process that advocates eight possible steps. You may or may not need every step, depending on the particular situation. A good solution to a well-posed problem is usually far superior to an outstanding solution to a poorly posed problem.[16] A systematic approach to decision making includes the following steps:

1. Address the right decision problem.

2. Clarify your real objectives.

3. Develop a range of creative alternatives.

4. Understand the consequences of your decision.

5. Make appropriate trade-offs among conflicting objectives.

6. Deal sensibly with uncertainties.

7. Take account of your risk-taking attitude.

8. Plan ahead for decisions.[17]

Problem-Solving Steps

Problem solving is not a skill that people are born with; it is an art that is learned and fine-tuned over the years. Typically in a work setting, the problem-solving process is learned by observing and emulating others.

One simple technique that a manager can use to speed a solution more quickly is to write the description of the problem he or she is trying to solve in the form of a question and display it in a prominent place in his or her office.

For example, the question "What is the single most important thing we should do to improve staff retention?" displayed on a whiteboard or on a sticky note near a work area can be seen throughout the workday.

Using the display technique helps to define the problem clearly, which is the first step to problem solving. The steps that follow represent one problem-solving approach:

1. Define the idea or problem that needs attention.

2. Collect, interpret, and analyze information.

3. Develop possible alternative solutions.

4. Analyze the implications of selected alternatives.

5. Select the preferred alternative.

6. Implement the decision.

7. Follow up, evaluate, and modify the decision, if necessary.

Message *for* AOMs

The ability to keep cool in a crisis is one of the qualities that distinguish the good manager from a run-of-the-mill one. Chapter 6 has identified several responsibilities of AOMs that *can* result in crisis situations. Not everyone is cut out to be an organizational leader. It is a tough job that includes making thoughtful decisions and understanding how to best interact with and motivate each of those people who report to you.

When you become a manager, remember to give sincere praise on a regular basis to those you supervise. The rewards from recognizing praiseworthy employees motivate them and results in making your job easier.

When you acknowledge good performance in others, be sure to specify the behavior, its results, and your feelings. Another idea is to let people tell you the story of their own success and how they did it, and then listen intently. After all, nothing encourages successful performance like a receptive audience.

1 Management entails completing the technical, more mechanical aspects of everyday tasks, while conforming closely to department policy, procedures, rules, and regulations. Leadership, in contrast, encompasses the spirit, vision, and ethical considerations that accompany the decision-making process.

2 Theory X includes assumptions that people generally dislike work, lack ambition, and work primarily because they have to get money to live. Punishment, threat, and close supervision might be necessary to motivate individuals. Theory Y, on the other hand, assumes that work is as natural as rest or play and that workers will accept responsibility when self-direction and self-control can be used to pursue valued objectives. Theory Z emphasizes long-range planning, consensus decision making, and strong mutual worker-employer loyalty.

3 Maslow based his concept of a hierarchy of needs on two principles: (1) human needs may be arranged in a hierarchy of importance, progressing from a lower to a higher order of needs and (2) a satisfied need no longer serves as a primary motivator of behavior.

4 The under-30 generation feels more comfortable than their predecessors in doing more than one thing at once; they can more easily make connections and are free from the constraint of a single path of thought; they tend to think differently about how to get information and solve problems; and they view the computer as a friend. Older workers are dependable, they have a work ethic, and they are willing to accept flexible schedules.

5 Some defensive behaviors include making an excuse, blaming others for your shortcomings; treating others in a condescending, overbearing, threatening, and demeaning manner; using aggressive behavior against those who cannot fight back; and avoiding conflicts by leaving a situation physically or mentally.

6 Formal authority to tell others what to do that is granted by the organization is called position power. On the other hand, personal power is informal power that is manifested by the extent to which followers are *willing* to follow a leader. Personal power, unlike position power, comes from below.

7 Some managers think of office politics as leveraging, positioning, and building alliances. In these cases, smart office politics refers to communicating well with superiors, drawing out the best in subordinates, and working easily with colleagues. Still others think of office politics in less glowing terms.

8 The seven steps in the problem-solving process are (1) Define the idea or problem that needs attention, (2) Collect, interpret, and analyze information, (3) Develop possible alternative solutions, (4) Analyze the implications of selected alternatives, (5) Select the preferred alternative, (6) Implement the decision, and (7) Follow up, evaluate, and modify the decision, if necessary.

QUESTIONS FOR CRITICAL THINKING

1. In your own words, distinguish between management and leadership.

2. Cite three situations in the life of an AOM where the behaviors of Theories X, Y, and Z might be appropriate.

3. What behaviors do you feel describe a poor decision maker?

4. Which one of the defensive reactions do you feel is the most serious one with which an AOM has to deal?

5. What are some basic differences between position and personal power?

6. In your opinion, what is the most dangerous aspect of office politics in the workplace?

Case Study 6-1: The Behavior Styles of Two Managers

Assume you are on an interview team to select a new president and CEO for your organization. During the course of the interviews, two of the candidates expressed the following behavior styles.

Candidate A said:

In turning troubled companies around, I would use this technique. I would first observe how people work and then reorganize. I would promote the top 10 percent and fire the bottom 10 percent. It's amazing how much energy it gives to the remaining 80 percent. Persuasion alone won't do the job. I would further pick role models on either end of the spectrum and do something with them. I believe this would promote a tighter team with a lot of deadwood and office politics gone. Actions speak louder than words!

Candidate B said:

I would push decision making down into the middle ranks and create a corporate culture that questions the status quo, welcomes change, and encourages teamwork. Both men and women thrive in a boundaryless environment. To that end, I would want to have my employees determine how to spend the day or week. If they believe they need to take a supplementary course or spend a week at a customer site to improve their knowledge of a key subject, then I say let them do it. It's understood that everyone is working toward our team's common goal, and we all want to be successful.

Discussion Questions

1. Discuss the advantages of each style of leadership, as well as some possible disadvantages that could surface with each style.

2. Given only these two candidates, which one would you choose to be president and CEO? Why?

Case Study 6-2: Office Politics Gone Too Far

Amber Siskowski, an office worker at Regal Technical School, is waiting for the office manager to return from lunch. Amber, who was recently promoted to executive assistant to the vice president, has been the brunt of several offensive office political games within the past six weeks. In her wait for Mr. Robert Wilson, the office manager, to return, she contemplates what she should do about this latest trick. Should she make a scene and confront the two women she suspects are behind these acts, should she quit her job, or should she seek legal counsel? This latest tactic has crossed the line, and Amber has had it.

When Mr. Wilson returns, Amber follows him into his office, lays down a letter addressed to her husband on Mr. Wilson's desk, and asks him to read it. Mr. Wilson is perplexed but begins to read. He can see real anger in Amber's face and overall demeanor. In a very few sentences, he ascertains that the letter strongly suggests to her husband that Amber is having an affair at work.

Amber wants to know what Mr. Wilson plans to do about this accusation and outright lie. She denies any affair is going on and is willing to confront her accuser(s)—whoever they may be. Her husband feels Regal Technical School should put an end to these games.

Discussion Questions

1. If you were Mr. Wilson, what would be your initial reaction?

2. In your opinion, does the company become responsible for serious allegations made by a co-worker to another co-worker?

3. If you were Mr. Wilson, how would you advise Amber?

Case Study 6-3: *Internet Research Activity*

Assume you are doing a report on *Generation X workers.* Use the Internet to research information needed to answer the following questions. Key your responses.

1. Which Web search engine did you use?

2. Write down three of the URL addresses that you accessed during your search.

3. As a result of your search, develop an outline of the topics you might use in your report.

Endnotes

[1] Genevieve Capowski, "Revving Up to Lead," *HR Focus,* January 1998, p. 2.

[2] Craig R. Hickman, *Mind of a Manager, Soul of a Leader* (New York: John Wiley and Sons, 1990).

[3] Deborah Stone, "Work and the Moral Woman," *American Prospect,* November/December 1997, p. 78.

[4] Jacqueline Stanfield, "On Our Own Terms: Portraits of Women Business Leaders," *The Social Science Journal,* April 1997, p. 260.

[5] Carolyn Wiley, "Create an Environment for Employee Motivation," *HR Focus,* June 1992, p. 15.

[6] Jennifer J. Laabs, "Targeted Rewards Jump-Start Motivation," *Workforce,* February 1998, pp. 89–90.

[7] Kevin Wallsten, "Targeted Rewards Have Greater Value—and Bigger Impact," *Workforce,* November 1998, p. 4.

[8] Roberta Maynard, "How to Motivate Low-Wage Workers," *Nation's Business,* May 1997, p. 36.

[9] Rosalind Jeffries, "Are Your Workers Unmotivated?" *Nation's Business,* May 1997, p. 23.

[10] Marc Prensky, "Twitch Speed—Reaching Younger Workers Who Think Differently, Literally," *The Conference Board,* June 1998, p. 44.

[11] Julia King, "All Work No Play? Gen X-ers; No Way," *Computerworld,* May 5, 1997, p. 2.

[12] Marilyn Gardner, "New Outlooks on Retirement," *Christian Science Monitor,* November 14, 1997, pp. 10–11.

[13] Helen F. Jailer, "Corporate Politics and the Information Professional," *Online,* July 1993, pp. 49–50.

[14] Susan M. Barbieri, "How to Win Allies and Influence Snakes," *Working Woman,* August 1993, p. 35.

[15] Adele Scheele, "Smarter Decision Making," *Working Woman,* January 1993, p. 22.

[16] John S. Hammond, Ralph L. Keeney, Howard Raiffa, "The Perfect Decision," *Inc.,* October 1998, pp. 74–75.

[17] John S. Hammond, Ralph L. Keeney, Howard Raiffa, *Smart Choices: A Practical Guide to Making Better Decisions,* Harvard Business School Press, 1998.

The Communication Process and Office Communication Networks

Chapter 7

> " A meeting is no substitute for progress.
>
> —*Unknown* "

objectives

After completing this chapter, you will be able to:

1. Describe the communication process.

2. List examples of nonverbal communication.

3. Discuss how filtering negatively affects the communication process.

4. Explain the importance of feedback in the communication process.

5. Describe the difference between upward communication and downward communication.

6. Explain the positive and negative aspects of the grapevine as an informal communication channel.

7. Describe ways in which information can be disseminated to employees who work away from the office.

8. Identify the purposes of organizational meetings.

9. Explain the importance of intercultural communication in business today.

Communication is the basis of all our relationships. Without it, each of us would live dreary lives in isolation. We need other people, and our connections to others are forged by communication. Yet, because we learned to communicate gradually as we grew up, most of us have never really thought about this valuable skill. The purposes for which oral and written communication are transmitted in the office and some of the media commonly used for their transmission are presented in Table 7.1.

THE COMMUNICATION PROCESS

Although most of us take communication for granted, its importance cannot be overestimated. According to communication experts, we spend about 70 percent of our waking hours communicating—speaking, listening, reading, and writing. We can choose the most appropriate communication medium from the following:

Roger Courts

Director and CEO
Sacred Heart League
Walls, Mississippi

Mr. Roger Courts, a native Mississippian, is in his thirty-fifth year of service for the League. The Sacred Heart League is a not-for-profit Catholic communications and direct-mail, fund-raising organization with member-donors in all 50 states and Puerto Rico. In his position as director and CEO, he is responsible for directing the entire operation of the Sacred Heart League, a 120-employee organization. All funding for the programs in education, social services, housing, and transportation is provided through the efforts of the League, which has a full line of services—from information systems and printing to a fully equipped mail department. In recent years, Mr. Courts has served as either chairman or board member for a number of local and national organizations, including chairman and board member of the National Federation of Nonprofits, a Washington-based grassroots organization, overseeing the concerns of the charitable sector in legislative, regulatory, and postal issues; and committee member of the United States Postmaster General's Work-Share Task Force, 1988. Mr. Courts received his B.A. in psychology and English from Memphis State University.

QUESTION:

How has electronic mail and networked microcomputers changed the way you communicate within the office?

Dialog *from the* Workplace

RESPONSE:

When I came to work at the Sacred Heart League 35 years ago, most of us were located in a large, open, cinderblock building. Our desks were in close proximity, and it was easy to physically pass documents to one another, along with a spoken message. As the organization grew, our workspace grew commensurately. Soon, we had to resort to an intercom system (at that time, intercoms were separate from the telephone system) and an interoffice mail system to prevent a significant waste of time, as employees at all pay levels trotted about the office, dropping off materials and, of course, visiting and "catching up on the latest" along the way. Then came the day when our office facility had expanded to a plant of over 50,000 square feet. A more efficient means of communication

was a necessity. Our office automation consultant, Mary Ruprecht, provided the answer: electronic mail.

At first, we were reluctant to explore the possibilities, feeling that virtually every information system need deserved a higher priority than this one. In time, we did install a mainframe electronic mail system for communicating and scheduling meetings. In no time, this e-mail system became as much a part of everyone's routine as a stapler and a coffee mug. Now, we are using a greatly enhanced electronic mail and scheduling system on our LAN that serves some 60 PCs throughout the organization. One out of every two employees has a PC.

The tremendous advantage afforded by an e-mail system was dramatically illustrated to me recently, when I returned to work after a two-week vacation. There were 65 e-mail messages awaiting me, along with a foot-high stack of interoffice envelopes (over 50 in number). The e-mail messages required 29 minutes to read, answer, or otherwise dispose of. It was mid-morning of my second day back before I was able to process the accumulation of interoffice envelopes.

Our goal is to decrease the volume of interoffice mail by transferring as much of it as possible to the e-mail system. A paperless office is not yet possible in our applications, but without a doubt, we are moving on an uninterrupted course in that direction. In today's climate of competitiveness, an organization simply cannot tolerate the inefficiencies of yesterday's technologies and processes.

face-to-face, telephone, electronic mail, written memos, or video.

Organizational communication effectiveness is directly proportional to the organization's basic philosophy of how employees should be treated and the ideal relationship that should exist between employees and management. Whether it is the organizational system we are talking about or our individual ability to communicate, we can improve the process.

Simply put, **communication** is the exchange of messages. Messages can be verbal, using spoken or written words; or they can be nonverbal, using symbols, gestures, expressions, and body language. For communication to take place, there must be a sender (a person who transmits the message) and a receiver (a person who gets the message). Whether it is one-way or two-way communication, effective communication occurs when the sender and the receiver have the same understanding of the message, as shown in Figure 7.1.

In one-way communication, the sender transmits a message, the receiver gets it, and the process is complete. For example, an employee calls in to report she is ill and will be out for the day. The person receiving the call understands the message, makes note of it, and hangs up.

In two-way communication, however, the sender transmits a message, the receiver gets it, and subsequently the receiver responds with another message. The process may continue with the sender and receiver alternating roles, giving one another feedback. Conversations and business correspondence are examples of two-way communication.

Nonverbal Communication

We think of words as the chief means by which we communicate. Being clear, concise, and courteous in your choice of words is important. However, studies of face-to-face communication have shown that 80 to 90 percent of the impact of a message comes from nonverbal elements such as facial expressions, eye contact, body language, and tone of voice.

Communication experts, for example, point out that in face-to-face communication, 55 percent of what we communicate is in our body language, 38 percent in how we speak, and 7 percent in what we say. Further, if we are on the

Management Tip

When communicating, try to keep your temper even when faced with unfair resistance. To lose your temper is to lose an opportunity to share your message.

PURPOSE OF COMMUNICATION	COMMUNICATION MEDIA
To Inform	<ul><li>Interoffice memo announcing a meeting</li><li>Telephone call in which a customer is quoted a price and shipping date for goods ordered</li><li>Sales meeting to present new products to staff</li><li>Press release announcing the selection of a new CEO</li></ul>
To Persuade	<ul><li>Personal conversation in which a co-worker is requested to serve as a volunteer in a fund-raising effort</li><li>Report to management on the need to purchase an upgrade version of desktop publishing software</li></ul>
To Evaluate	<ul><li>Performance appraisal records</li><li>Quality control report summarizing the customer complaints this quarter</li><li>Budget performance report that compares amounts budgeted with expenses incurred</li></ul>
To Instruct	<ul><li>Instruction manual for operating the new fax machine</li><li>Directions given orally to workers for preparing a form</li></ul>
To Meet Human and Cultural Needs	<ul><li>"Small talk" ("Hello, have a good weekend?"), etc., before, during, and after business hours</li><li>Note inviting workers to participate in annual fitness run</li></ul>

Table 7.1

Purposes of Communication and Commonly Used Media

telephone, we have only fifteen to thirty seconds to make a good impression. Only 10 to 20 percent of what we communicate on the phone is based on what we say—80 to 90 percent is in how we say it. According to these statistics, nonverbal communication can be far more revealing of the content of a message than the words used.[1]

Examples of the four nonverbal communication areas—facial expressions, eye contact, body language, and voice qualities—are given in Table 7.2.

Communication Feedback and Filters

Communication and feedback in business are important to reaching corporate goals and motivating employees. **Feedback** can be verbal and nonverbal responses that the receiver gives by further communicating with the original sender or another person.

It is not an easy task to give feedback in such a way that it can be received without threat to the other person. This technique requires practice in developing sensitivity to

Figure 7.1

A Model of the
Communication
Process

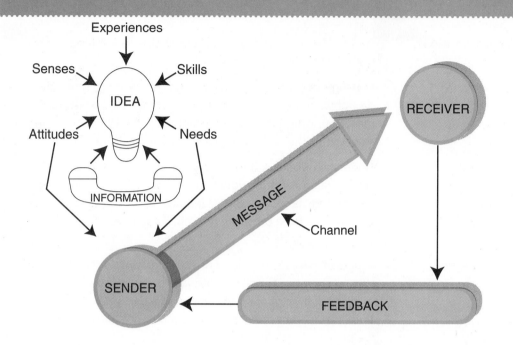

other people's needs and being able to put one-self in the other person's position.

Filtering is the tendency for a message to be watered down or halted completely at some point during transmission. Both speakers and listeners have communication "filters" or barriers through which messages must come. In other words, the speaker sends a message through his or her filters; the listener receives the message through his or her filters. As a result, total and accurate communication can be very difficult to achieve. Some examples of filters or barriers that cause people to misunderstand each other occur when the speaker or listener:

1. Does not listen or does not want to listen.

2. Does not understand the "language of feelings."

3. Does not say enough, or may not be given the chance to say enough.

4. Gets mixed up in definitions. For example, a speaker often assumes that the listener understands what he or she said.

5. Fails to indicate to the other person that the message was understood and it is not necessary to continue the dialogue.

6. Misinterprets information because of differences in culture.

7. Gives information too fast.

8. Is generally unwilling to ask questions.

9. Experiences personality conflicts or differences with the other person.

10. Jumps to conclusions.

11. Fails to read nonverbal messages.

TYPES	EXAMPLES
Facial expressions	Smiling, frowning, and raising your eyebrows are facial expressions that communicate feelings.
Eye contact	Making eye contact when speaking with someone is usually desirable. In the United States, for example, people who do not meet your eyes during conversations are thought to be hiding something. This, of course, differs in other cultures.
Body language	Nodding your head, shrugging your shoulders, gesturing with your hands, or shifting your weight from side to side are examples of body language. Body language can indicate a wide range of emotions from boredom (yawning) to impatience (tapping your fingers or feet).
Voice qualities	A person's voice can be loud or soft, high or low pitched, fast or slow, pleasant or harsh, monotonous or interesting. Not only can a voice tell a lot about how we feel in a particular speaking situation, but perhaps more important, it also tells much about how we personally are feeling physically and psychologically at the moment.

Table 7.2

Nonverbal
Communication

OFFICE COMMUNICATION NETWORKS

Communication networks in organizations are unique and reflect, to a large degree, what organizations see as their mission to customers and their vision to achieve that mission. One way to view communication networks is through upward, downward, and lateral communication; another way is through formal and informal communication channels. Still other communication networks are set up to communicate with the distant employee on an individual basis or with many employees at face-to-face meetings.

Regardless of which network or channel is used, effective communication occurs when the right people receive the right information in a timely manner. If any of these three conditions is not present, a particular communication event is ineffective.

Upward, Downward, and Lateral Communication Networks

Upward communication is feedback of data or information from lower levels in the organization to upper-management levels. This communication usually deals with problems, clarifications, attitudes, ideas, and accomplishments. To encourage upward communication, managers use suggestion systems, attitude surveys, team meetings, complaint procedures, and committees.

Downward communication, on the other hand, follows the organization's formal chain of command from top to bottom. This communication covers procedures, policies, goals, assignments, and directives. One concern with downward communication is that the message might decrease in accuracy as it passes through the chain of command. For that reason, managers use written materials such as employee handbooks, policy manuals, organizational newsletters, bulletin boards, videos, and meetings to clearly communicate downward within the organization.

Lateral communication, also known as horizontal communication, is communication that occurs between departments or functional units, usually as a coordinating or problem-solving effort. Organizations can set up short-term task forces to allow for colleagues to discuss unique projects, or they can set up more long-term committees for counterparts to get together and discuss a particular organizational concern or issue on an ongoing basis throughout the year.

Formal and Informal Communication Channels

In addition to communication networks in offices, there are also communication channels. These communication channels are different from each other and are usually referred to as formal and informal communication channels.

Formal Channels. Similar to downward communication, formal communication channels are the officially prescribed means by which messages flow normally inside organizations. Sometimes this is referred to as

Bulletin boards are a source of company and employee information for all personnel. © *PhotoDisc, Inc.*

"following the chain of command," which means that the correct channel to follow is to discuss issues or concerns with your immediate superior first before going over his or her head.

Informal Channels. The chain of command fails to consider informal communication between members. Informal communication channels describe communication that travels along channels other than those formally designed by the organization. Informal interaction helps people accomplish their jobs more effectively. The best known type of informal communication within an organization is the grapevine.

The Grapevine. The **grapevine** involves transmission of information by word of mouth without regard for organizational levels, and it often provides a great deal of useful information. Unfortunately, however, the grapevine can also distort information, create resentment, and work against organizational plans and objectives.

One example of grapevine chatter is the business of talking about the boss. It happens in the cubicle corners of every office across the country. Cliques of co-workers gather to trade complaints and gossip about the incompetence of the boss or an unpopular directive. Such talk is usually harmless, say organizational psychologists. They say it alleviates subordinates' sense of helplessness and strengthens bonds among colleagues. Nevertheless, when the gossip gets nasty, it may be time for a manager to intervene.

Rumors. It is generally recommended that a manager's best strategy is to let office rumors slide. Trying to refute gossip generally gives it more credence. But if negative gossip wrongly accuses superiors of not doing their jobs, suggests they are having affairs with subordinates, or provokes employees to gang up on their superiors, then a manager must take some action. Such talk sets a bad tone and hinders communication as well as productivity in the office.

The best approach to follow when clarifying rumors is to attack the source. Private one-on-one conversations with the gossiping perpetrators usually squelch further rumors and prevent

workplace mutiny. But if the gossip is true, a change in the boss's workplace behavior or personal life may be in order.

Table 7.3 recaps these communication networks and channels.

Long-Distance Communication Networks

Motivating a work team that is spread across the company—or even the globe—can be a real challenge to any manager. But with the right technology on your side, the whole group can stay synchronized. Whether you manage a team of telecommuters or staffers dispersed throughout the company, how well all of you communicate with each other is the key factor in how well work gets done.

Using the speed of electronic mail, voice mail, fax, and videoconferences are all effective ways to gather—and spread—information despite colleagues' divergent schedules and locations. These technologies minimize telephone tag and allow participants to respond at a distance and at a time that is convenient for them.

Electronic Mail. According to Forrester Research, Inc., in Cambridge, Massachusetts, about 60 million Americans have electronic-mail access.[2] **Electronic mail** (e-mail) is best suited to people already tied to a PC or desktop terminal. Essentially an electronic version of sending a memo, e-mail can also serve as a scheduling aid if all participants make a public version of their calendars available on the computer system. Most e-mail systems allow you to broadcast a single message to a predetermined distribution list, making team

Communication Networks	**Upward Communication Is . . .** feedback of data or information from the lower levels of the organization to upper management levels. *Examples:* suggestion systems, surveys, team meetings, complaint procedures, and committees
	Downward Communication Is . . . feedback of data or information that follows the organization's formal chain of command from top to bottom. *Examples:* employee handbooks, policy manuals, organizational newsletters, bulletin boards, videos, and meetings
	Lateral Communication Is . . . feedback of data or information that occurs between departments or functional units, usually as a coordinating effort. *Examples:* short-term task forces or committees
Communication Channels	**Formal** Communication that follows the formal chain of command as represented on the company's organizational chart. **Informal** Communication that allows for informal interaction between workers to help them accomplish their jobs more effectively.

Table 7.3

Communication Networks and Channels

messaging simple. In addition, e-mail allows participants to set up a "file folder" or "bulletin board" to handle ongoing discussions.

Some individuals like electronic mail because it is fast and does not require any movement. Other individuals prefer face-to-face meetings with eye contact, voice changes, and facial expressions. E-mail is a mixed blessing. It does promote efficiency, in that it carries a sense of urgency, so it helps expedite communication with consumers and advertisers, letters, or new product announcements. On the other hand, because it is so easy to reach people directly, there is no way of screening e-mail the way you can screen phone calls or letters.[3]

Very few companies have policies on the use of e-mail. E-mail is often stored for years and can later be used against the writer. A survey by the American Management Association in 1998 found that 20 percent of companies have some system for reviewing employee e-mail, usually by spot checks.[4]

While e-mail is necessary and beneficial, it is important to recognize that it is a medium that uses only text and offers no visual or non-verbal clues. E-mail can have a downside when communication is so easy that annoying and inappropriate messages are sent. It is wise, therefore, to develop an e-mail protocol among multinational organizations and their group members to minimize the chances for misunderstandings when using this tool. Consider the following guidelines.

- *Topics.* Which topics are appropriate for e-mail and which are not? Which topics should be addressed in person or over the phone instead?
- *Frequency.* How frequently should members use e-mail?
- *Urgency.* What constitutes urgency? Is it possible to define the terms ASAP and urgent?
- *Participation.* Who should participate? Does every team member need to be a recipient of every e-mail?
- *Time of day.* Should there be "blackout" periods when e-mails are not sent or received?

- *Jokes, profanity, intimacies.* What kinds of guidelines should exist regarding topics, language, or personal relationships?

Voice Messaging and Faxing. Voice messaging and faxing, on the other hand, are good alternatives for less computer-oriented businesspeople. Most voice mail systems and fax machines offer a "broadcast" feature—that is, the ability to send the same message to an established routing list.

While both voice mail and e-mail have their own set of rules, four general ones emerge.

1. Whatever type of medium you use, a business message should be professional; that is, it should be clear and courteous, follow spoken or written grammar rules, and (if applicable) contain correct spelling.

2. When dealing with extremely sensitive information, it is better to deliver the message face-to-face, or at least in a telephone conversation, so both parties can have questions answered and so no misunderstandings develop.

3. Neither e-mail nor voice mail is totally private or secure. Never send a message in either medium that would prove embarrassing to you, others, or to your organization if read or heard by the wrong person.

4. Prepare your message so that it pleases the recipients. Find out how they prefer to communicate and use that medium.[5]

Teleconferencing and Videoconferencing. If you need frequent status reports from your team, consider using a form of **teleconferencing**. Phone conferencing technology, for example, allows for audio-only conferences and permits in excess of sixty people to call in at once.

Videoconferencing is another long-distance communication option. It not only provides two-way audio but two-way video and two-way document exchange, as well. Although it is the most expensive form of teleconferencing, businesspeople agree that, by comparison, bringing out-of-state employees to a meeting is a far greater expense. With voice-activated video cameras, the picture is always coordinated with the person talking at the time. Care must be taken when using this technology because communication can be interrupted, even cancelled, when people, for example, interrupt others, slam down coffee cups, or shuffle papers.

For years, desktop videoconferencing has been plagued by high cost and lousy image and sound quality. Now sharp price reductions and quality improvements have made real videoconferencing capability a reality. For example, a complete desktop videoconferencing set-up, including camera, headset, microphones, and software suite, costs less than $800.[6]

Videoconferencing saves not only time but cash, since there are no costs for airfare, hotels, and other travel expenses.[7] Table 7.4 describes various types of long-distance communication devices.

Meetings and Presentation Skills

Meetings have always offered the most obvious way to network with others in organizations. Though meetings are intended to serve many purposes—information giving and exchange, fact finding, and problem solving—they often

Videoconferencing is a low-cost effective method of bringing distant workers together to meet and discuss issues.   © *PhotoDisc, Inc.*

turn out to be an unproductive use of people's time. One way to enhance meetings is to practice presentation skills.

Effectively Run Meetings. When you are in charge of a meeting, it is your responsibility to make it focused and efficient. You will earn the respect of colleagues and save your company valuable hours. As a guide, there are activities you can do before, during, and after for running short but productive meetings.

Management Tip

To put a dollar cost to meetings, try this. The next meeting you attend, silently guesstimate the hourly salary of each person in attendance. Even a half-hour meeting costs an organization lots of money.

Electronic mail (e-mail)	A system that enables a user to transmit letters, memos, and other messages directly from one computer to another, where the messages are stored for later retrieval.
Facsimile (fax)	A machine that can transmit and receive documents over regular telephone lines. The sending machine digitizes and transmits the document (text, graphics, signatures) over the telephone line to the receiving machine, which then reproduces a copy or facsimile of the document.
Teleconference	A method of conducting telephone conference calls among three or more people in different locations.
Videoconference	A method of conferencing in which people at different locations can see and hear one another and also communicate via computer where one-way or two-way TV supplements the audio channel.
Voice mail	A sophisticated, computerized telephone answering system that digitizes incoming spoken messages, stores them in the recipient's voice mailbox, and then reconverts them into spoken form when retrieved.

Table 7.4

Long-Distance
Communication
Devices

Before the meeting:

1. Have a clear purpose in mind about why you are meeting.

2. Prepare a written agenda. If possible, distribute copies of it to those attending at least one day prior to the meeting. Set a time limit for agenda items.

During the meeting:

1. Start on time. Rewarding latecomers by waiting for them and reviewing material when they do arrive only punishes punctual participants.

2. Cover big issues early.

3. Invite the right people. Keep in mind that employees who need information but have little input can be updated later with a copy of the minutes. If key people will be absent, try to reschedule the meeting for a more convenient time.

4. Plan your presentation. Define problems and identify possible solutions ahead of time. Have handouts and audiovisual materials ready. State your ideas in terms of benefits to the company and individuals.

5. Promote a professional atmosphere. Tolerate little, if any, chatter and discourage food and smoking. Speak in crisp, energetic tones and try to direct long-winded participants to a conclusion with appropriate questions and comments.

6. End on time. Put an end time as well as a start time on the agenda and make every effort to meet it.

After the Meeting:

1. Distribute copies of the minutes.

2. Follow up on decisions made.

3. Evaluate the need for "regularly" scheduled meetings. Regular meetings, particularly weekly ones, tend to become social hours. Should they be held monthly or on an as-needed basis instead?[8]

Approaches to Running Meetings. When you are responsible for running meetings, you can use two approaches: meetings that are leader controlled or group centered.

Leader-Controlled Approach. The leader is clearly in charge at this type of meeting. It is most effective with large groups or when the purpose of the meeting is simply to present information.

Group-Centered Approach. The leader's job is to keep the meeting moving and redirect the focus of comments. The purpose is generally for group members to interact freely and address one another in such a way as to promote the free flow of information.

Table 7.5 describes the advantages and disadvantages of each approach when conducting meetings.

Presentation Skills. Perfecting presentation skills is a "must do" in today's business arena because the ability to communicate effectively in today's business world is a "must have." The following pointers can help improve your delivery and increase your ability to deal with uncooperative participants.

- Use visual and audio aids.
- Involve the audience.
- Don't stand in one spot.
- Work from an outline.
- Avoid negative comments.
- Allow time for feedback.
- Handle audience criticism.[9]

A comfortable and friendly atmosphere promotes an effectively run meeting.
© *PhotoDisc, Inc.*

LEADER-CONTROLLED APPROACH

Advantages

1. Leader is in control and has an agenda. Fewer surprises occur during the meeting.

2. A great deal of material can be covered in a relatively short period of time.

Disadvantages

1. Free flow of information is often discouraged.

2. Members are not able to express themselves as well on sensitive issues.

3. There is little creativity allowed in discussions with this approach.

GROUP-CENTERED APPROACH

Advantages

1. Members of the group are encouraged to exchange and better understand other's viewpoints.

2. Usually, better decisions result from the free flow of information.

3. Generally, people feel better because they have been allowed to express their emotions and feelings on issues.

Disadvantages

1. Typically, these meetings take more time to complete.

2. Because the leader's role is more of a facilitator, his or her leadership skills are significant to the meeting's success.

3. This approach is not well suited to a large group.

Table 7.5

Conducting Business Meetings

Business Correspondence, Reports, and Forms

A discussion of office communication would be incomplete without a brief review of the major types of business correspondence, reports, and forms used in business today. Though there are other documents prepared by office professionals, you will find that letters, memos, reports, minutes, proposals, and itineraries constitute the majority of written communication prepared in the office.

Refer to Table 7.6 to clarify the purpose of preparing each of these communications and to

Figure 7.2 to see examples of how selected office documents should look.

INTERCULTURAL COMMUNICATION

The more international business becomes, the more important it is to recognize differences among people from different cultures, because these differences affect good communication. By taking advantage of opportunities to communicate outside our own cultural boundaries, we will become better communicators.

TYPES	PURPOSE	COMMENTS
Letter	One of the most common forms of written messages used by businesses to communicate with people and organizations outside the firm.	The standard letter parts are letterhead, date, inside address, salutation, body, complimentary close, and signature line.
Memo	The primary medium of written communication within companies. Memos are informal and provide a rapid, convenient means of communication between workers.	The increased use of e-mail is lessening the use of memos within organizations. The standard heading for memos includes To, From, Date, and Subject.
Report	These are documents that analyze and evaluate organizational activities of all kinds and provide critical information for decision making.	In preparing a report, follow these steps: 1. plan the report, 2. collect the data, 3. organize the data, and 4. draft the report.
Minutes	These official records of meetings list the items discussed, the results of votes, and the person responsible for carrying out any follow-up steps.	Minutes should be clear, correct, informative, factual, and free of judgmental words.
Proposal	A document that suggests a method for finding information or solving a problem. Proposals must be persuasive.	Typically, a proposal answers questions such as what problem you are going to solve, how you are going to solve it, when you will complete the work, and how much you will charge.
Itinerary	A document that is a record of travel plans.	Typically, an itinerary includes date, time, location of departures and arrivals, and hotel and car rental details.

Table 7.6

Business Correspondence, Reports, and Forms

Figure 7.2
. . . .
Examples of
Typical Office
Documents

LETTER

INTERNATIONAL BUSINESS SERVICES
4050 West Company Way
Phoenix, AZ 85008

June 7, 20—

Julia Stevens, Regional Manager
Explorer Products
2243 Indian School Road
Phoenix, AZ 85014

Dear Ms. Stevens

Thank you for your inquiry about International Business
Services. The enclosed material should give you a better
understanding of our company and services that we offer.

We are proud of our reputation for putting the customer first
in every area of our operations. We feel that this attitude is
one of the most important contributors to our success and to
the success of the customers we serve.

I will be contacting you within the next two weeks to see if
you have any questions or need any additional information.
Again, thank you for your interest.

Sincerely

Patricia Gibson, President

Enclosure

MEMORANDUM

Memorandum

DATE: February 13, 20—

TO: Cecilia Haynes & Woodrow Francis

FROM: Rosa Lee Saikley

SUBJECT: New Sexual Harassment Procedure

Attached is an update of the new sexual harassment
procedure, which we would like to commence using in one
month. Please review and address any questions or
comments to me by the end of the week. Thank you.

Attachment

MINUTES

RESOURCE COMMITTEE
Minutes of the Meeting December 11, 20—

ATTENDANCE	The Resource Committee met on December 9, 20__, at the Airport Sheraton in Phoenix, Arizona, in conjunction with the western regional meeting. Members present were J. Parker Davis, Cynthia Giovanni, Don Madsen, and Darrin Matthew. J. Parker Davis, chairperson, called the meeting to order at 2:30 p.m.
OLD BUSINESS	The members of the committee reviewed the sales brochure on electronic copyboards. They agreed to purchase an electronic copyboard for the conference room. Cynthia Giovanni will secure quotations from at least two suppliers.
NEW BUSINESS	The committee reviewed a request from the Purchasing Department for three new Mac computers. After extensive discussion regarding whether to buy Mac or IBM-based computers, the committee approved the request but only for IBM-based computers, since that is the company's standard.
ADJOURNMENT	The meeting was adjourned at 4:45 p.m. The next meeting has been scheduled for January 4 in the headquarters' conference room. Members are asked to bring with them copies of the latest resource-planning document.

Respectfully submitted,

D. S. Madsen, Secretary

ITINERARY

LAKE TAHOE SALES MEETING
Itinerary for Cecilia Haynes
March 12-15, 20—

Thursday, March 12
Phoenix/Lake Tahoe   **America West 83**
   Leave 5:10 p.m.; arrive 6:30 p.m.
   Seat 5D; nonstop; dinner

Sunday, March 15
Lake Tahoe/Phoenix   **America West 360**
   Leave 7:30 a.m.; arrive 9:15 a.m.
   Seat 10D; nonstop; breakfast

NOTES:

1. Jack Weatherford, Assistant Western Regional Manager, will meet
   your flight on Thursday and return you to the airport on Sunday.
2. All seat assignments are aisle seats.
3. A single-room reservation, (Reservation/Confirmation #368112-0)
   guaranteed for late arrival, has been made at the Golden Nugget for
   March 12-14.
4. You are to meet your co-presenter, Ronald Reynolds, in the lobby of
   the Golden Nugget Hotel on Friday at 8:00 p.m. to review handout
   materials for Saturday's presentation.

Important Phone Numbers:
   Jack Weatherford (880) 555-8029, ext. 87
   Golden Nugget Hotel (880) 555-7777
   American West Reservations (800) 555-1234

Cross-cultural communication is tough. The solution? Learn about the customs of your global colleagues. Americans doing business in Australia, for example, should not assume that they do not have to make significant adjustments just because the two countries share the same language, British heritage, Christian religion, and belief in democracy. Americans have a tendency to impose change and issue orders; Australians, in contrast, tend to resent being given orders and prefer a more collaborative approach to decision making.[10]

Skill in intercultural communication plays a significant role in the success or failure of U.S. firms participating in the global arena. The most successful multinational organizations are companies whose employees not only understand world economics and global competitiveness, but who also have the ability to communicate effectively with international counterparts.

The key to success in motivating employees from different cultures is to be watchful of cultural differences in attitudes and business practices of other countries—specifically, relative to perception of change, sense of time, use of communication, work orientation, and competition.[11]

In the April 1998 *Business Education Forum*, nine areas of international business are recommended as critical global business skills in the new millenium and beyond. They are:

- *Awareness.* Understand the role of international business and its impact on business activity locally as well as in international activities.
- *International business communication.* Apply appropriate communication strategies for effective business relations.

- *Environment.* Describe the social, cultural, political, and legal economic factors that impact on business activities.
- *Ethics.* Describe the environmental factors that illustrate ethical business practices.
- *Finance.* Explain the role, concepts, and importance of international finance and risk management.
- *Management.* Comprehend the challenges of operating a business and managing human resources in an international business setting.
- *International marketing.* Apply marketing concepts and skills to international business settings.
- *Import/export and balance of trade.* Relate the balance of trade concept to the import/export process.
- *Organizational structure of international business.* Identify business ownership opportunities in international settings.[12]

Message *for* AOMs

"

Few organizations exist in order to communicate. Most have another purpose: to sell a product or service, to supply a social need, and to implement plans and policies. Yet to do these things, organizations spend an enormous amount of time, energy, and money communicating.

Administrative office management is critical for successful organizational communication. Because language shapes the way organizations see reality, sometimes communicating is hard because our words reflect different understandings of reality. Communicating effectively in an organization requires understanding the way it produces messages and ideas and then projecting those messages with reality and self-confidence.

summary chapter 7

1 The communication process requires that there be a sender, the person who transmits the message; a receiver, the person who gets the message; and an understood message, meaning that both sender and receiver have the same understanding of the message.

2 Examples of the four nonverbal communication areas include facial expressions, eye contact, body language, and voice qualities.

3 Filtering is the tendency for a message to be watered down or halted completely at some point during transmission. Both speakers and listeners have communication "filters" or barriers through which messages must come. As a result, total and accurate communication can be very difficult to achieve.

4 Communication and feedback in business are important to reach corporate goals and to motivate employees. Feedback can be verbal and nonverbal responses that the receiver gives by further communicating with the original sender or another person.

5 Upward communication is feedback of data or information from lower levels in the organization to upper-management levels.

Downward communication, on the other hand, follows the organization's formal chain of command from top to bottom.

6 The grapevine involves transmission of information by word of mouth without regard for organizational levels, and it often provides a great deal of useful information. Unfortunately, however, the grapevine can also distort information, create resentment, and work against organizational plans and objectives.

7 Using the speed of electronic mail, voice mail, fax, and videoconferences are all effective ways to gather—and spread—information despite colleagues' divergent schedules and locations.

8 Meetings are intended to serve many purposes—information giving and exchange, fact finding, and problem solving.

9 The most successful multinational organizations are companies whose employees not only understand world economics and global competitiveness, but who also have the ability to communicate effectively with international counterparts.

QUESTIONS FOR CRITICAL THINKING

1. Give an example of one-way and two-way communication in which you have participated this week.

2. Explain what is meant by the idea that both speakers and listeners have communication filters through which messages must pass.

3. Give some examples of how organizations demonstrate both upward and downward communication.

4. In your opinion, is e-mail safe to use and will its use in business increase?

5. Describe how well a meeting was run that you attended recently (club, civic organization, church-related, school). As a guide, use the suggested activities on pages 142–143 that describe what to do before, during, and after a meeting.

6. In your own words, explain what is meant by intercultural communication.

Case Study 7-1: The Costly Communication Seminar

Hedy and Jonathan met in the hallway by chance and decided to have lunch together. Both top managers at Murphy Unified School District (Hedy is human resources manager and Jonathan is the comptroller), they got into a conversation about the value to the school district of employees' attending so many communication seminars. This was prompted by the fourth advertisement Hedy had received this week about such seminars coming to their town. Although they are friends who, in the past, have always regarded each other highly, the conversation got rather heated at times.

Jonathan's Position

These seminars are "rip offs." At $150 for an eight-hour session—on school time—the school district loses a day's wages for no work done, as well as the cost of the seminar. If employees need to improve their communication skills, then their immediate supervisors should let them know, and they can attend night school or the community college or a seminar like this at their own expense.

Hedy's Position

It is to the school district's advantage to support in principle, as well as in financial terms, employees who desire to improve themselves in an effort to become better employees. If 100 employees were to attend a school-district-paid seminar from the 1,000 employees on staff, then costs incurred in community misunderstandings at school board meetings could be minimized, and the $15,000 ($150 x 100) would be negligible. Look at the $50,000 legal fee for litigation the school district had to pay because of the recent "miscommunication problem" between an assistant principal and a parent of an eighth grader. A case in point, look how much difficulty we are having trying to communicate our positions right now!

Discussion Questions

1. What valid points does Jonathan make about this issue?

2. What valid points does Hedy make?

3. Which position would you support and why?

Case Study 7-2: E-Mail Abuse

As the office manager for a medium-size advertising agency, it comes to your attention that several employees are using their e-mail addresses to write to friends during office hours when they should be working. Since everyone has a computer terminal at his or her own desk, you realize it will be difficult to control, but you know you have to do something.

Discussion Questions

1. In your opinion, do you believe this issue to be a growing concern in business today?

2. Are there steps that businesses can take to assist workers in staying focused on the work at hand? If so, what do you suggest?

Case Study 7-3: Internet Research Activity

Assume you want to find a seminar or workshop coming to your area dealing with *business communication issues and trends.* Use the Internet to research information needed to answer the following question. Key your responses.

1. Which Web search engine did you use?

2. Write down three of the URL addresses that you accessed during your search.

3. As a result of your search, describe at least three seminars you might attend. For each seminar, indicate the following: the cost of registration, where and when it will be held, and key topics which will be covered and by whom.

Endnotes

[1] From material presented by Jerry Odell, human resources manager, at a communications workshop in Flagstaff, Arizona, in January 1993.

[2] Barb Cold-Gomolski, "E-mail's Double-Edged Sword," *Computerworld,* February 23, 1998, p. 28.

[3] "E-mail: Godsend or God-Awful?" *Folio: The Magazine for Magazine Management,* September 15, 1998, p. 84.

[4] Jerry Adler, "When E-Mail Bites Back," *Newsweek,* November 23, 1998, p. 45.

[5] "New Etiquette for Evolving Technologies," *Business Education Forum,* October 1998, p. 8.

[6] "Videoconferencing," *Fortune,* November 16, 1998, p. 134.

[7] Thomas Love, "A High-Tech Way to Save Time and Money," *Nation's Business,* June 1998, p. 14.

[8] Kay B. Johnson, "10 Steps to Meeting Management," *Women in Business,* March-April 1992, p. 15.

[9] David Crocker, "Bored-Room Meetings?" *Black Enterprise,* April 1998, p. 108.

[10] Brenda Paik Sunoo, "Adapting to the Land Down Under," *Workforce,* January 1998, p. 24.

[11] Bob Nelson, "Motivating Workers Worldwide," *Workforce,* November 1998, p. 4.

[12] Thomas Haynes, "Learning Activities for International Business," *Business Education Forum,* April 1998, pp. 31–32.

Groups, Teamwork, and Conflict Issues

chapter 8

"
Light is the task when many share.

—*Homer*

"

After completing this chapter, you will be able to:

1. State reasons people become part of a group.

2. Discuss the impact groupthink issues and hidden agendas have on accomplishing an organization's goals.

3. Explain why conflict management is an essential skill for any successful manager.

4. Briefly describe the five conflict management styles.

5. Identify the outcomes of win-lose, lose-lose, and win-win negotiating styles.

6. Describe the effects of stress on the job.

7. Discuss ways to overcome problems with time management.

Groups are something effective leaders learn to work with to get results. A **group** refers to two or more people who personally interact with each other in order to achieve a common goal. Since much of the work in organizations is accomplished through group effort, an understanding of how groups function and their impact on both organizational and individual behavior is essential for an effective administrative office manager.

THE NATURE OF GROUPS AND TEAM-BUILDING CONSIDERATIONS

Companies using a team structure may have team members evaluate each other, and sometimes bonuses are awarded to a team, with the members deciding how to distribute them. People working under a team structure often become cynical when they see teamwork go unacknowledged while individuals are rewarded. Some analysts believe the difficulty

Charles F. Nielson

Vice President of Human Resources
Texas Instruments, Inc.
Dallas, Texas

In 1992, Texas Instruments (TI) won a *Personnel Journal* Optimas Award, which was created to foster an increased awareness of human resources in the general business community. TI's award in the *Service* category honors departments that have developed a program or policy in an effort to support another constituency within the organization.

Charles E. "Chuck" Nielson received a B.S. degree from Brigham Young University in sociology, with minors in psychology and economics. Mr. Nielson did graduate work at the University of Utah and Utah State University.

Nielson's work experience began at Thiokol Chemical Corporation in Brigham City, Utah, where he was involved in the employment and supervisor training function. His next experience was with Fairchild-Hiller Corporation in St. Augustine, Florida, where he supervised the industrial relations function. Nielson joined Texas Instruments in 1965. He has had a variety of personnel responsibilities and is currently vice president of human resources.

Nielson was appointed by President Bush to the President's Drug Advisory Council, which advised and assisted the President on ways to mobilize the private sector against illegal drugs. Nielson is a member of The Business Roundtable Employee Relations Committee (ERC), which is comprised of the top human resources executives at the leading Roundtable companies. The ERC plays an active role in legislation affecting the relationship between employees, employers, and the government. Nielson is also a member of the board of directors of the Labor Policy Association, a group concerned exclusively with the development of the nation's human resources and employment policies.

QUESTION:

We have read about the formation of your policy committee that represents a joint venture between two teams of management—the operating people and the human resources (HR) people. How has this policy committee aided in ensuring that TI's policies and programs are responsive to the needs of your organization?

Dialog *from the* Workplace

RESPONSE:

It is becoming very evident that what differentiates one company from another is the effectiveness of the people. To provide an environment that enables the best performance from each individual requires policies which are insightful from a human resources perspective and which add value from an operating manager perspective.

The true significance of the current situation in TI can best be understood by looking at how things used to be. In the past, many times HR views and operating views were poles apart. HR viewed the operating perspective as being punitive and insensitive; operating managers viewed the HR perspective as soft.

The Policy Committee has accomplished a synergistic relationship between HR professionals and key operating managers. HR policies are now, in fact, aimed at enhanced performance, and both HR managers and operating managers jointly hold ownership of the policy.

U.S. workers experience when trying to work in teams is the result of our culture of individualism. Our American culture programs us to be the best individual we can.[1]

Types and Characteristics of Groups

When individuals associate on a fairly continuous basis, groups will form, with or without the approval of management. Individual members receive a great deal of satisfaction from being part of the group. A group can be either informal or formal.

The term *teamwork* has various interpretations and may not be the same thing as a real team. When some companies call for teamwork, the managers simply want people to work together. Other companies dismantle their entire managerial structures and reorganize in teams, requiring people to learn a whole new way of working. In between are organizations in which teams are formed for certain tasks and projects.[2]

Types of Groups. **Informal groups** arise spontaneously throughout all levels of the company and evolve out of employees' needs for social interaction, friendship, communication, and status. In contrast, **formal groups** are deliberately formed and created by management for the purpose of attaining organizational goals and objectives. Some examples of formal groups are problem-solving committees that meet on an as-needed basis and are relatively permanent, and task-force groups, which usually focus on a specific issue, meet a few times, and then disband.

Characteristics of Groups. Groups, in general, appear to have some common characteristics. Three of these characteristics are that groups set norms, instill conformity, and engender cohesiveness. If you think about it, not only do we see groups form with these common characteristics in the workplace, but we also see them in other group examples, such as professional organizations and even in our own family unit.

Norms. A **norm** is a generally agreed-on standard of behavior that every member of the group is expected to follow. For example, a norm for a dance group might be the way they wear their hair at performances and their lively dance expression. Human nature compels most of us to gravitate toward groups of like-minded individuals with a strong identity, so these norms ordinarily do not offend group members. If being a member of a group is important to an individual, he or she will change personality, beliefs, and behavior to conform to the group.

Conformity. Group pressure forces its members to conform, or comply, with the norms established by the group. Because nonconformity threatens the group's standards, stability, and longevity, the pressure placed on each member to conform is oftentimes intense. Compliance is important to the group because behavior is visible; for the group to succeed, its members must show they are united in their efforts.

Cohesiveness. Cohesiveness is an emotional closeness that exists among the group members, and its success depends on how well the group sticks together and acts as a single unit instead of as a group of individuals.

As you may recall from a previous chapter, the middle level on Maslow's hierarchy is the need for social interaction—a feeling of belonging, to be identified with one or more groups. Few people like being alone or working in isolation for extended periods of time.

Motivation to Join Groups. People become part of a group for one, or all, of the following reasons:

1. *Affiliation.* Group companionship provides feelings of security, belonging, and friendship.

2. *Power.* There is strength in numbers. Being a member of a group provides reassurance and support, often giving its members the courage to take a stand on an important issue, which they might not do on their own.

3. *Identity.* Along with membership in a group comes an increased awareness of personal identity—a sense of being somebody. Self-esteem is positively reinforced.

4. *Goal accomplishment.* In most situations, a group will accomplish goals more effectively than any individual effort, due in part to the variety of skills and knowledge that are collectively provided. The more brainpower used to solve a problem, the better the chance for a successful resolution.

Groupthink and Hidden Agenda Issues

Formal and informal groups are important to organizations and affect their performance in a variety of ways. The impact that groups have can be either positive or negative, and this impact often manifests itself in terms of groupthink and the hidden agendas of individual group members.

Groupthink Issues. **Groupthink** is the tendency of highly cohesive groups to lose their critical evaluative abilities and, out of a desire for unanimity, often overlook realistic, meaningful alternatives as attitudes are formed and decisions are made. At times, groupthink can contribute to unethical behavior in the workplace. Symptoms of groupthink are arrogance, overcommitment, and excessive loyalty to the group.

The more cohesive the group, the more likely the individual members tend to "agree not to disagree," especially when it comes to challenging the ideas of the group leader. Unfortunately, in that way, groupthink can undermine the analytical process, legitimize ignorance, and reinforce biases because people do tend to be influenced by their peers. Instances of groupthink occur most often at meetings where decisions have been made *before* the meeting even begins. In other words, the other members of the group are there merely to rubber-stamp the leader's choice.

Although a certain amount of groupthink can be expected from any group situation, some techniques are available to leaders to minimize its occurrence. Leaders can, for example, diversify the group membership to get different per-

People become part of a group for many reasons, such as affiliation, power, identity, or goal accomplishment.
© *PhotoDisc, Inc.*

spectives as well as provide opportunities and permission for open debate.

Hidden Agendas. Another pitfall of any group interaction is the possibility that someone will be safeguarding a hidden agenda or personal goal. **Hidden agendas** are comprised of attitudes and feelings that an individual brings to the group. While often planned, hidden agendas can also rise spontaneously as a result of a disagreement with some idea expressed or conflict with a member in the group.

When there is a hidden agenda present, goal orientation shifts from the group to the individual so that the individual with the hidden agenda nearly always, either consciously or subconsciously, places obstacles in the path of the group's planned agenda. Hidden agendas represent what an individual or group want, instead of what they say they want.

While hidden agendas are neither better nor worse than planned agendas, they are important to understand. At the very least, AOMs need to recognize their existence because they can profoundly interfere with the ability to focus and can block the process of groups.

If not recognized and understood, hidden agendas can waste a great deal of a group's energy and the organization's resources. Here are three ways you, as a leader, can help a group handle hidden agendas:

1. Realize that a hidden agenda is a natural part of the group process because individual members have individual goals and needs.

2. Recognize that a hidden agenda might be present when the group is having difficulty in reaching its goals.

3. Decide how to bring the hidden agenda to light.

Teamwork and Team-Building Elements

The process of supervising, managing, and leading employees in organizations will continue to change as team efforts become more pronounced. By combining the resources and skills of interdependent work-group members with the high energy and motivation created through effective teamwork, employees and supervisors can attain extraordinary levels of achievement through teams. What a team might look like is described in Table 8.1. From an ideal perspective, however, an effective team is one that is efficient, productive, and cohesive.

Who Are Team Members?	1. A team is composed of two or more persons in the organization, usually from dissimilar departments in the organization.
	2. The members are competent and knowledgeable in the way they carry out their duties.
What Does a Team Attempt to Do?	1. The team is constantly learning and growing—adapting itself to changing requirements and multiple goals.
	2. Its work is consistently superior in both quality and quantity.
How Does the Team Concept Work?	1. Problems and conflicts within the team are addressed quickly and professionally.
	2. The quality of decisions made by the team is high, and members share a sense of satisfaction in work accomplished.

Table 8-1

What Does a
Team Look Like?

Source: Adapted from a "Fundamentals of Teambuilding" seminar presented by Jerry Odell, August 1993, in Phoenix, Arizona. Used with permission.

With the advent and increased use of teams, a new and positive phenomenon called *multiskilling* is emerging in organizations. The informal training concept called **multiskilling** requires team members to learn every job on the team. In this way, team members can cover for each other and respond quickly when conditions change.

As shown in Figure 8.1, organizations must help build effective teams because team building does not just happen. Team building is one of many "interventions" used to create change in an organization. Its purpose is the creation of a work environment that enables and promotes achievement of organizational and individual goals. Modern team-building efforts usually include concentration on how team members relate to each other and how work is completed.[3]

Here are some ways leaders can contribute to and help make a team effort more effective:

1. Avoid arguing for your own viewpoint. Instead, state your point as clearly and concisely as you can and listen to others.

2. If the discussion reaches an impasse, do not assume that someone must win and someone must lose. Look for a new option that is the next best alternative for everyone.

3. Never change your mind just to avoid an argument. Encourage differences of opinion among team members.

4. If an agreement comes too quickly, take another look at the issue. Different interpretations of what was agreed to may be hiding differences. Make sure that everyone fully understands the intent and content of the agreement.

Figure 8.1

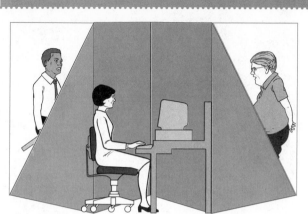 

Effective team-building efforts concentrate on how team members relate to each other and how work is completed.

5. Do not give way to other viewpoints unless you feel they have reasonable merit.

6. Avoid using conflict-reducing tricks to reach agreement, such as majority vote, calculating an average, flipping a coin, or bargaining.

7. Make sure that every member of the group contributes.

According to Nancy Austin, co-author with Tom Peters of *A Passion for Excellence,* making the transition to teams means a fundamental shift in power and authority. That means the familiar tenets of traditional management can make self-managing teams seem slippery and uncontrolled if the accountability issue is left vague. Of course, a shift to teams does not dilute the obligation of leaders to perform up to company expectations. With teams, however, the manager's role is rewritten. Organizational leaders must get used to being hands-off coaches who liberate, rather than overseers who confine.[4]

CONFLICT RESOLUTIONS

Managers are required to deal with different conflict situations almost routinely. Why is that so? Because no two people are exactly alike. And this uniqueness guarantees at least one thing—there will always be conflict. Since we all tote the baggage of our personal values, experiences, beliefs, and perceptions with us everywhere, the chance that our values will clash with those of someone else from time to time is very real. Conflict is an inevitable part of life, and the workplace is no exception. That is what makes effective conflict management an essential skill for any successful manager.

Conflict, itself, is not a bad thing. Disagreement can, in fact, be a healthy and creative

> **Management Tip**
>
> *Extreme conformity in group decision making can be destructive when it results in reduced mental efficiency, poor testing of reality, and lax moral judgments.*

Two situations involving conflict resolution in process—one at a standstill and the other making progress.   © *PhotoDisc, Inc.;* © *CORBIS*

exercise in the growth and development of an individual, team, or project. Further, conflict can ultimately strengthen work relationships. Trouble erupts, however, when conflict goes unmanaged and unresolved. Therefore, a manager's goal should not be to eliminate all conflict but to minimize and redirect dysfunctional discord by seeking and applying constructive resolutions.

Whether the outcome of a conflict issue is positive or negative is almost totally determined by the way it is managed. One could ask, "Why not let individual 'flash fires' burn themselves out?" A thoughtful response is because ultimately, the physical, psychological, emotional, and financial toll they take on an organization and its employees can be tremendous.

Understanding and Resolving Conflicts

Until recently, conflict of any sort in the office has been unwelcome—perhaps because many people associate it with a lack of harmony, emotional pain, or destructive behavior.

Benefits of Conflict. Though it is true that conflicts can have a devastating effect on productivity, morale, teamwork, and, ultimately, your organization's bottom line, there are some reasons why conflicts can actually be healthy for a business. Here's how:

1. *Conflict produces change.* Conflict often leads to the first step toward getting rid of outdated procedures, revising regulations, and fostering innovation and creativity.

2. *Conflict leads to unity.* Addressing rather than suppressing conflict opens the lines of communication, gets people talking to each other (instead of about each other), and makes people feel like they are part of a team that cares.

3. ***Conflict promotes compromise.*** People learn how to work harmoniously, come up with creative solutions, and reach outcomes that benefit everyone involved.

Conflict Resolution Process

Adhere to these steps, which are similar in nature to the problem-solving steps in Chapter 6, when you need to resolve conflicts:

1. ***Identify the problem.*** Sometimes the problem merely needs to be reframed. If you put a new frame on a picture, the picture looks different. If you put a new meaning on a problem, the problem can look different, too.

2. ***Look for solutions.*** Good solutions come most often from random, nonjudgmental brainstorming.

3. ***Choose the best solution.*** The best solution solves the problem, does not hurt anyone or interfere with their rights, and satisfies both parties. There should be no winner or loser; both sides should feel as if they have achieved something. That is called a win-win solution, which will be more thoroughly discussed later.

4. ***Act.*** Follow through on one of the solutions.

5. ***Evaluate.*** If your approach turns out to be ineffective, do not look on it as a failure. It just means you have eliminated one approach and you are ready to try another. We learn by our mistakes. (Go back to step 1.)

At every step during the conflict resolution process, communication is important. Communication does not mean just telling someone what you want. It means listening to what they want. It means establishing eye contact and being sensitive to body language. It means not making demands or ultimatums, but offering suggestions instead.

When conflicts become heated, and they sometimes do, follow these hints to control your impulses:

1. Be aware of your feelings. Although some people are ashamed of their angry, sad, or jealous feelings, these feelings are real, and you are entitled to the feelings you have. If you are angry, admit it to yourself and express your feelings using adult-like behaviors.

2. Take a break if your feelings get too hot to handle. Divert yourself. Do something else or go somewhere else.

3. Count to ten slowly. It will give you at least ten seconds to cool off and think about your approach.

4. Consult with someone such as a close friend, relative, or co-worker who has a calming effect on you, and whom you can trust in confidence.[5]

There is one final point to mention about understanding organizational conflicts. Organizations by their very nature create unique problem-solving obstacles. Be aware of these workplace realities that do, in fact, hamper honest conflict resolution attempts:

1. Employees are afraid to criticize their bosses.

2. People are self-protective of their positions and power.

3. Technical expertise is intimidating to those with less knowledge.

4. People see problems from their own viewpoints rather than the broader organizational perspective.

Managing and Negotiating Effective Solutions

According to research, the top-two things that managers don't want to deal with are conflict resolution and performance evaluation—because performance evaluation can cause conflict. However, conflict must be managed and not suppressed. Generally, the danger with workplace violence is not from that kind of extreme violence, but from lower levels of internal conflict. A company can be slowly poisoned by anger and hostility. It's critical, therefore, that clear rules for governing conflict must exist.

It's the job of senior management to establish the environment of an organization, which includes laying down rules governing disagreements. That means that you have rules for how you treat each other. You have rules about listening, about being respectful, and about trying to appreciate the differences in style and perspective.[6]

Managers spend a large amount of their time refereeing conflict—a lot of time dealing with issues that retard progress, productivity, support, and cooperation. The goal of productive problem solving and conflict resolution is for parties involved to move from some form of compromise to ultimate collaboration marked by a shared success.

Conflict Management Styles. Got a conflict with a colleague? Be aware of how you respond. Your reaction may de-escalate the situation or fan the fires. Keep in mind:

- If you compete, you're assertive in pursuing your own concerns. This style is useful when quick action is necessary or when you need to make an unpopular decision.
- If you accommodate, you're cooperative, but unassertive. This style is useful when you realize that you're wrong or that the issue is more important to the other person.
- If you avoid, you don't address the conflict. This reaction is useful when the issue is trivial, a confrontation could be damaging, or you need time to cool off or gather information.
- If you collaborate, you're both assertive and cooperative. Rather than avoiding a problem, you attempt to work with another person to find a mutually satisfying solution.
- If you compromise, you address rather than avoid an issue. Compromising means split-

Management Tip

Every time we face up to a problem and resolve it, we grow by learning to get along better with others and by taking responsibility for our own actions.

ting the difference or agreeing on a middle ground.[7]

According to an article in the *Journal of Business Ethics,* there are five generally accepted styles for dealing with conflict. Nothing is inherently right or wrong with any of these styles. In fact, each can be appropriate and most effective depending on the situation and issues to be resolved and the personalities involved. These conflict management styles are competing, accommodating, avoiding, collaborating, and compromising. Refer to Table 8.2 for a detailed description and understanding of each conflict management style.[8] When used appropriately, each of these styles can be an effective approach to conflict resolution. Recognize that any one style or a mixture of the five can be used during the course of a dispute to arrive at the collaboration and compromise required for ultimate agreement.

Conflict may be unavoidable in organizations, but the anger, grudges, hurt, and blame that often ensue from it are not. Although negotiation is defined as conferring, discussing, or bargaining to reach agreements, most managers realize that in practice, negotiations involve conflict and therefore can result in a win-lose, lose-lose, or win-win situation.

Negotiating Styles. Managers spend a good portion of their time negotiating with employees, suppliers, customers, or other work groups. When people bargain over positions, they tend to back themselves into corners defending their positions, which results in a number of either win-lose or lose-lose outcomes.

Win-Lose. The **win-lose negotiating style** assumes that one side will win by achieving its goals and the other side will lose. When engaging in a win-lose negotiation, the person with the most information is in the most powerful position. A win-lose approach to negotiations is sometimes obvious and appropriate, while at other times it is less apparent and destructive.

For example, groups often set themselves up for win-lose outcomes by following the principle of majority rule—if 51 percent of the group votes one way, then 49 percent are losers. Another example of the win-lose approach occurs when the parties start the negotiation process by stating the specific outcomes they want to see.

When the issues involved in a conflict are trivial or when a speedy decision is required, this style may be appropriate. It is also appropriate when unpopular courses of action must be implemented—for instance, when implementing the strategies and policies formulated by higher level managers. In general, use the win-lose style when:

- you have a clear conflict of interests,
- you are in a much more powerful position, or
- you are not concerned with promoting a long-term relationship.

Lose-Lose. The outcomes of the **lose-lose negotiating style** are common when one party attempts to win at the expense of the other. Lose-lose outcomes also occur when unreasonable union demands have forced companies into bankruptcy or when employers

STYLES AND DESCRIPTION	INVOLVES
Competing An aggressive and totally antagonistic style. A competitor pursues his or her own views at a colleague's expense. This is a power-oriented mode in which a group member uses whatever means that seems appropriate to win.	**Competing** could mean "standing up for your rights," defending a position that you believe is correct, or demonstrating a win-at-all-costs attitude.
Accommodating An unassertive, self-sacrificing, and hospitable style that is in direct opposition to competing. Colleagues who use this approach relinquish their own concerns to satisfy the concerns of another employee.	**Accommodating** usually takes the form of selfless generosity or blind obedience and yielding completely to another's point of view.
Avoiding Avoiding is an unassertive, sidestepping, and retreat-oriented conflict management style. An avoider generally chooses to dodge conflict at all costs.	**Avoiding** might take the form of diplomatically sidestepping an issue, postponing an issue until a better time, or simply withdrawing from a threatening situation either emotionally, physically, or intellectually.
Collaborating A more cooperative, synergistic, and multilateral conflict resolution style. Collaborators find mutually satisfying solutions as they dig into a problem to identify underlying issues.	**Collaboration** involves agreeing not to compete for resources or use confrontation to find creative solutions to mutually engaging problems.
Compromising Compromising means that both parties "split the difference" in order to settle disagreements. It might mean exchanging concessions or seeking quick, middle-ground solutions.	**Compromising** involves finding expedient, mutually acceptable solutions that partially satisfy both parties.

Table 8-2

Conflict Management Styles

Source: Adapted from Dawn M. Baskerville, "How Do You Manage Conflict?" *Black Enterprise,* May 1993, pp. 63–64.

destroy the effectiveness of their workers by taking advantage of them.

Mutually destructive outcomes can also surface from personal disputes among employees. For example, feuding co-workers may destroy their own careers by acquiring a reputation of being difficult to work with or not being team players.

Compromise can sometimes seem better than fighting a win-lose battle and risking a lose-lose outcome. When resources are scarce or limited, compromise may indeed be the best solution.

Win-Win. The **win-win negotiating style** assumes that a solution can be reached that will satisfy the needs of *all* parties. Instead of looking at their opponent as an adversary to be defeated, win-win negotiators see others as allies in a search for a satisfactory solution through collaborative means.

In most situations, the needs of the negotiating parties are not incompatible; they are just different. The four basic components of a win-win negotiation are as follows:

1. Separate the people from the problem.

2. Focus on interests, not positions.

3. Generate a variety of possibilities before deciding what to do.

4. Insist that the result be based on some objective standard.

As you can see in Figure 8.2, there is a vast difference in results among the three styles. By focusing on the end result instead of the means of getting there, win-win solutions can

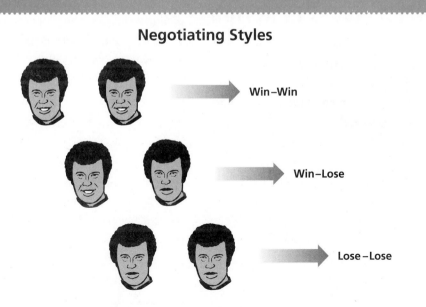

Negotiating Styles

Win–Win

Win–Lose

Lose–Lose

frequently be found. You will want to use the win-win style when:

- you have common interests,
- power is approximately equal, or you are in a weak position, or
- a continuing, harmonious relationship is desired.

When you can bring the conflicting parties together to discuss the issues face-to-face, you are using a powerful conflict management technique known as integration. **Integration** is a win-win method, instead of a win-lose or lose-lose method. In a win-win situation, all parties walk away with something gained by using their imagination to work out a mutually satisfactory solution. The major advantage of integration is the shared commitment for all parties to find a solution. Having shared this commitment, a strong foundation exists for future collaboration and resolution of future conflicts.

CONFLICT ISSUES IN ACTION

Other conflict issues can arise that demand a manager's attention. Increasingly, job stress and time management become issues with workers and managers alike. An overview of these two issues, therefore, is appropriate in this chapter.

Job Stress

Scenario: The phone is ringing off the hook. Your report on the new project is due in half an hour. Your boss asks to see you immediately. You have not had any time to eat lunch. And you cannot get the cap off the aspirin bottle. You are stressed.[9]

Stress in the workplace is costing American businesses staggering amounts of money. **Stress** may be defined as any external stimulus that produces wear and tear on a person's psychological or physical well-being. A person under severe or prolonged stress cannot function as effectively as a person leading a more balanced life. Although the implication is that stress is negative, a certain amount of it can have quite positive effects, such as improving one's health through athletic competition or high productivity and accomplishment as a community leader.

Although there are some positive aspects of stress, companies are primarily concerned with preventing the negative outcomes, most notably job burnout. **Burnout** is a stress-related affliction resulting when people invest most of their time and energy in a particular activity. Burnout candidates are those who tend to be idealistic and/or self-motivated achievers, tend to seek unattainable goals, and whose stress is primarily job related. Rising stress levels also are byproducts of the current corporate climate, when downsizing and mergers are common and can occur without warning.[10]

Work is the leading cause of stress for the majority of Americans. The Family and Work Institute's 1997 National Study of the Changing Workforce suggests that the emotional well-being of working Americans is three times more likely to be affected by job-related stress than other personal demands, such as children, spouses, elderly parents or housework. The National Safety Council reports that job stress causes one million employees to be absent from work on an average workday, which translates to around $200 billion in costs for employers in terms of lost productivity, workers' compensation claims, and medical care.[11]

More folks are calling in sick, but it may not be a virus that has them down. Illness accounts for only 22 percent of no-shows, reports CCH Inc., a tax and business information firm that surveys absences. Consultants say firms can reduce costs and disruption by recognizing family and other demands for a "sickless day off." Suggestions include flexible work schedules, emergency childcare, and combined accounts from which to draw sick, personal, and vacation days. With absenteeism projected to grow, some employers may crack down; but others are likely to offer new options to mesh work and personal time.[12]

In summary, business organizations are now acknowledging that job-related stress can result in employee illness, turnover, job dissatisfaction, reduced productivity, and other workplace problems. It has been estimated that days lost from work due to stress have risen from just 1.1 days in 1995 to 1.5 days in 1998 and that this costs employers around $200 billion to $300 billion every year as measured by such factors as employee turnover, absenteeism, direct medical costs, workers' compensation, lower productivity, and accidents. The factors identified to have the greatest effect on stress are degree of control over work, demands on employees, and lack of support from co-workers and superiors. Other leading stressors are poor working conditions, inability to voice complaints, responsibility without authority, and inadequate recognition.[13]

Effects of Stress. The symptoms of stress are often invisible, but the effects are unmistakable.

Going beyond productivity, the impact on the individual is substantial. Stress prevents people from feeling fulfilled, from feeling happy, and from feeling valued both on and off the job.

In her book *Toxic Work,* Barbara Reinhold makes the case with research and case experience that many Americans "don't like what they do for a living and are becoming sick of it." She cites evidence: A national study estimates that about 20 million adults hate their jobs and stay with their current employer only to retain health insurance. The result of job unhappiness can be recognized in physical symptoms—weight problems, headaches, muscle soreness, fatigue, digestive troubles, and lower back pain. The concept goes beyond such ergonomic issues as bad posture in front of your computer or breathing poorly ventilated air in an office building. It is deeper than not having enough time to exercise or eating poorly on deadline.[14]

Simply put, as job pressure rises, productivity drops. While everyone can handle a certain amount of stress, if you give employees too much for too long, they won't be producing at their peak. When employees are asked about on-the-job stressors, they often complain of such things as inadequate training, frequent schedule changes, poor new-hire screening, lack of communication, a misguided reward system, and a dingy work environment. More often than not, they also have in mind some workable solutions, but employers must ask.

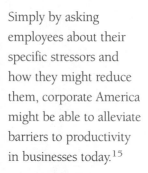

Management Tip

Perfectionists beware! Workers who expect flawless performance from themselves may experience more stress-related illnesses than those who set and achieve realistic goals.

Simply by asking employees about their specific stressors and how they might reduce them, corporate America might be able to alleviate barriers to productivity in businesses today.[15]

Managing Stress.

Stress in the workplace is not a clear-cut issue with tried and true solutions. A question often asked is which comes first— life stress or work stress? Progressive employers are facing the challenge by forging partnerships with employees to reduce workplace stress by improving safety, increasing communication, and returning as much control as possible to the individual doing the job.

Stress is not based on what happens to you, but on *how you deal with what happens to you.* The key to stress is "choice" in how to deal with the stressors. Because you cannot build a life completely free from stress, it is important that you develop some ways of dealing with stress. Doctors have come up with a few suggestions on how to live with stress:

1. Work off stress with some physical activity.

2. Talk out your worries with someone you trust and respect.

3. Learn to accept what you cannot change.

4. Avoid self-medication like alcohol or other chemicals because, in the end, the ability to handle stress comes from within you, not from the outside.

Just giving yourself *time off* for an activity you enjoy can minimize the effects of job stress.   *©PhotoDisc, Inc.*

5. Get enough sleep and rest.

6. Balance work and recreation by scheduling time for recreation to relax your mind.

7. Do something for others; this gets your mind off yourself.

8. Take one thing at a time.

9. Give in once in a while, instead of fighting and insisting you are always right.

10. Make yourself available and get involved in life and the business of living.[16]

Time Management

Many of us are victims of our attitudes about time. We put things off, we complain about the lack of time, and we misuse the time we have. The purpose of time management is to help us overcome these problems. Time is an important element and resource and is often mismanaged. Insulating oneself and starting time management on a personal note are two methods that work for many managers. Handling interruptions by others is a necessary skill.[17]

Procrastination. If procrastination is a problem, how can you overcome it? How can you avoid putting things off? Of the several basic approaches, one or more may work for you:

1. Set a deadline for starting a task and stick to it.

2. Get going with something easy and routine; then shift into the harder aspects of the task.

3. Reward progress, but save the biggest reward for completing the task.

4. Set short-term and long-term goals.

5. Make a daily "to do" list and then prioritize the items.

6. Always ask yourself during the course of the day, "What's the best use of my time right now?"

7. Use a daily planner or calendar, and keep it current.

8. Do it now . . . if at all possible.

Six tips to help you overcome procrastination and become more productive:

- *Consider potential consequences.* Write down possible negative outcomes of your behavior. Will delaying a task be worth a missed deadline, poor-quality work, or loss of a customer?
- *Take smaller bites.* Divide a big task into little steps and focus on completing them one at a time.
- *Delegate responsibility.* Don't try to do it all yourself.
- *Affirm yourself.* Give yourself a pep talk daily.
- *Set deadlines and promise results.* Self-imposed deadlines and the expectations of others are often enough to get us to act. No one wants to lose face.
- *Reward yourself.* Give yourself a pat on the back or treat yourself to something nice— but only when you've deserved it.[18]

Setting Priorities. People who believe they do not have enough time to accomplish everything they want to accomplish may be misusing time by not setting priorities. In most people's work responsibilities, there are three types of activities. Let's call them A, B, and C:

- *A activities* are most important and crucial to the job and should be the main focus of your time and energies.
- *B activities* have medium priority. They are important, but less so than A activities.
- *C activities* are low-priority activities. These are routine and relatively unimportant.

To use the work hours available in the best way, the effective AOM should spend a greater percentage of his or her time performing A-type activities. For example, delegate to an assistant or colleague those tasks that are routine and that can help others improve their skills, like checking the paper in the copy machine or filing papers.

Time Wasters. Many people complain that they do not have enough time when the real problem is that they spend too much time on unimportant matters while spending too little time on what is important.

While it is true that people with family and work responsibilities have many demands on their time, some people are able to get more done in the same amount of time than others. The truth is that each of us has the same 24 hours each day. How we use those hours is the critical factor. When pinned down, most people cannot account for where their time goes.

The following list contains nine common time wasters in the office that most of us are guilty of occasionally and that can account for why it takes more time to finish a task than necessary.

1. unnecessary phone conversations

2. ineffective meetings

3. unannounced visitors

4. poor delegation

5. excessive paperwork

6. putting off making decisions

7. stress

8. personal disorganization and office clutter

9. general distractions and interruptions[19]

In today's work environment, with the tremendous influence on downsizing and right-sizing, many employees are now assuming management duties and responsibilities. Another way to look at time wasters is relative to the basic management functions. Is time being wasted by inadequacies in basic management functions?

- *Planning function.* Are there any objectives? Is crisis management the norm? If so, your time is being wasted.

- *Organizing function.* Do you have multiple bosses? Is there confusion over responsibility and authority?

- *Staffing function.* Is your office over- or under-staffed? Do you have untrained personnel?

- *Directing function.* Is there any coordination of teamwork? Do you look for ways to delegate?

- *Controlling function.* Are your measurements and controls in place and reasonable? Do you have effective methods for handling the telephone and drop-in visitors?

- *Communicating function.* Are directions, objectives, and missions clearly communicated and easily understood? Are you and your boss always in meetings? How much socializing is going on?

- *Decision-making function.* Are managers indecisive? Are snap decisions made frequently? Do committees make decisions?[20]

Message *for* AOMs

AOMs can help group members learn that in group efforts, even though their ideas are disputed, their personal competence is not being questioned. Phrases like "we are all in this together" and "let's find a solution that is good for everyone" indicate the appropriate attitude for the group, rather than "I'm right and you're wrong." As an AOM, you will want to help group members look for shared successes and rewards—as well as shared responsibility for failures—not individual recognition.

This chapter introduced critical elements in handling job stress and managing time. Both of these work-related issues erode office productivity and steal valuable time. You should put into practice each day the task of breaking large projects down into small, manageable parts. Smaller tasks are attractive because they are short, easy, and produce immediate gratification. This technique makes it easier to delegate because it forces you to be clear and concise about the project boundaries. Remember that all projects, no matter how massive, are only a series of small items reassembled.[21]

1 People become part of a group for one, or all, of the following reasons: affiliation, power, identity, and goal accomplishment.

2 Groupthink can contribute to unethical behavior in the workplace. Symptoms of groupthink are arrogance, overcommitment, and excessive loyalty to the group. When there is a hidden agenda present, goal orientation shifts from the group to the individual so that the individual with the hidden agenda typically will place obstacles in the path of the group's planned agenda.

3 Conflict must be managed and not suppressed because a company can be slowly poisoned by anger and hostility and undermine the mission of the organization.

4 If you compete, you're assertive in pursuing your own concerns. If you accommodate, you're cooperative, but unassertive. If you avoid, you don't address the conflict. If you collaborate, you're both assertive and cooperative. If you compromise, you address rather than avoid an issue. Compromising means splitting the difference or agreeing on a middle ground.

5 The win-lose negotiating style assumes that one side will win by achieving its goals and the other side will lose. The outcomes of the lose-lose negotiating style are common when one party attempts to win at the expense of the other. The win-win negotiating style assumes that a solution can be reached that will satisfy the needs of *all* parties.

6 Stress prevents people from feeling fulfilled, from feeling happy, and from feeling valued both on and off the job.

7 Some suggestions on how to overcome problems with time management are (1) not to procrastinate, (2) set priorities, and (3) don't waste time on unimportant matters.

QUESTIONS FOR CRITICAL THINKING

1. Why would an office worker want to be identified with an informal group at work?

2. Which need, according to Maslow's needs' hierarchy, does belonging to a group meet? In your opinion, how well do organizations in general meet that need?

3. Some people say that there are more disadvantages of groupthink to an organization than advantages. Do you agree? Why or why not?

4. In your opinion, what is the most effective way for a leader to help a group handle hidden agendas?

5. Why is it not a good idea for organizations to let a conflict run its course?

6. Based on your experience, what percentage of time have you tried to follow most of the five steps when resolving personal conflicts? Was it effective?

7. In your own words, briefly describe each of the three negotiating styles.

8. When you experience job stress, how does it affect you? In other words, what symptoms show up?

9. What techniques do you personally use daily to manage how you spend your time?

Case Study 8-1: The "Me" Committee Member

Assume you are a member of a strategic planning committee, and the goal is to review the correct wording and intent of the organization's mission statement. There is one member on the committee who exhibits the following behaviors and attitudes during discussion: "I must have everything my way. Everything has to be perfect."

Discussion Question

Using the five steps to resolve conflicts that were covered in this chapter, describe how you and/or other committee members should deal with this committee member.

Case Study 8-2: What's the Worst Thing That Can Happen?

The comptroller's secretary came in on Monday morning and announced she had attended a seminar on stress management at the local university over the weekend. As a result, she announced that she's going to manage her stress better. One thing she will do is, to every stressor, she will ask, "What's the worst thing that can happen if I don't do this . . .?"

Her boss, the comptroller, is happy she is continuing her self-improvement and attending workshops but is unclear about how her new approach to getting things done will affect his position as comptroller of the organization.

Discussion Questions

1. Do you see any problem with the approach the secretary is taking?

2. Does the comptroller have a valid concern about his secretary's new attitude?

Case Study 8-3: *Internet Research Activity*

Assume you are doing a report on *stress on the job.* Use the Internet to research information needed to answer the following questions. Key your responses.

1. Which Web search engine did you use?

2. Write down three of the URL addresses that you accessed during your search.

3. As a result of your search, list three items of current information you might use in your report.

Endnotes

[1]Margaret Steen, "Managers Seek to Balance Individual Rewards with Group Goals," *InfoWorld,* September 14, 1998, p. 91.

[2] Ibid.

[3]Ronald R. Sims, "Linking Groupthink to Unethical Behavior in Organizations," *Journal of Business Ethics,* September 1992, pp. 653–654.

[4]Nancy K. Austin, "Making Teamwork Work," *Working Woman,* January 1993, p. 28.

[5]Sandra R. Arbetter, "Resolving Conflicts Step by Step," *Current Health 2,* September 1991, p. 15.

[6]Michael Barrier, "Putting a Lid on Conflicts," *Nation's Business,* April 1998, pp. 34–35.

[7]Beblon Parks, "Got a Conflict with a Colleague? Here's How to Resolve it Now," *Instructor,* April 1998, p. 74.

[8]M. Afzalur Rahim, Jan Edward Garrett, and Gabriel F. Buntzman, "Ethics of Managing Interpersonal Conflict in Organizations," *Journal of Business Ethics,* May 1992, pp. 426–428.

[9]Paul Cornell, "Stress Busters," *The Secretary,* January 1995, p. 18.

[10]Stephanie Armour, "Workplace Stress Takes Increasing Toll," *USA Today,* May 4, 1998, p. 5.

[11]Shari Caudron, "On the Contrary, Job Stress is in Job Design," *Workforce,* September 1998, pp. 22–23.

[12] "Ever Thought of Calling in Well?" *U.S. News & World Report,* November 9, 1998, p. 82.

[13]Gail Dutton, "Cutting-Edge Stressbusters," *HR Focus,* September 1998, p. 12.

[14]Barbara Bailey Reinhold, *Toxic Work,* Dutton Publishing Co., 1996, pp. 34–35.

[15]Ibid.

[16]From a "Positive Ways to Deal with Stress" seminar held in December 1998 at Northern Arizona University in Flagstaff, Arizona.

[17]Jacob Weisberg, "A Time Management Survival Guide," *Folio: The Magazine for Magazine Management,* October 1, 1998, p. 85.

[18]Iris Randall, "Realizing the Dream Deferred," *Black Enterprise,* February 1998, p. 196.

[19]Daniel Janal, "Killing Time Is Killing You," *Computer,* October 1992, p. 23.

[20]Ellen L. Gray, "Time Management in Today's Working Environment," *The Secretary,* May 1996, p. 25.

[21]Odette Pollar, "Conquering the Inner Demon," *The Secretary,* January 1995.

Part II:
Debate the Issue

1. Retrieve the file Part II—Debate, which contains the table shown below, from the template disk. Using the form for each of the three issues listed in step 3, quickly key some ideas you have as initial rections to each statement.

2. Prepare to role play either point of view in a mock in-class debate.

3. Part II debate issues follow:

   a. "Women leaders are less likely to derive satisfaction from competitive achievement than men leaders."

   b. "In today's world, communication is based on the speed of the message, not the effectiveness of the message."

   c. "Companies should help employees deal with stress."

POINTS OF AGREEMENT	POINTS OF DISAGREEMENT
1.	1.
2.	2.
3.	3.
4.	4.

training

performance

ethics

Managing Human Resources in the Office

Staffing Practices: Trends, Laws, and Job Analysis

chapter 9

> There is something that is much more scarce, something rarer than ability. It is the ability to recognize ability.
>
> —*Robert Half*

objectives

After completing this chapter, you will be able to:

1. **Discuss factors that make today's U.S. workforce a challenge for administrative office managers.**

2. **List major legislation that affects the employment process in organizations.**

3. **Describe the role of the AOM in the job analysis process.**

4. **Distinguish between the information contained in a job description and a job specification.**

5. **List the advantages of the compressed workweek, job sharing, and telecommuting for the worker.**

6. **Describe the advantages of telecommuting to the employer and to society.**

Technology is redefining the concept of work. It is spurring a radical rethinking of work processes, human capital, and knowledge in a growing number of organizations. Increasingly, companies and human resources departments are examining work processes, human capital, and knowledge in radically different ways. Technology will permeate almost every business practice and drive enormous strategic and practical progress.

As a result, managers will have to focus on measuring efficiency and productivity, rather than tracking a group of employees and tasks.[1] People and their complex behavior patterns are the lifeblood of any organization. The next three chapters contain essential information every administrative office manager must know to manage people and human resources activities effectively.

Tony Norris

PC Specialist
Sears Merchandise Group
Hoffman Estates, Illinois

In 1968, Tony Norris joined Sears in California. He was later promoted to the Chicago home office, and by 1980 he had become a shoe buyer for the retail chain and its catalog.

In 1986, a spinal tumor paralyzed Norris from the neck down, forcing him to leave Sears and a job he dearly loved. In 1988, after a coma and a 20-month hospital stay, his former boss called, asking if he would like to come back to work at Sears. Norris accepted and currently works as a PC specialist, planning and budgeting for Sears shoe departments in some 800 stores across the country.

QUESTION:

Tony, think about today's management students who tomorrow may be interviewing job candidates with disabilities. What suggestions can you offer that will aid in reducing job bias during the interview?

Dialog *from the* Workplace

RESPONSE:

I never tell people ahead of time that I'm in a wheelchair. They shouldn't do anything different for me than they'd do for anybody else—and it's no different for a job interview. I don't put that information on my resumé either. I just concentrate on my qualifications and I hope the interviewer will do the same.

My advice to new interviewers would be to never prejudge any applicant, especially one with a disability. Keep an open mind and focus on capabilities, not disabilities.

If I were applying for a position, I'd want the interviewer to tell me what the job description requires and then leave it up to me as to how I'd meet those requirements. In other words, focus on the final outcome, not how the person actually performs the task.

It's probably human nature to say, "Gee, if I were in that person's shoes, I could never do this job." But an unbiased interviewer won't fall into that trap. Don't underestimate a person with a disability and don't try to

second-guess what his or her abilities are.

It always irritates me when I go into a restaurant and the waitress asks my nurse, "What would he like for dinner?" Don't let that scenario happen on the job. If, for example, you're interviewing someone who is deaf, always address the applicant, not the interpreter. The interpreter is just the go-between. It's the job applicant that you want to get to know.

I don't know why people do this, but many times they'll be overly nice to me simply because I'm in a wheelchair. Sometimes I think they are going to reach out and pat me on the head like a little child. Perhaps they are uncomfortable or just uninformed, but I'd prefer that they see me as a professional in a business environment.

What I want from a work situation is to be treated as an equal—whether it's an interview or just an average day on the job. Just because I've got splints on my hands doesn't mean you shouldn't offer to shake hands with me.

As your company's recruiter, it's your job to ask all the tough questions, evaluate each candidate fairly, and select the best person for the company. I'm sure you'll make the right decision if you keep this one thing in mind: There's no relationship between the disability and the capabilities of a person.

What major functions in human resource management do AOMs perform? We start our study of this subject with a better understanding of the laws that affect human resource management and the job analysis and design process. Chapter 10 will cover on-the-job practices, specifically employee recruitment and the selection process, as well as employee orientation, training, counseling, and appraisals. Chapter 11 will examine work ethics and business etiquette issues—stateside and abroad.

First, however, we examine the American workforce to better understand the type of employee AOMs manage today and follow with an introduction to the laws that affect human resource management.

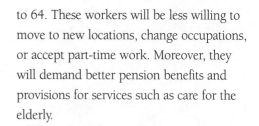

Management Tip

As you read magazines and newspapers or watch news telecasts, continually look for new information that describes societal trends. These trends will affect how you work.

U.S. WORKFORCE TRENDS

Today's labor market looks different from yesterday's to many seasoned administrative managers. Managers see changes in overall workforce trends that have an effect on the way people perform their jobs.

Some demographics and trends prepared by the U.S. Small Business Administration put today's workforce challenges in perspective.

1. Hispanics account for more than 25 percent of the workers joining the labor force; Asians, 15 percent; and blacks, 14 percent.

2. The aging of the workforce will be a bigger challenge as the Baby Boomers reach ages 45

to 64. These workers will be less willing to move to new locations, change occupations, or accept part-time work. Moreover, they will demand better pension benefits and provisions for services such as care for the elderly.

3. The number of immigrant workers, with differing cultural and educational backgrounds, will increase and pose challenges to employers.[2]

The trends just listed and other demographic trends have already produced demands for changes in public policy such as mandatory family leaves for employees as well as an increased awareness of and compliance with civil rights and equal employment opportunity legislation. Of importance to managers is their influence on cultural diversity in society, which in turn is directly reflected in the workplace.

With these changes in the U.S. workforce, managing human resources as part of your overall responsibilities will be a challenge. It requires an administrative office manager who can handle change, anticipate trends, and move calmly and quickly to reach effective solutions.

LAWS AFFECTING HUMAN RESOURCE MANAGEMENT

During the past three decades, federal legislation has changed the rules for employers by granting employees specific rights. Failure to comply with these laws subjects employers not only to the risk of litigation, but it also invites negative public attitudes and can damage employee morale. Among the most important legislation that influences how people are managed are the Equal Pay Act of 1963, the Civil

Rights Act of 1964 (and its numerous subsequent amendments), the Americans with Disabilities Act of 1990, and the Family and Medical Leave Act of 1993.

Equal Pay Act of 1963

One of the first equal employment requirements resulting in a mandate to employers was the **Equal Pay Act of 1963,** which provides equal pay for equal work, regardless of sex. This law requires that men and women working under similar working conditions must receive the same pay if their jobs require equal skill, effort, and responsibility.

The concept of comparable worth applies to jobs that are valued similarly in the organization, whether or not they are the same. **Comparable worth** implies that jobs with comparable levels of knowledge, skill, and ability should be paid similarly even if actual duties differ significantly.

Civil Rights Act of 1964

Beginning with the Civil Rights Act of 1964 and specifically with its Title VII, known as "Equal Employment Opportunities," employment practices in organizations were put on notice to be nonbiased, consistent, and fair in the treatment of *all* employees. The agency authorized under Title VII to oversee compliance with the Civil Rights Act is the **Equal Employment Opportunity Commission (EEOC).** This agency handles complaints relative to race, sex, color, religion, and national origin, plus age and disability discrimination and compensation charges.

The primary functions of the EEOC are to investigate and mediate equal employment opportunity (EEO) complaints. Normally, most complaints are either settled privately or litigated in the courts. The EEOC has the legitimate power, however, to issue an injunction in an attempt to mediate and remedy the complaint. An **injunction** is a court order requiring a person or corporation to do or to refrain from doing a particular act.

Over the years, significant amendments have been made to this act. These amendments have dramatically affected employment practices in the United States and, as a result, have changed the way managers manage. Noted in the next paragraphs are four significant mandates with which managers must comply that affect employment of office support workers.

Age Discrimination in Employment Act of 1967. Originally, the age discrimination legislation prohibited mandatory retirement below age 65 for most employees. However, with longer productive years predicted among older workers, this mandatory retirement age was raised to age 70 in the late 1970s. Then, again, in 1986, the act was amended. This time it prohibited mandatory retirement at *any* age for almost all employees.

Equal Employment Opportunity Act of 1972. Title VII of the Civil Rights Act was amended in 1972. Its effects were sweeping because the act applied to virtually all forms of job discrimination, such as discriminatory treatment in hiring, promoting, testing, training opportunities, evaluating, compensating, disciplining, and terminating employees. This amendment became known as the **Equal Employment Opportunity Act.** It forbids discrimination on the basis of race, sex, religion, or national origin.

Equal employment opportunity is not only a legal issue; it is also an emotional issue. The topic is of concern to everyone regardless of sex, race, religion, age, national origin, color, or position in the organization. Perhaps no other regulatory agency has so thoroughly affected human resource management as has the EEOC. For example, if you, as an employer, behave as described in the employment situations listed in Table 9.1, you may be in violation of EEO.

Pregnancy Discrimination Act of 1978.

Under the Pregnancy Discrimination Act, employers are required to treat disabilities related to pregnancy the same as other disabilities. For example, if employees who have absences resulting from illnesses not connected to pregnancy are excused without medical evidence, asking pregnant women for such evidence could violate the act.

Sexual Harassment Law of 1991.

The sexual harassment law has its roots in Title VII of the Civil Rights Act of 1964, which prohibits discrimination on the basis of sex. Beginning in 1991, however, events such as the Anita Hill–Justice Clarence Thomas harassment suit and the U.S. Navy "Tailhook" scandal involving sexual harassment of women attending a convention of naval aviators led not only to an increase in legal action but also to major shifts in the way people *think* about sexual harassment at work.

Sexual harassment cases have continued to increase dramatically since 1991. Because of this increase, lawyers are now drafting consensual sex agreements that both the client and the client's partner sign, contracting their amorous intentions and promising not to bring a harassment suit if the affection ends. In addition, many businesses are purchasing employment practices liability insurance (EPLI) coverage as a method to defray unwanted but perhaps inevitable sexual harassment charges.[3]

As a practical matter, the Supreme Court's most recent sexual harassment rulings in the summer of 1998 required companies of any size to have:

- A written policy outlawing all forms of sexual harassment.
- Sexual harassment training for supervisors.
- A strategy for responding to sexual harassment complaints.[4]

A federal act in 1978 prevents discrimination against pregnant workers.
©PhotoDisc, Inc.

EXAMPLES OF DISCRIMINATION BASED ON RACE, RELIGION, NATIONAL ORIGIN, AGE, OR DISABILITY

Employment Practice	Discrimination Examples
Hiring	"I don't care if he is the right person for the job, I think we are going overboard in this company by hiring so many minorities."
Promotions	"Perhaps we can have dinner some evening after work and discuss your future with the company."
Testing	"We are going to have to change our entire testing procedure to accommodate him (applicant has a disability)."
Evaluations	"I have a problem with anyone who cannot look me in the eyes when I give them an evaluation—even though I realize certain ethnic groups are that way."
Compensation	"We can get by paying Mr. Ziede minimum wage because he has lots of retirement income coming in."
Discipline	"Women always cry when they receive a reprimand!"
Termination	"I'm afraid if she gets fired, I'll have her entire church congregation in my office tomorrow. You know how they stick together."

Table 9.1 Equal Employment Opportunity Act of 1972

Organizations are committed to maintaining a work environment free of discriminatory intimidation and sexual harassment and typically have a policy covering these actions. In addition to defining prohibited behavior, a written sexual harassment policy should also:

- Make clear that the company won't tolerate misbehavior from anyone, including supervisors and customers.
- Encourage harassed employees to complain to their supervisor—or, if the supervisor is the harasser, to some other designated person.
- Assure employees of confidentiality.
- Assure employees that retaliation will not be tolerated.[5]

Sexual harassment is broadly defined as unwelcome sexual advances, requests for sexual favors, and other verbal or physical conduct of a sexual nature that creates an intimidating, offensive, or hostile work environment.

There are two kinds of harassment that the courts have recognized. The first, *quid pro quo*—a Latin term meaning "this for that"—forbids a supervisor from telling a subordinate he or she must have sex with the supervisor or else suffer

When news of a sexual harassment complaint reached a recently promoted top manager, he dismissed it with a wisecrack about "those nutty feminists." As a new administrative manager who overheard his comment, what would you say?

adverse consequences on the job, such as a promotion, a raise, or benefits. The other is **hostile work environment,** where supervisors or co-workers do things that make the work atmosphere more difficult for people based on their gender.

Hostile work environment harassment really isn't about sexual exploitation. It's about exclusion—one group trying to make the work atmosphere more difficult for another because they would really rather not have the person around. Sometimes it is sex, but sometimes other things are used to make women look less serious, less capable, different, and out of place on the job.[6] A hostile environment is determined by the circumstances of each case. However, four factors that contribute to a hostile environment are (1) frequency of the discriminatory conduct; (2) the severity of the conduct; (3) whether the conduct is physically threatening, humiliating, or an offensive utterance; and (4) if the conduct interferes with an employee's work performance.

Harassment can be prevented if informal actions are taken before incidents escalate into full-blown problems. This strategy thwarts the harassing behavior at the lowest level possible, which requires addressing the situation *before* it

becomes a formal complaint. Formal complaints are more difficult to handle because they are often confrontational and unpleasant. Informal options available to employers are:

- Appointing an ombudsman who is designated as a neutral and usually reports directly to the CEO.
- Planning an intervention whereby the manager or human resources representative sits down with all parties to review the issue.
- Hiring a professional to mediate who is an impartial expert and who guides the disputing parties through a process that encourages open discussion of the problem, listening, and empathizing.
- Fact-finding and investigation are used with situations that are more complex.[7]

The challenge for employers and managers is to find a resolution to sexual harassment charges that is fair to all parties involved. Table 9.2 outlines steps a company can take to reduce the risk of sexual harassment on the job.

Americans with Disabilities Act of 1990

Many people feel that the Americans with Disabilities Act (ADA) of 1990 is the single most important piece of antidiscrimination legislation to be enacted since the Civil Rights Act of 1964. As previously stated in an earlier chapter, the ADA prohibits, in companies with twenty-five or more employees, discrimination against people with disabilities in the use of public services, transportation, public accommodations, and telecommunication services. More important to managers, the ADA prohibits discrimination in

STEPS TO REDUCE THE RISK	
Create a company policy with procedures covering sexual harassment.	Ensure that the policy is communicated and understood by all employees.
Educate managers and employees.	All employees must understand what sexual harassment is so they can avoid it or so they can recognize it if they become targets.
Treat complaints seriously.	Investigate complaints as soon as possible, and take appropriate action while respecting your employees' rights to confidentiality.
Recognize that harassment is not just a crime of men against women.	While their numbers are still relatively small, cases involving same-sex harassment or females harassing males are on the rise.
Consider mediation if a complaint is made.	Mediation is always less expensive than a lawsuit.
Be prepared to take action against third-party harassment.	Remember that harassers can come from the ranks of vendors, clients, and other outsiders.
Consider purchasing employee-practices liability insurance (EPLI).	EPLI protects employers against claims such as wrongful termination, discrimination, and sexual harassment.

Table 9.2

Sexual Harassment on the Job

employment against qualified applicants with disabilities.

For organizations, the passage of the ADA legitimizes the purpose of completing a job analysis (to be discussed next) with its resulting job description and specifications. This is because a key element in ADA is the requirement for organizations to identify *essential* functions of jobs. For example, when current employees with disabilities apply for job transfers or promotions or when any applicant applies for a first-time position with the organization, managers need to state clearly the physi-

cal activities and characteristics the position requires of the worker. In other words, the job description must clearly state what percentage of time and with what frequency seeing and hearing; standing and walking; climbing and balancing; kneeling, crawling, reaching; and fingering, grasping, and feeling will be required to perform a particular job.

The ADA is not without controversy. Those who take issue with the provisions in this act feel that, while aiding some handicapped people in their quest to enter the workforce, the law serves mainly to help injured or impaired workers. According to figures released by the EEOC, people already in the workplace have brought 85 percent of the discrimination claims under review. In fact, two-thirds of all severely disabled adults remain unemployed. The most commonly cited disabilities of office workers are back pain and ailments such as carpal tunnel syndrome and depression, which together account for 40 percent of the ADA cases. By contrast, the blind and the deaf have filed only 6 percent of all the actions to date.[8]

Another controversial issue is that requirements of the ADA are broad and vague. Employers, for instance, must make "reasonable accommodation" for "impairments" that include everything from drug addiction to obesity. Many activists, on the other hand, vigorously defend the law, which has forced public buildings and businesses to install wheelchair ramps and Braille signs. The issue to be debated relative to the ADA is not one of should the law exist, but whether the scope of the law needs to be modified.

Family and Medical Leave Act of 1993

The Family and Medical Leave Act of 1993 requires employers with at least fifty workers to provide employees up to twelve weeks of unpaid parental/family leave for one or more of the following situations:

- birth, adoption, or foster-care placement of a child,
- caring for a spouse, child, or parent with a serious health condition, or
- serious health condition of the employee.

A **serious health condition** is defined as one requiring inpatient, hospital, hospice, or residential medical care by a continuing physician and one that prevents a person from going about his or her regular activities for three or more consecutive days.

Congress passed the law in response to increasing pressures on Americans to juggle work and family needs. Frequently, workers find it necessary to take leave or unpaid time off for family and medical problems. Under this act, while a worker is on leave, the company must continue to pay group health insurance if the employee is already signed up to participate. Moreover, the employee must be allowed to return to the same job or an equivalent position.

How do organizations go about achieving fairness in the application of equal employment opportunity? As an administrative office manager, you can do the following:

1. Eliminate irrelevant job requirements.

2. Open job and promotion opportunities to the handicapped, minorities, and women.

3. Facilitate childcare through job variations in the work schedule, such as job sharing, a compressed workweek, and telecommuting opportunities.

4. Provide equal pay for equal work.

5. Provide training in EEO requirements and sensitivity training to minority needs.

6. Modify employee benefits to meet the needs of women, minorities, and working families.

In addition to the laws already mentioned, there are other EEO laws and executive orders that are applicable to agencies of and contractors with the federal government. Table 9.3 describes the general provisions of four mandates.

JOB ANALYSIS AND DESIGN

The foundation of the staffing function is the job analysis. **Job analysis** is the process of collecting and organizing information about jobs performed in the organization. Specifically, it is a systematic way to gather and analyze information about the content of the jobs, the human requirements, and the context of jobs. The core of a job analysis is the distinction that is made among jobs in an organization relative to these seven criteria:

1. work activity and behaviors,

2. interactions with others,

3. performance standards,

4. machines and equipment used,

5. working conditions,

6. supervision given and received, and

7. knowledge, skills, and abilities needed.

Without a job analysis as a basis, it would be difficult to develop complete, accurate, and effective job descriptions and job specifications. As previously mentioned, it would also be difficult to comply with the Americans with

GENERAL PROVISIONS	
Laws	
Vocational Rehabilitation Act of 1973	▪ Prohibits discrimination against handicapped individuals. ▪ Requires development of an affirmative action plan.
Vietnam Era Veteran's Readjustment Assistance Act of 1974	▪ Prohibits discrimination against Vietnam-era veterans. ▪ Mandates affirmative action to employ and advance disabled and qualified veterans.
Executive Orders	
EO #11246 (1965)	▪ Prohibits employment discrimination based on race, color, religion, sex, or national origin. ▪ Requires development of affirmative action plans. ▪ Established Office of Federal Contract Compliance Programs.
EO #11478 (1969)	▪ Requires the federal government to ensure that all personnel actions regarding employment be free from discrimination based on race, color, religion, sex, and national origin.

Table 9.3

EEO Laws and Executive Orders Applicable to Agencies of and Contractors with the Federal Government

Disabilities Act mandate to list essential skills if you had not given thought to what those skills are.

The Job Analysis Process

Who typically performs the job analysis and what steps are usually followed? First, a job analysis can be conducted by someone inside the organization or by an outside consultant trained specifically in this process. If the job analysis is performed internally, a human resource department professional or you, as an administrative manager, may be assigned the task.

Although the steps can vary from organization to organization, a job analysis follows these customary steps:

1. Identify the job that will be studied.

2. Determine how to collect information about the job's tasks, responsibilities, and skill requirements.

3. Identify who in the organization—employees and/or managers—has this information.

4. Inform employees and managers alike as to the purpose and procedures that will be followed during this analysis to allay any fears and to elicit their cooperation.

5. Gather all pertinent data that exist about those jobs, such as job descriptions, organization charts, and industry-related resources.

6. Conduct the job analysis by gathering complete information through interviews, questionnaires, records, and observations.

7. Evaluate and verify the accuracy of the data collected with other employees and managers.

8. Prepare job descriptions and job specifications with input from employees and managers.

A **job description** defines in written form the tasks, duties, and responsibilities of a particular job; the **job specification** goes further and clarifies the knowledge, degree, skills, and abilities a worker needs in order to do the job competently.

Job Description. When preparing a typical job description, the administrative office manager should make sure certain factors are considered. For instance, a job description needs as many of the following items listed as possible: job title, department, code, salary range, and supervisor. In addition, this description should include the following information:

1. physical demands of the job and minimum physical requirements needed,

2. working conditions, including responsibilities for other people, money and equipment, and relationships with others,

3. duties and responsibilities of the job,

4. days and hours of work, and

5. machines, tools, and equipment used.

Job Specifications. After the job description is written, the specifications of the job need to be detailed. Consider such employee characteristics for the job as these:

1. educational background and knowledge, skills and techniques, and training and experience required to perform the job, as well as any special training needed, and

2. personal characteristics such as sociability, and organizational and communication skills.

An example of a completed job description and job specification for an office worker is shown in Figure 9.1.

Table 9.4 describes the nature of the job analysis and its elements. In addition, it shows how elements are related and become the basis for other actions an AOM may need to take during the employment process.

Figure 9.1

INTERNATIONAL BUSINESS SERVICES
JOB DESCRIPTION AND SPECIFICATIONS

JOB TITLE: ADMINISTRATIVE ASSISTANT

POSITION SUMMARY: Reporting to the Administrative Office Manager, this 30-hour position is primarily responsible for providing secretarial support.

Essential Job Functions:

1. Receives and screens telephone calls and visitors and assists visitors or calls by answering questions or providing information regarding company procedures.
2. Keys, formats, and proofreads material such as forms, newsletters, advertisements, and corrects grammatical, punctuation, and spelling errors.
3. Organizes, establishes, and maintains recordkeeping systems for records, sets up files and records, and follows up on missing information.
4. Records and tracks account expenditures, creates worksheets on computer or in a manual system, prepares periodic reports, and submits to supervisors.
5. Assembles and distributes or mails general information requested by employees, visitors, and customers.
6. Initiates responses to customer inquiries and requests for information by composing correspondence of a nontechnical nature, such as explanation of established procedure.
7. Performs other duties as assigned.

Knowledge, Skills, and Abilities:

1. Knowledge of general office practices and procedures.
2. Knowledge of written communication formats, business English, and composition.
3. Skill in use of personal computers with word processing, spreadsheet, and database software.
4. Skill in both oral and written communication.
5. Skill in operating various office equipment, such as ten-key adding machine, calculator, copy machine, facsimile machine, postage scale, and telephone system.
6. Ability to communicate with employees and other business contacts in a courteous and professional manner.
7. Ability to work on your own with minimal supervision.
8. Ability to lift up to fifteen pounds on a frequent basis.

HOW THE JOB ANALYSIS, JOB DESCRIPTION, AND JOB SPECIFICATION CAN BE USED BY THE ADMINISTRATIVE OFFICE MANAGER	
Job Analysis describes	and is the basis for
▪ what the employee does	▪ determining job requirements
▪ how and why the employee does it	▪ compliance with ADA relative to essential skills required for the job
Job Description presents	and is the basis for
▪ a summary statement of the job	▪ employee orientation
▪ a list of duties and responsibilities	▪ employee instruction
	▪ supervision and control
	▪ disciplinary action
	▪ grievance handling
Job Specification lists	and is the basis for
▪ the personal qualifications required in terms of skills, education, experience	▪ recruitment
	▪ selection
	▪ development
▪ the working conditions affecting health, safety, and comfort	▪ job evaluation and wage determination
	▪ health and safety programs

Table 9.4

Nature of the Job Analysis

Alternative Work Styles

Advances in technology affect our culture. Changes in how information is produced and exchanged will allow for more flexible working styles and schedules.[9] *The Futurist* magazine recently offered insights that help individuals build their personal bridges to the new millennium. Relative to alternative work styles, a few of the predictions are as follows:

• Information technologies will allow increasing numbers of people to work at home.

• Telecommuting and advances in videoconferencing will largely replace face-to-face business settings by 2020. More than half of all workers in advanced information era societies will work out of their home or from decentralized offices.

• Computer use will continue to accelerate. Today, over 100 million individuals use the Internet with regularity.[10]

Many employers are finding that, in order to get and keep good workers, they have to adopt alternative employment patterns. Success with alternative work patterns requires certain qualities that are desirable but not always found in all office workers. For example, at-home workers must be self-starters who can work without supervision, and job sharers should combine flexibility with good communication skills. New policies covering flextime workdays, compressed workweeks, job sharing, independent contracting, part-time employment, and telecommuting are emerging. The law has had to struggle to keep up with all these changes, and questions include who is entitled to benefits, what constitutes a workplace, and how the employer-employee relationship is defined. Notwithstanding, flextime issues have made an appearance in various employee lawsuits.[11]

Flexible work arrangements send the message that there is no one right way to get work done. To be consistent with definitions, consider the following explanations:

- Flextime—core hours with flexible start/stop times
- Part-time—less than full time
- Job share—two people share one job
- Phases retirement—transition into retirement by working less than full time
- Flexplace or telecommuting—working from another location or from home
- Compressed work schedule—working a full schedule in fewer days.[12]

We will now discuss some alternative work styles.

Flextime Workday. Flextime in its most simple form is where workers are required to report for work on each working day and work

Telecommuting and other flexible work arrangements require workers to be computer literate. © *Comstock, Inc.*

a given number of hours. However, the times at which they arrive and leave are flexible as long as they are present during certain core times. For example, employees might be permitted to begin their day anytime after 6:30 A.M. and work as late as 6:30 P.M., as long as they put in eight hours and are present during the core times of 9:00 A.M. until noon and 2:00 P.M. until 4:30 P.M.

Compressed Workweek. The **compressed workweek** condenses the hours worked each week into fewer days. The most common compressed workweek is the 4–40 system, in which employees work four ten-hour days each week rather than the traditional five eight-hour days. To better serve customers with enough staff coverage, some organizations lengthen their workday by staggering hours among work groups. For example, certain employees begin

A well-equipped telecommuter uses up-to-date technology to communicate with a distant business office. © *CORBIS*

and end their workday two hours earlier than other groups.

Job Sharing. Job sharing allows two people to share the duties—and prorate the salaries and benefits—of one full-time position. Teaming up for job sharing is an innovative approach that is gaining popularity, especially among working parents. To ensure success, job sharing requires that day-to-day tasks be clearly spelled out in writing for each member of the job-share arrangement and commensurate responsibilities defined and agreed upon.

Telecommuting. As home computers, fax machines, and handy new phone technology make telecommuting more practical, the ranks of at-home workers are growing by 15 percent a year. About 7 percent of U.S. white-collar

employees now say they telecommute at least part of the time. A study from the Society for Human Resource Management found that a person who works at home just two days a week saves his or her employer between $6,000 and $12,000 a year in office space requirements, equipment costs, turnover, and increased productivity.[13]

A growing number of American workers are telecommuting and doing their work at home. At the home office, telecommuters are connected to office database and information systems through the screens of their personal computers. The problems of physical commuting, pollution, and the changing family and workforce have brought greater pressure from employees and employers alike to substitute phone lines for traffic lanes.

Office and clerical workers are beginning to dominate the workforce, and many of their tasks can be done at home. Further, employers are beginning to act on the belief that the employee's knowledge is the most valuable asset for a company—and probably for most businesses. This appears to be one of the factors that is driving companies to manage from a distance.

Research indicates that companies save money by reducing costs and more work gets done when employees work at home. As a result, more companies are turning to telecommuting to solve some very tough problems. Some employers are driven by the need to shrink real estate budgets. Others want another option available to comply with new laws such as the Americans with Disabilities Act and the Family and Medical Leave Act. Still other employers are using telecommuting as a way to meet worker demands for a better balance between work and family. The advantages of telecommuting to the employee and employer as well as the benefits to society are presented in Table 9.5.

Modern telecommuting introduces the computer, modem, fax machine, telecommunications, and phone line as substitutes for being in the office. Most telecommuters work at home or at a nearby satellite office two or three days a

week. The worker reports to the manager just as any other worker would, but as you can imagine, this calls for innovative approaches to management.

Technology makes working at home possible and can give the smallest home office the illusion of a fully supported main office. A well-equipped telecommuter has up-to-date communication technology. Equipment requirements vary with the job and could include any of the following: a personal or laptop portable

To the Employee	Provides flexibility for disabled employees and working parents.
	Schedules work projects within 24-hour period, rather than 8-hour workday.
	Takes advantage of self-motivation and self-directed behavior toward task completion.
	Reduces costs associated with office dress and gasoline required for commuting to work.
To the Employer	Stretches the usage of existing office space.
	Increases productivity because it appears telecommuters do more and better work with better on-time performance.
	Hires someone it especially wants, but who will not, or cannot, relocate.
To Society	Reduces transportation and energy requirements.
	Encourages greater community stability, since employees don't have to move every time they change jobs.
	Deepens the emotional relationships in the home and the neighborhood.

Table 9.5

Advantages of Telecommuting

computer, phone, modem, voice mail, electronic mail, fax machine, and printer. Equipment that makes it possible to teleconference is a real plus.

Telecommuters and their managers are unanimous in what telecommuting requires from both sides: trust. To manage telecommuters effectively, managers have to change their thinking from keeping tabs on people from 9 to 5 to the quality and quantity of output produced. To make telecommuting work, jobs must be able to be measured by some kind of results, filled by people who are self-starters, and managed by managers who can adapt and support this arrangement.

In the final analysis, the essence of telecommuting is a manager's ability to feel comfortable with a person away from the office. It is worth repeating that managers of telecommuters must change their focus from observing activity to managing for results.

Not everyone agrees that telecommuting and working at home really works. They argue that the office gives discipline, structure, and social interaction to the job. A further concern is that, in time, telecommuting may not be so voluntary. Opponents to telecommuting feel that it is only a matter of time until companies discover that they can cut their real estate costs or more easily comply with Clean Air Act mandates to reduce the number of employees commuting by car if they clear out a few floors.

To ensure its success, a telecommuting arrangement should begin with a formal agreement covering the work expectancies of the supervisor, employee, and organization. Above all, there should be no surprises for anyone. Table 9.6 describes eleven essential elements in a formal telecommuting agreement.

In summary, telecommuting makes good business sense to organizations. In addition to the advantages already mentioned, it allows many companies to create a "shared workspace," whereby one desk can serve six or eight people. Companies are hopeful that office efficiencies, such as telecommuting, will account for about half their real estate savings.

It is not just cost savings that companies might realize; it is also a realization that for some workers, the office is sometimes a less-than-desirable place to work. It is not just the wear and tear of getting there. It is the noise, the interruptions, and the endless meetings. As a growth industry, telecommuting has such a strong appeal that many people are giving up fast-track careers for the chance to work at home.

Temporary Employees

Many U.S. employers say they like having the option of a just-in-time workforce. The fact that Manpower Inc., the Milwaukee-based staffing firm, is now the largest employer in the United States attests to the popularity of the demands by businesses for temporary employees. In 1997, the U.S. Bureau of Labor Statistics (BLS) estimated 12.5 million workers were employed

Management Tip

When you state the requirements for administrative-assistant-type jobs, be very clear and thorough. These requirements set the screening criteria in action, and it is difficult to avoid problems later should this information be mistaken or inaccurate.

I. TRUST

II. A SECURE MANAGER

III. A FORMAL AGREEMENT

1. Makes sure performance meets the organization's mission statement and all parties agree with the statement of performance.

2. Looks at equipment needs and costs ahead of time.

3. Establishes a start time and tries to project the reasons for why, when, and how the telecommuting arrangement might end.

4. Establishes times and frequency of face-to-face meetings at the office.

5. Makes training available to the telecommuter, especially on unfamiliar telecommunications equipment.

6. Explains clearly the impact and/or changes this new arrangement may have on compensation and benefits.

7. Details the relationship with the supervisor, particularly how often employee and supervisor must communicate.

8. Spells out performance standards.

9. Works out exactly how the employee will be involved in departmental meetings.

10. States how often performance will be reviewed.

11. Establishes terms of eligibility for bonuses and salary increases.

Table 9.6

Essentials for Successful Telecommuting

in "alternative work arrangements" out of a workforce of 126.7 million people. The BLS broke the total down further:

- 8.5 million are independent contractors,
- 2 million are "on-call" workers,
- 1.3 million are employed by temporary-help agencies and
- 800,000 are employed by contract firms.

Noteworthy also is that the number of workers employed by temporary and leasing agencies (professional employer organizations) has doubled in just the last 10 years alone.[14] All this newfangled contingent work is changing the very nature of work contracts. It is becoming less of a full-time worker world and more of a *work-as-needed* world.

The idea of hiring temporary employees to fill permanent positions on an "audition" basis isn't new. From an employer's point of view, the "employee audition" can be simple. It doesn't include the time wasted on all the searching, interviewing, testing, negotiating, and hoping that the next candidate will be the one hired. What employers are finding is that in almost any field or specialty, the skills needed can be found on the rosters of temporary-help firms.[15]

Years of corporate downsizing and the high-tech labor shortages have forced companies to rely heavily on temporary workers. However, with the move toward so-called **permatemps**, or long-term temporary employees, many employees feel the permatemp system creates a stratified workforce composed of permanent and temporary employees. This situation makes it hard for employees to work effectively as a team. Temps and permatemps are different from contractors in that they are employed by a temporary employment agency. Contractors typically either work for themselves or are permanent employees of a consulting firm.[16]

In summary, though temporary employees offer tremendous benefits in today's fast-moving, redefining organization, there are increasing challenges ahead—many of which are only surfacing for today's administrative office manager.

Message *for* AOMs

Human resource managers often use the expression "the right fit" or "firmfit" when referring to having selected the *right* person for the *right* job in the *right* firm at the *right* time. This chapter details for the AOM pertinent facts, options, and processes involved in getting that "right fit." As a manager on the job, refer to the tables for critical steps to be followed in staffing practices.

To a large extent, Chapter 9 is analogous to planning any project, trip, or event. If it's done right from the beginning, you can expect fewer problems as you progress, and the entire process will not take as long and will follow the dictates of the law. Administering staffing practices in today's workplace is critical to the success of any organization because employees are not only an organization's most valued asset but also its most expensive one.

1 In the U.S. workforce, diversity of cultural, ethnic, racial, and generational backgrounds will continue to challenge the AOM.

2 Among the most important legislative acts that influence the manner in which people are managed are the Equal Pay Act of 1963, the Civil Rights Act of 1967 (and its numerous subsequent amendments), the Americans with Disabilities Act of 1990, and the Family and Medical Leave Act of 1993.

3 Depending on the organization, the job analysis process, including approximately eight steps, could be performed either by the administrative office manager or a human resources department employee.

4 A job description defines in written form the tasks, duties, and responsibilities of a particular job; the job specification goes further and clarifies the knowledge, skills, and abilities a worker needs in order to do the job competently.

5 Some of the advantages of alternative work styles for the worker include flexibility and the fact that there is no one right way to get work done. The flextime workday, compressed workweek, telecommuting, and job sharing allow workers more latitude in accommodating family needs.

6 Advantages of telecommuting to the employee include flexibility in scheduling and dealing with family issues and reduced costs relative to clothing and gasoline required for getting to the office. For the employer, the advantages are less cost for office space, hiring the right person who does not need to relocate, and increased productivity from telecommuters.

QUESTIONS FOR CRITICAL THINKING

1. Discuss the effects of three demographic trends that influence today's management styles.

2. In your opinion, why are there major amendments to the Civil Rights Act of 1964?

3. What are some problems you might face as an AOM in maintaining a work environment free of sexual harassment?

4. In your opinion, what are some problems you might face as an AOM in maintaining a work environment free of disability discrimination?

5. Given the description of the Family and Medical Leave Act of 1993, do you feel it is too broadly defined to be enforced successfully by an AOM? Discuss.

6. Why is it beneficial to the organization and to the employee to perform a job analysis?

7. Describe a typical office worker who might benefit from each of the four alternative work styles discussed in the chapter.

Case Study 9-1: Sexual Harassment

Keith had just been recognized by his advertising agency for preparing an exemplary ad campaign presentation book for the agency's top client by using desktop publishing software. Keith is studying to be a graphics artist in night school, and he had prepared a "model" document that could be used with all future clients. Kristy, an advertising executive, asked Keith to join her at lunch to celebrate and to discuss his "future in advertising."

During the course of the meal, the conversation took an unexpected turn. Kristy began commenting on how attractive and sexy she thought Keith was and expressed a desire to spend more time with him. Keith refused her advances and felt embarrassed. However, Kristy continued to make uncomfortable statements and to remind him how the agency could advance an "attractive" employee like him.

The working relationship between Keith and Kristy deteriorated after this luncheon. Unwelcome suggestions now became common, and Kristy seemed to wind up around his work area. When they were alone, she playfully winked at him and touched his arm or shoulder. Although Keith was certain he was being subjected to sexual harassment, he was hesitant to pursue it any further with his supervisor, the agency's administrative office manager. Keith believes that the AOM actually saw Kristy "coming on to him" when she recently walked up on them at the water cooler.

Discussion Questions

1. Does this scenario constitute grounds for sexual harassment? If so, discuss what action you think Keith should take.

2. If you were the AOM and saw the scene at the water cooler, what would you do?

3. Would the situation be any different if the advances had been made by a man to a woman? Explain.

Case Study 9-2: Moving from Temporary to Full Time

Friday afternoon, Marjorie Rivo, office supervisor of Lee's Software, called a local temporary help service and requested a payroll clerk for several days' work during the end-of-the-year rush. Monday morning, Alan Stein reported for work. After two days, Rivo found that Stein was a highly competent worker, got along well with his department head and co-workers, and took on responsibility as if he had been with the firm for years and expected to be there for years to come.

Toward the end of Stein's first week, a permanent vacancy occurred in the accounting department, and Rivo approached him with a full-time job offer. She was pleased to find that Stein liked the company and would like to become a full-time employee.

Discussion Questions

1. Was Rivo unethical in approaching Stein with an offer of full-time employment?

2. What steps should Rivo now take to obtain Stein's services on a full-time basis?

3. What are the ethics and business practices involved in hiring a temporary worker on a permanent basis?

Case Study 9.3:
Internet Research Activity

Assume you are doing a report on *alternative work styles*. Use the Internet to research information found specifically in the publications *Vital Speeches* and *The Futurist*. Key your responses.

1. Which keywords did you use?

2. Write down three of the URL addresses that you accessed during your search.

3. As a result of your search, list three items of current information you might use in your report.

Endnotes

[1] Samuel Greengard, "How Technology Will Change the Workplace." *Workforce,* January 1997, p. 79.

[2] Dale D. Buss, "Coping with Faster Change," *Nation's Business,* March 1995, pp. 27–29.

[3] Mark Hansen, "Love's Labor Laws: Novel Ways to Deal with Office Romances after the Thrill Is Gone," *ABA Journal,* June 1998, p. 79.

[4] Michael Barrier, "Sexual Harassment," *Nation's Business,* December 1998, p. 14.

[5] Ibid.

[6] Ellen Yaroshefsky, " Sex @ Work: More Thank Sex," *MS.,* May/June 1998, pp. 58–59.

[7] Jennifer Blalock, "Informal Harassment Policies Key to Prevention," *Workforce,* October 1998, p. S10.

[8] Leslie Kaufman-Rosen and Karen Springen, "Who Are the Disabled?" *Newsweek,* November 7, 1994, p. 80.

[9] Arno Penzias, "Technology and the Rest of Culture," *Social Research,* Fall 1997, p. 1020.

[10] Graham T.T. Molitor, "Trends and Forecasts for the New Millennium," *The Futurist,* August-September 1998, pp. 58–59.

[11] Lisa Stansky, "Changing Shifts," *ABA Journal,* June 1997, p. 55.

[12] Karol L. Rose, "The Business Case for FLEX," *HR Focus,* August 1998, p. S2.

[13] Anne Fisher, "How Do I Persuade My Boss to Let Me Work at Home?" *Fortune,* November 9, 1998, p. 264.

[14] Jennifer Laabs, "Global Temps Fill the Workforce Void," *Workforce,* October 1998, pp. 61–63.

[15] Stewart C. Libes, "The Audition: A New Trend in Hiring," *USA Today (Magazine)*, July 1997, p. 54.

[16] Barb Cole-Gomolski, "Reliance on Temps Creates New Problems," *Computerworld,* August 31, 1998, p. 1.

On-the-Job Employee Practices

objectives

After completing this chapter, you will be able to:

1. List several sources that are successful for internal and external recruitment of employees.

2. Describe the content of a new employee orientation session as conducted by an administrative office manager (AOM).

3. Discuss the systems approach to training.

4. Determine the feasibility of and under what circumstances an office worker is best trained on the job or outside the organization.

5. Distinguish among the three categories of discipline problems.

6. Describe the importance of the performance appraisal process to the employer, AOM, and employee.

> One cool judgment is worth a thousand hasty councils. The thing to do is to supply light and not heat.
>
> —*Woodrow Wilson*

In this chapter, we begin our study of other practices in managing human resources as they relate to the AOM's role in employee recruitment, selection, orientation, training, counseling, performance appraisals, terminations, and exit interviews. More and more, employees are looking to their companies to hire the right people, train them correctly, and develop their potential. Some suggestions on how to select, train, and develop employees include

- Screen and select for the skills that are needed: both hard skills (such as problem solving, math, and reading) and soft skills (such as attitudes, motivation, and communication skills).
- Use behavior-based interview questions.
- Provide training that enhances the skills of employees.
- Unify organizations around shared values.[1]

Peter Pesce

Managing Director, Human Resources Worldwide Arthur Andersen & Co., SC Chicago, Illinois

Peter Pesce, a native Chicagoan, graduated from DePaul University in 1970. Shortly thereafter, he joined the account and audit staff of Arthur Andersen & Co., Chicago office. A few years later, he transferred to the human resources and administration area and in 1976 was promoted to manager. In 1989, he was appointed to his current position of managing director, human resources worldwide.

Pete is also a member or consultant of several organizations, including the American Council of International Personnel, Society for Human Resources Management, and Conference Board.

Dialog *from the* Workplace

QUESTION:

What are the major problems you have encountered in determining the salaries for exempt and nonexempt personnel? How have you solved these problems?

RESPONSE:

Some of the problems in salary determination center around the following characteristics of a sound pay program:

- Internal equality
- External competitiveness
- Legality
- Ease of understanding by both employees and managers
- Affordability to the employer
- Efficiency in administration
- Appropriateness of the program for the employer

The points noted here, while not necessarily mutually exclusive, do conflict in some areas. An objective of pay programs is to find the correct balance in order to provide a pay plan that is fair and equitable to the employees while being manageable and cost effective for the employer. We attempt to balance these needs by establishing sound market-based pay plans for each group.

For exempt and nonexempt administrative personnel, we use a job evaluation program that aligns positions in one of several salary bands based on a point factor evaluation system. A number of compensable factors are identified for each job to arrive at relative values. The results are reviewed for internal equality and are compared to benchmark positions in the marketplace to establish external competitiveness. Salary bands are used as part of a career-development plan, as well as one of the features in the administration of our merit pay program.

The pay plans are supported by market surveys for exempt and nonexempt administrative personnel in each of our locations and professional personnel on a national basis. The results of these surveys are used to help ensure the proper application of pay policies after consideration of the compensation objectives appropriate in each market. Guidance is provided from central sources; however, as noted, each business unit develops application compensation philosophies and applies them locally in accordance with individual market conditions.

In summary, we manage the sometimes conflicting objectives of a compensation program by developing plans appropriate for each employee group, obtaining market survey data for each of these groups, and encouraging the application of local initiatives as both appropriate and necessary.

EMPLOYEE RECRUITMENT

Employee recruitment is the process of generating a pool of qualified applicants for organizational job vacancies. This process should take into account the current and projected needs for employees in various job categories. Prior to starting any recruiting efforts, however, an administrative manager needs to take some preliminary steps. To begin, the AOM must recommend to the human resources department the number of people needed, any special skills and experience required of the candidates, and possible recruitment sources for the best job candidates.

It is advisable to consider all recruitment sources when vacancies occur in organizations. Generally, these sources fall into two categories: internal and external.

Internal Sources

When recruiting internally, vacancies are advertised only within the organization, usually on a job-posting bulletin board. Interested applicants generally come from current employees, former employees, and previous applicants who might regularly check the bulletin board postings. When job vacancies arise, many companies use internal sources for upgrading, transferring, and promoting to new positions within the organization. Additionally, companies find internal recruiting advantageous because it

1. costs less to fill vacancies internally,

2. provides a worker whose strengths and weaknesses are already known,

3. ensures continuity of employment,

4. promotes loyalty to the organization,

5. builds morale, and

6. motivates employees to achieve better performance.

External Sources

There are several sources for recruitment outside the organization. Some external recruiting sources include computerized on-line job announcements, private and public employment agencies, temporary employment services, college placement offices, and job fairs, as well as media want ads in newspapers and magazines and on television, radio, and billboards.

Why is recruiting externally a good step for companies to consider? Some reasons are that (1) qualified employees within the organization may be unwilling to apply for a position or they may lack the skills needed, (2) the different perspectives and varied experiences of new hires can rejuvenate an organization, and (3) organizations sometimes develop complacency among current employees, which stymies growth. Refer to Figure 10.1, which shows the relationship among these various recruiting sources for office workers.

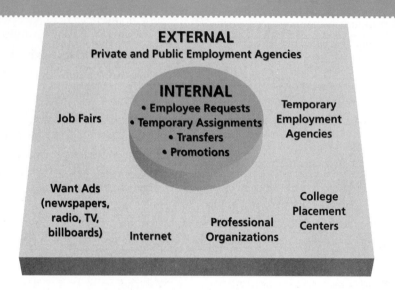

For companies, the hiring process can be both time-consuming and expensive. On-line advertising has become the least expensive method of attracting employees for employers, who can perform a nationwide search for the appropriate job candidates without placing ads in different newspapers (where word count can limit job descriptions).

New information technology has created options that were unthinkable a few years ago, which has revolutionized the way job seekers and employers connect. The Internet and World Wide Web are where many job seekers are turning for information and resources. Job searches can now be conducted 24 hours a day, seven days a week. A job seeker can e-mail a resumé and expect it to reach its destination within seconds.

The main drawback of electronic resumés and computers conducting searches for potential job candidates based on keyword searches is not having the appropriate terminology or buzzwords. In other words, if the resumé is not worded correctly, it is invisible to the company seeking job candidates through its Internet site. Computers also do not evaluate intangible but important human factors like motivation, interpersonal skills, creativity, a positive attitude, or sense of humor.[2]

EMPLOYEE SELECTION

Employee selection is the process of choosing individuals who have relevant qualifications to fill jobs in an organization. Although each organization adapts the process to its own needs, the seven steps described on the next few pages are normally followed in a typical selection process.

1. *Forward position requisition.* To begin the process, the administrative office manager completes a position approval form. The **position approval form** identifies the position title and related classification information, essential functions of the position, and the duties, experience, education, and training needed to perform the duties. For an

example of a position approval form, see Figure 10.2.

2. *Complete application form.* Each applicant completes an **employment application form,** which will serve as the basis for initial screening of minimum qualifications and become the basis for any subsequent

interview. Many applicants submit resumés, but employers still require completion of an application. Why? Legally, the same information must be collected on all applicants, and the application form is used for that purpose. Figure 10.3 shows an example of a two-page employment application form. Note that specific questions related to

Figure 10.2

Example of a position approval form.

INTERNATIONAL BUSINESS SERVICES
REQUEST FOR POSITION APPROVAL

☐ NEW POSITION ☐ EXISTING POSITION ☐ FULL-TIME ☐ PART-TIME/TEMPORARY
☐ EXEMPT ☐ NONEXEMPT ☐ BUDGETED ☐ NOT BUDGETED

Proposed Position Title _____ Department _____ Location _____

Proposed Position Reports To _____ (Title) Position Implementation Date _____

Position Classification _____ Salary Range _____ Funding Source: Account Number _____

Describe Funding Source: _____

Primary Purpose of the Position: _____

ESSENTIAL FUNCTIONS OF THE POSITION: _____

Minimum Amount and Kind, if any, of Education REQUIRED to Perform These Duties.

Minimum Amount of Experience (Years and Kind) REQUIRED to Perform These Duties.

Licenses, Certification, or Registration REQUIRED, if any.

Does This Position Supervise Anyone? If So, List Name and Title.

Is Anyone Currently Performing These or Similar Duties? If So, Explain.

JUSTIFICATION OF NEED FOR THE POSITION (Why the position is needed).

BUDGET IMPLEMENTATION
Acct. Name/# _____

EXPLANATION OF ANY EXCEPTIONS TO BUDGET ALLOCATIONS: _____

Request Approval: _____ _____
Initiator's Signature—Date   Department Head Signature—Date

Financial Department Approval: _____
Signature—Date

Human Resources Department Approval: President Approval:

_____ _____
Signature—Date   Signature—Date

DISTRIBUTION: White—Human Resources   Yellow—Payroll   Pink—Department

Figure 10.3

Example of an employment application form.

INTERNATIONAL BUSINESS SERVICES
4050 West Company Way
Phoenix, AZ 85008

APPLICATION FOR EMPLOYMENT

It is necessary to answer each question as completely as possible even if you attached a resume.

A separate application is required for each position for which you apply (copies acceptable)

POSITION APPLYING FOR _____

JOB NUMBER _____ DEPARTMENT _____

PERSONAL INFORMATION

Social Security Number _____ Application Date _____

Applicant Name _____
              (Last)   (First)   (Middle)

Address _____
       (Current Address)   (City)   (State)   (Zip Code)

Residence Phone Number _____ Message Phone Number _____

NOTICE TO APPLICANT
Please read carefully

International Business Services reaffirms its commitment to the policy of equal opportunity in employment regardless of race, color, religion, creed, age, gender, national origin, physical or mental disability, or veteran status in accordance with applicable federal and state statutes and regulations.

All information given by me in this application is true. I understand that false information (misrepresentation or omission of information) will disqualify me for employment or cause my subsequent dismissal. I authorize investigation of all statements contained herein. I also authorize the employers and/or references listed (exceptions noted under Employment History) to release any and all information concerning my previous employment and any pertinent information they may have and release all parties from any liability for any damages that may result from furnishing such information.

Signature of Applicant _____ Date _____

EDUCATIONAL HISTORY

Circle last grade completed in elementary or high school   Name and Location (City/State) of Last High School
  1 2 3 4 5 6 7 8 9 10 11 12 ☐ GED

SCHOOL NAME/LOCATION	Dates Attended From	Dates Attended To	Credit Hours Completed	Type of Degree Earned	Curriculum Major	Curriculum Minor
College or University:						
College or University:						
Other Training (Business, Vocational, or Technical School)						

Have you taken any additional courses or attended any seminars which have a bearing on the job for which you are applying?

OTHER IMPORTANT INFORMATION

Specify office machines that you can operate and years of experience (if applicable to position for which you are applying).	Shorthand WPM	Typing WPM
Specify word processing or computer equipment you can operate and years of experience (if applicable to position for which you are applying).	W/Processing WPM	Data Entry WPM

Specify computer software you can use (if applicable to position for which you are applying).

Specify other equipment you can operate and years of experience (if applicable to position for which you are applying).

Have you ever been convicted of anything other than minor traffic violations? ☐ NO ☐ YES
Have you ever been warned about, disciplined, or discharged for sexual harassment, ☐ NO ☐ YES
fighting, assault, or related offenses?
Have you ever been warned about, disciplined, or discharged for violating safety rules? ☐ NO ☐ YES

If you answered yes to any of the above, please explain on a separate sheet of paper.
Note: A conviction will not necessarily bar you from employment. Each conviction will be judged on its own merits with respect to time, circumstance, and seriousness.

Figure 10.3

Example of an
employment
application
form.
(Continued)

RECORD OF EMPLOYMENT

Fill in completely, beginning with current or last position held.
THIS SECTION MUST BE COMPLETED EVEN IF A RESUME IS ATTACHED.

| Name of current or last employer & address (include city and state) | ☐ Full-Time ☐ Part-Time |
| | Hours worked per week _____ |

| Type of Business/Name of Supervisor | Starting Date | Leaving Date |

| Job Title | Phone Number | Starting Pay | Ending Pay | Reason for Leaving |

Description of Work and Responsibilities

| Name of next previous employer & address (include city and state) | ☐ Full-Time ☐ Part-Time |
| | Hours worked per week _____ |

| Type of Business/Name of Supervisor | Starting Date | Leaving Date |

| Job Title | Phone Number | Starting Pay | Ending Pay | Reason for Leaving |

Description of Work and Responsibilities

MAY WE CONTACT ALL EMPLOYERS/SUPERVISORS LISTED?   ☐ YES   ☐ NO

Indicate exceptions: _____
_____
_____
_____

REFERENCES

Please provide the names of three additional references.

1. _____
   Name   Address/Telephone No.   Position

2. _____
   Name   Address/Telephone No.   Position

3. _____
   Name   Address/Telephone No.   Position

ADDITIONAL INFORMATION

Please give any additional information which may more fully describe your qualifications, skills, experience, education, background, and interests.

_____
_____
_____
_____
_____
_____
_____
_____
_____
_____
_____
_____
_____
_____
_____
_____
_____
_____
_____

If more space is needed, please attach additional sheets

Employers can conduct nationwide searches posting on-line job announcements. © *EyeWire*

marital status, age, number of dependents, information on spouse, height, and weight do not appear on the application because they are illegal questions to ask. The Equal Employment Opportunity Commission requires that data requested on application forms be job related.

3. ***Complete preliminary screening.*** The preliminary screening checks the application form to ensure that minimum requirements as specified on the position approval form have been met by each candidate. Normally, a human resources specialist performs this step. The purpose of the screening process is to eliminate any applicants early in the process who do not meet the minimum requirements as stated in the position approval form.

4. ***Administer employment tests.*** Employers are relying more on personality and aptitude

tests to ensure that new employees have the necessary skills and personality for the job. However, managers must be careful in using these tests because of possible litigation from Title VII of the Civil Rights Act of 1967, which forbids discrimination due to race, color, religion, sex, or national origin. The Civil Rights Act of 1991 also explicitly made illegal the use of test scores for discrimination purposes.[3] If the applicant meets minimum qualifications for the job, a variety of tests may be administered to assess the applicant's job-related aptitudes and skills. Here we list three of the more common testing instruments used to screen office workers:

a) *Aptitude test.* This is a paper-and-pencil test that measures general ability to learn

The setting for an interview should be inviting and should put the applicant at ease. © *PhotoDisc, Inc.*

or acquire a skill. Example: Sales or marketing aptitude test.

b) *Ability test.* This is also a paper-and-pencil test that assesses the skills the candidate has learned. Example: English, filing, or math ability.

c) *Work sample test.* This performance-based test requires an applicant to perform a simulated job task that the position requires the applicant to be able to do. Example: Using a computer to produce a form letter, a financial statement, or a simple brochure.

5. ***Conduct job interview.*** A selection interview is designed to assess job-related knowledge, skills, and abilities and to clarify information from other sources. Table 10.1 lists ten

reminders administrative office managers should follow when conducting the employment interview. As an AOM, you may choose to select other colleagues to serve with you as part of an interview team, or you may choose to conduct the interview yourself. Whichever approach you take, you will need to prepare your interview questions ahead of time. Moreover, to be fair and legal according to Equal Employment Opportunity Commission rulings, the same set of structured

1. Establish the objectives and scope of each interview.

2. Establish and maintain rapport with each candidate.

3. Be an active listener.

4. Pay attention to body language and nonverbal cues given by the candidate in his or her responses to questions.

5. Provide information about the job and company as accurately and honestly as possible when asked.

6. Use questions effectively and consistently with all candidates.

7. Separate facts from inferences as candidates respond to questions.

8. Control the course of the interview to ensure all objectives are met.

9. Keep careful notes.

10. End the interview effectively by asking the candidate if he/she has any questions and letting the candidate know when he/she will be contacted with the decision.

Table 10.1

Hints for the Employment Interviewer

interview questions must be used during each job candidate's interview. Structured questions are fair to all candidates, and the responses are more easily compared.

Three types of interview questions commonly used are structured, situational, and behavioral. We present a brief description and examples of interview questions that might be used for each of the three types:

a) *Structured interview questions.* These standardized questions are typically asked of each applicant. For example:

- How does your experience qualify you for this job?

- Please take a few minutes and tell us about yourself. Conclude your response with a statement summarizing your preparation for this position.

b) *Situational interview questions.* These questions are related to the job requirements and knowledge, training, and educa-tion needed for the position being advertised. For example:

- Suppose you worked for two bosses, and both came to you with a rush project that had to be completed in the next two hours. How would you proceed if you only had time to do one of the projects well?
- If you were required to take minutes at evening meetings (not to exceed three nights per month), would this job requirement give you any concern?

c) *Behavioral interview questions.* These questions usually elicit a response detailing how the applicant did a certain part of a job in the past or performed a particular task. Sample questions include:

- Describe a work situation where you took a project from start to finish and were complimented on the results.
- Have you ever had an ethical dilemma on the job? If so, describe the nature of the dilemma and how you dealt with it.

6. **Check references and verify prior employment.** Prior to extending a job offer to the top candidate, background checks on prior employment and references are conducted. The reference checks are usually very good sources of information and can help confirm or question any impressions you have formed about the candidate.

7. **Give physical exams.** Depending on the nature of the job, a medical examination

and/or drug test may be appropriate parts of the selection process for the top candidate prior to final acceptance or rejection of the job offer by either party.

Finally, it is a good idea to take some time to review all information about the top candidate prior to extending the job offer. By the end of this seven-step process, you have collected substantial data on each of the candidates from many sources. Remember to recheck the information on the application forms, transcripts of courses taken or degrees and certificates received, interviews, tests, reference checks, and medical exam. Selecting the right employee is critical to your success as the manager, to the organization, and to the person you hire.

EMPLOYEE ORIENTATION

Once employees have been selected and report for work, a series of orientation activities becomes critical to the eventual success of the employee and the organization. **Orientation** is the activity that specifically prepares employees for working in a particular organization and working environment. An orientation meeting can be formal, with several new hires in a conference room, or it can be informal, with the supervisor on a one-on-one basis. Regardless of the method, however, an orientation meeting is a necessary first step for every new employee.

In general, a good orientation should provide information about the physical workplace, policies, procedures, and expected performance, as well as routine information such as payroll arrangements, breaks, benefits, and working hours. Some orientations also prepare the new

hire with a review of policy and procedures manuals, an introduction to fellow employees, a review of emergency procedures relative to safety or weather conditions, and a preview of upcoming training programs.

In many organizations, the responsibility for new employee orientation is shared between the human resources department and the administrative office manager. When this occurs, it is important to clarify what each area person will cover. Table 10.2 provides a checklist to follow when conducting an orientation. This checklist is divided according to the items covered by the AOM and those normally covered by the human resources department.

The success of an employee's first week on the job is as important to the company as it is to the employee. © *PhotoDisc, Inc.*

HUMAN RESOURCES DEPARTMENT	ADMINISTRATIVE OFFICE MANAGER
First Day of Work:	**First Day of Work:**
1. Ask employee to fill out the following forms (if applicable in your state):	1. Introduce to co-workers.
■ I-9 employment eligibility verification	2. Tour department and show around work area (coat closet, restroom, copy and fax machines, etc.).
■ W-4 federal income tax withholding form	3. Discuss specific working hours relative to lunch, breaks, starting and stopping the workday, and overtime.
■ A-4 state income tax withholding form	4. Clarify parking and dress issues.
■ Employee information sheet	**Second Day of Work:**
■ Loyalty oath	5. Introduce to "buddy" who will then mentor new employee.
■ Retirement enrollment form	6. Discuss training programs.
■ Group insurance enrollment forms	7. Clarify questions regarding job duties.
2. Discuss the following:	8. Discuss emergency contingency plans (medical, power failure, fire, personal safety, etc.).
■ Time cards	**Second Week of Work:**
■ Pay dates	9. Discuss any questions the new employee has relative to the content in the employee handbook.
■ Direct deposit availability	
■ Attendance policies	
3. Hand out employee handbook and sign form showing receipt.	
4. Give tour of facilities and discuss emergency evacuation procedures.	

Table 10.2

Employee Orientation Checklist

Role of the Human Resources Department

In general, the human resources department explains the conditions of employment, security requirements, and how pay and benefits will be dispensed. A human resources specialist also may provide a tour of the facilities and give each new hire an orientation packet containing necessary forms to complete and other information new employees need to know. To get some idea of what is included in an orientation packet, an example of a cover transmittal memorandum describing the contents of the orientation packet is shown in Figure 10.4.

Figure 10.4

INTERNATIONAL BUSINESS SERVICES

MEMORANDUM

To: New Employee

From: Human Resources Department

Welcome to International Business Services and best of luck in your new position! The enclosed information and forms have been gathered together to provide you with a practical introduction to the employment environment at IBS, and also to ensure a timely collection of necessary paperwork to initiate your official status as an employee. If you have any questions, please feel free to contact us any time during business hours at (602) 555-8314.

The following items must be completed and on file with the Human Resources office within 3 days after your starting date:

_____   I-9 Employment Eligibility Verification
                    (You must present your social security card and a photo ID in person at the Human Resources
                    office to properly complete this form.)

_____   W-4 Federal Income Tax Withholding form

_____   A-4 Arizona State Income Tax Withholding form

_____   IBS Employee Information Sheet

_____   Selective Service Certification Statement

_____   Loyalty Oath

_____   Group Insurance Enrollment Forms

These following items are provided for your information and convenience:

_____   Direct Department Authorization

_____   Most Recent *Human Resources Update*

_____   Benefits Summary Sheet

_____   List of Paydays and Holidays

_____   Essential Policy Information
                    (Affirmative Action, Drug-Free Workplace, Sexual Harassment)

_____   Pamphlets on Vision Care, Prescription Options, and "Managed Care"

_____   Medical and Dental Insurance Certificate Booklets and ID Cards

An orientation package contains not only a welcome to the organization but also important items that must be legally completed and returned to the human resources department within a certain period of time.

Role of the Administrative Office Manager

Normally, when the human resources department is finished with its portion of the employee orientation, the AOM discusses with the new employee the job duties, hours of work, and how overtime, sick leave, absences, and tardiness will be handled. Usually, it is at this time that the new employee is introduced to current employees and is shown workplace facilities including his or her desk area, break room, and restroom.

Management Tip

Establish a good working relationship with the human resources department. This department can make you, as a manager, look good through its support and periodic assistance.

"Buddy" System

A popular practice in some organizations is to use a buddy system to supplement the new employee orientation process. The **buddy system** matches a new employee with an experienced employee who maintains close contact with the new employee and lends support by answering routine questions. Psychologically, this system is believed to have significant advantages for new employees by relieving anxiety and stimulating the feeling of belonging. In general, new employees seem more comfortable asking a peer questions rather than an immediate supervisor.

Regardless of whether you use a follow-up "buddy" system approach or whether you schedule a second orientation session with new employees, a systematic orientation program should have some follow-up to clarify questions the new employee may have after spending some time on the job. Orientation should be seen as a continuous process because organizations are constantly undergoing changes and employees need to be informed of new processes that will affect their attitude and success on the job.

Retention—Keeping Workers Happy

In 1998, Aon Consulting concluded a three-year study of employee loyalty to create an annual index of workforce commitment. This study examined the organizational factors and conditions that affect the level of worker commitment. The results indicate that employee commitment has fallen across all industries, job functions, and levels; that job-related stress has increased; that the number of employees having difficulty balancing their professional and personal lives is growing; and that more employees are willing to change jobs if offered higher pay.

The study also identified five factors that strongly influence the decision of employees to stay with an organization. These are a fearless corporate culture, job satisfaction, opportunities for personal growth, organizational direction, and recognition of employees' need for work/life balance by the company.[4]

Given these outcomes, companies need to work harder to find ways to retain good employees. Although most managers agree that the following employee retention techniques alone will not keep employees on board, they also say that low-cost ideas such as these are an essential piece of a company's retention puzzle.

1. Flexible hours

2. Telecommuting

3. Praise

4. Employees training employees

5. Clear career paths

6. Work with cutting-edge technology

7. Emphasize value of benefits package

8. Supportive culture

9. Small gifts and cash prizes[5]

Exit interviews indicate that many employees leave a company because of their need for greater flexibility. To succeed, flexible work arrangements necessitate a redefinition of the manager-employee relationship. Managers must learn to coach, mentor, and empower their employees to work harder and smarter and to control their own time.[6]

EMPLOYEE TRAINING

In today's office, many businesses agree that the cost of keeping people—even if you have to spend money to train them and to make them feel better about what they are doing—is minor compared to the cost of replacing them.[7] One way to keep good employees is through continual training to upgrade their skills. Sometimes this is referred to as lifelong learning. **Lifelong learning** is a concerted effort to invest continuously in the collective talents of people. Motorola is one example of a company that has invested heavily in training its employees. Motorola already gives all employees at least forty hours of training a year, and it hopes to quadruple that figure by the year 2000. Top management at Motorola views the dollars it spends today as a return on investment in the form of a significant competitive weapon.

Training is broadly defined as specific preparation to carry out the tasks and functions of a particular job. Given that work skills are becoming more sophisticated because of emerging technologies and that today's information will be replaced within three to five years, training efforts must be offered and encouraged. Otherwise, workers' skills will become obsolete in the jobs they hold. In most organizations, administrative office managers are directly

responsible for training and upgrading the skills of their employees.

The Systems Approach to Training

Before meaningful training can occur, the organization needs to assess what the training needs are and then develop, design, and make arrangements for delivering educational programs for employees at *all* levels. Specifically, the systems approach to training emphasizes formulating instructional objectives, developing learning activities to meet those objectives, establishing performance criteria to be met, and evaluating the results of training. Table 10.3 shows the necessary activities involved in each phase of planning and delivering training according to this formalized systems approach.

Methods of Training

The companies that train best deliver instruction when and where the employee needs it—sometimes in a classroom, sometimes by satellite TV, or sometimes on a personal computer. The most effective training is concise and interactive, interspersed with group projects,

Emphasis of Systems Approach to Training:

- To formulate instructional objectives.
- To develop learning experiences that achieve those objectives.
- To establish performance criteria to be met.
- To obtain evaluative information.

Phase I: ASSESSMENT	Phase II: TRAINING AND DEVELOPMENT	Phase III: EVALUATION
Steps:	**Steps:**	**Steps:**
1. Analyze organizational needs (who needs what, problem areas, etc.).	5. Develop the training environment to effectively achieve the objectives.	8. Use the instructional objectives as a basis for evaluation.
2. Analyze the tasks of the job (difficulty of learning, how performed, etc.).	6. Determine what methods and interactive media will be most effective in delivering the instruction.	9. Give trainees a pretest and a posttest and compare the results.
3. Analyze what characteristics, skills, knowledge, and attitudes are needed in the person doing the specific job.	7. Deliver the training or development program.	10. Ask for feedback from trainees at the end of the program and again in three to six months to determine if training objectives were met.
4. Develop instructional objectives.		

Table 10.3

Systems Approach to Training

role-playing, and hands-on experiments. In general, AOMs can train employees on the job or by using outside training sources.

On-the-Job Training (OJT). This training is best described as "learning by doing." Organizations provide a variety of in-house

training programs, such as one-on-one supervisor training, job rotation, computer-assisted instruction, special projects or assignments, and mentoring.

The main advantages of OJT are that (1) production is carried on while the employee is being trained and (2) OJT results in low out-of-pocket costs. On the other hand, the major disadvantages of OJT are (1) the poor learning environment, which can be one of interruptions and other working distractions, and (2) the awareness by the employee that work still has to get done—either after training or after hours—or a backlog will occur.

In 1998, a $1.6 million study funded in part by the Labor Department and conducted by the Center for Workforce Development concluded, after taking one of the most comprehensive looks into when and where workers learn, that 70 percent of workplace learning is informal. In other words, along with teamwork, the study found that most informal learning occurs during meetings; interactions with customers, mentors and supervisors; on-the-job training and site visits; cross-training; shift changes; peer-to-peer communication; and just by doing one's job.[8]

Many companies have brought their training activities in-house as a result of downsizing and cost reductions. In doing so, these companies utilize fellow employee experts to train other employees on a wide range of issues. Peer experts are often more effective because of their personal knowledge of job processes. In addition, companies find that their presence and availability to others help build stronger working relationships. To support effective in-house training, many companies offer **train-the-trainer workshops.** These workshops teach peer experts interactive and instructional skills.

Outside Training. Outside training occurs when learners are sent to some outside source, such as a school, college, professional workshop or seminar, or equipment manufacturer, to learn the job. Learning a new computer application or software package off-site is an example of outside training.

Because organizations realize how important training is to their eventual success, many companies provide total or partial educational benefits, such as payments for tuition, fees, and books, to defray costs associated with employees' attending training off-site. Moreover, if the training is directly applicable to work, many companies release employees during the workday to attend classes.

Coaching Techniques

To realize maximum performance, most workers expect coaching on how to do their jobs well. As an effective manager, you will want to recognize an employee's need for effective performance feedback and systematically follow through in providing it. When effective job skill training is conducted, some of the time-tested coaching steps used by a manager or trainer are as follows:

1. Explain the purpose and importance of what you are trying to teach.

2. Explain the process to be used.

3. Show how the process is done.

4. Observe while the person practices the process.

5. Provide immediate and specific feedback.

6. Express confidence in the person's ability to be successful.

7. Agree on follow-up actions.

COUNSELING AND DISCIPLINING EMPLOYEES

Counseling and, if necessary, disciplining employees are actions administrative office managers will perform. However, good leadership and motivational skills on the AOM's part tend to have a minimizing effect on the need to counsel and discipline in the workplace.

Counseling Employees

There are a number of areas in which you as an AOM may need to perform employee counseling. Primary counseling occasions include consultations about job performance, career planning, safety, layoffs, termination, and retirement. Other areas of a more personal nature are counseling about physical, mental, or emotional illness and substance abuse problems.

Critical to on-the-job counseling is centering the dialogue *only* on job performance. Do not get personal. Give specific counseling comments, rather than general ones. For example, instead of saying, "You have to do more work," say instead, "Your work output must increase 20 percent to reach minimum standards." Or, instead of saying, "You have got to do a better job of communicating with me," say instead, "You must notify me in advance when you cannot keep an appointment or are going to be late."

If you are counseling a troubled employee who needs more than you can offer, point out to him or her the availability of internal or external counseling services and further explain that only the employee can decide whether to seek assistance. Emphasize the confidentiality of your conversation. But do not leave until you get a commitment from the employee to meet

specific work criteria that will be monitored in line with a plan for improvement based on work performance.

To make counseling more effective, act natural and listen attentively. The benefits of counseling will be worth it. As a result of effective counseling, you should see these changes in the worker:

1. a reduction in anxiety, fear, and distrust;

2. more cooperation; and

3. a sense of direction that stimulates personal growth.

Handling Discipline Problems

Every organization's objective should be to reduce the need for discipline, but if discipline becomes necessary, it should be administered immediately after the infraction in a fair, consistent, impersonal manner and only after advanced warning has been clearly given to the employee.

Categories of Discipline Problems. Organizations generally classify discipline problems according to their severity. In other words, determine whether the behavior is a minor infraction, a major violation, or an intolerable offense.

Minor Infractions. These instances do little harm but may be serious when they happen frequently. Some examples include absenteeism and tardiness.

Major Violations. These actions are disciplinary problems that substantially interfere with orderly operation in a business. For example, major violations include violating safety rules, stealing, failure to carry out an order, and lying.

Intolerable Offenses. These misconducts are disciplinary problems of such drastic, dangerous, or illegal nature that they endanger employment relationships. Possession of deadly weapons and use of drugs on the job are examples of intolerable offenses.

Progressive Discipline. Discipline is dispensed in a progressive way. Figure 10.5 shows that before an employee can be discharged, a sequence of steps must take place. These could be one or more warnings, a written reprimand, or a suspension. Care must be taken to follow due process in any disciplinary action. Table 10.4 provides some factors to consider to determine whether due process was followed.

To reduce employee complaints as well as the need for disciplinary actions, successful managers introduce these factors into the workplace:

1. Make sure employees are aware of the performance and behavioral requirements for their jobs.

2. Place employees in jobs for which they are qualified or can qualify.

3. Provide effective orientation, training, and coaching.

4. Evaluate employees often during training.

5. Provide a quality work environment.

6. Motivate employees through the use of incentives and effective leadership.

7. Provide for corrective rather than punitive disciplinary action.

PERFORMANCE APPRAISALS

Computer-based programs are helping to bring consistency and legal peace of mind to the evaluation process. Much of what a manager needs to know to conduct employee evaluations is now packaged as computer software. A particular software package, for instance, takes reviewers through a logical review process, rating employees on a scale of 1 to 5 for eleven job elements, such as job knowledge, initiative, and

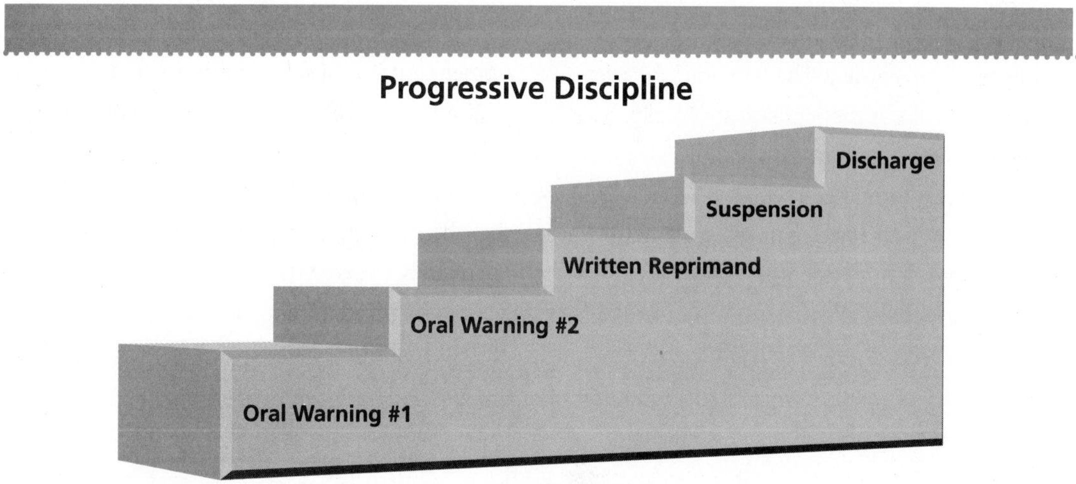

Progressive Discipline

Figure 10.5

Before an employee can be discharged, an AOM first must take several steps to correct any behavior.

Steps (bottom to top): Oral Warning #1, Oral Warning #2, Written Reprimand, Suspension, Discharge

WHEN HANDLING DISCIPLINARY PROBLEMS, CONSIDER THESE FACTORS AND ASK YOURSELF IF DUE PROCESS WAS FOLLOWED:

1. Did the employee have prior warning that his or her conduct would result in disciplinary action, including possible discharge?

2. Was the misconduct related to the safe, efficient, and orderly operation of the organization?

3. Was an investigation held?

4. Was the investigation fair and objective?

5. Did the investigation obtain circumstantial evidence that the employee was guilty?

6. Was the disciplinary action nondiscriminatory?

7. Was the disciplinary action reasonably related to the seriousness of the offense and the employee's record with the organization?

Table 10.4

Was Due Process Followed?

Note: YES answers to these questions indicate that due process was followed.

oral and written communication. Each element can be weighted according to its importance to the employee's job function.[9]

Performance appraisals have the potential to advance or derail careers. As a supervisor, you will notice things about your employees' attitudes, their performances, and their work habits nearly every day. That is your job. Eventually, you will use these observations as a basis for employee performance appraisals.

Annual performance reviews of employees are an effective and necessary management tool. Reviews should document employee shortcomings as legal protection in case of a dismissal. Fairness and consistency are key requirements. A good review should reinforce previous feedback.[10]

Objectives of an Appraisal

The objectives of a performance appraisal are to (1) recognize subordinates for outstanding performance, (2) help subordinates improve performance, (3) change behavior, and (4) provide data for making personnel decisions involving compensation, promotion, training and development, and discipline or termination.

Certain conditions must be present for an employee to feel he or she has been given a fair performance appraisal. These conditions are that the manager (1) has had an opportunity to adequately observe the employee, (2) understands the job requirements, and (3) has a fair and appropriate point of view. Most importantly, a performance appraisal should never surprise the employee. That is to say, managers should never save either criticism or compliments for the once-a-year review. The employee should be constantly and consistently counseled or praised throughout the year.

Conducting an Appraisal

Imagine you are going to be giving a performance appraisal tomorrow morning. In general, what steps might you take today to prepare adequately?

1. You might first want to prepare for the appraisal by completing the performance appraisal form and by anticipating the tone of the conference (friendly, stressful, or otherwise) as well as what you want to have accomplished for the good of the company and employee when the appraisal is over. An example of a performance appraisal form is shown in Figure 10.6.

2. Then, you could make performance and development of the employee your major concern. In other words, think ahead and study past employee performance. Be prepared with specific examples that will clarify the reasons for your ratings should the employee question your evaluative judgments.

3. Finally, anticipate and decide on the specific steps that you will suggest the employee take to improve performance on the job. Set a date to review performance within the month.

Delivering constructive criticism during a performance evaluation is a delicate business and is generally difficult for most managers to do. You must, however, present any problems you have observed strongly enough to elicit a desired change in behavior. Yet, you do not want to spark resentment or undermine your employee's confidence by being too harsh. It is a delicate balance.

How do you meet this challenge? Most managers find it helpful to start by giving positive feedback about the employee's work before bringing up the negatives. You will find that by planning ahead and organizing the sequence and timing of your comments, delivering the appraisal will be clearer and better received.

If your criticism is accepted as justified, reiterate your confidence in the employee by scheduling a meeting within a few weeks or a month to review his or her progress. If, on the other hand, the employee denies that there is a problem or gets angry, try to get beyond the reflexive response. Provide specific examples of the performance problem and ask about any obstacles that may have stood in the employee's way of being successful on the job.

> **Management Tip**
>
> *When correcting an employee, don't use the following words: "always," "never," "ever," "perpetually."*

> **Ethics/Choices**
>
> During an appraisal, an employee apprehensively reveals to you that her inattentiveness at work has been due to a recent event in which she was assaulted. She tells you in confidence and asks specifically that you not write it down in her personnel file. Would you honor her request?

Figure 10.6
....
Administrative
support
performance
appraisal form.

INTERNATIONAL BUSINESS SERVICES
PERFORMANCE APPRAISAL
Administrative Support

NAME: POSITION:

PLEASE EVALUATE THE EMPLOYEE'S PERFORMANCE AGAINST THE FOLLOWING PERFOR-MANCE FACTORS. Circle the numerical rating: 5. Outstanding 4. Good 3. Satisfactory 2. Fair 1. Unsatisfactory. Circle NO (not observed) if unable to evaluate the item. Each factor rating must be explained in the justification comment section.

PERFORMANCE CRITERIA AREA	5	4	3	2	1	NO	COMMENTS
KNOWLEDGE OF THE WORK Understanding of the various phases, knowledge of the technical fundamentals of the position. Understands work output relationships and interdependencies within IBS.	5	4	3	2	1	NO	
QUALITY OF WORK Thoroughness, neatness, accuracy, completeness.	5	4	3	2	1	NO	
QUANTITY OF WORK Amount of work accomplished, ability to function effectively within time or work schedule, prompt completion of work.	5	4	3	2	1	NO	
INITIATIVE Ability to act on his/her own. Displays understanding of task or project and moves forward on own.	5	4	3	2	1	NO	
CARRY OUT INSTRUCTIONS Willingness and ability to take instructions and effectively follow through. Makes positive effort to suggest task/process improvement.	5	4	3	2	1	NO	
ATTITUDE Accepts suggestions, responsibility, improves work techniques. Displays cooperative, positive behavior patterns. Exerts positive influences on morale of co-workers. Exhibits effective interpersonal skills that contribute to department team goals and to IBS's mission.	5	4	3	2	1	NO	
ATTENDANCE/PUNCTUALITY Consistency in avoiding absenteeism and tardiness. Provides adequate notice of absence.	5	4	3	2	1	NO	
OVERALL EVALUATION	5	4	3	2	1	NO	

MAJOR STRENGTHS AND/OR WEAK AREAS NEEDING IMPROVEMENT—RECOMMENDATIONS
(ATTACH ADDITIONAL NARRATIVE SUMMARY SHEET, IF REQUIRED)

Signature

SUPERVISOR DATE

Signature

EMPLOYEE DATE

Note: By signing this form, the employee acknowledges only that this evaluation was discussed and a copy has been received. It does not necessarily signify the employee concurs with the evaluation.

Outcomes of Appraisals

A positive performance evaluation allows an employee to capitalize on the moment by asking for additional responsibilities that could lead to a promotion or a substantial raise. If, on the other hand, an employee had an "off" year, it is smart to mitigate the damage by demonstrating how a program of improvement will begin.

If a performance appraisal backfires, the manager should reflect and consider the reasons that may have made it unsuccessful. Could it be that—

1. The manager dislikes face-to-face confrontations?

2. The manager lacks interviewing skills?

3. Too many forms must be completed?

4. Rater bias exists?

5. There is no top-management support of the rating or consequences?

6. The judgmental and helping roles of the manager conflict?

In summary, there are a number of personnel actions that can be taken as a result of a performance appraisal. On the positive side, the employee can be rewarded with a pay increase, a promotion, additional training, or a career move. On the negative side, the employee can receive a layoff or discharge.

Message *for* AOMs

Issues that affect workers on the job are as varied as they are many. An AOM is not expected to perform in an exemplary fashion 100 percent of the time. No one is superhuman. However, the AOM is expected to understand organizational processes and know where to quickly find answers to common workplace questions and issues of concern to workers.

As you attempt to be the best AOM you can be, read as many articles as you can from newspapers, magazines, and journals to stay updated on better approaches to improve your "people" skills. In addition, network with fellow managers in and out of your company by attending trade shows, conferences, and seminars. Chances are your colleagues will want to share ideas and talk through problems with you as much as you do with them. One final suggestion: find a person you admire and regard highly. Study the techniques and attributes that draw you to that person. If it feels right during your association with each other, propose a mentoring relationship to help you become a better manager and stay focused on ways to improve on the job.

1 Internal sources for recruitment include employee requests, temporary assignments, transfers, and promotions; external sources for recruitment include the Internet, private and public employment agencies, job fairs, temporary employment agencies, want ads, professional organizations, and college placement center.

2 An AOM typically introduces the new workers to co-workers, gives a tour of the department, clarifies parking and dress issues, and discusses specific issues relative to working hours, training, job duties, and emergency contingency plans.

3 The systems approach to training emphasizes formulating instructional objectives, developing learning activities to meet those objectives, establishing performance criteria to be met, and evaluating the results of training.

4 Organizations provide in-house training programs because of cost reductions and downsizing; outside training occurs when learners are sent to some outside agency when it is most cost effective to do so.

5 Minor infractions do little harm but may be serious when they happen frequently; major violations are those that substantially interfere with orderly operation in the business; and intolerable offenses include misconducts of such a drastic, dangerous, or illegal nature that they endanger employee relationships.

6 Performance appraisals give the employee a snapshot of his or her strengths and weaknesses and supply the AOM and employer with organized data on which to promote or expand on responsibilities for the employee.

QUESTIONS FOR CRITICAL THINKING

1. In your judgment, should new employees attend an orientation or be assigned a "buddy"?

2. Of the two approaches—OJT and outside training—which do you feel best meets the needs most of the time as a means of training office workers?

3. If you were asked to coach a worker on converting from WordPerfect software to Microsoft Word, how would you proceed?

4. Interpret this statement made by an AOM: "The worst part of this job is having to do performance appraisals. I hate them." Do you think managers feel this way? If so, why?

5. What is meant by progressive discipline? Give an example.

Case Study 10-1: Criticizing an Employee's Work

Walter Blue, the administrative office manager at Kids' Toys Inc., is not looking forward to the day. He has a performance appraisal with Sarah at 10 A.M. and has had it on his mind since arriving at work. He feels prepared—he's got his notes ready, the performance appraisal form is already typed, and he has a sense about how he wants to proceed in the interview.

Sarah comes into his office at 10 A.M. sharp, and the conversation goes like this:

Mr. Blue:

Sarah, I'm generally very pleased with your work—especially the way you're handling the arrangements for the sales conference next week. But there is one thing you need to work on. Maybe I haven't made it clear that you're also responsible for supervising all the promotional material, but lately I've found quite a few mistakes and some sloppy work.

Sarah:

Mr. Blue, you know I have been working ridiculous hours to get everything done for the sales conference on time. I can't believe you're complaining about this, given all that I've done for you.

Mr. Blue:

Let me show you what I mean, Sarah. Here are copies of the last three promotional pieces that you OK'd. I've marked the problem areas.

Sarah:

I think you're being very unfair. On the whole, my work is excellent—you're just nit-picking. Mr. Blue, you've been overly critical of me since the first day I started working for you.

Discussion Questions

1. In your opinion, how is this performance appraisal going? How do you think it is going to end?

2. Could Mr. Blue have said or done anything differently?

3. Should Sarah be issued a warning about her attitude? If so, how should Mr. Blue proceed?

Case Study 10-2: Falsifying an Employment Application

In a desperate moment three years ago, you misrepresented your educational background when you completed the application form at your current place of employment. Ever since, that little lie has been like a time bomb ticking away in your personnel file. Tomorrow, you face an employee appraisal and a review of your qualifications for promotion. Today, you are in a quandary.

Discussion Questions

What should you do? Ask for your personnel file and delete the "padded" degree? Live with the lie and keep your mouth shut? Or what?

Case Study 10-3: Internet Research Activity

Assume you are doing a report on *counseling and disciplining employees.* Use the Internet to research information needed to answer the following questions. Key your responses.

1. Which Web search engine did you use?

2. Write down three of the URL addresses that you accessed during your search.

3. As a result of your search, list three items of current information you might use in your report.

Endnotes

[1] Jennifer Laabs, "Pick the Right People," *Workforce,* November 1998.

[2] "Electronic Resumes and Online Job Searches, " *Keying In,* January 1998, pp. 2–3.

[3] Michael Delikat and Rene Kathawala, "Personality and Aptitude Tests: Insurance Against Hiring Mistakes or Invitation to Litigation?" *Managing Office Technology,* March 1998, p. 16.

[4] David L. Stum, "Five Ingredients for an Employee Retention Formula," *HR Focus,* September 1998, p. S10.

[5] Steve Alexander, "Keeping Workers Happy: Ten Low-Cost Strategies Can Keep Employees from Job Hunting," *InfoWorld,* December 14, 1998, p. 91.

[6] Karol L. Rose, "The Business Case for FLEX," *HR Focus,* August 1998, p. S2.

[7] Michael Barrier, "Develop Workers—And Your Business," *Nation's Business,* December 1998, p. 25.

[8] Maggie Jackson, "It's Not Chitchat, It's Training," *San Francisco Chronicle,* January 7, 1998, p. D2.

[9] George V. Hulme, "Using Software for Worker Reviews," *Nation's Business,* September 1998, p. 35.

[10] Michael Barrier, "Reviewing the Annual Review," *Nation's Business,* September 1998, p. 32.

Work Ethics and Business Etiquette Issues

chapter 11

66

Politeness goes far, yet costs nothing.

—*Samuel Smiles*

99

objectives

After completing this chapter, you will be able to:

1. **List six ethical behavioral and moral standards leaders should model.**

2. **Cite two examples of ethical codes found in society today.**

3. **Describe changes in the workplace that have affected business behavior and etiquette.**

4. **List examples of up-to-date business manners.**

5. **Discuss the appropriate standards of business attire for men and women.**

6. **Describe etiquette tips that should be followed when conducting international business.**

Although work ethics and business etiquette reflect social and cultural factors, they are also highly personal and are shaped by an individual worker's own values and experiences. Oganizations pay attention to ethics and etiquette because the public expects a business to exhibit high levels of ethical performance and social responsibility.

CORPORATE VALUES AND BUSINESS ETHICS

Sound values, purposes, and practices are the basis for an organization's long-range achievement and continued growth. Value-driven management is a concept whose time has come. **Value-driven companies** find ways to link their daily operations to social and environmental concerns and integrate employee and community well-being into their decision making. Moreover, a value-driven company is one that consistently produces a high-quality product or service, treats employees with respect, and has

227

Josephine Soviero Sessa

*Director, International
School of Naples
Naples, Italy*

The International School of Naples, Naples, Italy, has an enrollment of 185 students and a staff of 28. Ms. Josephine Sessa, director, received her B.A. degree from Hunter College, CUNY. Her M.Ed. is from Framingham State College. In her position as director, she has many responsibilities and duties. Working with the personnel and overseeing the smooth functioning of the total system are important aspects of her job.

QUESTION: *What are your responsibilities in the total system in which you are involved? What types of problems do you experience in working with such a diverse group of people in your organization? How do you solve these problems?*

Dialog *from the* Workplace

RESPONSE:

My responsibilities in the functioning of the total system of the International School of Naples include:

- Coordinating the activities of the school administration and, through them, the activities of all employees.
- Maintaining high academic standards through the periodic review of curricula and methodology.
- Recruiting and selection of personnel.
- Ensuring evaluation of all personnel.
- Overseeing and coordinating the short- and long-range planning of the school, including responsibility for the building program and participation in fundraising activities.
- Stimulating, supervising, and evaluating the school's entire

program in relation to school objectives, board policies, community desires, and the best current educational practices.

- Representing the school and seeing to the proper and effective projection of the school's image.

- Maintaining systematic and open communication with the Board of Governors and all constituencies.
- Preparing the annual budget and long-term financial plan for the school.
- Recommending appropriate policy additions and changes to facilitate the fair and smooth functioning of the school.

Breakdowns in communication are inevitable in an international environment. The fact that my staff is made up of people from diverse backgrounds, customs, and cultures has contributed to this breakdown.

Initially, I find that teachers are reluctant to accept suggestions of change in their classroom management and teaching styles because they feel such suggestions imply inadequacy in their performance. Often, standard methods practiced "back home" are not always valid in this type of organization. Many times, teachers do not take into consideration that they are working at an international school in a foreign country and that their colleagues come from as diverse a background as their students.

I have tried to overcome these obstacles in a variety of ways. Peer coaching has proved to be a very effective method of bringing new ideas into the classroom without the negative effects of supervisory observations. In addition to this, I have allowed teachers to take on the responsibility of trying new methods and techniques to increase overall achievement. This empowerment of responsibility makes them feel more confident in their jobs. They share in the decision-making process at the school. They share their ideas with colleagues at weekly staff meetings and play a vital role in the overall functioning of the school on an organizational level. All of this heightens their interest and cooperation level and helps eliminate possible communication problems.

demonstrated ways in which it incorporates its values into the fabric and culture of its business.

When an organization's values statement is crafted, it should show the best side of a company's personality. The statement usually offers ambitious commitments to quality, service, and personnel growth. Unfortunately, for many organizations, the values statement is window dressing—an image thing. When companies put statements on paper and then ignore them, it is an easy and almost certain way to lose credibility with the workforce and revered customers.

Ethics and Ethical Issues Defined

Ethics is the systematic thinking about the moral consequences of decisions. In business, examples of ethical issues include, but are not limited to, sexual harassment, employee privacy, nepotism, environmental issues, security of company records, usage of computer and network systems, workplace safety, product safety standards, and financial and cash management procedures.

When leaders make ethical decisions, those decisions are usually based on the following six behavioral and moral standards: honest communication, fair treatment, corporate social responsibility, fair competition, responsibility to the organization, and respect for the law. Table 11.1 offers some business-oriented examples for each of the six standards.

The ability to make ethical decisions relative to work is one of the most important tools that today's worker can possess. Some of the most important ethical characteristics that organizations actually look for to ensure new worker success are reliability and trustworthiness, willingness to work, willingness to learn, responsibility for one's actions, and the ability to work cooperatively.

Management Tip

The very definition of business ethics requires institutional thinking. This type of thinking focuses on management that reflects the needs of the community, rather than on management that focuses on profits.

1.	**Honest communication**	Evaluate subordinates candidly; don't slant proposals to senior management.
2.	**Fair treatment**	Pay equitably; don't use lower-level people as scapegoats.
3.	**Social responsibility**	Show concern for employee health and safety.
4.	**Fair competition**	Avoid bribes and kickbacks to obtain business; don't fix prices with competitors.
5.	**Responsibility to the organization**	Avoid waste and inefficiency; act for the good of the company as a whole, not out of self-interest.
6.	**Respect for the law**	Avoid taxes, don't evade them; follow the letter and spirit of laws.

Table 11.1

Six Ethical Standards for a Value-Driven Company

Many organizations publish and then display their code of ethics. Two familiar examples of ethical codes in society today are the Golden Rule and Rotary International's four-way test, as shown in Table 11.2.

The Ethical Employee

The goal of organizations is to hire employees who have the ability to make ethical work decisions. A worker with this work ethic has the ability to recognize ethical problems, exercise

The Golden Rule

Do unto others as you would have them do unto you.

Rotary International's Four-Way Test for Code of Ethics

1. Is it the truth?
2. Is it fair to all concerned?
3. Will it build goodwill and better friendships?
4. Will it be beneficial to all concerned?

Table 11.2

Examples of Ethical Codes

ethical reasoning skills, resolve ethical conflicts, and implement ethical decisions.

There is a strong consensus in Western society concerning moral values and principles that historically have provided a practical guide to determining and doing what is *right*. The Josephson Ethics Institute has translated the following list of moral values or ethical principles into operational language. They incorporate the characteristics and standards that most people associate with ethical behavior in business. Adapted more closely to an ethical office professional, they are as follows:

1. **Honesty.** Office professionals are honest and truthful. They do not mislead or deceive others by misrepresentations.

2. **Integrity.** Office professionals demonstrate the courage of their convictions by doing what they know is right even when there is pressure to do otherwise.

3. **Trustworthiness.** Office professionals are trustworthy and candid when supplying information and in correcting errors.

4. **Loyalty.** Office professionals avoid conflicts of interest, do not use or disclose confidential information, and respect the proprietary information of their employer.

5. **Fairness.** Office professionals are fair and equitable in all dealings. They do not abuse power arbitrarily or take undue advantage of another's mistakes or difficulties.

6. **Concern and respect for others.** Office professionals are concerned, respectful, compassionate, and kind. They respect the rights and interests of all those who have a stake in their decisions.

7. **Commitment to excellence.** Office professionals are willing to put more into their jobs than they can get out of them.

8. **Leadership.** Office professionals realize that the best way to instill ethical principles and ethical awareness in their company is through example.

9. **Reputation and morale.** Office professionals seek to protect and build the company's reputation and the morale of its employees by engaging in conduct that builds respect.

10. **Accountability.** Office professionals are personally accountable for the ethical quality of their decisions as well as those of their subordinates.[1]

Loyalty in the Workplace

Loyalty dilemmas usually arise when an employee is promoted or protected for the wrong reasons. Some examples of loyalty dilemmas are:

- Changing or concealing incriminating documentation;
- Lying;
- Creating a false impression or allowing a false impression to persist;
- Choosing to do nothing or remaining silent while some wrongdoing occurs;
- Choosing between favorites—say, choosing between your boss and co-worker or your boss and the company; and

• Responding by trying to protect or promote the wrong person or cause for the wrong reason.[2]

According to a 1998 survey conducted by International Survey Research, about half of all U.S. workers admit to taking unethical or illegal actions. These actions included cheating on expense accounts, accepting kickbacks, and secretly forging signatures. In addition, the survey revealed employee theft, at $120 billion a year, is costing companies more than shoplifting.[3]

Four social trends are emerging today and influencing decisions employees make about work/life. They are:

1. *Anti-institutional bias.* The federal government has been the major focus of skepticism and distrust, but the sense that established structures are out of control extends to business. A decade of downsizing has taken a heavy toll on the worker.

2. *Self-reliance.* Feeling betrayed or abandoned by the corporations they once looked to for security, guidance, and the means to the good life, Americans increasingly value and depend on their personal resources.

3. *Less willing to take risks.* The recent years of no growth, cost cutting, and downsizing have caused many workers to begin behaving in self-protective ways.

4. *Family and child-centeredness.* Americans believe the institution of the family has been in crisis long enough, and they lay some of the blame on the business environment. Generation X parents don't want their kids

to grow up as latchkey children. The ideal, once again, is to have one parent at home.[4]

What these trends point to is a new moral focus relative to work and living. Because values precede behavior, it's safe to predict that companies need to take employees' values seriously. The choices people are making point to a desire for more meaning in work and in life. People at all levels want to know what the organization stands for and whether it is something they can feel a part of. Knowing that their company stands for values they themselves hold can help employees decide to devote their loyalty and best effort.

Ethics in the Workplace

The business world is not a separate universe of economic values and goals distinct from society but an aspect of the behavior of society as a whole. To be effective, ethics cannot be a mere restraint on the unsocial or criminal behavior of managers or a pragmatic response to consumer pressure. The total ethics concept is analogous to the zero-defects concept in operations management.

Many companies develop detailed codes of conduct and policies or introduce "hotlines" for workers; yet, many of these firms actually pay only lip service to the ethics they supposedly espouse when it comes to their daily activities. The gap between what the company actually practices and what it supposedly upholds promotes cynicism, which in turn nurtures and reinforces mistrust. Cynicism and mistrust foster unethical behavior.[5]

The morals and ethics of employees can be a determining factor in the success or failure of a company. Employees with a great work ethic are usually more productive and trustworthy, so employers can mentor them instead of police them. Such environments allow more creativity. Ethical behavior contributes to the bottom line in companies by reducing the cost of business transactions, establishing trust among stakeholders, increasing the likelihood of successful teamwork, and preserving the social capital necessary for doing business.[6]

To visualize the structure of an ethical business environment, imagine a pyramid divided into four parts. Companies can create an ethical environment in their organizations by ensuring the presence of ethical awareness, reasoning, action, and leadership. An organization is said to possess:

- *Ethical awareness* if employees are able to recognize ethical problems when they occur.
- *Ethical reasoning* if employees are provided with the right tools for understanding and dealing with ethical dilemmas. These tools include a common language and method of evaluating the courses of action they can take in the face of moral dilemmas.
- *Ethical action* when structures and approaches enabling employees to freely discuss and resolve ethical issues are established.
- *Ethical leadership* when leadership is applicable to all levels of the organization and can be achieved by allowing everyone to be a moral leader.[7]

Ethics should form the foundation of an organization's mission and permeate its statement of business objectives. If the ethic is to serve the common good of all who have an interest in the business, then all the stakeholders, not just those with a financial interest, must contribute to meeting the business objectives and exercising some control.

To some, ethics is often considered a matter of personal behavior, but the need for ethical behavior of corporations is just as real. Managers should make it a point to support ethical behavior in their organizations; otherwise, they must take responsibility for misdeeds and run the risk of both corporate and personal liability. It is this threat of legal punishment that has prompted many organizations to put compliance-based ethics programs into effect.

The Pygmalion in Management Theory argues that managers' expectations of their subordinates serve as self-fulfilling prophecies. In other words, managers who expect creativity, productivity, and ethical behavior from their employees usually get it. Unfortunately, the reverse is also true, which may explain why bad followers happen to bad leaders.

Management can take five steps to establish an ethical workplace:

1. ***State corporate values in three sentences or less.*** Make sure all employees understand what these values are and how they *apply* to daily activities. Publish the values so that associates and customers also understand them. Some examples of value statements:

    a) Our customers are the only reason we are in business.

    b) Quality is #1 with us.

    c) Every college employee helps students to learn.

2. *Act according to these published values.* One interpretation of this simply states: "We are what we do, not what we say."

3. *Outline specific responsibilities for decision making to ensure accountability.* It is important that policies and lines of responsibility be clearly stated. Be willing to take action if your code of ethics is violated.

4. *Encourage open discussion.* Discussions about controversial issues, ethical questions, and anything that might fall into gray areas should occur with frequency. Keep in mind that people must feel safe before they will speak openly.

5. *Conduct ethical-awareness training for employees.* Allow workers to see how the company's ethical system applies to everyday problems and gray areas. For example, Citicorp has developed *Work Ethic,* a board and card game to teach business ethics to its employees. The game, which is divided into groups of entry-level employees, supervisors, managers, and senior managers, presents employees with ethical problems. The consequences of decisions become more serious at higher levels. The ethical problems presented by the game include issues such as insider trading, client confidentiality, and sexual harassment.[8]

By virtue of their positions, office professionals have always had to deal with ethical issues.

These issues ranged from the "little white lie," told over the telephone and face-to-face, to being asked or forced to perform illegal, immoral, and unethical tasks on the job.

BUSINESS ETIQUETTE AND BEHAVIOR—STATESIDE AND ABROAD

In light of our shrinking world, our "global village," and expanded media coverage throughout the world, good business etiquette is crucial; behaviors are more closely scrutinized today than ever in the past. Business etiquette, stated simply, is doing unto others as you would have them do unto you. A U.S. Office of Consumer Affairs' study confirmed this when it found that 91 percent of all customers will never do business again with a company that offends them. In short, good manners are cost-effective.[9]

Business etiquette is much more than knowing how to use the correct utensil or how to dress for certain occasions. Today's businesspeople must know how to be at ease with strangers or in groups; they must know how and when to congratulate someone; they must know how to make introductions; and they must know how to conduct themselves at company social functions, receptions, and meals. Table 11.3 describes new business etiquette rules of the workplace relative to general office etiquette, general courtesy, introductions, and travel.

Elements of Business Etiquette

Elements of business etiquette focus on work behavior, meeting people, telephone etiquette for meetings, dining etiquette, and correct etiquette when dealing with other cultures.

General Office Etiquette	▪ Business casual dress does not mean that it is acceptable to wear sloppy attire; it is better to dress conservatively than to dress too casually.
	▪ Offensive language, be it gender, culture, or race based, does not belong in the workplace.
	▪ Sexual innuendoes and off-color jokes should be avoided.
General Courtesy	▪ Business etiquette is genderless and generationless—everyone should be treated equally.
	▪ Men or women should never loosen their ties or remove their jackets unless the host or hostess does.
	▪ A person should never be kept waiting longer than 10 minutes.
	▪ Thank-you letters should still be sent after meals and interviews.
Introductions	▪ Men and women should always extend the right hand when being introduced.
	▪ Men and women should both stand when a guest from outside the company enters a room.
Travel	▪ Men no longer need to feel obligated to assist women with their bags.
	▪ A male or female driver should unlock all doors for passengers before getting into a car.

Source: Jim Rucker and Jean Anna Sellers, "Changes in Business Etiquette," Business Education Forum, *February 1998, pp. 43–45.*

Table 11.3

General Business Etiquette Rules

At Work. Etiquette at work includes all aspects of the work environment—completing work on time, getting to work on time, being courteous to others, being an active member of the work team, practicing good human relations, listening, following through on commitments made, and solving problems in a manner that involves good etiquette.

For Meeting People. Office courtesy should be a matter of policy. Etiquette for meeting people involves receiving guests, making their visit pleasant and worthwhile, introducing people, presenting gifts, shaking hands, and remembering names.

With Telephonic Devices. The telephone naturally de-emphasizes status, gender, and age distinctions. One way to look at the telephone is that it allows us to respond to content, not context, thereby facilitating democracy and equality. On the other hand, telephone rudeness can inadvertently occur and may have a devastating and long-term effect on an organization. Recent studies find that when companies lose clients, most of the time it is due to indifference or negative treatment on the phone.

For Dining Out. Etiquette for breakfast, lunch, or dinner meetings involves planning the meeting, arranging for seating, paying the bill, tipping, using proper table manners, and knowing how to deal with alcohol in a business meeting situation.

Table 11.4 offers a brief list of etiquette rules to keep in mind for the four business situations.

Shifting Standards

Never before has there been so much confusion about what is appropriate behavior in the workplace—and never before has it been so important

to get the rules of workplace conduct right. Already under pressure to improve productivity and to hang onto their jobs, managers and employees at every level now face the added strain of trying to adjust their attitudes, for example, to shifting standards on racial and gender issues.

The biggest change in the workplace, some say, has been the diversification of the workforce—the entry of women and racially mixed persons. Much of what passed for humor in the office in the 1980s may now be questionable or perhaps even downright dangerous. A casual compliment could be construed as inappropriate and result in a career-limiting move. Some American workers are asking whether the movement to enforce strict workplace conduct has gone too far and thrown a chill over normal human interactions, resulting in driving prejudice underground.

Employers cannot avoid getting involved in conduct issues. Companies, however, are putting the burden on employees to make judgment calls on each encounter with a co-worker. However, inappropriate comments of a racial or sexual nature that are intimidating, hurtful, or hostile are unacceptable.

Business Manners, Attire, and Image Skills

As businesses continue to reduce staff and compress layers of management, companies are catapulting administrative and technical professionals into positions of increased responsibility and exposure. Today, you must look and act the part—exude style, competence, and authority—to ensure that your ascent up the ladder does not end in a crash landing.

At Work
1. Positive attitudes are practiced.
2. "Please" and "thank you" are said frequently.
3. Smoking is not allowed.
4. Vulgar language is not used.

For Meeting People
1. Visitors will be seated in a reception area that is attractive and comfortable.
2. Appropriate magazines will be available to make waiting time more interesting.
3. Coffee, tea, or soft drinks may be offered.
4. Waiting time should be as short as possible, no longer than ten minutes.
5. Visitors should be informed of accommodations, such as restroom facilities or the water cooler.
6. The person with the highest rank is introduced first. If rank is equal, the older person is introduced first.

With Telephone Devices
1. Answer the phone by the third ring.
2. Say "Good morning" or "Good afternoon."
3. Identify your company, your department, and yourself.
4. Listen to the caller to determine the nature of the call.
5. Try to direct the caller to a person who can help him/her.
6. If you must put a caller on hold, do not keep the caller waiting longer than thirty seconds before checking back.
7. Always end the call on a pleasant note and by saying "Goodbye." Never say "Bye" or "Bye bye."

For Dining Out
1. Arrange seating for meetings in advance.
2. Establish with the waiter that you will be paying the check.
3. The guest should order first (unless guest asks host to do so), and the guest should be served first.
4. You will be served from the right, so be prepared to lean slightly to the left to allow the waiter to serve you.
5. Eating utensils are used from the outside in; that is, the salad fork will be placed on the outside of the dinner fork.
6. The napkin, when placed to the side of the plate, is placed on the left.
7. Tip the waiter approximately 15 percent, more if service is especially good, less if service is bad. Never make a scene about bad service.

Table 11.4

Business Etiquette Guidelines

Source: Adapted from Annette Vincent and Melanie Meche, "It's Time to Teach Business Etiquette," Business Education Forum, October 1993, pp. 39–41.

Business Manners. In an increasingly competitive business environment, good manners can make the difference in completing a sale and getting or keeping a customer. Keep these up-to-date hints in mind:

1. When men and women are involved in business dealings, defer to professional rank instead of gender. Women no longer expect to get out of an elevator first or be automatically introduced first.

2. When making introductions, follow business rank—which means introducing client, boss, and then colleagues, in that order. Stand for introductions when clients or executives enter the room. Do not call clients or business associates by first name, unless they request it. Never use an honorific when referring to yourself. Say, I am John, or Jane Jones, not Dr. Jones.

3. With business correspondence, use proper forms of address and salutation, and be extra careful to spell names correctly. In the near future, we can expect technology to come to the rescue with computerized business etiquette programs that flag protocol mistakes in a document and suggest polite alternatives but, until then, check your work carefully.

Business Attire and Image Skills. You must have technical skills, communication skills, and interpersonal skills; but, to succeed, you also need image skills. The importance of image and attire in the business world is very real. Your image is like the weather—people notice when it is extremely good or extremely bad. Put another way, your image is your repu-

Your image is like the weather. People notice when it is extremely good or extremely bad.   © *CORBIS*

tation and a reflection of how others perceive you, either through your conversation, appearance, or written words.

A positive public image is a way of life in which your wardrobe style, voice tone, grooming habits, etiquette, office decor, body language, and business presentations (oral and written) denote a style of performance commensurate with success.

Given the standard five seconds it takes a person to make a visual first assessment, most experts agree that your appearance sends a powerful message. For some women and men, what one wears to work is almost as important as job performance.

In recent years, corporate managers have noticed more casual styles invading the workplace. Fancy shorts outfits, sheer and lacy blouses, short body-clinging skirts, designer jeans, sandals, and tennis shoes have infiltrated corporate America. Many female executives—as well as administrative assistants and executive secretaries—feel that such attire is inappropriate, especially for the woman who hopes to advance her career. Business suits, dresses, and sensible shoes are still the best way to dress for success.

The standard of business attire, however, is changing somewhat. Many companies are relaxing their dress codes when employees are not meeting with customers. What are the new rules?

1. *Observe what everybody else is wearing.* "Casual dress" can mean different things at different companies. Blue jeans and tennis shoes may be perfectly fine at a small advertising agency but be off-limits at a bank.

2. *Respect geographic customs.* The standard for business attire can vary depending on whether you work in a large metropolitan area or in a small town, and depending on the region of the country. A good idea is to ask a trusted associate for some tips on appropriate dress.

The bottom line, however, is that people want to be taken seriously, and attire can help

or hurt in that regard. When people look at you and see the way you act, as well as the way you dress, they draw impressions concerning your ability, your credibility, and, most importantly, whether you are serious and should be taken seriously.

When you go to work, be dressed and prepared for anything, because you could be in contact with people in all stations of life. Work attire should reflect the position you hold, the organization you represent and, of course, a little about you personally. Being well groomed from head to toe is part of that preparedness. Men and women should bear in mind the dress-for-success tips given in Table 11.5.

Generation Xers and Business Etiquette

Unlike several generations ago when good manners were drilled into young minds during childhood, today's Generation Xers were raised in a much more casual, laid-back atmosphere. Nowhere is that more evident than when they enter the corporate halls. Interpersonal skills and the ability to adapt to corporate culture are critical for their success, and savvy companies take control of this situation by outlining expectations upfront and providing training.

Following are some tried-and-true tips on corporate etiquette that are important for *all* workers.

1. Show respect and deference to your colleagues. Don't sit at a meeting until being shown where to sit, or ask, "Where would you like me to sit?"

1. If you want to get ahead, look around. Emulate and imitate in dress those men and women you admire who are moving up in the company. Dress not only for the position you hold now but also for the position you aspire to hold.

2. Dress appropriately and blend in, yet maintain your personal style.

3. Dress classically. For women, that means wearing suits, dresses, sensible heels, or flats. For men, that means wearing suits, slacks, and sportcoats combined with contrasting dress shirts and ties. Stick to the basics. Purchase classic cuts as opposed to trendy styles. The classic cuts can be worn year after year.

4. Save dressy short sets, tight skirts, leggings, jogging suits, jeans, stretch pants, and other casual attire for leisure activities.

5. Stay away from clothes that wrinkle easily.

6. If you are in a conservative environment, choose suits and dresses with jackets. If unsure, go conservative. Avoid a situation in which you have to be told what not to wear at work. Good taste is the key; if an outfit is questionable, then don't wear it.

7. Invest in classic, quality accessories such as a briefcase, trench coat/overcoat, watch, pen, and daily planner. These items suffer considerable wear and tear, so they should be purchased with longevity in mind.

8. Clunky jewelry, garish makeup, and overpowering cologne or aftershave speak volumes without your ever saying a word. Moderation is the key in these areas.

Table 11.5

Tips for Dressing for Success

Source: Adapted from Anne Russell, "Fine-Tuning Your Corporate Image," Black Enterprise, *May 1992, pp. 74–76, and "What to Wear to the Office,"* Ebony, September 1993.

2. Rise with respect when greeting colleagues, managers, or clients who enter your office or workspace.

3. Develop a positive handshake, rather than a casual wave and the word "Hey!"

4. Cultivate conversation skills.

5. Pay close attention to your appearance with professional grooming and dress. Colleagues, management, and customers do not always understand trends and other forms of expression.

6. Navigate business events with customers, such as business luncheons, with ease.

7. Present a polished image on paper by sending sincere, thoughtful notes as often as possible.[10]

Politeness takes on greater importance when you are interfacing within an international business setting.   ©*PhotoDisc, Inc.*

International Politeness

People from other countries spend a great deal of time studying the American culture. A good host should be willing to spend time and effort studying his guest's culture. Attention to the details is not only a polite practice, but in today's global economy it is also the smart business practice.[11]

As Americans gain greater access to other countries and as businesspeople from abroad come here, our knowledge of etiquette needs to become more universal. We have to learn about and remain respectful of each other's particular ways of greeting people, eating, dressing, and making conversation. Even though more Americans are learning other countries' customs and languages, the image of the "ugly American" still persists. With international business competition heating up, manners

Management Tip

Take time now to read books or magazine articles on international etiquette so you are prepared when those skills are needed.

could mean the difference between deals and debts.

Expect international etiquette of the future to become more streamlined and homogenized as the pace of life increases. There is speculation that America's casual manners are being adopted around the world. But do not assume that local proprieties will fade away. Variations in etiquette will always be with us due to climate and regional differences.

The etiquette of tomorrow will include many cross-cultural do's and don'ts. Many ref-

erences are available to consult when doing business with non-Americans. Table 11.6 is adapted from an article that appeared in *The Secretary* magazine. Though not intended as a comprehensive list of social and business customs abroad, the guidelines for doing business in Europe, the Middle East, along the Pacific Rim, and in Latin cultures will whet your appetite to study customs and cultures around the globe.

Table 11.6

Good International Manners Could Mean the Difference Between Deals and Debts.

Latin Cultures	European Cultures	Middle East Cultures	Pacific Rim Cultures
■ Handshakes are common.	■ Gift-giving is expected—candy and flowers are excellent choices.	■ Friday is a day of rest; business resumes on Saturday.	■ Writing (or typing) "thank-you" notes is vital following meetings and interviews.
■ Eat their main meal at midday.	■ Use a firm handshake—both when you arrive and when you leave.	■ Never drink alcohol.	■ People in these countries use three names—the first is their family name.
■ Will stand close when talking—much closer than in the United States.	■ Toasting is very important in most countries.	■ Pointing with one finger is considered impolite; use your open hand instead.	■ Gift-giving is common. Present gifts with both hands, then bow.
■ First names are seldom used.	■ Punctuality is appreciated, except in Spain, Greece, and Italy, where it is less important.	■ Women do not cross their legs.	
■ May be more interested in you personally than as a representative of your company.			

Source: Adapted from Roger E. Axtell, Do's and Taboos of Hosting International Visitors *(New York: John Wiley & Sons, 1990).*

Message *for* AOMs

"The best of all worlds for organizations is to create a climate whereby all employees, at all levels of responsibility, consider themselves accountable for their own actions. To do this, managers have to make a special effort to regard ethics as a top priority, and companies need to create their own codes of ethics.

Many would say that ethics, manners, and profit complement each other. In the book *Letitia Baldridge's Complete Guide to Executive Manners,* the author promotes the theory that good manners are cost-effective because they not only increase the quality of life in the workplace, contribute to optimum employee morale, and embellish the company image, but they also play a major role in generating profit.[12] AOMs generally accept these ideas because a company with a well-mannered reputation attracts and keeps good employees.

1 The behavior and moral standards for ethical decisions are honest communication, fair treatment, corporate social responsibility, fair competition, responsibility to the organization, and respect for the law.

2 Two moral codes popular in society today are the Golden Rule and the Rotary International's four-way test.

3 Two changes in the workplace that have affected business behavior and etiquette are shifting standards on racial and gender issues.

4 A few examples of up-to-date business manners are: when making introductions, follow business rank; stand for introductions; and always use proper forms of address when preparing business correspondence.

5 Emulate and imitate in dress those men and women you admire who are moving up in the company. Dress not only for the position you hold now, but also for the position you aspire to hold.

6 When conducting international business, become aware of particular ways of greeting people, eating, dressing, and making conversation.

summary chapter 11

QUESTIONS FOR CRITICAL THINKING

1. Of the six ethical behavior and moral standards described in Table 11.1, which two do you feel should most influence good business decisions?

2. In your opinion, what is the most significant change in the workplace that has affected business behavior?

3. Given the ten characteristics associated with ethical behavior in business, which three do you feel best describes you? Explain.

4. Describe a businessperson you know who projects a positive public image.

5. What negative effects do America's casual manners have on international etiquette?

Case Study 11-1: Breakout Session at an Ethics Workshop

Ken Rowe, president of a large grocery chain in Helena, Montana, attended an ethics workshop recently. In one of the breakout sessions, he was a member of a four-person group that had the following activity to discuss and present to the other attendees: His group was asked to first reach consensus on their collective definitions of ethics, work ethics, and ethical behavior. They could prepare three separate definitions or only one definition encompassing the three terms.

Second, his group was asked to duplicate the form and assign a ranking order (1–7) to each ethical issue by importance. To make the activity more challenging, his group was asked to consider the same seven ethical issues as applied to three different types of organizations. In other words, would they rank the issues for each organization in the same way? As it turned out, Mr. Rowe's group found it difficult to reach consensus. Assume that you worked for Mr. Rowe and that he asked you to complete the same project and indicate your results.

Discussion Questions

1. What is your definition(s) of the three terms?

2. Indicate your rankings below for each ethical issue by importance for a community college, automobile manufacturer, and retail store.

ETHICAL ISSUES	RANKINGS		
	Community College	Automobile Manufacturer	Retail Store
Sexual harassment			
Employee privacy			
Environmental issues			
Security of company records			
Workplace safety			
Product safety standards			
Financial and cash management procedures			

Case Study 11-2: Former Model Turns Receptionist

Roxanne Frederick recently went to work for an interstate transportation company in Detroit as its receptionist. The first week or so, several of the employees went out of their way to go through the lobby to take a second look at her. She was very attractive and most soon learned she was a former model for car shows at General Motors Corporation.

Her image, however, started to create problems in the company. Though Roxanne was a nice person and didn't appear conceited, she was unique to the organization. As the AOM is finding out, work has slowed down since she was hired. For instance, truck drivers were stopping by and spending time chatting with her; other female workers were saying "catty" things behind her back and seemed to be spending more time in negative conversations. Three comments from the other women that were overheard were "She's too perfect," "She wears heavy makeup," "She dresses too nice for this place."

Discussion Questions

1. Do you think the AOM should view this problem as one that will work itself out with time?

2. If it doesn't, what steps might you take as the AOM to enable this trucking company to get work back on track?

3. In your personal opinion, is it wrong for someone to be regarded as "not fitting the image" of the organization?

Case Study 11-3: Internet Research Activity

Assume you are doing a report on *ethics in the workplace.* Use the Internet to research information needed to answer the following questions. Key your responses.

1. Which Web search engine did you use?

2. Write down three of the URL addresses that you accessed during your search.

3. As a result of your search, list three items of current information you might use in your report.

Part III: Debate the Issue

1. Retrieve the file *Part III-Debate,* which contains the table shown below, from the template disk. Using the form for each of the three issues listed in step 3, quickly key some ideas you have as initial reactions to each statement.

2. Prepare to role play either point of view in a mock in-class debate.

3. Part III debate issues follow:

   a. "The office is a terrible place to work. Companies save more money and more work gets done when employees stay at home and work."

   b. "I'm for 3 strikes and you're out. Forget this due process stuff. If someone wants to work, there will be few, if any, problems. It is those workers who mess up time and time again that need to be fired after the third incident."

c. "A person's behavior and professionalism are reflected by their appearance on the job or in school."

POINTS OF AGREEMENT		POINTS OF DISAGREEMENT	
1.		1.	
2.		2.	
3.		3.	
4.		4.	

Endnotes

[1]From materials received at an "Ethics" seminar presented by Dr. William E. Miller at Northern Arizona University in Flagstaff, January 1999.

[2]Nan Demars, "A Fine Line," *The Secretary,* May 1997, p. 11.

[3]Del Jones, "Workplace Loyalty: Not Dead Yet, But Strained," *USA Today,* February 4, 1998, p. 4B.

[4]Ed Emde, "Employee Values Are Changing Course," *Workforce,* March 1998, p. 84.

[5]Craig Dreilinger, "Get Real (and Ethics Will Follow)" *Workforce,* August 1998, p. 101.

[6]Norman E. Bowie, "Companies Are Discovering the Value of Ethics," *USA Today (Magazine),* January 1998, p. 23.

[7]Dawn-Marie Driscol; W. Michael Hoffman, "Spot the Red Flags in Your Organization," *Workforce,* June 1997, p. 136.

[8]Karin Ireland, "The Ethics Game," *Personnel Journal,* March 1991, p. 73.

[9]Jim Rucker and Jean Anna Sellers, "Changes in Business Etiquette," *Business Education Forum,* February 1998, p. 44.

[10]Amy Mills Tunnicliffe, "Helping Generation Xers Decipher Protocol." *HR Focus,* December 1997, p. 5.

[11]Melinda M. McCannon, "Don't Use Your Left Hand (and Other Taboos of International Entertaining)" *The Secretary,* August/September 1996, p. 9.

[12]Letitia Baldridge, *Letitia Baldridge's Complete Guide to Executive Manners* (New York: Rawson Associates, 1985).

Internet

groupware

mobility

part **4**

Managing the Office Environment and Systems

Computer Systems and Related Equipment

chapter 12

> How dangerous it is to reason from insufficient data.
>
> —*Sherlock Holmes*

objectives

After completing this chapter, you will be able to:

1. **List the five classifications of computers and describe the characteristics that make them different from each other.**

2. **Identify the basic hardware devices for most computer systems.**

3. **Define computer peripherals and give examples of three peripherals.**

4. **Contrast the uses of system software and application software.**

5. **List popular application software used in the business office today.**

6. **Describe how other automated office equipment such as facsimiles, shredders, electronic typewriters, and dictation machines are used in today's businesses.**

Buying technology is easy. Using it intelligently is the real challenge. Chapter 12 will describe the components of computer systems and cover the major aspects of managing those computer systems. Two recommendations companies are increasingly implementing to avoid technology management problems are creating a strong technology committee and recruiting top-notch technology managers.[1] The 1998 *Inc. Tech* issue reported survey results from companies that were asked if they had a technology plan. Sixty percent reported that they do; 52 percent of the input on the technology plan was reported to come from the chief executive officer.[2]

MANAGING INFORMATION SYSTEMS AND COMPUTERS

Managers need information to effectively manage operations, people, and resources. A computer system converts data into information that managers can use to make decisions critical to an organization's success.

John E. McKever

Executive Director, Information Technology
Coconino Community College
Flagstaff, Arizona

Mr. McKever has worked in several information technology positions over the past 17 years. Currently, he is executive director of Information Technology at a community college and is responsible for all aspects of information technology, with oversight of all computer/software systems including college LANs, WANs, Web sites and Internet connectivity. His other work experience includes serving as the director of management information systems in the behavioral health field, as an applications manager and senior systems analyst for Circle K Corporation and as a systems analyst and database administrator at Northern Arizona University.

Mr. McKever received his B.S. in business administration in June 1982 from Northern Arizona University.

Question:

Technology is in a constant state of change. What current trends in technology do office professionals need to be aware of when working in a business environment? Further, what are some skills business people should bring to their positions or acquire over time?

Dialog *from the* Workplace

Response:

Currently, trends in technology are moving the industry more to a Web-based/Web-enabled architecture, meaning that more processes/systems will be more dependent on other systems as sources of information than was the case in the past.

This means that more powerful data management/executive information systems will reside on the desktop, using remote information. So, while individuals will be able to make more timely decisions locally, it will remove them from the context of the information they are using to make the decisions.

As a general skill overall, I would emphasize flexibility or an ability to synthesize what one system/application does and equate it to another system. Learning MS Word extremely well, for example, could be a handicap in an office using Corel, but someone who understands the concepts of a word processing application should be able to transfer their skills and abilities across multiple word processing applications.

An additional skill would be a basic understanding of the desktop hardware (Mac versus Intel/IBM), the operating system (Win98, Win95, Windows NT), and network interfaces. Note that I say *basic*. Workers should not worry about the low-level stuff or the merits of one operating system over another, but it is essential that office professionals understand the electronic world they live and work in.

And finally, a basic understanding of software applications (Word/WordPerfect, Excel/Quattro/Lotus, or Access/dBase/Paradox) is critical at a conceptual level, even if workers do not use them on a daily basis.

The AOM plays a major role in an organization by not only understanding the information needs of all managers but also by having the knowledge and global perspective to get the right information to the right manager at the right time to make the best decision possible.

Information Technology

Information technology (IT) is the study, design, development, implementation, support, and management of computer-based information systems—particularly software applications and computer hardware. In other words, IT workers help ensure that computers work well for people, and most companies need their skills to keep their businesses running smoothly. The point is that, as an AOM, you will work closely with colleagues with these emerging IT job titles: database administration associate, information systems operator or analyst, network specialist, technical support representative, programmer, and analyst.[3]

Management Information Systems (MIS)

One way businesses meet information needs is to use management information systems (MIS). A **management information system** is an integrated computer system that provides information and aids in decision making in organizations.

MIS and Management Functions. An MIS helps supervisors perform the following functions:

1. *Planning.* Goal setting, scheduling, and inventory planning

2. *Organizing.* Decentralization of processes and scheduling

3. *Controlling.* Production control, inventory control, quality control, environmental control, budgetary control, and financial control

Information Management. Information is data that has been processed and is useful in decision making. It helps decision makers by increasing knowledge and reducing uncertainty. For decision making to be credible, it must possess the following six characteristics:

1. *Accessible.* Information must be relatively easy to obtain without excessive effort.

2. *Relevant.* Information must be meaningful and pertinent in and of itself.

3. *Clear.* Information must be in a format that is easily understood, specific, and unambiguous.

4. *Accurate.* Information must be precise, accurate, and free from error.

5. *Objective.* Information must be unbiased and not slanted by the views of particular parties.

6. *Timely.* Information must be available when needed and should be sufficiently current to aid recipients.

The Computer and MIS

For many years, computers have been used to perform routine and repetitive operations formerly done manually, such as payroll preparation and sales order writing. Each organization has particular needs that must be met by its computer systems. The types of information that can be provided by a computer system are just as diverse as an organization's use of information. A management information system ensures that computer-processed information is useful to a company by focusing on the information needs of the organization.

COMPUTER SYSTEMS

Computer systems should always be purchased with a clear knowledge of *how* they will be used and *what types* of components will be needed to comprise the system. Buying a computer system is one of the most important, but also one of the most difficult, decisions in which AOMs participate. It requires an eye to future needs so that existing systems can be updated and adapted to tomorrow's needs.

A **computer** is an electronic device operating under the control of instructions stored in its memory. Computers can accept data in the form of words and numbers and process that data arithmetically and logically to produce usable output; they can then store those results for future use. A computer system is a group of computer devices that are connected, coordinated, and linked in such a way that they work as one to complete a task. In an office setting, you may find relatively small and simple computer systems composed of only one or two small computers serving an entire office. In contrast, you may find large computer systems that store large amounts of data and information that everyone in an organization can access by simply using a keyboard-type device on his or her desk.

Computers are useful because they are very fast, they are accurate, and they can store vast amounts of data. Typically, computer systems are classified according to their physical size, memory capacity, speed, and cost. In general, there are five classifications of computers: microcomputers, servers, minicomputers, mainframe computers, and supercomputers.

Microcomputers

The computer system that is the smallest in size, has the least amount of memory capacity, is slower than the other four, and costs the least is the **microcomputer.** The microcomputer, also called the personal computer (PC), is the system used by most office workers. These computers can sit on desktops or be portable and as small as a notebook held on one's lap. Microcomputers range in price from several hundred dollars to $10,000. Though notebook computers will be covered more thoroughly in Chapter 14, it is important to mention a noteworthy issue now. With prices of notebook PCs dropping and their power and expandability rising, the decision to go with a notebook or its desktop brethren as the corporate standard gets tougher when it's time to upgrade company PCs.[4]

Server Computers

Server computers are designed to support a computer network that allows all employees to share files, application software, hardware (such as printers), and other network resources. Server computers usually have the following characteristics:

- They are designed to be connected to one or more networks.
- They have powerful CPUs.
- They have large memory capacity and large disk storage capacity.
- They are capable of and are used for high-speed internal and external communications.

Minicomputers

Minicomputers are often larger than desktop microcomputers and, like a PC, can be used with standard electrical outlets with no environmental controls necessary. They are popular for multiuser applications, such as numerical control of machine tools in manufacturing operations and industrial automation robotics. Minicomputers range in cost from a few thousand dollars to hundreds of thousands of dollars.

Mainframe Computers

Mainframes are very fast and powerful units and for a long time were the largest of all computer systems. They are freestanding and larger than most minicomputers. In addition, they are different from the previous three systems because mainframes require special wiring and environmental controls to operate efficiently. Because these computer systems operate 24 hours a day, primarily large businesses and government use them. They range in cost from approximately $200,000 to millions of dollars.

Supercomputers

Supercomputers are the largest, fastest, and most expensive computer systems available. They can cost up to $20 million and are used primarily for scientific applications, such as weather forecasting and other applications requiring complex and lengthy calculations. The demand for and use of supercomputers is increasing.

Table 12.1 provides a comparative summary of the users and applications for each of the five categories of computer systems.

COMPONENTS OF A COMPUTER SYSTEM

When purchasing a computer, an AOM is faced with many choices. One of the most important and first questions you will have to answer is, "What do I want the computer to do for me?" With that answer in mind, questions pertaining to what processor, keyboard, and monitor to buy; how much memory and how large a hard disk to buy; and what type and size diskette or CD-ROM drives to buy will become easier to answer. The following information will help you make informed decisions about computer needs.

Hardware, Memory, and Storage

The basic hardware devices for most business computer systems include those items you can physically touch, such as a monitor, a keyboard, a printer, and a computer system unit containing the memory chips, storage devices, and other electronics.

Hardware Devices. The following are considered the essential hardware devices that every system should have.

Monitor. The **monitor** resembles a television screen in that it displays information. Monitors

CLASSIFICATION	USERS AND APPLICATIONS
Supercomputer	Government agencies for designing weapons, rockets, and military devices; businesses and universities for commercial and scientific applications.
Mainframe Computer	Large businesses and government agencies, such as banks, airlines, and insurance companies.
Minicomputer	Small businesses or divisions of large companies. Used by engineers, architects, commercial artists for speedy number crunching and graphics.
Server	Schools and businesses to allow a network of other computers to share data, application software, and hardware resources.
Microcomputer	Available in a range of sizes to fit individual user's needs. Used extensively in businesses, the home, and educational institutions.

Table 12.1

Comparison of Users and Applications for Computer Types

range in cost from less than one hundred dollars to several hundred dollars depending on their size and features. The more expensive

A color monitor.   © *PhotoDisc, Inc.*

monitors are high resolution, which produce more attractive, crisp, and clear images on the screen. The purpose of the monitor is to show you what you are doing as you use the computer. Your choice of a monitor will depend on your needs and preferences, as well as your budget. The choices include monochrome and color, with screen sizes varying from 15 inches to large, full-page and two-page monitors.

Keyboard. The most common input device is the basic keyboard. Most newer keyboards, however, consist of three distinct sections: the typewriter (or alphanumeric) keypad with function keys at the top, the cursor movement area, and the numeric keypad. As you enter or type data on the keyboard, it is simultaneously displayed on your monitor screen and stored in the computer's main memory. For comfort and ease of operation, many computer users prefer

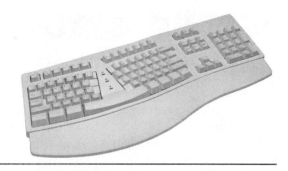

Examples of computer keyboards. © *PhotoDisc, Inc.*

the ergonomically designed keyboard, which slants naturally in a soft V-shape.

Printer. Printers produce paper output in the form of text and graphics. Numerous types of printers are available with price tags ranging from one hundred dollars to many thousands of dollars. Most office printers today are nonimpact, which means they do not print characters by striking the paper. Some common types of nonimpact office printers are the DeskJet or inkjet, laser, and xerographic printers.

The printer of choice in most offices is the laser printer. Laser printers usually can produce a number of different typefaces, or fonts, of varying design and size. Many laser printers can print in excess of 18 pages per minute. Although companies like Lexmark and Epson are manufacturing fine printers, Hewlett-Packard continues to dominate both the low end and the high end of the laser printer market.

Computer System Unit. The system unit in a typical personal computer generally includes a microprocessor, which is a single silicon chip containing the central processing unit (CPU), and a small amount of special-purpose memory. In addition, the system unit contains one or more memory chips mounted on a main circuit

board called the motherboard. The microprocessor, with its increasing speed and processing power and ever-decreasing prices, has helped revolutionize the way companies do business. Major manufacturers of microprocessors today are Intel, IBM, and Motorola.

Memory and Storage. The two types of memory chips used in computers today are the ROM and RAM chips. The hard drive, floppy disks, and optical disks such as compact disk read-only memory (CD-ROM) disks are the most common computer storage devices.

Read-Only Memory. Read-only memory (ROM) chips are used for the permanent storage of certain instructions, most frequently parts of the computer's operating system software that check computer hardware when you turn on your computer. Instructions stored on ROM chips cannot be written over or altered and are not lost when electric current is disrupted or turned off. Some leading manufacturers of memory chips are Motorola, NEC, Toshiba, and Texas Instruments.

Random-Access Memory. Random-access memory (RAM), also called main memory or primary storage, resides in the system unit. This high-speed memory area is where your program and document are stored while you are working on them. Computer memory is measured in bytes. A byte is the space required to store one character (a letter, digit, or symbol). The minimum recommended amount of RAM on microcomputers is 32 megabytes (MB) or approximately 32 million bytes. However, most users working in the Windows environment prefer at least 64 MB of RAM memory or greater.

RAM is only active when the computer is on; therefore, RAM depends on the flow of electrical current. If the current is turned off or disrupted by a power surge, a brownout, or electrical interference generated by lightning or nearby machines, the contents of the RAM chips will be lost. For this reason, RAM memory is said to be volatile. Fortunately, storage on the hard disk or diskette is available that is not volatile. As a consistently applied technique, operators should save their work frequently; that is, copy the document on the screen from RAM onto a diskette or the hard disk.

Hard Disks. In contrast to RAM, **hard disks** are nonvolatile storage devices. In other words, when the power is turned off, the software and documents stored on the hard drive are not lost. Hard disks are thin but rigid metallic platters that are coated with a substance that allows data to be recorded in magnetic form.

The hard disk is a permanent part of a hard disk drive encased within the system unit and cannot be removed. Because hard drives have a number of moving parts, they are also more susceptible to failure than most other parts of a

A Printer. © *EyeWire*

computer system. For this reason, it is very important to back up, or make a duplicate copy of, the data stored on a hard disk drive.

One of the most important questions to ask when you buy an office microcomputer system is "How large a hard disk will I need?" The most prudent response is to buy as much storage as you can afford that meets your current and projected needs. Just like computer memory, storage is measured in megabytes or, increasingly, in gigabytes. The preferred amount of hard disk space for today's office ranges from 2 gigabyte (GB) to 9 GB. A **gigabyte** is a measure of computer storage capacity that is equal to approximately one billion bytes. The **terabyte (TB)**, or one trillion bytes, is the next level for measuring disk storage.

Optical Disks. Optical disks are an important form of storage media. Created by the same kind of laser technology as the compact disks (CDs) that have revolutionized the music business, these disks have had a similar impact on the computer industry. Optical disks can provide tremendous storage capacity at a relatively inexpensive price.

The **compact disk read-only memory (CD-ROM)**, probably the most familiar kind of optical disk, is prerecorded. A single CD-ROM can hold up to 660 MB, equal to 330 high-density floppy disks. In other words, a CD-ROM can hold about 300,000 pages of information. Because of their capacity to store large quantities of infrequently updated information, they are great for reference materials like encyclopedias and catalogs. Large storage capacity also makes CD-ROMs a good choice for storing both sound and images. Therefore, they are frequently used for multimedia applications.

The technology used to create CD-ROMs is filtering down to the desktop. CD-recordable drives, now available for under $400, allow the user to write data onto a specially manufactured disk that can then be read by any standard CD-ROM drive.

Peripherals and Accessories

In addition to the major hardware components, computer users also use peripheral devices and other accessories.

Hardware Peripherals. **Peripherals** are hardware devices that are optional to the operation of the basic unit. Some examples of peripheral computer hardware are the mouse, modem, scanner, and digital camera.

Mouse. To move around in the Windows environment, you will probably work with a mouse. The **mouse** is a device used for moving the cursor-like insertion point around the text and for pointing. The mouse has a small ball on its underside that rolls around as you move it around on the mouse pad.

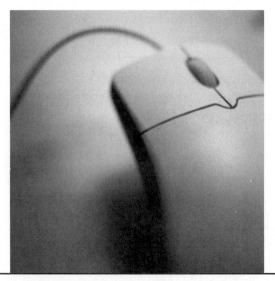
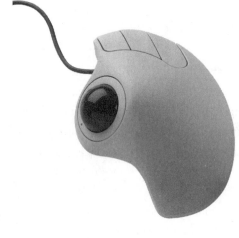

Two examples of mouse-type devices. © *PhotoDisc, Inc.*

When you move the mouse up (away from you), the pointer on the screen moves up; moving the mouse left, right, or down causes a corresponding movement of the pointer on the screen. Basic mouse techniques include point, left and right single-click, drag, and double-click. Computer users often find that the mouse is more efficient, easier to learn, and quicker to use than the keyboard or other types of pointing input devices.

Modem. An essential business tool, the **modem,** is used to link a computer to telephone lines, so that communicating with other computers is possible. Businesses depend more and more on **connectivity,** or being able to move electronic information from point A to point B efficiently. To do so, businesspeople are dependent on the computer and the phone—the modem is the link that joins these two communication tools.

The modem is ideally suited to some tasks. Because of modems, files in computer form arrive at their destination in minutes, rather than the hours previously required when sending a disk or documenting by overnight mail. With modems, users can conduct instant on-line research, gathering information from virtually any publication around the world. Moreover, modems provide answers to computer or business questions from a pool of on-line experts through networking with other users. Major considerations when choosing a modem are:

1. *Internal versus external.* Internal modems come in the form of add-in boards that are installed inside your computer; external

Digital technology has brought video conferencing capabilities to the desktop.   © *PhotoDisc, Inc.*

modems are stand-alone units that plug into a port at the back of the system unit.

2. *Speed.* Common modem transmission speeds are 33,600 and 56,000 bits per second (BPS) or greater. A faster modem may be worth the extra cost if you plan to consistently transmit large files.

3. *Fax capability.* Modems often combine fax capabilities with standard data transmission, as more mobile workers travel with portable computers.

Scanner. A **scanner** is an input device that acts like a miniature photocopy machine connected to a computer, copying graphic images into the computer and allowing typewritten pages to be scanned and entered without retyping. A scanner does this by using optical character recognition software, which converts the image into a pattern of dots, and transmitting the results to the computer, where it is stored as a graphic file on the hard disk. The images then can be viewed, altered, or enhanced through the use of various graphics programs.

Scanners include both hand-held and desktop models. One measure of the quality of a scanner is the number of dots per inch (or resolution) it produces when converting the image. The greater the resolution, the better the control over the gray levels, colors, contrast, and brightness of the transferred image.

Digital Camera. New cameras and software bring photography into the computer age. **Digital cameras** capture images with sensors and computer memories rather than with traditional film. Pictures taken with digital cameras can be edited with computer programs and can be printed on an inkjet or laser color printer.[5]

With no film and no processing, a digital camera creates a computer file as soon as you snap the shutter. It looks and operates much like a 35-mm point-and-shoot camera, but everything is instant. If you don't like your results, erase them. You can transfer the images to your PC for viewing, manipulate them with a digital "darkroom" program, and then print them, post them on a Web site, e-mail them, or store them.[6] Digital cameras can range in price from approximately $500 to over $1,000.

Computer Accessories. Hundreds of computer accessories have been developed to complement desktop systems and eliminate the clutter that accumulates around peripherals. Several companies offer products designed to help employees organize their spaces. Some examples of computer accessories are magnifier antiglare radiation filters for monitors, extendable monitor arms, above-the-desk computer platforms, under-the-desk keyboard drawers, and mouse pads.

Software

Software, also known as a program, is a group of instructions executed by the computer. Business and office software used on microcomputers or PCs can be categorized as either system software or application software.

System Software. One of the most basic software decisions you make when buying a computer system is which operating environment you will use. The popular choice for system software is Windows 98, which uses a graphical user interface (GUI). Using icons or symbolic pictures to represent programs, files, and common operations, this Windows-environment approach of using graphics, or pictures, and menus simplifies the user's task of working with a computer, making it more user friendly. However, office professionals will also find Windows NT and UNIX.

Windows 98. Building on the groundbreaking innovation of Windows 95, Microsoft's latest operating system, called Windows 98, provides an enhanced graphical environment. Like its predecessor, Windows 98 provides essential operating system commands and features that give you the ability to add and remove programs, start and exit programs, install and uninstall peripheral devices, control hardware settings, and manage data on storage devices. Yet, Windows 98 also capitalizes on the latest technologies of the Internet to give you a truly Web-integrated environment from which you can work seamlessly with local or Internet resources. With the new features of Windows 98, you can customize your desktop to behave like a Web browser.

Windows NT. Like Windows 98, Windows NT is also a complete operating system designed to take advantage of the capabilities offered by 32-bit microprocessors. Aimed primarily at the business market, Windows NT is an operating system for high-performance workstations and network servers.

UNIX. UNIX is a popular nonproprietary, portable operating system developed at AT&T Bell Lab in 1969. Unlike other operating systems, UNIX allows application programs to work across the full range of platforms— from microcomputers to supercomputers— and across manufacturers' lines. UNIX supports multitasking, multiuser processing and networking, and it is commonly used on server workstations, minicomputers, and mainframes.

Application Software. Application software is productivity software that allows you to use a computer to solve a specific problem or perform a specific task. The biggest market for application software is the office.

As an AOM, you will oversee the use of several major software packages, as computers input and process office data and then convert it into usable information or output. The five types of application software most often used in today's offices are word processing, spreadsheet,

database management, graphics, and desktop publishing.

Word Processing. A word processor makes writing and editing everything from a brief memo to a novel much easier and faster. **Word processing** software allows you to create, edit, format, print, and save documents such as letters, memos, reports, and other text with greater ease and efficiency than using a typewriter.

The real strength of word processors is their ability to edit previously stored material and to format documents and arrange written material so it is presented attractively on a page. Printing features can create headers, footers, and page numbers. In addition, most word processing packages contain a spell checker, a thesaurus, a grammar checker, and mail merge options, as well as drawing tools, tables, and help features.

The most popular full-featured word processing programs are Microsoft Word and Corel WordPerfect.

Spreadsheets. **Spreadsheets** are financial planning tools that perform mathematical calculations and are used by businesses large and small, nonprofit organizations, scientists, professors, and private individuals in their homes. The power to record, organize, analyze, and present all sorts of financial and statistical

> **Management Tip**
>
> *When selecting a computer system, the first step is to determine how you will use the computer. Then, select the software, and finally determine the hardware. Once the process is followed, you will have a better idea about how much speed, RAM, hard disk storage capacity, as well as the software, you will need to buy.*

information is available within spreadsheet programs.

When businesses need to calculate and analyze figures quickly and easily, they use spreadsheets. A spreadsheet software program, for example, makes it easy to calculate depreciation, prepare financial statements, track and analyze financial results, develop a budget, manage cash flow, and analyze alternatives. Popular spreadsheets on the market today are Microsoft Excel, Lotus 1-2-3, and Corel QuattroPro.

Database Management. Database management software computerizes and manages record-keeping and information tasks by helping you store, organize, and retrieve information much more efficiently than using paper file folders in cabinet drawers. As a result, it is often called an electronic file cabinet. Database management involves using a computer rather than a manual system to store, manipulate, and retrieve data, as well as to create reports from stored data and information.

Data managers allow you to enter information once, perform a complex calculation or sorting routine on that information, and then produce, for example, three different reports based on the results. Databases can store almost any type of data, and organizations realize computerizing this data can yield enormous gains in managing their business. These gains result from making better use of information and having accurate and up-to-the-minute reports on which to base critical decisions.

Suppose you want to send collection letters to customers who are more than 30 days late on their payments. Billing information is collected

in an invoice file, and customer data is stored in another file. This is an application made for a database management system (DBMS). DBMS software allows you to construct a database environment for a set of related files and to quickly access and manipulate the information located in several separate files. DBMS reduces data redundancy and confusion because information can be more easily shared across department and division lines. When information needs to be updated, for example, it is updated in only one place. DBMS software common in offices today includes Microsoft Access, Oracle, dBase, and Paradox.

Graphics. Graphics software presents data clearly and quickly in visual form on a computer. There are two basic forms of business graphics software: analytical graphics and presentation graphics. Analytical graphics software allows you to take data from an existing spreadsheet or database file and create, view, and print charts and graphs.

When more professional-looking charts and graphs are needed to accompany an oral presentation, for example, presentation graphics software is appropriate to use. These packages allow you to create slides of charts and graphs, diagrams, and other presentation materials from scratch.

Why do business professionals use graphs? They use graphs to define and analyze problems, summarize and condense information, and spot trends or trouble spots. Further, business reports that summarize ideas graphically are preferred because they are more interesting to read and more persuasive with customers.

Which type of graphics software you should buy depends on your needs. If you plan to use graphics to convey data and do not plan to use your computer as an artist's tool, look at stand-alone presentation software or the charting programs that come with many popular spreadsheet and database software.

If, on the other hand, you plan to use individualized graphics, your choice depends on whether you want to start from scratch and create your own work or modify other images from a draw or paint program. There are many fine presentation graphics and drawing packages from which to choose, such as Microsoft PowerPoint and CorelDraw!

Desktop Publishing.
Desktop publishing (DTP) refers to the use of a microcomputer to assemble words and illustrations on pages and to print those pages on a high-quality printer, such as a laser printer. For example, desktop publishing systems allow you to produce professional-looking newsletters, reports, manuals, brochures, advertisements, and other documents that incorporate text with graphics. For a businessperson, desktop publishing helps present ideas powerfully and dramatically.

Using desktop publishing within a company can be much less expensive and more controllable than going to an outside printer. With desktop publishing, charts, diagrams, drawings, and even photographs can be easily added to documents to enhance and clarify the message. Today, the technology for producing desktop-published documents is a part of the total integration of information systems in the office.

Even though desktop publishing can be done with high-end word processing packages

such as Word or WordPerfect, the most popular complete desktop publishing software sold includes Adobe PageMaker and QuarkXPress.

Table 12.2 lists some of the most popular software used in offices today and how these packages are used to produce specific office documents.

Voice Recognition Software. Documents and other written communications can now be created faster and more economically with the use of voice recognition software. With speech converted directly into text on the computer screen, the often-slow process of keyboarding and the need for transcription are both eliminated. Software prices range from $50 to $500 and are determined by such factors as number of users, support for applications, and vocabularies. Though this software is not perfect and makes mistakes about 5 to 10 percent of the time (correction can be made as soon as spotted or after dictation), it is becoming a serious business tool that can revolutionize the way documents are created.[7]

OTHER AUTOMATED OFFICE EQUIPMENT

Because so much is written about computers today, at times it is easy to forget that other automated systems are just as vital in helping an

TYPE	POPULAR PACKAGES	OFFICE APPLICATIONS
Word Processing	Word WordPerfect	Letters, memos, reports, contracts, multipage documents
Spreadsheet	Excel QuattroPro	Budgets, financial statements, what-if analysis, statistical information
Database Management	Access Oracle dBASE	Customer listings, personnel listings, inventory items, vendor information
Graphics	PowerPoint CorelDraw!	Slides, graphs, charts, draw-and-paint projects
Desktop Publishing	PageMaker QuarkXPress	Brochures, advertisements, newsletters, price lists, catalogs

Table 12.2

Application Software in the Office

office run smoothly. When processing office information, you can expect to use equipment other than computers to get a job done. In the office, for example, you will use a fax to send a letter to a customer in another city, a paper shredder to safeguard personnel and financial records, an electronic typewriter to fill in preprinted forms, and dictation machines to speak your thoughts when processing business letters and reports.

Facsimiles

In offices around the world, the fax revolution is underway. A **facsimile (fax)** is a machine that translates copies of text or graphics documents into electronic signals, which are then transmitted over telephone lines or by satellite.

Uses of the Fax. There is no doubt that facsimile machines are permanently changing the way clients place orders and how headquarters acquires data from field offices—altering the very nature of business. Today, an office without a fax machine is about as rare as one without a computer.

The fax is impacting the U.S. Postal Service and overnight express mail services in delivering business communications. With the speed and convenience of a phone call, fax machines speed business communications in a relatively inexpensive way. As previously discussed, many businesses install modem/fax cards inside the computer and use fax software to send and receive paper messages.

Challenges of Using the Fax. Fax users are becoming aware of some concerns, such as proliferation in the use of the fax and security issues.

Proliferation. As businesses and institutions rely more on faxes, concerns over product speed and quality, training and usage, and cost containment have taken on a new urgency. Fax machines provide speed and convenience, to be sure; yet, most offices currently lack the organization or discipline to control this powerful technology. By establishing clear, simple guidelines for using the fax, unnecessary transmission is reduced, thereby saving both time and money.

Security. Relative to fax usage, security is an increasingly worrisome issue. The sheer number of fax machines in use increases the possibility of sending confidential information to a wrong number. Additionally, as more fax machines are connected to networks, the chances of unauthorized tapping are growing. Cellular phones are particularly vulnerable to eavesdropping, making mobile faxing risky, as well.

Shredders

Office paper **shredders** provide document security and, at the same time, help the environment. Many companies use shredders to destroy sensitive material to ensure that it stays confidential. Shredded paper is easier to recycle and more biodegradable when placed in a landfill. Paper shredders, which are experiencing marked growth each year, vary greatly in productivity and price.

Although some models fit over wastebins, larger machines placed in central locations are generally more powerful and accept more paper. When purchasing paper shredders, buyers should consider the materials they will be destroying and the overall capacity in terms of their current and future needs. Paper shredders range from over-the-trashcan models costing less than $50 to heavy-duty models costing several thousand dollars.

It is interesting to note that paper shredders used to be considered expensive, but now some companies are paying for them by selling the shreds to recycling centers and to animal breeders who use the shreds for bedding. Also, many companies now reuse shreds as packing material for fragile items.

Multifunction Devices

These all-in-one document machines print, fax, copy, and scan. The number of less expensive models introduced recently makes them affordable at under $300. This device offers two primary advantages: it requires less space and costs less than separate units. The one obvious risk of a multifunction device is that if the machine breaks down, you lose all four functions. Yet, many users are willing to take the risk.

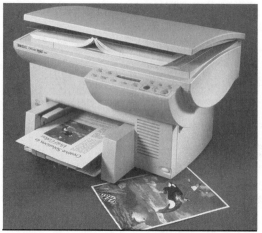

A multifunction device that prints, faxes, scans, and copies documents. *Courtesy of Hewlett-Packard Company*

Typewriters and Dictation Machines

There is no question about the impact that increased use of computers among managers has had on the use of typewriters and dictation machines in the office. Increasingly, offices use neither of these devices, which were so prevalent a decade ago. Nevertheless, they are still found in many offices and used by office support workers.

Typewriters. Some users of office electronic typewriters often prefer these machines to personal computers for tasks such as printing mailing labels, addressing envelopes, and filling in multipart forms and index cards.

Dictation Machines. A dictation machine is a device used to capture thoughts on magnetic voice media. The use of dictation machines, however, has shrunk in recent years. The reduced use of dictation machines can be directly attributed to the advent of portable computers and a lack of trained transcriptionists.

Message *for* AOMs

Today's conventional wisdom is quick to declare that if you want to save time and get organized, use high technology. Get a computer or a fax. Put a cellular phone in your car. High tech today means unsurpassed speed and maximum availability, which supposedly equals massive amounts of time saved.

Availing yourself of all the electronic wonders on the market today—from special telephones to laptop computers—can indeed free your time. But there are pluses and minuses to consider when looking at electronic wonders as time-savers, because these machines can also be great users of time. If you make efficient use of technology, you will be able to save time; an overindulgence or overdependence on machines, however, can wind up wasting far more of your time than those machines will save.

As an administrative office manager, you will discover that perhaps one of the most important benefits of prying information off paper and cramming it into computers is getting the opportunity to rethink thoroughly how the company conducts its business. Clearly, computers are not about to push paper completely out of the office overnight. Many hurdles remain. However, the more managers know about how computer systems and related equipment operate, the greater asset they will become to any organization that hires them.

1 The five classifications of computers are microcomputers, servers, minicomputers, mainframe computers, and supercomputers. The characteristics that make them different from each other are their size, amount of memory capacity, processing speed, and cost.

2 The basic hardware devices for most business computer systems include those items you can physically touch, such as a monitor, a keyboard, a printer, and a computer system unit containing the memory chips, storage devices, and other electronics.

3 Peripherals are hardware devices that are optional to the operation of the basic unit. Some examples of peripheral computer hardware are the mouse, modem, scanner, and digital camera.

4 Software, also known as a program, is a group of instructions executed by the computer. System software controls the operations of the computer; application software applies the computer to solving particular document processing problems.

5 The five types of application software most often used in today's offices are word processing, spreadsheet, database management, graphics, and desktop publishing.

6 In the office, you will use a fax to send a letter to a customer in another city, a paper shredder to safeguard personnel and financial records, an electronic typewriter to fill in preprinted forms, and dictation machines to speak your thoughts when processing business letters and reports.

summary chapter 12

QUESTIONS FOR CRITICAL THINKING

1. Of the five classifications of computers, in your opinion, which ones will an AOM most likely manage?

2. In order for a computer system to operate, what four hardware devices should be present?

3. What is the major difference between RAM and the hard disk drive?

4. Describe the function of a modem in a computer system.

5. What types of office documents can scanners scan?

6. In your opinion, which types of application software are most used in today's business offices and why?

Case Study 12-1: Stingy Co-workers

Tracy Gilson has just been hired as a computer operator in an old, established real estate office in town. She wants to do her best and learn as much as she can on the job. Tracy hopes to get her real estate license someday and sell residential properties herself. She views the job as a way to learn the business from the ground up.

Almost immediately, Tracy senses something is wrong when she asks the other three office workers questions to clarify her work assignments and office procedures. Two of them, Scott and Denise, seem to withhold important information from her intentionally. It appears to Tracy that they are going to dole out information only when it is needed. The third office worker, Marion, is more helpful. Tracy finds herself feeling closer to Marion and using her as a role model.

Discussion Questions

1. Why do some office workers have the attitude that they must keep, rather than share, certain knowledge and special procedures? Do you feel this applies to persons in management, as well?

2. The attitude practiced by Scott and Denise leads to human relations problems. What are some other outcomes that businesses can expect when employees practice this attitude and are allowed to get away with it?

Case Study 12-2: The "MIS"— To Get or Not to Get

Events in the temporary employment services industry have been changing so quickly that it has been hard for Benson's Personnel Specialists to keep up. As a result, President J. Michael Benson recently hired an executive assistant, Beth, primarily because she has previous experience with working on management information systems (MIS). Beth knows and has commented that with an MIS system in place, Mr. Benson would have information at the right time to make decisions with greater confidence.

In addition to the expense of changing their current decentralized computer system, Mr. Benson is concerned with the best way to approach his 25 employees about an MIS system, which he hopes to install within the year.

Discussion Questions

1. Why do you think employees feel threatened by the placement of an effective management information system in their organization?

2. What can management do to calm those fears?

Case Study 12-3:
Internet Research Activity

Assume you are doing a report on the *rise in information technology departments.* Use the Internet to research information needed to answer the following questions. Key your responses.

1. Which Web search engine did you use?

2. List three URL addresses that you accessed during your search.

3. Develop an outline of topics to be used in your report.

Endnotes

[1]Dana H. Schultz, "Technology Management: Three Keys to Success," *Law Office Technology,* April 1998, p. 3.

[2] "What IT Planning Does Your Company Do?" *Inc. Tech 1998,* July 1998, p. 19.

[3]Christopher J. Bachler, "What Exactly Is Information Technology?" *Workforce,* July 1998, p. 53.

[4]Mark Brownstein, "Notebook or Desktop?" *InfoWorld,* November 24, 1997, p. 93.

[5]"Digital Imaging," *Fortune,* Winter 1998, p. 132.

[6]Richard Folkers, "Digital Darkroom: Digital Cameras Don't Click," *U.S. News & World Report,* May 4, 1998, p. 72.

[7]John Dykeman, "Talking to Your Computer Starts to Pay Off: The Case for Digital Dictation," *Managing Office Technology,* September 1998, p. 22.

Telecommunications and Office Network Systems

chapter 13

" Look ahead. Always aspire to the job above yours, and learn what's necessary to do it.

—*Andrew Sherwood*
"

objectives

After completing this chapter, you will be able to:

1. **Discuss the importance of telecommunications with respect to information movement and management.**

2. **List several devices that may be connected to form a computer network.**

3. **Explain how local-area networks (LANs) are set up.**

4. **List several benefits to organizations that use LANs.**

5. **Describe the role of electronic mail in today's offices.**

6. **Distinguish between a client/server-based and a peer-to-peer LAN system.**

7. **Identify several ongoing managerial activities that must take place to keep LAN systems in operation.**

Transmitting and receiving information is vital to American business. The ideal way for people to work is to be able to say at any time, "I need some information." They will not care whether the information is on a CD-ROM disk, a company file server, or thousands of miles away in some central repository. They will simply import the needed information and proceed.

TELECOMMUNICATIONS SYSTEMS

Telecommunications is the transfer of data from one place to another over communication lines or channels and includes the communication of all forms of information, including voice and video. Computer users will simply be "in touch," with data or information available whenever and wherever they wish. Getting documents into the hands of the people who need to see them and getting them back at the right

Leonard D. Troy

Senior Manager,
Network Operations
MCI Telecommunications Corp.,
Central Division
Cincinnati, Ohio

Mr. Troy attended Purdue University, where he received a B.S. in math. His MBA was awarded from Xavier University. Beginning at MCI in Kansas City, Missouri, in 1978 as a switch technician, Mr. Troy moved rapidly into a Washington, DC, position as a circuit engineer. From there, he moved to Cincinnati in 1980 as a supervisor. After a promotion to manager, Cincinnati-Dayton, in 1984, he moved up in 1991 to his current position of senior manager, Southern Ohio, Cincinnati–Dayton–Columbus.

QUESTION:

What changes have you seen at MCI in communication activities? Have you seen any changes in the amount and/or levels of communication problems both from upward and downward communications?

Dialog *from the* Workplace

RESPONSE:

The last ten years have seen an explosion in the amount of computer-based technology being applied to communication tasks and problems. These technologies include personal computers, electronic phone systems, electronic mail systems, voice mail systems, voice and videoconference systems, pagers, cellular phones, etc. All of these have been geared to make communications easier, faster, and more complete.

At MCI, the single technology that has made the largest impact on the way we communicate has been our MCI Mail electronic mail system that we originally developed and deployed in the early 1980s. Currently, there are many public and private electronic mail systems throughout the world. These systems are interconnected to allow the easy exchange of messages between the systems. This allows anybody on any one of the systems to communicate with virtually anybody else in the world who has a computer, fax machine, telex terminal, or other type of electronic communications device on a near real-time basis. At MCI, virtually all written communications, including memos, reports, data files, etc., are transported from one person to another by the electronic mail system. In a large, growing company like MCI, having the ability to rapidly move critical information to the people who need it is a key problem to have solved.

Electronic mail systems present some issues concerning the security and control of information. Information can be easily misdirected and could end up in the hands of people who should not have the information. Since the electronic mail systems are interconnected and shared, an unintended recipient could be someone outside the organization.

When information is presented to people, there is no

guarantee that the people will absorb the information and use it. Getting people to read memos and reports was a problem before electronic mail and remains a problem. Here the communication problem is not in the message or the medium, but with the people themselves who are involved in the communication. Simply changing the medium to an electronic format has no effect on this issue.

On the whole, MCI has found the electronic mail system to be a very useful communications tool that has assisted the company to grow and prosper. With a little care, the problems are controllable and not a major concern. This also sums up the experience that other organizations have had with electronic mail systems. These systems will not totally replace written documents as a form of communication in the near future, but they have proven their usefulness and will continue to grow and to be enhanced.

times is of greatest importance in the business office in the Information Millennium.

Experts foresee a rich and varied range of information services and links promoting information movement and management becoming increasingly commonplace. These information services are already in place and include e-mail, fax, delayed delivery, text-to-voice, voice-to-text, video and image-file transport, and video-conferencing.

The medium of choice for innovations in telecommunications is fiber optics. Such a fiber, roughly the diameter of a human hair, can transmit as many as one billion bits of information per second in the form of digitized pulses of light. Compared to twisted pair wire or coaxial cable, fiber optics promises superior fidelity, protection from electrical disturbances and security breaches, and a lower cost than copper wire. Data superhighways, utilizing the power and speed of fiber-optic networks, provide the infrastructure for standardized communication that allows users to interface with each other, regardless of the equipment or data type they have.

NETWORKS IN THE OFFICE

Businesses have long sought to improve the ways their employees work together, gain access to information, and operate outside the office. It is not economically feasible or realistic for an organization to maintain all the resources its members might like or need. However, it is possible to provide connectivity resources that give people access to the tools they need to work better. That is precisely what American business is attempting to do.

Networking leverages investments made on hardware and software. Some predict that it won't be long until stand-alone equipment will be the exception, because the next step for many companies will be to take their stand-alone equipment and connect it to a network.[1]

Connectivity and Geographic Coverage

Connectivity can enhance access to important data needed for making decisions. This data is often collected through diverse channels. Connectivity gives equal support to members of a work group, a client, or a customer, regardless

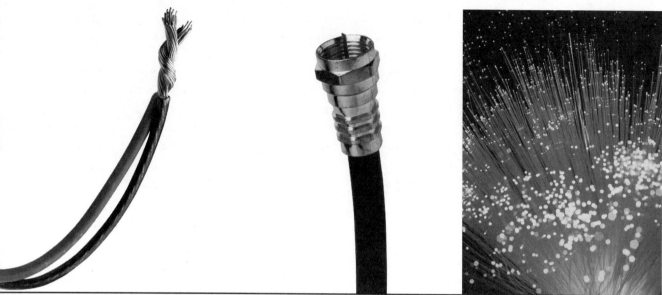

Examples of twisted pair wire (left), coaxial cable (middle), and optical fiber (right).   © *PhotoDisc, Inc.*

of geographic location. Connecting people and computers is the key to delivering cost-effective services in today's computing environment. The concept of connecting with colleagues over a network, wherever they are, is growing rapidly.

Such new forms of communication and cooperation go under various names, from "virtual networking," "ad hoc networking," and "telecommuting" to "spider-web organizations," "virtual employees," and more.

Networks can be conveniently typed, based on their geographical coverage and connection lines. A computer network using leased lines from telephone company vendors over a wide geographical distance, for example, is called a wide-area network (WAN). A network extending over a few miles or within a city is a metropolitan-area network (MAN). Whereas in the past, a local-area network (LAN) system extended only within a building or group of buildings and used privately controlled connection lines, we now see wireless LAN networks entering the picture. Figure 13.1 illustrates the geographical scopes of networks.

Wireless LAN technology makes a huge difference for end users. For one thing, their equipment suddenly becomes mobile. Employees can take it anywhere in the facility where they happen to be working and keep the same capabilities. For another, they suddenly have the possibility of networking in a facility where there may not have been the option before, simply because of the building's situation. The

Figure 13.1

Networks are described based on local (LAN, metropolitan (MAN), or world (WAN) access.

company may be in an older building where the walls are solid brick or a building where the insulation is asbestos. Wireless LANs can go anywhere and can run in complement to wired LANs within a facility. There is a tradeoff, however. There is currently a speed difference between wired and wireless LANs. Wired LANs run at 10 to 100 MB per second, and wireless LANs run at 1 to 2 MB per second. Depending on the applications running on the wireless LAN, however, that slower speed may be perfectly acceptable in many organizations.[2]

Local-Area Networks

Lower costs, versatility, ease of use, and the convenience of thousands of options and application programs make LANs a popular choice in companies of any size. A **local-area network** is a computer and communications network that covers a limited geographical area; allows every node to communicate with every other node; and does not require a central node or processor. A **node** is a station, terminal, computer, or other device in a computer network. For growing companies, LANs make sense. Even an

office with only two or three PCs can enjoy the advantages of local-area networking.

Networks work well because of a special control program called a **network operating system (NOS)** that resides in a file server within a LAN. The NOS is critical to LAN operations because it handles the requests for data from all the users or workstations on the network. A **file server** is a computer device and part of the LAN that allows for sharing of peripheral devices such as printers and hard disk storage units. A server is usually a microcomputer or minicomputer with the following characteristics: fast CPU speed, large RAM, large disk capacity, fast disk-access speed, plenty of expansion slots available, reliable hardware, and an operating system that is compatible with standard software drivers such as network, disk, and video drivers. Figure 13.2 shows how LANs work between workstations with access to file servers.

Benefits of LAN. Many companies are replacing minicomputers and even mainframes with PCs connected to LANs because of the wider availability of software and the speed and

Figure 13.2
. . . .
Even an office
with only two
or three PCs can
enjoy the
advantages of a
LAN system.

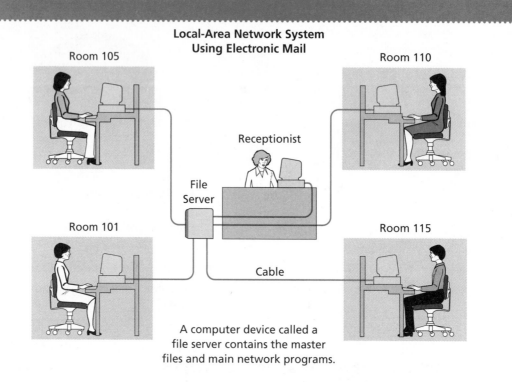

**Local-Area Network System
Using Electronic Mail**

Room 105

Room 110

Receptionist

File
Server

Room 101

Room 115

Cable

A computer device called a
file server contains the master
files and main network programs.

memory capacities available now on microcomputer technology. From just about anywhere on earth, you can use a modem-equipped computer and remote-control software modem to dial into a computer on your office LAN. As you key in data from wherever you are, you can do everything you could do if you were sitting at your desk, and you can see it all on the screen in front of you.

Organizations use LAN systems because they offer several benefits and make good business sense. Specifically, LANs assist companies because they:

1. Improve work-related communications among people in a work group.

2. Make the sharing of information easier, with less wasted time among work group members.

3. Provide easy access to a variety of printers, without the necessity of buying an expensive printer for every group member.

4. Give easy, low-cost access to fax facilities.

5. Allow group members access to office resources while at home or on the road.

6. Share selected application software, such as a word processor and a spreadsheet, for consistency of presentation and ease of upgrading and maintenance.

7. Have a common database accessible by all members of the group.

8. Furnish a method for scheduling people, meetings, and group resources.

9. Connect all varieties of equipment, allowing for easy communication, for instance, between formerly incompatible Macintosh and IBM personal computers.

Server-Based and Peer-to-Peer LANs. In practice, there are two general design philosophies for LANs: server-based and peer-to-peer. Recall from an earlier discussion that servers can be a file server, printer server, or communications server.

Server-Based LANs. In a client/server LAN, a central computer (server) stores the majority of the applications of the organizations and manages printing and communications activities. Each desktop PC (client) accesses the server when it needs to run a shared program or use network services. Any organization with more than five PCs on the network should consider the client/server mode. A major benefit of a client/server network is that it lets you centralize management and security for the network.

Client/server networks also make it easier to back up important documents and other information. The server can be set to automatically back up the entire network, including individual PCs; in a peer-to-peer model, users are responsible for backing up their own information.[3]

With server-based LANs, it is necessary for a user to attach or "log in" to the central file server before engaging in any LAN activity. The

Connecting people and computers is the key to delivering cost-effective computing services throughout an organization. *©Comstock, Inc.*

log-in command finds your user profile and authorized privileges in the server; prompts you for a password, if needed; and then sets up your access rights to the file server resources.

To log into a default server, you type a log-in username; the username is the user identification given to you by the network system administrator. Then, you will be asked for and must key in your password. The system often requires you to change your password periodically after so many uses. When you type everything correctly, the computer will respond with a log-in welcome screen, and you can begin using the LAN system. When you are finished working with the system, it is important to log out. Logging out is a process for disconnecting your workstation from the LAN system.

Peer-to-Peer LANs. By way of contrast, a peer-to-peer LAN can communicate directly with any other computer without going through a central server first. A peer-to-peer network is best if you have five or fewer PCs, and light file and printer sharing is your main reason for implementing a network. Peer-to-peer is the least costly method of connecting PCs and requires little set-up and maintenance, but it doesn't have the network security and management features of a client/server network.

Still, in a peer-to-peer network, the computers can exchange files and use each other's resources. This set-up requires that shared applications and resources be stored in a particular PC, with access given to the other users. One or more PCs store the resources, which are shared by others.

The peer-to-peer model can be counterproductive, however, if there are too many users trying to share an application or resource simultaneously. For instance, continuous requests to print or run a shared program will slow the host computer. Imagine an office where the accountant has the only copy of a spreadsheet application that is shared by everyone in the office. When it is time to prepare budgets, several users may need to access the program simultaneously, creating a logjam on the accountant's PC at the most crucial time of the year.

Computer Networks

The future of document processing will not be paperless but will consist of new documents and document management that can truly capitalize on networked microcomputers. A computer network is made up of several devices (computers, terminals, or other hardware devices) connected by an electronic communi-

cations system. In general, communications networks (such as the telephone system) can exist without computers, but computer networks cannot exist without communications systems.

Business offices and organizations that have as few as two or as great as ten personal computers can network. With networks, small organizations benefit, because as files and resources are shared, the costs of operation are lowered significantly. In addition, with the help of a wide mix of software and hardware vendors, users on Macintosh and IBM-based PC networks work together using tools that make it easy to assemble, store, find, exchange, and track electronic documents over a network without the necessity for enormously expensive mini- and mainframe-based systems.

Groupware

Work group software, frequently called groupware or collaborative software, is one of the most publicized, fastest growing computer applications on the market today. **Groupware** is the combination of electronic technology and group processes that supports teams and organizations as they work together on projects and share information over a network. Local-area networks, wide-area networks, and electronic mail together constitute, in effect, the backbone of groupware. Most groupware provides an electronic appointment calendar, an address book, and notepad. One of the more widely used groupware packages is Lotus Notes.

At a minimum, groupware requires personal computers that are networked in such a way that files may be transmitted from one computer to many others on request. In addition to computers and printers, copiers, fax machines, and telephones may need to be attached to the network to serve the needs of work groups.

Groupware is a technology that is clearly being driven by users' needs. In today's flattened, downsized, and networked organization—in which cycle times have been reduced, responsibilities have been pushed downward, and all effort is directed toward working closer to the customer level—important information that was once the property of an elite few must be accessible to a greater number of lower level staff. Groupware allows these people to share, analyze, and use information across vast distances and time zones.

The next step in groupware software, according to a November 1998 article in *Fortune* magazine, will include data conferencing, streaming video, and Internet telephony, or so-called real-time technologies. Millions of consumers and business users rely on the Internet every day. Yahoo! has become a household name, and electronic commerce is now a top priority for large and small companies alike. The American workplace is being reengineered to take advantage of the inherent interactivity of the Web.[4] With groupware, dozens or even hundreds of people can work together on-line to share documents, hold meetings, and bring teams of experts together over the World Wide Web.

Microsoft has its own term for the collaborative Internet—the two-way Web. With Microsoft Office 2000, the company has committed to using Internet standards as companions to its own proprietary format for files. That should make tasks easier. For example, it will enable Office users to create a document and save it *directly* to a Web site without having to worry about converting their work from the proprietary format like Microsoft Word. They will also be able to download and edit files directly from the Internet.

Collaborating in real time with colleagues over the Web will inevitably change the way people work and share information. Gone are the days when managers hoarded information to retain power. To work on Internet time, teams of managers, engineers, and marketers need to make decisions on the fly—even if they're in different time zones. The Internet has become a highway between dispersed workers, and collaborative software paves the way for further gains in productivity.[5]

Electronic Mail

Within today's organizations, little takes place that is not a team effort. Team members need communication tools such as electronic mail to enhance teamwork. Electronic mail (e-mail) is a system used to send messages between or among users of a computer network. E-mail is most effective when it facilitates communication among people who work in physically disparate places or who work different shifts.

Suppose, for example, the human resources manager wants to set up a meeting with seven employees throughout the company to discuss a change in the medical insurance plan. With e-mail, the meeting schedule could be sent to each of the seven employees simultaneously, and a survey form requesting completion of strategic departmental information could also

E-mail has enabled people to communicate instantly throughout the world.
©Comstock, Inc.

accompany the e-mail message. This would allow the human resources manager to receive those completed surveys (employees would e-mail them back) prior to the meeting. E-mail makes it easy to send, receive, save, respond to, delete, or print messages.

Moreover, today's electronic mail systems are not mere replacements for interoffice memos. Among other services, they provide access to shared fax resources, allow accounting and other software systems to send automatic alerts to appropriate officers, provide a means for distributing reports, and allow the transfer of files among co-workers.

To make e-mailing easier for the business traveler who needs capability to access office networks via the Internet, a new service is being provided by hotels and airports. Hotels, for example, can contract with third parties to

implement Internet access. An Internet service provider (ISP) can provide hotel access and add the charges to a guest's bill. Billing can be at a flat rate of $9 or $10 a day, or by the hour. According to reports, so far this service has been greeted with enthusiasm by its users. Although the installation cost per room is approximately $200, there is a definite market for those travelers who do not travel with their laptop computers and who have a need to periodically send and receive e-mail messages.[6]

There is one word of caution, however. Although communication networks offer the promise of more personalized media and widespread telecommuting, they also threaten individual privacy. Ethics will continue to be an important issue among users and designers of all networked systems.

MANAGING NETWORKS AND INTEGRATED TECHNOLOGY

The management of telecommunications networks in a corporate environment is a job that requires long hours and a regimen of upgrading knowledge through continuous training. Increasingly, data communications and the management of information systems are blending with telecommunications management as illustrated in Figure 13.3.

Typically, the telecommunications manager needs to know not only the physical telephone system but also the circuits and technologies that are involved in the firm's data processing operations. This can include knowledge of local- and wide-area networks, videoconferencing, data communications technology, and voice

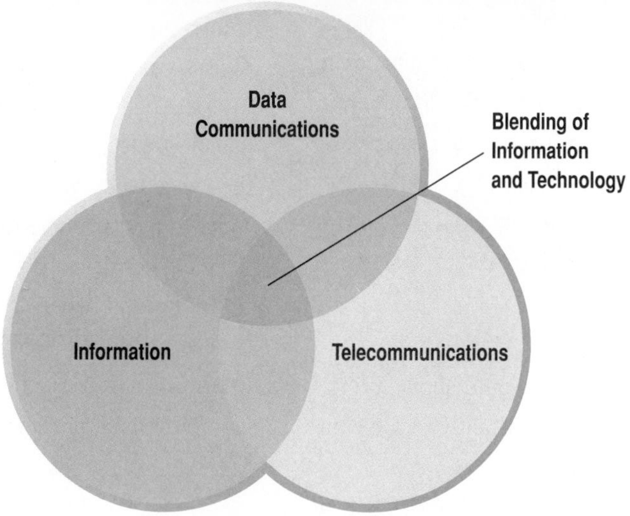

Figure 13.3

Data communications management, the management of information systems, and telecommunications management have blended and are creating new challenges for administrative office managers.

messaging. Most managers, lacking the time for formal training, rely on seminars, books, sales representatives, and conferences to keep up with the rapidly changing technology.

LAN Managerial Activities

Apart from the primary installation of a LAN system, there are ongoing managerial activities that must take place to keep the LAN in operation. If an organization does not have a network administrator, then these activities more often than not shift to the administrative office manager. Some of these activities include the following:

1. Setting up new users.
2. Deleting users who should no longer have access.
3. Specifying user access rights.
4. Ensuring that printer output can be properly captured.
5. Training users to make effective use of the LAN.
6. Providing technical support to users.

Management Tip

Winners in business are people who are open to new ideas. Be among the first in a group to say to a new idea, "Let's investigate this further and see if we can make it work!"

Integration Issues

Another management concern dealing with the rush of technology is the integration of networked fax machines, copiers, and telephones. New office software systems connect computers, phones, copiers, fax machines, and printers into a seamless digital web, thus permitting them to exchange information and circulate documents electronically. For example, a new wave of advanced office machines would allow you to write a memo and send it instantly to the computer screens of staff members, to the photocopier down the hall, as well as to the boss's printer and fax machines and computers of division managers around the world.

Most businesses today assign management of data and telephones to separate groups, but they need to be blended and jointly managed in order to realize efficient integration of office technologies. If managers handle this integration well, they will benefit handsomely from having created a more efficient system for computing information, sending faxes, and for managing voice and mail messages.

Message *for* AOMs

Communication networks offer widespread connectivity, yet they also increase the potential for misuse of information. As an AOM, you will be one of the critical organizational managers charged with the task of safeguarding information and making sure information is safe, secure, yet available for immediate use when the need exists.

The well-connected office in the future will allow for networks to keep all of a company's data at its fingertips, regardless of how much or how fast the business expands. Managing information is not just an option for global business; it is a requirement. It is also a never-ending task. For those reasons, AOMs will be required to put in long hours and pursue a continual regimen of training. There is just no way around it.

1 With telecommunications, computer users will simply be "in touch" with data or information whenever and wherever they wish, by getting documents into the hands of the people who need to see them and getting them back at the right times.

2 Some of the devices that can be connected in a computer network are computers themselves, hard drive storage units, printers, and scanners.

3 Whereas in the past, a local-area network (LAN) system extended only within a building or group of buildings and used privately controlled connection lines, now we see wireless LAN networks entering the picture.

4 LANs benefit organizations because they improve work-related communications among people in a work group; make the sharing of information easier; and provide easy access to a variety of printers and files on servers.

5 E-mail is a system used to send messages between or among users of a computer network and is most effective when it facilitates communication among people who work in physically disparate places or who work different shifts.

6 In a client/server LAN, a central computer (server) stores the majority of the applications of the organizations and manages printing and communications activities; in a peer-to-peer LAN, computers communicate directly with any other computer without going through a central server first.

7 Some of the LAN managerial activities include setting up new users; deleting users who should no longer have access; specifying user access rights; ensuring that printer output can be properly captured; training users to make effective use of the LAN; and providing technical support to users.

QUESTIONS FOR CRITICAL THINKING

1. List two examples of telecommunications in the office today.

2. Consider two types of networks described in the chapter and discuss their advantages in an office environment.

3. Cite two reasons driving organizations to install LANs.

4. What does a server-based LAN system require a user to do before he or she can use it?

5. What is the difference between a LAN and a WAN?

6. Of the ongoing managerial activities, which one would challenge you most in keeping a LAN system operational?

7. To you, what is the most exciting aspect about the future of groupware?

Case Study 13-1: I'm from the Old School . . .

That's how the banking vice president described himself to anyone who would listen. As a 52-year-old veteran with more than 25 years of personalized banking experience, Charlie was used to giving his requests for computerized information to his secretary and having them on his desk within the hour. Now all that has changed. He has been told that he now must use a computer to perform his own data entry activities, perform searches on customer files, and generate his own reports—including his own daily production reports.

On his desk this morning were two large boxes that contained a computer system. There was also a note for him to phone the computer technician's extension to have his computer system installed and to arrange for training. Charlie's first reaction was "They can't do this to me!" His second thought was "Maybe they are trying to force me to retire."

Since the bank he started with 25 years ago has already merged with other banks on three previous occasions, Charlie feels that the bank doesn't care anymore and is starting to treat valued customers and employees like a number. With those thoughts, his enthusiasm for his job is deteriorating fast. He is contemplating visiting the human resources department to discuss an early retirement.

Discussion Questions

1. In your opinion, is Charlie overreacting or are his reactions typical of the older worker in today's workplace?

2. If you were a close colleague of Charlie's and he asked your advice about whether he should quit or stay with the bank, what would you say?

Case Study 13-2: Preferential Treatment

Northland State University is on-line with its network system. The problem, however, is that not everyone is connected. In general, the administrative staff members, top administrators, and a few chosen faculty members are connected. When Gail, for example, asked if she could get on the network in order to have access to e-mail and the Internet, she was told to write a memo to her manager. Her manager needs to authorize funds to pay for a line drop to her workstation and the purchase of a computer network card, at a cost of approximately $100.

This is starting to cause division within the ranks between those who are and those who are not connected to the network.

Discussion Questions

1. In your opinion, how should an organization go about deciding who will be on the network initially and who will be phased in later?

2. What can the organization expect if this situation is allowed to continue? Could this situation have been avoided? If so, how?

Case Study 13-3:
Internet Research Activity

Assume you are doing a report on *groupware and collaborative software.* Use the Internet to research information

needed to answer the following questions. Key your responses.

1. On which site did you locate the most information on this topic?

2. Research specifically the software package Lotus Notes. Discuss cost, features, and training issues involved for this product when an organization installs it on its server.

Endnotes

[1]Lura K. Romei, "The Office Cosmos: The Connectivity Universe," *Managing Office Technology,* June 1997, p. 22.

[2]Ibid., p. 23.

[3]Tarik K. Muhammad, "Look Before You LAN: Is a Local Area Network Right for Your Home or Office?" *Black Enterprise,* January 1998, p. 25.

[4]"Productivity Gains," *Fortune,* November 16, 1998, p. 188.

[5]Ibid.

[6]Stephen H. Wildstrom, "Easier E-Mailing on the Road," *Business Week,* June 29, 1998, p. 20.

Internet Services, Distant Office Systems, and Other Computer Issues

chapter 14

"
Business is like riding a bicycle—either you keep moving or you fall off.

—*John D. Wright*
"

objectives

After completing this chapter, you will be able to:

1. Describe the purpose of on-line information and database services, such as the Internet and commercial providers.

2. Contrast the differences between the Internet and the intranet.

3. Identify two emerging technologies that help workers in physically distant locations conduct productive meetings.

4. Discuss some advantages of notebook computers over desktop models.

5. Describe the relationship between computers and the wise use of energy.

6. Cite some examples of mobile office equipment.

Connecting all the parts of an organization that are physically located apart from one another is becoming easier with computer and telecommunications technology. Covered in this chapter are issues related to distance management; these issues include on-line information and database services, and employee meetings at a distance.

ON-LINE INFORMATION AND DATABASE SERVICES

With telecommunications, a much broader access to a myriad of business information is possible. Access is made possible through on-line information and database services such as the Internet, intranet, and commercial on-line services that include America Online, CompuServe, Prodigy, Earthlink, and Sprynet.

Internet

The **Internet** is an international "network of networks" comprised of government, academic,

Rodney W. Scheyer

Director of Finance
Boeing Computer Services
Seattle, Washington

Mr. Scheyer has been director of finance for Boeing Computer Services since 1988, having previously been a systems analyst in Boeing's Aerospace division. He holds a B.A. in accounting from the University of Washington and an MBA from Seattle University. He has also participated in the Program for Management Development at Harvard University.

Dialog *from the* Workplace

QUESTION:

In your experience, what is usually the most difficult aspect of upgrading the system within your organization?

RESPONSE:

System upgrades can be a source of considerable aggravation. Change happens! Customers' needs change. Technology provides more alternatives. Environments change. New employees require changes in training and preparation. Cost pressures require management to seek the most effective and efficient means of process and product management. Since our administrative systems must constantly be evaluated and changed because of these factors, a critical requirement for the manager today is to transition to a more effective and efficient system with a minimum amount of disruption and cost.

The most effective management technique we have found is *planning.* We start with a careful understanding of customer requirements, followed by a detailed understanding of the "as is" condition. Next, we work with our systems and technology people to bring the most current technology and products to bear on the problem. The result of these activities is a detailed plan.

In many cases, the management of a system application can be illustrated by an old sports analogy. When you throw the forward pass in football, three things can happen, and two of them are bad! In managing a system upgrade, three things can happen, and all of them can be bad, including the functionality and expectation of the system design, the schedule, and the cost. The secret to making sure that all three don't turn out badly is the creation of and the attention to a carefully constructed milestone plan.

and business-related networks that allow people at diverse locations around the world to communicate through electronic mail, to transfer files back and forth, and to log on to remote computer facilities.

Because the Internet is a collection of huge supercomputers, telephone cables, and satellite transmission systems that relay data to and from thousands of points across the globe, users have access to millions of computer files, many with sound clips, pictures, and even video. For example, business leaders can obtain data on current market trends and conditions through the network each day. Employees can use the network to communicate with each other. Sales representatives can use it to market products and services.

Businesses, libraries, and academic institutions should all be concerned about proper use of the Internet. Employees and management usually agree that company time should not be spent on personal affairs. While that restriction once meant personal telephone calls and mail, today it includes electronic mail, Web surfing, chat rooms, and other on-line no-nos.

Internet Access Policy. Paid time spent on personal Internet use can be the least of a company's worries, given the vast world that lies within reach via the Internet. Opportunity to commit felonious crime exists, as does the chance to violate a company's privacy. Some companies already have clear-cut policies that dictate the limits of employee Web access and e-mail, but many do not, and Internet use is left to the discretion of the employees. Policies regarding Internet access, in general, should be concise and made well known to employees, staff members, or the public.

Any Internet access policy is intended to work more as a deterrent than act as a legally-binding document. The intent is to avoid potential problems before they arise. If employees, for example, know e-mail is not private or secure and that superiors may read it, that alone often eliminates many problems.[1]

Internet Activities. The Internet isn't just for sending e-mail and surfing the Web anymore. It is turning into a low-cost and nearly universal communications medium, helping to send faxes, retrieve voice mail, and carry two-way conversations. Because the cost of connecting via the Internet is essentially independent of time and distance, you can save big and benefit from all sorts of nifty automated features that just aren't possible with traditional telephones.[2]

Although the Internet itself is based on communications technology, it offers a variety of services that also are based on this technology. Some of these services are presented in the following sections.

The Web. One of the more popular uses for communications is to access the **World Wide Web, WWW,** or **Web.** The Web consists of a worldwide collection of electronic documents (Web pages) that have built-in links to other related documents. Connected users browse pages on the Web and are able to access a wide range of information, including news, research, educational material, and sources of entertainment.

Telephony. Internet telephony enables you to talk to other people over the Web. Using Internet telephony allows you to use the Internet instead of the public switched-telephone network to connect a calling party and one or more called parties. As you speak into a computer microphone, Internet telephone software and your computer's sound card digitize and compress your conversation and then transmit the digitized conversation over the Internet to the called parties. At the receiving end, the process is reversed, so the receiving parties can hear what you have said.

E-Commerce. More and more Internet users are using the Web for e-commerce. **Electronic commerce (e-commerce)** includes activities such as shopping, investing, and banking by using either electronic money (e-money) or electronic data interchange. **Electronic money (e-money)** is a means of paying for goods and services over the Internet. **Electronic data interchange (EDI)** is the transmission of business documents or data over communications media. Many companies use EDI to transmit routine documents, such as purchase orders, shipping information, or invoices.

Other Emerging Services. New ultra-low-cost Internet services are emerging that will perhaps replace long-distance telephone services someday. These new services will enable telephone communications globally for less than a penny a minute and faxing for between 7- and 14-cents per page. The quest to offer such services has not just start-up businesses but also such giants as AT&T, MCI, IBM, Intel, and Microsoft scrambling to offer Internet-based alternatives to the standard telephone network. The Internet, after all, is more efficient in handling simultaneous long-distance traffic than traditional networks.[3]

Cookies on the Internet. The Internet's sheer size and the fact that it is not owned by anyone are weaknesses as much as strengths. It has been said that the Internet is a vast network of electronic roads, boulevards, dead ends, and circles that seemingly take you everywhere—and nowhere. While it is a vast and exciting resource, the Internet is a public place, and you should use common sense while there.

One reason electronic commerce is so popular is that it often relies on cookies to track information about viewers, customers, and subscribers. A **cookie** is a small file that a Web server stores on your computer. Cookie files typically contain data about you, such as your user name or viewing preferences. Be aware that

On-line buying and selling are changing the way business is conducted all over the world.   © *Comstock, Inc.*

some Web sites sell or trade information stored in your cookie to advertisers. If you do not want your personal information being distributed, you should limit the amount of information you provide to a Web site. It is possible to disable cookie use altogether.

Table 14.1 provides a list of Internet terms used by "net surfers."

Intranet

Now that you have figured out what the Internet is, along comes the next piece of trendy **technojargon**—the "intranet." Don't panic: just think of an intranet as a World Wide Web site that is used only within a company. Companies using intranets can simplify life for users and network managers because they work on any kind of computer. Moreover, employees reach the intranet site with standard Web-browser software, such as Netscape. Table 14.2 outlines pros and cons relative to setting up an intranet.[4]

Simple intranet applications include electronic publishing of basic organizational information, such as telephone directories, event calendars, and employee benefit information. More sophisticated uses of intranets include groupware applications, such as project management, group scheduling, and employee conferencing.

While some intranets operate on a LAN at a single location, other intranets use many public and private networks to connect remote

- **E-mail:** Allows the user to send messages to other individuals or groups across the electronic highway.

- **FAQs:** Directories and files throughout the Net that answer frequently asked questions. FAQ files are always a good place to start learning about a new service or Internet location.

- **FTP:** Stands for *file transfer protocol*. FTP enables the user to make a copy of a file on a remote host and bring it *back* to his or her computer.

- **HTTP:** Stands for *HyperText Transfer Protocol*. Protocols are instructions computers understand that tell them how to handle and send hypertext documents from computer to computer. You see *http* at the beginning of World Wide Web URLs.

- **URL:** Stands for *uniform resource locators*. A URL is an address or reference code that makes it possible for GUI browsers to find specific hypertext documents on any host server in the world.

- **WWW or the Web:** Stands for *World Wide Web*. It is based on hypertext and allows the user to move from one document to another simply by clicking on a keyboard or mouse.

Table 14.1

Internet Terms

REASONS TO SET UP AN INTRANET	REASONS NOT TO
Your business uses several different types of computers—and the users all need to reach the same company information	You don't have a local area network, or your network's operating system does not use TCP/IP, the Internet communications standard.
You need to centralize data in an easy-to-access way.	You don't have any compelling business justification for one.
You'd like to give employees controlled use of more of the information stored on your networks, but . . .	Many of your employees don't use computers.
You don't want to administer network versions of various software packages.	

Table 14.2

Intranet Pros and Cons

locations. Anytime a private network connects to a public network, an organization must be concerned about security and unauthorized access to organizational data. To prevent unauthorized access, organizations implement one or more layers of security called a firewall. A

Ethics/Choices

Your company has recently subscribed to America Online. As you are walking by a colleague's office, you notice he is "cruising the Net" and has pulled up pornographic files on his screen. Do you ignore this episode, or as a friend would you say something to him to prevent him from getting in trouble?

firewall is a general term that refers to both hardware and software used to restrict access to data on a network. Firewalls are used to deny network access to outsiders and to restrict employees' access to sensitive data such as payroll or personnel records.[5]

On-Line Services

Commercial on-line services, such as America Online, CompuServe, and Prodigy, as well as local Internet service providers (ISPs), make information and services available to paying subscribers. Once you subscribe to an on-line service, you can access it by using communications equipment and software to connect to the service provider's computer system. Services that are available through commercial ISPs like America Online include electronic banking, shopping, news, weather, hotel and airline reservations, and investment information. All on-line services offer Internet access and electronic mail to their subscribers.

Databases available for a basic subscription fee (for example, $20 per month) to one of the commercial on-line services generally include channels (databases) on news and sports, reference libraries, games, shopping, financial services, travel, and leisure. One of the main advantages of paying for and using a commercial on-line service over the Internet is that with a toll-free 800 or 888 number, subscribers can talk to technicians who can help with problems they might have. In summary, with on-line services, business professionals now have available at an instant incredible, quality information for very little money that drives, and is the basis for, good business decisions.

EMPLOYEE MEETINGS AT A DISTANCE

With distant employees, a group meeting may be necessary to exchange ideas. Emerging technologies can help workers in physically distant locations conduct productive meetings. Two methods of "virtual conferencing" or "virtual meetings" can reduce travel expenditures and increase productivity. These methods are videoconferencing and collaborative screen sharing.

Videoconferencing

As businesses look for ways to operate more cost-effectively, they often try to minimize travel. For years, only the largest companies could afford in-house videoconferencing equipment and facilities. Recently, some Kinko's stores—

Videoconferencing saves money and increases productivity.
.   *© CORBIS*

best known for copying and printing services— have started offering videoconferencing for as little as $150 per hour. As with so many applications, videoconferencing is now turning to the Internet. Both Microsoft and Netscape, for example, have included videoconferencing capabilities in their latest Web browsers.[6]

Videoconferencing is not a new idea, but its cost has plummeted, and its quality has improved greatly. This technology allows people to see each other and to interact in a manner similar to that of a conventional meeting in which all of the participants are in the same room. No one loses work time traveling or sitting in airports. No one suffers jet lag, and more importantly, meeting attendees do not run up travel expenses.

On the other hand, some participants feel there is a downside to videoconferencing, but not enough so that it overshadows its benefits. Two of the major concerns about videoconferencing are that the video renders jerky images and the spontaneous give-and-take in meetings is hard to do.

Collaborative Screen Sharing

Collaborative screen sharing, on the other hand, needs only two modem-equipped microcomputers and appropriate software. Unlike videoconferencing, screen sharing does not show participants' faces. All that is required is a simple audio hookup to link conversation and the ability to view and manipulate the same-page layout or diagram on a computer screen.

For example, suppose an AOM were collaborating with an architect across town regarding the final floor plan and design for a new office area. Collaborative screen sharing allows the AOM and the architect, through conversation, dialog, and revising screen designs on each of their own computers, to reach agreement quickly and clearly on critical design issues.

The advantage of screen sharing is that it is inexpensive and easy to set up. All you need besides a basic desktop computer is the software, a modem, and standard telephone lines. It is as simple as sitting down at your desk and dialing your remote co-worker. The disadvantage is that it can be awkward unless you have worked previously with the other participants.

The versatile notebook computer comes in a range of prices with a corresponding range of features.   © *EyeWire*

Executive Suites for Business Travelers

In addition to videoconferencing and collaborative screen sharing, executive suites are gaining in popularity for employees who travel. Executive suites offer a number of cost-effective advantages to the business traveler who needs to use an office with adequate business-support services, if only for a day or two. Here are some services businesspeople can take advantage of—and many are available without making an advance reservation:

- Use of a private office or computer workstation;
- Use of a conference or training room and videoconferencing equipment;
- Word processing, desktop publishing, copying, faxing, color printer output, and digital scanning;
- LAN access and dataport hookup, and
- Phone calls professionally handled during their stay.[7]

THE MOBILE OFFICE EQUIPMENT SYSTEM

For businesspeople on the move, portable technologies can make every moment (if desired) a working moment. People who buy mobile office equipment are trying to get more minutes of productive time out of the ordinary workday, whether they're checking their voice mail while in a traffic jam or finishing a speech in a hotel room. What were once thought of as novelties have rapidly evolved into mainstream business tools.[8] The so-called "road warriors" basic equipment checklist should include, at a minimum, a cellular phone, a pager, a modem, and a notebook computer.

Notebook computers, or laptop computers, are small enough to be carried in a briefcase but often are transported in their own carrying cases. Notebooks are considered general-purpose computers because they can run most application software packages. They have standard keyboards and usually have at least one disk drive for storage. Notebooks usually weigh between four and eight pounds.

Notebook computers continue to be enhanced in terms of features and performance, making them more suitable as replacements for desktop systems. The notebook's portability provides numerous benefits, such as the capability to make sales presentations, offer training remotely, give formerly desk-bound workers the option to work at home, and communicate through videoconferencing.[9]

Notebook computers come in a range of prices with a corresponding range of features.

- At the top of the price range are high-end notebooks that offer all of the office capabilities of a desktop system. These are usually powered by the 300 MHz (megahertz) Intel Mobile Pentium II and can cost well over $5,000.
- The second category of notebooks contains the biggest sellers; so-called "value machines" that range from $1,000–$2,000. They offer enough power and performance to meet the needs of most students, families, and mobile workers. Notebooks in this range often use technology that is only months behind that of the high-end models.
- In the third category are high-performance notebooks that are also thin and extremely lightweight. Costing $3,000 or more, these are favored by executives and workers whose travel habits require the sleek and light style.[10]

In addition to notebook computers, digital technology is providing many new electronic office machines for the mobile office. Many combine functions such as copying, printing, faxing, and scanning into one machine. Though these products tend to be a bit more expensive than one-function peripheral devices, they are cheaper than the total prices of the several stand-alone peripherals they can replace.

> **Management Tip**
>
> *Keep in mind that tactless electronic messages have cost companies millions in damages and cost employees their jobs. Remember that e-mail messages survive just as paper copies do and can be produced in a court of law.*

OTHER COMPUTER ISSUES

There are additional network and computer issues to mention prior to leaving our discussion of these popular home and business machines. An AOM will, at some point, be concerned about computer issues, specifically dealing with energy consumption of computers; the qualifications and ethics of office computer users; and, critical to every organization, security of the data on company networks.

Computers and Energy Use

Computers are the fastest growing users of electrical power consumption in the business world. In the last ten years, computer-related energy consumption has increased fivefold. Computer use is now estimated to account for 5–10 percent of all commercial electrical consumption.

Each year, more and more computers are purchased and put to use. But it is not just the number of computers that is driving energy consumption upward. The way we use computers also adds to the increasing energy burden. Research reveals that most desktop personal computers are not being used most of the time they are running. When buying computers, make the decision with energy use in mind. Consider the following suggestions:

1. Buy a monitor that is only as large as you really need. A 17-inch monitor uses 40 percent more energy than a 14-inch monitor does when in active mode.

2. Buy only as much monitor resolution as you need. Higher resolution monitors use more energy.

3. Consider an ink-jet printer. These printers are slower than laser printers but use 80 to 90 percent less energy.

4. Consider purchasing retrofit power management devices. These devices power-down computer equipment when it is not actively in use.

5. Buy laser printers with low or no ozone emissions to maintain indoor air quality.

6. Request that packaging materials used by your computer vendor be recyclable or biodegradable.

However, the most basic energy conservation strategy for any type of equipment is *turn it off whenever possible*. Table 14.3 lists ten additional energy-saving strategies for using computers.

Qualifications for Computer Users

The rate at which job functions are computerized continues to accelerate, and employees and businesses must learn to adapt quickly. That is the conclusion of "Managing Today's Automated Workplace," a report published by The Olsten Corporation. Researchers found that many companies have personnel who are inadequately qualified to use the advanced technology profitably.

The Olsten survey of more than 1,400 executives indicated that higher productivity, better communication, quality improvement, and lower administrative costs were some of the benefits of the increased reliance on automated computer systems. Word processing and spreadsheet programs are the most widely used software applications. Computerized databases and records management systems are also popular. In the survey, 70 percent of companies reported a strong need for basic keyboarding skills, such as data entry and word processing. Other capabilities in demand include desktop publishing/graphic design and the management of network communication.[11]

Ethical Use of Computers

Several ethical issues surround information technology. Ethical choices are more complex and difficult either when laws do not exist or when their applications to new situations are unclear. AOMs are faced with such complications because rapid technological development has left many "gray areas" not yet defined by law.

Specific ethical topics that influence office computer use include the security and privacy

1. Turn off your computer and/or peripherals when they are not in use. A modest amount of turning computer equipment on and off will not harm the equipment.

2. Do not run computers continuously (unless they are in use continuously). Also, if possible, don't run your computer all the hours you are in the office.

3. Look for ways to reduce the amount of time your computer is on without adversely affecting your productivity.

4. Break the habit of turning on all your computer equipment as soon as you enter the office each day. Turn on each piece of equipment only when you intend to start using it.

5. If practical, informally group your computer activities and try to do them during one or two parts of the day, leaving the computer off at other times.

6. Do not turn on your printer unless you are ready to print. This especially applies to laser printers since they consume a considerable amount of electricity even while idling.

7. If for some reason you must leave your computer on while you are not working on it, turn off your monitor to reduce energy consumption.

8. Turn off your entire computer system (CPU, monitor, and printer) when you go to lunch or will be out of the office for a meeting or errand. Rebooting when you resume computer work usually just takes a minute.

9. Do not use a "power strip" master switch if you do not need all of your equipment all the time you are working on your computer.

10. Be an energy educator and gently remind your co-workers and colleagues to save energy by changing their computer habits.

Table 14.3

Energy-Saving Computing Strategies

Adapted from "Green Computing" by Walter Simpson, The Secretary, *April 1995, pp. 20–21. Reprinted with permission.*

of data, employee loyalty, and the copying of computer software.

1. *Hacking* is a computer term used to describe the activity of computer enthusiasts who are challenged by the practice of breaking computer security measures. **Hacking** is a crime, and gaining unauthorized access to another computer can be as serious as breaking into someone's home.

2. Because the field of information processing is a dynamic environment with a shortage of qualified workers, there are many job opportunities. Although court rulings differ, there should be some degree of loyalty to the

employer on the part of the employee. Actions taken in the process of changing jobs should be conducted in an ethical fashion. For example, taking data files belonging to your previous employer that you are unauthorized to take with you would be unacceptable and disloyal.

3. Software copying or *piracy* is the unauthorized copying of a computer program that has been written by someone else. Whether done for personal use or to sell for profit, software piracy is a crime.

An April 1998 survey sponsored by the Ethics Officer Association shows that the expanding use of technology and eroding business ethics may be on a collision course in the modern workplace. As a result, companies are scrambling to rewrite policies and develop security methods that work. The study reported that 45 percent of workers say they have committed at least one of a dozen actions over the past year that are either unethical or fall into a gray area.

The ethical abuses range from the relatively minor—13 percent of workers say they have used company computers to shop the Internet—to the potentially catastrophic—4 percent of workers say they have done something to sabotage the computer system or data of their company or co-workers. Other ethical abuses included accessing private computer files without permission; listening to private cellular phone conversations; copying company software for personal reasons; and reporting to work, logging on, and searching the Internet for another job.[12]

Security of Data on Networks

Today's computer networks pose a very real threat to corporate security. Yet, keeping data safe requires more than technological solutions. It's about policies, procedures, and education. According to the Computer Security Institute of San Francisco, 75 percent of companies have suffered financial losses, such as financial fraud, theft of proprietary information and sabotage, from computer security breaches. The Institute found that the biggest security threats typically come from inside an organization.[13]

As more and more data goes electronic, the risks and threats to the modern organization grow. Examples abound. An unencrypted e-mail sent over an intranet or the Internet can allow crucial information to fall into the wrong hands. A PC without the proper password protection can easily become a source of illicit knowledge. And a network without the proper safeguards, including firewall and audit capabilities, can allow crooks to steal or destroy sensitive data. Many security breaches occur when a disgruntled employee—usually someone who has been fired—is allowed access to his or her PC. A strict termination policy which deals with passcodes must be in place. A person should immediately be locked out of the system upon release from a job.

New technology is making it easier to nab crooks and maintain solid security. Biometrics is beginning to filter into the workplace. Using thumbprint, retina, or facial recognition, **biometrics devices** allow only authorized personnel access to the network, without the hassle of passwords. Yet, no amount of technology will ever eliminate all cybercrime. Five ways to ensure employees keep data secure are:

1. *Use passwords.* No other tool can provide as much protection so inexpensively. However, passwords are only as good as the systems and policies surrounding them. It is important that employees use a password they are able to recall and that log-off procedures are also in place.

2. *Turn systems off when not in use.* Getting employees to switch off systems at night and on weekends is one of the best ways to avoid someone using it, especially if password protection is in place.

3. *Rely on encryption when sending sensitive e-mail.* The latest generation of encryption tools allows a user to click an icon and encrypt a file. Use encryption tools especially when a sensitive or confidential e-mail is being sent across the Internet.

4. *Maintain clearly defined policies.* When employees know what is expected of them and what actions they're supposed to take,

it's far easier to ensure they are following policies and guidelines.

5. *Provide ongoing education and reinforcement.* If recurring reminders, paper shredders, and spot checks are in place, people are going to think a lot more about security in general.[14]

Trust is an important aspect of computer-based business transactions, such as those involving electronic commerce. Over the years, people have put their faith in ordinary technologies such as computers, fax machines, and copiers. However, the advent of the Internet and electronic commerce are compelling users to trust a huge network of computers that they cannot control. They are required not only to trust the network but also to trust the information it contains. This is why companies that want to sell their products and services over the Net should cultivate trust among their customers and clients. If they are not a trusted organization to begin with, their on-line businesses are not likely to flourish.[15]

Message *for* AOMs

Somewhere along the line, we changed from a society of people who believed only what we could see with our own eyes and touch with our own hands into a society that freely accepts the intangible, almost mystical workings of technology. In just a few decades, we have come to believe in computers, fax machines, copiers, and other forms of technology as immutable facts of life. We have them, we need them, and they (for the most part) work. Administrative office managers owe it to their company's customers to respect their privacy and earn their trust in daily interactions with them.

summary chapter 14

1 With telecommunications, a much broader access to a myriad of global and personal business information is possible through on-line information and database services, such as the Internet, intranet and commercial on-line services.

2 The Internet is an international "network of networks" comprised of government, academic, and business-related networks that allow people at diverse locations around the world to communicate through electronic mail, to transfer files back and forth, and to log on to remote computer facilities; the intranet is a World Wide Web site that's used only within a company.

3 Two emerging technologies that help workers conduct productive meetings at a distance are videoconferencing and collaborative screen sharing.

4 The notebook's portability provides numerous benefits, such as the capability to make sales presentations, offer training remotely, give formerly desk-bound workers the option to work at home, and communicate through videoconferencing.

5 The number of computers is driving energy consumption upward. In addition, the way we use computers also adds to the increasing energy burden, because most desktop personal computers are not being used most of the time they are running.

6 Mobile office equipment should include, at a minimum, these items: cellular phone, pager, modem, and notebook computer.

QUESTIONS FOR CRITICAL THINKING

1. Why is the Internet described as the "network of networks"?

2. What are the services that America Online and CompuServe offer to subscribers?

3. Why do business travelers use executive suites?

4. What is a major difference between videoconferencing and collaborative screen sharing?

5. Argue the reasons corporations might purchase a notebook computer instead of a desktop computer system at replacement time.

6. Describe some ethical abuses of using computers found among employees in the workplace.

Case Study 14-1: A Notebook Computer or Desktop Model?

Your friend, who is studying for a Ph.D., knows you are taking computer courses and seeks your help in acquiring a computer for her immediate needs: writing her dissertation and use in her future career. She asks you to provide a plan for purchasing a computer system that will satisfy both of her needs. On one hand, you feel a notebook computer rather than a desktop model would best serve her needs, but you aren't quite sure.

Discussion Questions

1. What further questions would you ask to determine her needs?

2. What type of PC would you ultimately recommend she buy, and why?

Case Study 14-2: Boss Travels More

Assume that you work as an administrative assistant for an executive in an advertising firm. He has just learned that with the merger of your company with a *Fortune* 500 advertising firm, he will be traveling 60 percent of his time. Your boss has asked you to research the type of equipment he will need to acquire in order to work at a distance and still communicate with you.

Discussion Questions

1. What equipment would you recommend he requisition your company to buy?

2. In what ways do you see your job responsibilities changing as a result of your supervisor's new work assignment?

Case Study 14-3: Internet Research Activity

Many computer crimes come under the jurisdiction of the Federal Bureau of Investigation. Assume that you are doing a report on *computer crime in the workplace*. Use the Internet to research this topic. Key your responses.

1. Go to the Federal Bureau of Investigation home page and gather information about current cases the FBI is investigating that cover computer crime.

2. Determine from other searches how the FBI is anticipating and preventing the most catastrophic crimes that computer hackers could commit.

3.   Research recent computer viruses that have infected business computers on a widespread basis (e.g., the Melissa virus from April 1999 or the worm virus in June 1999).

4.   As a result of your search, outline several items of current information you might use in your report.

Endnotes

[1]Melissa Everett Nicefaro, "Internet Use Policies," *Online,* September–October 1998, p. 31.

[2]"Conversation Piece," *Fortune,* Winter 1998, p. 281.

[3]Ibid, p. 282.

[4]Phaedre Hise, "Intranets Explained," *The Secretary,* March 1997, p. 2.

[5]Gary Shelly and Thomas Cashman, *Discovering Computers: A Link to the Future* (Course Technology: Cambridge, MA, 1997).

[6]Dana H. Shultz, "Videoconferencing," *Law Office Technology,* April 1998, p. 2.

[7]Tracy A. Fellin, "Suite Alternatives," *The Secretary,* May 1996, pp. 9–10.

[8]Doug Stewart, "Power Trips," *Inc.,* June 1994, p. 39.

[9]Mark Brownstein, "Notebook or Desktop?" *InfoWorld,* November 24, 1997, p. 93.

[10]"Frequent Fliers," *Fortune,* November 16, 1998, p. 68.

[11]"Demand Is High for Computer Literacy," *The Secretary,* February 1995, p. 4.

[12]Del Jones, "Survey Indicates Employees Misuse Employer's Technology," *USA Today,* April 26, 1998, n.p.

[13]Sam Greengard, "How Secure Is Your Data?" *Workforce,* May 1998, p. 53.

[14]Ibid, p. 56.

[15]Kelli D. Meyer, "Believing What You Can't See: The Importance of Trust in Business and Technology," *Managing Office Technology,* June 1998, p. 7.

Trends and Challenges in Administrative Office Management

chapter 15

> "It is our attitude, more than anything else, that will affect a successful outcome.
>
> —*William James*

objectives

After completing this chapter, you will be able to:

1. Identify three trends in the business world that will most affect how the AOM manages now and in the future.

2. Describe the four information technologies that will affect the ways in which workers retrieve, process, and output information.

3. List job titles that office workers can have based on distinct, specialized skills for each position.

4. Discuss the concept of the "Infotech" worker as it is applied to the office environment.

5. Describe the advantages of computer monitoring as applied to the work performed by office workers and managers.

6. Describe the typical stages of career development.

7. Identify the benefits to an office worker in joining professional associations.

8. Explain what is meant by a mentoring relationship.

Throughout the previous chapters, you studied changes that will affect the AOM's work patterns. These changes have been extensive in comparison to the work patterns of just a few years ago. The purpose of this chapter is threefold: First, to provide a realistic look into the trends that will affect an AOM; second, to spotlight impending activities the AOM will assume in managing the "Infotech" worker; and, third, to discuss ways the AOM can stay challenged through career development and participation in professional growth activities.

TRENDS IN ADMINISTRATIVE OFFICE MANAGEMENT

Three trends in the business world are most prominent in their effect on how the AOM manages the office environment. (1) The workplace is experiencing a new facelift; (2) the information sector, where AOMs work, will experience a huge growth in the number of

Andrea L. Schutz

Vice President for Human Resources Educational Testing Service, Inc. Princeton, New Jersey

Andrea's background is one of diversified and progressive experience in human resources management, including benefits, employment, affirmative action, compensation, records management, personnel policy development, organizational and staff development, and labor relations. She also has experience in risk management, including property and casualty insurance, loss control, and fire protection.

Previously, Andrea worked at Lenox, Inc., Mathematica, Inc., and Princeton University. She received her B.A. in sociology from Tougaloo College, Tougaloo, Mississippi, and her master of public affairs from the Woodrow Wilson School of Public and International Affairs, Princeton University.

QUESTION:

What is the nature of the employee benefits program provided by Educational Testing Service, Inc.? As you look ahead to the twenty-first century, what new kinds of benefits do you believe will emerge for ETS's employees?

Dialog *from the* Workplace

RESPONSE:

Educational Testing Service, Inc. is a private, nonprofit corporation devoted to measurement and research, primarily in the field of education. In the provision of a benefits program for its approximately 3,000 employees, ETS is committed to:

- Optimizing the value of each benefit plan to both employees and the organization while maintaining quality in every aspect of benefit administration and communication.
- Designing plans that add to the employees' quality of life and help protect them from financial loss due to illness, injury, death, or loss of income.
- Conferring certain benefits to reward employees for outstanding performance and service.
- Applying sound business judgment to create and modify an employee benefits package that is flexible and responsive to values and objectives of the corporation.
- Complying fully with all government laws and regulations.

The ETS benefits program is very broad-based and includes insurance programs, wellness programs, dependent care programs, education/ training, disability benefits, and time-off benefits.

The shape of the ETS benefits program in the future will be heavily influenced by factors internal to the organization such as demographics; the company's academic traditions; the culture and its emphasis on equity, openness, and employee choice; program utilization; and financial considerations. External influences that will affect what ETS chooses to do include our marketplace for obtaining clients and attracting staff; laws and regulations; the shape of government programs; social and political developments; vendor developments; and technological innovation.

So what's likely to be considered? Health maintenance (i.e., prevention, early diagnosis, and improving medical outcomes), will be the leading influence of our benefit program design.

Communications, which emphasize educating the staff about the programs available to them, optimal use of those programs, and overall support for effective decision making will grow.

Finally, work/family concerns will become increasingly important in our programs. The makeup of ETS contributes heavily to our attention in this direction.

Overall, the direction will be one that facilitates healthy, satisfying, and productive lives.

workers; and (3) the office support person will perform more "management-type" tasks.

Corporate Culture and Trends in the Workplace

Employees who work for companies whose values closely match their own tend to stay in jobs longer and with greater satisfaction. Job seekers who want to achieve a good match should decide their own workplace priorities and identify companies where those qualities are valued. A **corporate culture** can be defined succinctly as a set of behaviors or qualities that are valued not because competition forces all companies to value them, but simply because . . . that's the way things are. When evaluating a potential employer, keep in mind that you can learn a lot just from nonverbal observations. What do the work spaces look like? How are employees dressed? Most important, what are they doing— standing around chatting or sitting alone in their offices?[1]

According to the World Future Society's *Outlook '95* newsletter, the future work world was painted in the following way. Interestingly, this picture is now very real and gaining momentum:

1. *"Virtual" organizations are replacing traditional companies with collaborative networks.* By integrating computer and communications technologies, corporations have created collaborative networks linking thousands of people at separate locations.

2. *Lifetime jobs are a thing of the past.* Creating a strategy for one's career is requiring new, more portable skills that can be marketed to a variety of potential employers. For example, an individual worker can expect to work as a temp at one place and a consultant at another within the same month.

3. *Businesses are outsourcing more functions to stay flexible in times of rapid change.* Computerized training and support systems enable temporary and part-time workers to keep pace with core employees.

4. *"Road warriors," the new ultra-mobile workforce, increasingly work out of "briefcase offices."* A single computerized palmtop unit now can serve as mailbox, fax machine, and notebook.

Growth in the Information Sector

Careers in the information sector of the economy are in a growth stage. These office careers involve collecting, analyzing, synthesizing, storing, and retrieving data. In this new century, a vast array of electronic information technologies have melded, changing the way we work, play, learn, and live. The "big four" information technologies—computer networks, imaging technology, massive data storage, and artificial intelligence—have had revolutionary effects on how workers retrieve, process, and output information. Increasingly, these key technologies are reshaping today's occupations as vital tools most office workers use every day.

1. *Networks* are indispensable for sharing and communicating information with anyone, anywhere, anytime.

2. *Imaging technology* makes information more user friendly and enables the rapid transmission of images.

3. Massive *data storage systems* handle information and store it electronically in readily accessible, attractive, and concise formats.

4. *Artificial intelligence systems,* including expert systems, "knowbots," and agent software, are partnering with workers in doing routine office tasks.

Role of the Office Worker

As the structure of business continues to change, so does the role of the secretary, or administrative assistant. Offices will increasingly rely on secretaries to perform details once reserved for supervisors as companies scramble to achieve further savings and efficiencies.

According to Office Team, a support-personnel placement service, during the past decade secretarial career possibilities have grown from three traditional titles—receptionist, secretary, and executive secretary—to include nearly twenty different classifications with distinct, specialized skills required for each position. New opportunities range from word processing and desktop publishing to transcription services and data management. Table 15.1 shows administrative career job titles—then and now.

Coping with change will test an AOM's flexibility and foresight—the *flexibility* to change yourself and the *foresight* to anticipate the changes and prepare for new ways of doing what you have always done. These are some of the on-the-job trends office professionals can anticipate:

1. offices with fewer walls and more shared space,

2. cabinets or lockers for personal projects and belongings that replace individual offices,

3. flexible schedules, odd work hours, and working in satellite offices, and

4. growth of the "virtual office," or the office in a briefcase or a car, complete with high-tech equipment and conveniences.

More than ever before, continuing education is necessary for everyone. Those who continue to

ADMINISTRATIVE CAREER JOB TITLES

THEN	NOW
▪ Executive Secretary	▪ Administrative Assistant
▪ Receptionist/Clerk	▪ Administrative Office Manager
▪ Secretary	▪ Administrative Information Specialist
	▪ Administrative Receptionist
	▪ Desktop Publishing/Graphics Specialist
	▪ Executive Assistant
	▪ Office Specialist
	▪ Office Professional

Table 15.1

Technology Has Allowed for More Specialists in the Office.

learn *make change their friend.* Those who do not will find themselves in a very threatening new world.

MANAGING THE "INFOTECH" WORKER

Restructuring the organization around information is something that will, of necessity, have to be done by *all* businesses. Employees will be known as "**Infotech**" workers.

Information technology, or Infotech, consists primarily of computing, combined with telecommunications and networking. By the year 2010, Infotech will result in many positive changes, making many jobs more challenging and rewarding. Realistically, however, it may also lead to job loss, depersonalization, and boredom. Primarily, Infotech will affect workers on two levels:

1. It will be an important tool that allows workers to do more of their jobs through an intermediary, such as a personal computer or expert system.

2. It will change the nature of jobs because organizations will redesign computer-based jobs to take advantage of telecommunications and networking.

It is, therefore, safe to assume that practically no one will be exempt from the effects of Infotech on workers. In general, the future worker's primary activities will be gathering, creating, manipulating, storing, and distributing *information* related to products, services, and customer needs.

Infotech workers will present AOMs with several challenges—managing alternative work and outsourcing arrangements, as well as overseeing the computerized monitoring of employees' work habits, personal behavior, and their use of the Internet.

Managing Alternative Work Arrangements

In telecommuting situations—such as the virtual office, the mobile office, and the home office—the work travels, not the person, in the form of digital information. How well will these "virtual" workers use the extra time?

In a survey of 7,300 AT&T telecommuters, 29 percent said that with the alternative office situation, they use the extra time, which they would have spent driving to work or dealing with office politics, to do even more office work. Once the commute, personal chit-chat, and other office distractions are eliminated, the report stated that the employees' extra time is realized through increased "quality" work time.[2] The AOM's challenge will be to find ways to encourage the Infotech worker who is managed at a distance and out of sight.

Managing Outsourcing Services

Due to a shortage of skilled labor and the prospect of lowering costs, companies of all sizes are expected to increase their spending on outsourcing in the years to come, according to a 1998 survey from International Data Corp. The research group expects that outsourcing spending will increase at a compound annual growth rate of 10 percent in the United States, creating a $75 billion market in 2001. The most sought-after outsourcing services are data center, network operations, computer desktop and application services, and help desk technicians.[3]

Beyond the need to save money and gain access to specialized technical skills, outsourcing allows companies to better deliver service-level agreements and gives companies more agility in reacting to business changes. It should be noted that there have been numerous outsourcing failures, and some companies have rejected the idea outright. Poor outsourcer performance, loss of control of information, and

issues regarding layoffs are some of the inhibitors companies state as their reasons not to outsource services.

Computer Monitoring

The words "computer monitoring" sound threatening to most workers, but in the future computer monitoring may become a worker's friend. **Computer monitoring** involves using computers to observe, record, and review an individual's use of the computer, including communications such as e-mail, keyboard activity (used to measure productivity), and the Internet sites visited. For example, a computer that counts keystrokes and identifies errors might not result in a reprimand and snitch to the boss but instead suggest that the worker take a short breather. Other monitors could act as prompters, reminding the office worker of special details when talking with customers, or as coaches, giving tips on improving performance.

It is predicted that the year 2000 will see as many as 30 million people constantly monitored in the performance of their jobs. Monitoring can be done in a humane fashion if employees are guaranteed several rights—including access to all information gathered through monitoring. In fact, some argue that it might be motivational to give employees personal access to this information. Information given to the supervisor often turns out to be a club; but, when it goes directly to the worker, it can become a positive motivator.

Advanced computer systems will be able to make suggestions based on information that the employee enters. Not only will these computers keep closer tabs on employees, but, based on this added information, the computer will also be able to help employees do their jobs more effectively. Overall, the use of prompts will be positive because employees will not have to worry as much about remembering countless details.

For the AOM, information gathered via computer monitoring will increasingly be used to coach employees. Currently, many organizations use the information gathered as a basis for criticism. Companies are realizing, however, that it is more motivating for employees to be coached rather than reproached.

Internet Usage Monitoring

As a result of hooking employees to the World Wide Web, management is painfully aware that these workers have access to everything from marketing data to porn sites. To exercise a little control over just what Internet waves they surf, a software program that allows managers to monitor Internet usage patterns is now on the market.

The software, which costs about $500 plus $10 or so per employee, also has other uses as an Internet traffic cop. It can be programmed to block access to sites deemed inappropriate and to generate reports ranking various departments according to amount of time spent on-line.[4]

Corporate types say monitoring Internet usage makes workers more productive, conserves network resources, and helps limit legal liability by discouraging workers from downloading objectionable material to company computers. On the other hand, critics say the practice is unnecessary and misguided.[5]

Employee Monitoring

Workplace monitoring is nothing new—it's as old as employer-employee relationships. The main difference today is so much of the monitoring is from information that is gathered in secret, thanks to technology.[6] Employees may think their privacy is protected by the Fourth Amendment, which protects against unreasonable searches and seizures; but courts have ruled that the Constitution doesn't apply to employees of private firms. And, while some states have passed privacy legislation, the protections are scattershot. Few states have legislation, for example, to protect workers from being secretly videotaped or from employers reading their e-mail.

More than one-third of the members of the American Management Association, the nation's largest management development and training organization, tape phone conversations, videotape employees, review voice mail, and check computer files and e-mail, a 1997 report states. Personal behavior is no longer off limits: Some firms have adopted rules that limit co-workers' dating. Others ban off-the-clock smoking and drinking. Many companies regularly test for drugs. While companies say they collect information on their employees to comply with the law and protect their business interests, a survey of *Fortune* 500 companies showed that nearly half collect data on their workers without informing them.[7]

One way to help ease employees' apprehension about monitoring and at the same time set up some fair boundaries for workplace surveillance is for companies to create a formal privacy policy. A good privacy policy should not only articulate the reason for monitoring, but also specify when, where, and how employees will be monitored. The policy should also outline how that surveillance data will be used. A copy of the policy should be distributed to every employee upon hiring.

Advancement opportunities as an office professional are plentiful.
© *PhotoDisc, Inc.*

STAYING CHALLENGED AS AN AOM

Any job has its good and not-so-good days. To stay challenged, AOMs must take charge of their careers by dealing with career development issues on a regular basis (not just on not-so-good days) and by being open to participating in professional growth opportunities, which are plentiful.

Career Development Issues

Career development cannot be taken for granted. In other words, it will not take care of itself. Your career must be planned and managed in such a way that your personal and professional goals are frequently adjusted as circumstances change and new events occur.

Personal and Professional Goals. Adults usually consider four broad categories of goals when evaluating where they are at any one point in time. The four categories, which are the same for an administrative office manager, are financial, power, status, and career goals. Once you have identified your personal and professional goals in each category, mapping out a career strategy should be easy.

A career strategy should be flexible and based on your own personal experience and values. What steps should you take?

1. Identify your opportunities. What *might* you do?

2. Clarify your ambitions and hopes. What do you *want* to do?

3. Inventory your competencies and resources. What *can* you do?

4. Acknowledge your obligations. What *should* you do?

5. Recognize your personal values. What are you *willing* or *not willing* to do?

6. Develop a clearly defined plan of action with time lines for completion. How *will* you proceed?

Stages of Career Development. Workers who are on a career track realize that there are stages to career development that can be expected at particular ages. For example, most of us spend the years between ages 1 and 25 preparing for work. Between ages 18 and 25, we find our first job and enter the world of work. After age 25 through approximately age 40, we focus on our career and usually make some significant career accomplishments. Then,

from ages 40 through 55, we continue to progress and, in some cases, advance to higher levels in an organization. Finally, from age 55 to retirement, we begin to make some late career choices to phase out the present job. Table 15.2 lists some major tasks at each of the five career stages.

When preparing for or furthering a career choice, keep these suggestions in mind:

1. *Be flexible.* Administrators, accountants, information systems technicians, and administrative support personnel are in demand in almost every field from medicine, insurance, and education to law enforcement.

> ## Management Tip
>
> *What career-oriented workers should strive for is to make every effort to be ready for the next step when an opportunity knocks.*

STAGE	AGE RANGE	MAJOR ACTIVITIES
Preparing for Work	1–25	Develop occupational self-image, evaluate alternative occupations, develop initial occupational choice, pursue necessary education.
Selecting Job Opportunities	18–25	Secure job offer(s) from desired organization(s), select suitable job based on accurate information.
Making Early Career Choices	25–40	Learn job responsibilities, learn organizational rules and norms, fit into chosen occupation and organization, increase competence, pursue goals.
Making Mid-Career Choices	40–55	Reappraise early career and early adulthood, reaffirm or adjust goals, make choices appropriate to middle adult years, remain productive in work.
Making Late Career Choices	55–retirement	Remain productive in work, maintain self-esteem, and prepare for active retirement.

Table 15.2

Stages of Career Development

2. ***Develop communication and people skills.*** Employers mention over and over that they want employees who can speak and write well and who can interact and accomplish tasks with others.

3. ***Think globally.*** Trade barriers are dropping, meaning more and more companies will be competing internationally. As a result, opportunities will increase. To be marketable to such companies, you may need to learn another language, learn about other cultures, and learn how business is conducted in other countries.

4. ***Learn and advance your knowledge about computers.*** Stay on top of new technologies, software packages, and operating systems.

5. ***Get an edge on your competitors.*** Any extra skill, knowledge, or ability that will help you stand out from other applicants—computer skills, an extra degree, or a foreign language, for example—can be the plus that makes you the person chosen for the job.

6. ***Keep learning.*** Once you're employed, make learning a lifelong endeavor by attending seminars, conferences, in-house training programs, and pursuing college classes, certificates, and degrees.[8]

Managing Your Career. Most people can expect to have six to seven employers and perhaps three to four careers during their lifetime, so careful self-management of your career is critical. As you work to manage your career, begin by asking, "What will give my life meaning?" Be honest with yourself regarding your values, those things that are important to you.

A good recommendation is to reevaluate your goals soon after you have experienced any significant life change, such as obtaining a higher level of education, getting married, separated, or divorced, having a child, moving to another city or state, or being a part of a company's downsizing. Do not wait for others to "develop" you; it is up to you to create and seek out your own developmental opportunities. In that way, when timing and luck seek you out, you will be ready to launch yourself into your next job. Use on-line career resources and develop a professional portfolio as you manage your career.

On-Line Career Resources. You can discover career resources along the information superhighway in a communications bulletin board called "careers BB." There are messages from correspondents who are not only new to the secretarial profession, but those who are also considering secretarial careers and are seeking information on techniques, career tracks, training, and membership in professional organizations.

In addition, job seekers are finding lots of help when using the Internet to do job searches. It is possible to search for job openings with companies around the world on the Internet and to apply for positions by electronically transmitting your resumé for consideration. Take some time now to review various Web sites that have an employment link to become familiar with on-line hiring.

Your Portfolio. Career-minded office professionals should consider putting together one of the most important books a prospective employer would read about you—your portfolio. A **portfolio** is a collection of items that documents and chronicles the accomplishments that can give your career a boost. This book can offer unparalleled benefits during evaluations and job searches because it enables your current bosses or prospective employers to see your documented achievements.

One way to organize your portfolio is according to projects you have completed, training you have had, and skills you have developed and can do. Here is an overview of each of those categories and the materials and information you may want to include in each part:

1. *Projects.* Include copies or templates for such forms as inventory, billing, timesheets, style books, and manuals you helped create; include your time- and money-saving ideas that the company adopted.

2. *Training.* Include copies of certificates, academic degrees, courses, and seminars, as well as documentation of self-directed computer training you have completed and used on the job.

3. *Skills.* Create three subcategories such as management, computer, and interpersonal skills.

   - Under management, include samples of management responsibilities such as communication, time management, problem solving, and delegating.
   - Under computer, include how you helped your workers improve their computer skills as well as any technical skills you have learned, such as solving soft-

ware problems and minor hardware repair.
   - Under interpersonal, document situations that demonstrate you are a team player, showing your flexibility and adaptability in the workplace.

Professional Growth Opportunities

Seeking opportunities to grow in a career is not always an easy task, depending on where you live and work and other family and personal obligations you might have. Many successful office workers have used several sources to help them. They have joined professional associations, developed a mentoring relationship with others, and continued their training in critical skill areas needing development.

Professional Organizations and Associations. Joining a professional association is one way that people in many fields pursue career development. In an association, people with similar career interests share information and teach each other. By joining a professional association, you become an "insider."

At meetings or by reading association publications, you can learn about the concerns of the people in the profession and observe the strategies that successful people use to get ahead. Through professional organizations, members are provided opportunities to acquire skills and

Joining associations and attending conferences are excellent ways to stay on top of your chosen field.
© *EyeWire*.

professional credentials, to find or become a mentor, or simply to enjoy the social aspect of the group and network with others.

Table 15.3 provides a limited list containing information on some of the professional associations available to office professionals. Although this list is not complete, each association listed has some relevance for office professionals. You are encouraged to contact any of these organizations to find out additional details about membership.

One of the professional associations, International Association of Administrative Professionals (IAAP), sponsors a certifying exam for office professionals known as the **Certified Professional Secretary (CPS)** rating. The CPS rating is awarded to those who pass a one-day, three-part examination and have the required experience in the secretarial profession. The CPS examination is administered twice a year, at more than 250 locations around the world, on the first Saturday of May and the first Saturday of November. The exam covers the following areas: finance, business law, economics, office technology, office administration, business communications, behavioral science in business, human resources management, organizations, and management. Candidates have 3 years to pass all parts of the examination.[9]

The benefits of being a CPS holder are many and include self-esteem, self-fulfillment, greater job recognition, and sometimes higher pay. Many administrative office managers have achieved the premier status of their profession by becoming Certified Professional Secretary holders.

Mentoring Relationships. As you strive to make progress in your career, you will at times encounter obstacles. Some barriers to career progress, such as the lack of a particular skill, are obvious. But sometimes you may find yourself confused and discouraged by your unexplained lack of progress. At these times, having someone to advise, teach, and encourage you could make the difference between being on a temporary plateau and finding your career at a permanent standstill.

A **mentor** is an adviser, teacher, sounding board, cheerleader, and critic, all rolled into one. A mentoring relationship gives you someone with whom you can freely talk through problems, analyze and learn from your mistakes, and celebrate your successes. You quickly learn things you might normally find out only through the long process of trial and error.

American Society of Corporate
Secretaries (3,400)
1270 Avenue of the Americas
New York, NY 10020
Members are officers of corporations who
deal with boards of directors, sharehold-
ers, and senior management.

Association of Certified Professional
Secretaries (300)
RO. Box 9223
Phoenix, AZ 85068
A support network for individuals who
have successfully completed the CPS
examination.

National Association of
Executive Secretaries (4,000)
900 S. Washington
Suite G13
Falls Church, VA 22046
Publishes the *Executive Salary Survey
Report* biennially.

National Association of
Legal Secretaries (17,000)
2250 East 73rd Street
Suite 550
Tulsa, OK 74136
Has certification program leading to
designation as a Professional Legal
Secretary (PLS).

Business Professionals of America (55,000)
5454 Cleveland Avenue
Columbus, OH 43231
A nonprofit vocational organization for
students enrolled in high school and post-
secondary business and/or office education programs.

Executive Women International (6,000)
515 S. 700E
Suite 2-3
Salt Lake City, UT 84102-2801
Members are firms, each of which is represented by individuals engaged in executive and administrative positions.

Office Automation Society
International (600)
RO. Box 374
McLean, VA 22101
For managers, educators, administrators,
and consultants involved with integration
and application of automated office sys-
tems and technology.

International Association of Administrative Professionals (38,000)
10502 NW Ambassador Drive
Kansas City, MO 64195
Sponsors the Institute for Certifying Secretaries and awards the CPS designation.
Coordinates and authorizes research and
provides public instruction related to the
secretarial profession. Publishes *Office Pro*
magazine.

Table 15.3

Professional
Associations of
Interest to Office
Professionals

Some organizations provide formal mentoring programs. However, in many cases, mentor-
protégé relationships evolve spontaneously and
exist informally. In any case, when you choose a
mentor, look for someone in a position you
aspire to, who is a role model, and who

Suppose an executive in your company has assumed a mentoring relationship with an individual that you and most other workers do not respect—in a professional sense. Is this an issue of importance to the mentor? Could there be something else going on with these feelings?

possesses skills you wish to develop. The ideal mentor will have navigated some of the same paths you hope to travel and can alert you to potential pitfalls.

Training Opportunities. Training opportunities for an administrative office manager abound both on and off the job. Look for opportunities to grow and learn.

On-the-Job Experiences. Be open to coaching, understudy assignment, job rotation, lateral promotion, project and committee assignments, and staff meetings.

Off-the-Job Experiences. Participate in case studies, management games, role playing, and sensitivity training.

Message *for* AOMs

The words of Elnor G. Hickman, CPS and past president of Professional Secretaries International, perhaps best sum up the major content areas in this chapter. Allow me to quote her, because I believe her words are inspirational and realistic for those preparing to enter the world of work and who aspire to become an administrative office manager.

"Each of us enter the administrative office profession for different reasons, but we should focus on unified goals that will help office workers reach higher degrees of excellence:

• Embrace the changes that are transforming our jobs and our profession; learn new skills; assume new responsibilities; further our education;

• Recognize that ours is a diverse, demanding, and dynamic profession. Network with colleagues and use the resources offered by Professional Secretaries International and other groups to attain our professional best; and

• Prepare for the future by mentoring, training, and accepting leadership positions that will ensure the profession's ongoing growth and success.

John Ruskin, an English essayist, once said: 'A profession is not only a way to make a living, it is a way to make a life.' For us, the secretarial/office profession is a way to make a living, a way to make a life, and a way to make a difference."[10]

1 Some trends are (1) "Virtual" organizations will replace traditional companies with collaborative networks; (2) Lifetime jobs will be a thing of the past; (3) Businesses will outsource more functions to stay flexible in times of rapid change; and (4) The new ultra-mobile workforce will increasingly work out of "briefcase offices."

2 Computer networks, image technology, massive data storage, and artificial intelligence are the new technologies that will reshape today's occupations and become vital tools for most office workers.

3 Administrative career job titles include administrative assistant, senior secretary, executive secretary, desktop publishing/graphics specialist, production word processor, and administrative receptionist.

4 "Infotech" consists primarily of computing, combined with telecommunications and networking, and best describes the way in which all workers will perform their job tasks.

5 Computer monitoring may act as a prompter, reminding the office workers of special details when talking with customers, or as a coach, giving tips on improving performance.

6 The five stages of career development are preparing for work (1–25), selecting job opportunities (18–25), making early career choices (25–40), making mid-career choices (40–55), and making late career choices (55–retirement).

7 In professional organizations and associations, members are provided opportunities to acquire skills and professional credentials, to find or become a mentor, or simply to enjoy the social aspect of the group and network with others who share common interests and professional goals.

8 A mentoring relationship is one which gives you someone with whom you can freely talk through problems, analyze and learn from your mistakes, and celebrate your successes.

summary chapter 15

QUESTIONS FOR CRITICAL THINKING

1. Of the predictions about the workplace mentioned in the chapter, which two do you think will affect your life most? Why?

2. Of the information technologies mentioned in the chapter, which two do you think will affect your life most? Why?

3. Describe why you either agree or disagree with this statement: "Today's secretary is a goal-oriented manager."

4. Give your reactions to working in an office that has only a shared space where your personal projects and belongings are kept in a cabinet or locker instead of a traditional office.

5. Is the Infotech worker already on the job? Explain.

6. In your opinion, if a person does not want to be monitored on the job by a computer, should he or she have a choice in the matter?

7. At this point in your life, which one of these goals motivates you most now: financial, power, status, or career? State why you selected the one you did.

8. Would you personally go through the time and effort to prepare a portfolio as described in the chapter? Why or why not?

9. Based on your own experiences, do you know people who currently belong to professional associations? Why do you think they do?

10. Do you believe you would feel comfortable in a mentor-protégé relationship? Why or why not?

Case Study 15-1: Impressions and Promotions

Estelle Lopez has been on her new office job for about 15 weeks. She likes the job very much and eagerly continues to learn as much as she can about it. You, as her supervisor, consider Estelle an excellent employee because of her enthusiasm and her willingness to take on new responsibilities.

Though Estelle tries to do her best in all areas of her employment, she has a problem with grooming. She doesn't realize it, but the clothes she wears are more appropriate for a rock concert than an office setting. You call Estelle in for her 3-month evaluation and praise her for her excellent working habits, her punctuality, and her dependability.

Then you ask her about her career goals. Estelle responds that she eagerly looks forward to advancement and more responsibility. In fact, she says that someday she would like to become an AOM, just like you. You look surprised and tell Estelle that you thought she was more of a fun-loving gal than a serious career-minded woman. You explain that you arrived at these conclusions strictly from the way she dressed, not from her job performance.

Estelle is very surprised, and a little hurt; her attitude about the job is still good though.

Discussion Questions

1. What would you do as the AOM at this point, assuming Estelle wants to change her

image as quickly as possible and have you regard her more seriously?

2. In your opinion, is this a realistic "dress and grooming" situation that occurs in offices today on a regular basis?

Case Study 15-2: Updated Job Titles

Aspen Rental Company, a time-share condominium rental service that primarily serves the ski areas of Colorado, employs approximately 100 employees. Thomas Calvin, managing partner, has asked Kimberly Bruckner, AOM, to help him redefine career titles in the organization using a list similar to that of Table 15.1.

Kimberly is to review the list and come up with six job titles that would "fit the company." Currently, most of the thirty employees who primarily do office-related work are referred to as "secretaries."

Discussion Questions

1. List a minimum of six job titles; use Table 15.1

2. Tell why you selected those specific job titles for this particular organization.

Case Study 15-3: Internet Research Activity

Assume you are giving a speech entitled *Predictions About the Workplace.*

Use the Internet to research information needed to answer the following questions. Key your responses.

1. As two of your sources, use the publications, *The Futurist* and *Vital Speeches.*

2. As a result of your search, prepare an outline of your speech.

Endnotes

[1]Matt Siegel, "The Perils of Culture Conflict," *Fortune,* November 9, 1998, p. 257.

[2]Galen Bangsund, "Welcome to the Future," *The Secretary,* June/July 1995, p. 10.

[3]"Market Research: Outsourcing Services on the Upswing," *InfoWorld,* December 14, 1998, p. 22.

[4]Justin Martin, "Hunting Down the Porn Freaks," *Fortune,* July 21, 1997, p. 116.

[5]Deborah Branson, "Big Brother @ the.Office.com: Your Boss Can Track Every Click You Make," *Newsweek,* April 27, 1998, p. 78.

[6]R. J. Ignelzi, "Privacy: The Workplace Under Scrutiny," *Beacon-News* (Aurora, IL), April 7, 1996, pp. D1+.

[7]Dana Hawkins, "Who's Watching Now?" *U.S. News & World Report,* September 15, 1997, pp. 56–57.

[8]"Seven Tips for Career Preparation," *NBEA Keying In,* January 1995, p. 8.

[9]Paulette Gladis, CPS, "Reach for the Stars: Become a Certified Professional Secretary Holder," *The Secretary,* October 1994, p. 3.

[10]Elnor G. Hickman, "Degrees of Excellence," *The Secretary,* April 1995, p. 8.

Part IV:
Debate the Issue

1. Retrieve the file *Part IV-Debate*, which contains the table shown below, from the template disk. Using the form for each of the three issues listed in step 3, quickly key some ideas you have as initial reactions to each statement.

2. Prepare to role play either point of view in a mock in-class debate.

3. Part IV debate issues follow:

   a. "We live in a society fraught with information overload. Before long, we will become so paralyzed by all this information that it will be impossible to sort out what we need from what we don't need."

   b. "The computer has become an intruder in many homes because it negatively affects the quality and quantity of family communication, in much the same way that television has."

   c. "In terms of career advancement for an administrative office manager, there has never been a better time."

POINTS OF AGREEMENT	POINTS OF DISAGREEMENT
1.	1.
2.	2.
3.	3.
4.	4.

systems

compensation

safety

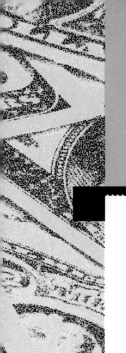

part 5

Managing Office Environment Issues

Other Essential Communication Skills

chapter 16

> "Speech is power: Speech is to persuade, to convert, to compel.
>
> —*Emerson*"

It becomes clearer every day that good communication skills are critical in attaining success in life. How effectively you communicate can make your daily activities either easy and pleasant or difficult and upsetting. The ability to communicate effectively is a skill that you can acquire just like any other skill. For example, the same practice and awareness of basic principles needed to become a good basketball player are needed to become a good communicator.

READING, WRITING, AND SPEAKING SKILLS IN BUSINESS

To be a good communicator in business, workers must practice effective reading, writing, and speaking skills, as well as listening skills, which are discussed later in the chapter.

Madelyn P. Jennings

Senior Vice President of Personnel
Gannett Company
Arlington, Virginia

Madelyn Pulver Jennings is senior vice president of personnel for the Gannett Company, a news and information company that publishes 81 daily newspapers, including *USA Today*. Gannett also has television and radio stations in major markets across the country and operates the largest outdoor advertising company in North America.

Madelyn joined Gannett in 1980. She previously held executive positions at Standard Brands and General Electric. She has a bachelor's degree in business and economics from Texas Women's University.

Madelyn serves on many boards of directors and committees, including the American Press Institute, Emory Business School's Center for Leadership and Career Studies Board of Advisors, George Washington University's School of Business and Public Management Associates Council, the Conference Board's Advisory Council on Human Resources Management, the University of Illinois Institute of Labor and Industrial Relations Advisory Committee, and UCLA's Human Resources Outlook Panel.

QUESTION:

I understand that your company uses the Standard Metropolitan Statistical Area (SMSA) figures as one criterion when setting the advancement goals for your operating unit's workforce. How has the diverse ethnic and gender mix reflected in the SMSA figures affected your career-advancement program?

Dialog *from the* Workplace

RESPONSE:

Our goal is that our workforce reflect the makeup of the communities where we operate.

To do that, we focus on the top four of the nine EEO categories—managers, professionals, technicians, and sales jobs—the positions with the most economic clout. We compare the SMSA minority and female labor force percentages for each of those categories as well as the total labor force percentage as indicators of available people. For jobs recruited on a regional or national basis, we use those labor force statistics for comparisons. Managers' compensation is based in part on achieving employment parity in each job category with the labor force availability.

This method has served to focus our efforts using an easily understood goal. Beyond that, we periodically review our ranks from an organizational standpoint to make sure minorities and women are fairly represented throughout, from the board room to the mailroom.

Each year, we review our progress to see how we're doing. We analyze the number of openings that occurred. When you have an opening, that's your opportunity for outreach efforts which enable you to help make change happen. Of all the openings which occurred, we look to see how many minorities and women were selected. If a unit's employee population is not representative of the makeup of its community, we expend extra efforts to find diverse slates of candidates.

We make sure that once employees are hired, they have access to training and development opportunities locally through a satellite network of educational programs and through the corporate training and development library. We recently introduced a career development program called "Where Do I Go from Here," which is made available through workshops and for self-directed study.

The result of these programs is a diverse workforce which we're convinced represents a "competitive edge" for us . . . in attracting and retaining people of promise and in the bottom line performance of our company.

Effective Reading Techniques

You may have discovered in preparing for exams that time spent reading materials can be either well spent or lost. Whether preparing for an exam or reviewing a business report, you can get more out of your time, energy, and efforts by following a few basic steps. The basic steps in reading for information are (1) previewing, (2) questioning, and (3) reviewing (PQR). This method is sometimes called the PQR system.

Previewing. Experienced readers preview the material before they start to read for comprehension. **Previewing** means scanning the selection, looking for main points, and discovering how the material is organized. To preview a report, for example, skim the preface, then turn to the table of contents and examine it to see how the main ideas are related to one another. Finally, leaf through the report to get a feel for what is there. If there is a summary, read it. If not, read the first and last paragraphs of each major section to get a general idea of what the report is about.

Questioning. Become an active reader by taking a questioning approach to the material. Ask yourself: Why am I reading this? How will this material meet my needs? What do I already know about this topic? Asking and answering questions as you read helps you master the material and keeps you focused.

Reviewing. Most of the time, reading something once is not enough. You should review what you read to fix it in your memory. You can do this by using three processes: seeing, saying, and writing. First, go back over the material, skimming each section of the article. As you *see* the material, *say* the answers to your questions aloud. Then *write* brief reference notes that summarize the main points. This review method helps you remember by organizing and repeating the material.

Effective Writing Techniques

Knowledge may be power, but communications skills are the primary raw materials of good

Effective writing relies upon adhering to the 5 Cs: complete, clear, concise, coherent, and correct.   © *PhotoDisc, Inc.*

client relationships. Regardless of your technical skills, you probably won't move up in an organization until your writing skills measure up. Writing ability is especially important in customer communication. Business proposals, status reports, customer documentation, or even e-mail replies all depend on clear, written communication.[1]

Related directly to reading office letters, memos, reports, and other related paperwork is the skill of writing business documents. Researchers estimate that American businesses generate more than 30 billion pieces of original writing each year. Workers on average spend one-third of their time on the job writing letters, memos, and reports.[2] Much of the writing, however, is unnecessary; most of it is poorly written; and all of it has to be read. Thus, a great amount of time is wasted not only by the millions of people who have to write on the job but also by those who have to read all of this writing. Companies can cut the waste of this less-than-effective writing by encouraging everyone to write succinctly and in plain English. Table 16.1 suggests ten steps you can take to become a more effective writer.

Use of the 5 Cs to check your writing is an effective method to use. The five Cs are *complete, clear, concise, coherent,* and *correct.* Briefly, when you "fine tune" your writing effort according to these five criteria, you question your written words and ideas by asking the following:

1. *Complete.* Are all of the reader's questions answered? Does the reader have enough information to evaluate the message and, if necessary, to act on it?

2. *Clear.* Does the reader get the meaning you intended? Does the reader have to guess what is meant?

3. *Concise.* Does the style, organization, and visual impact of the message help the reader to read, understand, and act on the information as quickly as possible?

4. *Coherent.* Are the ideas presented in a logical, consistent manner that makes it easy for the reader to follow and understand and, if necessary, lead to a decision or conclusion?

5. *Correct.* Is the information in the message accurate? Is the message free from errors in punctuation, spelling, grammar, word order, and sentence structure?

Some additional business writing suggestions:

1. *Be specific.* Misunderstandings usually arise when your writing lacks clarity. For example, don't write "I will get the report to you in a couple of weeks." Instead, write "I will get the report to you by September 15."

2. *Avoid redundancies.* Many writers like to use two words with nearly the same meaning in their sentences, erroneously thinking these add emphasis to the message. Instead, these redundancies add bulk. Two examples are *pleased* and *delighted, help* and *support.* Using either word, not both, gets your message across just as effectively.

3. *Be positive, even when the message is negative.* Think about it; don't you find yourself responding more to positive statements rather than negative ones? For example, instead of writing "The budget will not cover

1. Determine the purpose of the correspondence. Ask yourself: What is the reason for writing the letter? What response is required?

2. Decide which kind of letter or report is needed. If you are writing a letter, should it be good news, bad news, or persuasive? If you are writing a report, should it be direct or indirect?

3. Make notes of important points to bring out in the letter. List everything that needs to be said, in no particular order.

4. Organize the notes by topics. Arrange the points as you want to present them.

5. Free write. Write the correspondence as you talk. In other words, let your writing do the talking. Don't worry about spelling, grammar, and punctuation at this point. These can be corrected later.

6. Use appropriate sentence structure and length. Your writing should contain a variety of sentence lengths. Remember, long sentences may be difficult to read, and too many short sentences may make your writing seem choppy.

7. The writing should contain several paragraphs. Short paragraphs permit the reader to identify the facts and points of emphasis.

8. Revise. Read the correspondence for content. If it is not correct, revise.

9. Edit. After writing the initial draft, you should take a break from the task of writing. After this break, you should read the draft, correcting the spelling and grammar as you read.

10. Ask for input. Ask a colleague to read the letter for you. Welcome any feedback.

Table 16.1

Ten Steps to More
Effective Writing

Source: "Basics for Better Business Writing," by Annette Vincent, Ph.D., The Secretary, *March 1995, p. 8. Reprinted with permission from the March 1995 issue of* The Secretary® *Copyrighted 1995 Professional Secretaries International®.*

trip expenses over $100." Write "The budget will cover trip expenses up to $100."

4. ***Turn passive voice into active voice.*** Readers can visualize an active statement more easily than they can a passive one. For example, "A meeting will be held on Thursday" is better stated in this way: "We will meet on Thursday."

Effective Speaking Techniques

From the time you get up in the morning until you go to sleep at night, you use your voice to communicate. At home, you converse with your family about the events of the day. With your friends, you chat about whatever concerns you. You use the telephone to talk about business and personal matters. At school, you ask and answer questions in class and speak with other students. At work, you give directions, explain things, ask and answer questions, participate in meetings, and talk with customers and co-workers. In addition, you may occasionally give oral presentations at school, clubs, church, or work.

When addressing a group, it is important to keep your voice in top form and your nerves from showing. Here are some fine points used by professional speakers. First, avoid ice water because it tends to constrict the throat. Also avoid milk products, as they are inclined to coat your throat. In addition, it is best to drink lukewarm water with lemon instead of carbonated drinks, coffee, or tea because caffeine dries your mouth. Petroleum jelly on your teeth will keep your lips from sticking to them. Thus prepared, you can concentrate on your message.[3]

When you speak, try to give clear examples, use appropriate language, repeat information, ask questions, and use your voice effectively. Remember, when we speak, our voices tell others a lot about us. Here are some facts about your voice that you need to know:

1. ***Your voice has a vital role in confirming another person's first impression of you.*** If you sound harsh and abrasive, timid and insecure, or strong and confident, you will likely be viewed that way.

2. ***Your voice has a physiological effect on your listener.*** Speak rapidly and the listener's heart rate and adrenaline level increase. Shout at someone and their blood pressure rises. Speak calmly, and they feel a soothing effect.

3. ***Your voice is a barometer of your physical and emotional state.*** It reveals stress before other physical signs, reflects how tired you are, or gives clues to other emotions. For example, the voice of a person who is upset, tense, angry, or afraid rises.

> **Management Tip**
>
> *Stage fright in public speaking can be substantially reduced if you know **what** you want to say, **why** it is an important message for your audience, and **how** you will best communicate the importance of that message.*

Endless opportunities are available to improve your speaking skills and learn more effective speaking techniques. You may consider, for example, joining a local Toastmasters Club, taking a Dale Carnegie class, or signing up for a public-speaking course at a local college.

LISTENING AND HELPING SKILLS IN BUSINESS

Good listening habits foster success on the job. Think of the times that someone has asked you a question that you had just answered. Or remember the times when someone cut you off and just started talking when you were trying to communicate a problem and needed someone to listen and help you through that process. If this is unpleasant in casual conversation, think how annoying it is when conducting business, especially when you are on the receiving end of the "poor listener" or nonhelping agent.

Actively listening to and empathizing with what other people have to say are two important qualities of leaders. Effective leaders recognize that people have a need to be heard,

Management Tip

When taking a message for someone, the three most important things you can remember to do, other than take the message accurately, are to record the date, time, and your name on the message. The receiver of the message can contact you about it, if necessary.

especially in the turbulent work environment of today. In this environment, empathy is as valued as the willingness to listen. Employees, who are given greater responsibilities and are under more and more pressure, are looking for people who understand what they are going through.[4]

Effective Listening Skills

Most of us are not rude or insensitive to others when we lapse into poor listening practices. There are some realistic and honest roadblocks to effective listening that all of us experience from time to time:

1. Our minds will not wait; our thoughts race along four to ten times faster than most people speak.

2. We think we know already, so we listen with "half-an-ear."

Ethics/Choices

Georgia Candelaria, a co-worker of yours, has a son who was recently diagnosed with nonoperative cancer. Since being told by her son's physician, she has understandably been unable to focus and get her work completed on schedule. As a result, most people in the department have been covering for her. She considers the matter too personal to discuss and wants to protect her family's privacy. Do you continue to tell management nothing?

3. We are looking, but not listening. Have you ever been introduced to someone and failed to catch the person's name because you were focused on his or her clothes or mannerisms?

4. We are busy listeners; we try to do too many things while we listen.

5. We miss the big ideas; we are listening to words, not ideas.

6. Our emotions make us deaf when someone offers opposing ideas on matters about which we have strong opinions.[5]

Active Listening

Good listening skills in the office do not just happen. Instead, they are practiced through an awareness that listening is one of the most essential business skills you can have. One technique to develop and use is called active listening. **Active listening** is a restatement of the sender's total communication (thoughts and feelings), helping the sender to understand both the thoughts and feelings of his or her communication as you view them.

How do you listen actively? You do this by feeding back the underlying feelings you hear as well as the content of the message. Examples are "You sound upset when he uses your equipment" or "You are not pleased with the way the report is coming, are you?" Evaluate your abilities as an active listener by answering the questions posed in Table 16.2.

Effective Helping Skills

Effective leaders listen empathetically. When someone quietly asks, "Do you have a minute?"

Instructions:

Respond to each of the following ten questions with either a *yes* or *no* response, and check your score according to the scale at the bottom.

Do You . . .

1. Limit your talking during conversations? (You can't talk and listen at the same time.)

2. Think like the customer? Can you understand and appreciate the customer's point of view?

3. Ask questions? If you don't understand something, do you clear it up now so it doesn't embarrass you later?

4. Interrupt another speaker? (A pause, even a long one, doesn't always mean that the sender has finished what he or she wants to say.)

5. Concentrate on what is being said and practice shutting out distractions?

6. Take brief notes to help remember important points?

7. Listen for ideas, not just words?

8. Turn off personal fears, worries, and problems when dealing with others?

9. React to ideas, not the person?

10. Allow the speaker to complete sentences? Or do you jump to conclusions by mentally or verbally completing sentences for the speaker?

Score Your Yes Responses

8–10   You're a good active listener.

5–7   You're making an effort to become an active listener.

4 & under   Oops, have you wondered why it is difficult to get a conversation going?

Table 16.2

Are You an Active Listener?

they may really be crying out, "I need you to hear (and feel) this!" When you take the time to listen with empathy, you build the trust and commitment that creates an environment poised for success.[6]

Sometimes a customer or co-worker is upset and needs someone just to listen while he or she talks through a problem. When you perceive cues that the other person is experiencing a communication problem like this, and you *choose* to be a helping agent, there are a number of communication skills that you can use. These skills are listed in order of increasing activity and involvement on your part:

1. ***Silence.*** Simply listening passively with accompanying nonverbal behaviors (posture, eye contact, nodding of the head, etc.) communicates your interest and concern.

On the phone, your voice speaks volumes. Be energetic and enthusiastic.
© *PhotoDisc, Inc.*

2. ***Noncommittal acknowledgment.*** Brief expressions that encourage the person to continue talking toward an eventual solution communicate your understanding, acceptance, and empathy. Examples: "Oh, I see" and "Mm-hmm."

3. ***Door openers.*** Gently inviting the speaker to expand or continue the expressions of thoughts and feelings shows you are interested and involved. Examples: "Tell me about it." "Would you like to talk about it?"

4. ***Content paraphrasing.*** Putting the factual portion of the message into your own words and sending it back to check your accuracy indicates an attempt to understand the situation. Examples: "So you really told your boss off." "You're saying that if your plan works, the problem will be solved."

COMMUNICATING EFFECTIVELY ON THE TELEPHONE

In modern office technology, the telephone is the most sophisticated tool used by the largest number of employees. This tool is utilized to generate revenue, provide services, and resolve problems all in the course of any normal business day. Conversely, the telephone can also be the vehicle by which revenue is lost and problems are created.

In face-to-face business dealings, first impressions are both visual and physical in nature. The proper attire, a warm smile, and a firm handshake are the entree to the business activity. In telephone business dealings, abrupt or improper greetings are virtually impossible to recover from, because the caller holds the ultimate power in the telephone business deal by his or her ability to simply hang up and call someone else.

The visual dimension of communication is lost when you talk on the telephone. Power of facial expression, eye contact, and gestures to communicate are gone. Instead, you must rely only on your words and voice to convey your message. You must concentrate on identifying yourself and being courteous and attentive in order to communicate effectively on the phone.

Telephones are everywhere, and you have been using them all your life. But do you use the telephone properly? Tips on telephone etiquette, as well as how to place and receive calls, are critical to personal and business success. Regardless of the particular business situation, the following general tips can help you effectively master using the common piece of office equipment called the telephone:

1. Talk directly into the mouthpiece with your lips about an inch from the phone. Do not let the telephone slip below your chin.

2. Speak at a normal volume. If the connection is bad, place the call again.

3. Enunciate clearly so you will be understood.

4. Tell the other person what you are doing if you have to leave the line. Give the caller a choice regarding whether to hold for you or not.

5. Handle the receiver gently as you put it down on a table or desk. The noise it makes can amplify and disturb the person calling.

6. Gently put the receiver in the cradle when you hang up the phone.

In addition to these tips, Table 16.3 lists some time-tested procedures to follow when placing outgoing and receiving incoming calls.

DESIGNING AND WRITING OFFICE PROCEDURES

Every office needs some order and organization, as we have previously discussed. Part of the process in successfully managing office technologies is to develop work procedures. A **procedure** is a written, step-by-step standardized pattern of behavior that is followed when completing a specific task or activity. Written procedures are especially helpful when training new workers or when retraining current workers in new methods. Procedures further add continuity to the organization by providing some consistency among workers in handling routine tasks.

Although all office tasks are not routine and predictable, the majority of them are and should have written procedures. If you are the one responsible for writing a procedure, how do you go about the task? Although the content of a procedure is most important, it is best for all procedures to be written in a consistent manner. You will be more successful if you keep these few simple ideas in mind:

1. Number each step in sequence.

2. Always start each numbered step with an action verb, such as *sort, verify, key,* or *open.*

3. Use simple words and easy-to-understand language.

PLACING CALLS	RECEIVING CALLS
1. Choose the right time. Try to call during business hours and avoid lunchtime. Take time zones into consideration.	1. Pick up within three rings.
2. Be on the phone before the other party is, should someone else place a call for you. When you make people wait for you, they may feel that you think your time is more important than theirs.	2. Identify yourself immediately, and smile to make your voice sound pleasant. If the call came through a switchboard, answer by first giving the department name and then identifying yourself. If the call came directly, answer by first giving the company name and then your name.
3. Assume that someone is available to pick up the phone until after at least eight rings.	3. Transfer calls only if necessary. If you transfer a call, tell the other party the name of the person and extension of the other party in case the call gets disconnected during transfer.
4. Identify yourself promptly, and then give the name of the person to whom you want to talk.	4. Put calls on hold or leave the line only if you cannot avoid doing so. Always ask the caller's permission first. If you must keep a caller waiting more than thirty seconds, check back and explain the delay. If the delay is going to be long, ask if you may call back.
5. Make the call brief. Show that you value the other person's time. Make a checklist of subjects you wish to cover and have all the necessary information needed to ask or answer questions. This may include file folders, notes, and a calendar.	5. Give your undivided attention to every phone call. Stop any work you are doing so you can concentrate entirely on the caller. Always have a message pad or notepaper and pen or pencil ready. Set aside the problems of the day and have a positive attitude.
6. Say the first "good-bye" or "thank you" when you have initiated the call.	6. Avoid using slang such as "yeah" or "huh."
7. Be prepared to leave an accurate and complete voice mail message.	7. Always get the caller's telephone number when taking a message for someone. This saves looking it up. If you cannot spell the caller's name, ask the caller to spell it for you. Before you hang up, read the information back to the caller to ensure accuracy.

Table 16.3

Procedures to
Follow When
Placing and
Receiving Calls

Message *for* AOMs

"People judge you by what they hear from you. You may be the most efficient, best-intentioned, smartest manager in your organization, but neither efficiency, good intentions, nor brains will do you much good unless you can communicate—that is, get your message across.

Your professional image depends on your communication skills.

Communication plays another role that is equally important in your professional life. Your success in business depends on your ability to influence others. A businessperson is a leader. To lead, you must be able to get people to listen to you, to understand you, and to react to you—as you want them to behave. People judge your ideas—as they judge you—by your ability to communicate.[7]

When you communicate as a manager, remember the power of these words and phrases:[8]

The SIX Most Important Words: "I admit I made a mistake."
The FIVE Most Important Words: "You did a good job."
The FOUR Most Important Words: "What is your opinion?"
The THREE Most Important Words: "If you please"
The TWO Most Important Words: "Thank you."
The ONE Most Important Word: "We"
The LEAST Important Word: "I"

1 The steps in the PQR reading system are previewing, questioning, and reviewing. Previewing means scanning the selection, looking for main points, and discovering how the material is organized. Become an active reader by taking a questioning approach to the material. Review what you read to fix it in your memory.

2 One method is to check your writing according to the five Cs, which are *complete, clear, concise, coherent,* and *correct.*

3 Our voices tell others a lot about us in that (1) Your voice has a vital role in confirming another person's first impression of you; (2) Your voice has a physiological effect on your listener; and (3) Your voice is a barometer of your physical and emotional state.

4 Behaviors of active listeners are many, but some are that active listeners limit their talking during conversations, think like the cus-

tomer, ask questions, don't interrupt another speaker, take notes on important points, listen for ideas, react to ideas, and allow the speaker to complete sentences.

5 Some general tips to follow while using the telephone are (1) Talk directly into the mouthpiece with your lips about an inch from the phone; (2) Speak at a normal volume; (3) Enunciate clearly so you will be understood; (4) Tell the other person what you are doing if you have to leave the line; (5) Handle the receiver gently as you put it down on a table or desk; and (6) Gently put the receiver in the cradle when you hang up the phone.

6 An office procedure must be written with these items in mind: number each step in sequence; always start each numbered step with an action verb, such as *sort, verify, key,* or *open;* and use simple words and easy-to-understand language.

QUESTIONS FOR CRITICAL THINKING

1. Why is the PQR system for reading information effective?

2. At work, what are some examples of important speaking opportunities workers have to promote the well-being and image of an organization?

3. List some realistic and honest roadblocks to effective listening.

4. What are some thoughts to keep in mind when writing a procedure?

Case Study 16-1: Creating Effective Communication

Your organization has recently promoted several area managers. The employees in your company have been experiencing difficulty in understanding communications from these area managers, who work in the international arena. The vice president, Pat Montesanto, has asked you to develop a short checklist to orient managers on good communication and wants you to include intercultural considerations. She plans to have a training session soon.

Discussion Question

What items will you present on your checklist?

Case Study 16-2: Writing More Clearly

Georgia Moschou, vice president of office services at Mint Savings and Loan, believes that many of the reports prepared by the department managers are so poorly written that the messages become garbled in transmission. As a result, those receiving the messages have diffi-culty determining what action, if any, they are to take. Moschou's beliefs are confirmed by samples of her manager's reports that have been collected and analyzed over the past six months. Some of the findings of Moschou's audit are given here:

1. Words and phrases should be simplified. What short, simple words can the managers use instead?

   a. afford an opportunity   f. interrogate
   b. prioritize   g. utilization
   c. voluminous   h. finalize
   d. consummate   i. profitwise
   e. automatization   j. substantial portion

2. There are a few "static-loaded" sentences. How can these sentences be revised to communicate more clearly by using simple words?

   a. The antiquated electronic calculator housed in my office is ineffectual for solving the sophisticated mathematical problems I encounter.

   b. It is imperative that all unwarranted absenteeism be adequately investigated so reminders can be promulgated to the parties at fault.

   c. The customer's dilatory actions precipitated the necessity for our loan people to respond with exiguous information.

Instructions

Give Moschou a helping hand by answering the questions she has raised.

Case Study 16-3: Internet Research Activity

Assume that you are doing a report on *business communication over the telephone.* Use the Internet to research information needed to answer the following question. Key your responses.

1. Which Web search engine did you use?

2. Write down three of the URL addresses that you accessed during your search.

3. As a result of your search, list three items of current information you might use in your report. You might want to find the web pages of your local telephone company (US West, Sprint, MCI, etc.), as they may contain some links that would assist in gathering this information.

Endnotes

[1]Paula Jones, "Strong Writing Skills Essential for Success, Even in IT," *InfoWorld,* July 6, 1998, p. 86.

[2]Jim Evers, "Write On! Tips for Effective Communication," *HR Focus,* August 1993, p. 54.

[3]Roberta Maynard, "How to Speak with Confidence," *Nation's Business,* September 1995, p. 12.

[4]Alexander Lucia, "Leaders Know How to Listen," *HR Focus,* April 1997, p. 25.

[5]From material presented by Jerry Odell, human resources manager, at a communications workshop in Flagstaff, Arizona, in January 1993.

[6]Ibid.

[7]George Shinn, *Leadership Development* (New York: McGraw-Hill Book Company, 1986).

[8]From material presented by Jerry Odell, human resources manager, at a communications workshop in Flagstaff, Arizona, in January 1993.

Employee Recognition and Compensation

chapter 17

o b j e c t i v e s

After completing this chapter, you will be able to:

1. Identify the effects on the dismissed employee when he or she is terminated from a job.

2. Describe the difference between the worker who is exempt and one who is nonexempt.

3. List the general categories of indirect compensation plans.

4. Contrast the power of the union-represented worker with the power of the employer.

5. Describe the relationship between a policy and a procedure.

> As within, so without: your outer life will tend to be a mirror-image of your inner life. In other words, your external world of material accomplishment will correspond to your internal world of preparation.
>
> —*Anonymous*

The responsibilities of the administrative office manager in promotion and compensation matters are primarily to monitor employee attendance and productivity for compensation purposes and ultimately to match performance with commensurate rewards. The AOM also assists the human resources department in ensuring that compensation is in line and competitive with community and/or industry ranges to retain workers.

Typically, of course, wage rates and salary schedules are formulated by top management, by the human resources department, by union

Robert J. Sahl

Founder and General Partner
WMS and Co., Inc.
King of Prussia, Pennsylvania

The management consulting firm, WMS and Co., Inc., provides broad-base consulting service to clients in many areas, including compensation plan design, performance appraisal, individual assessments, management development, and management succession planning. Dr. Robert J. Sahl is a general partner of the firm and directs its Applied Behavioral Sciences consulting.

Prior to founding WMS and Co., Dr. Sahl was a principal with Hay Associates, where he aided companies in the selection, placement, and development of management personnel through psychological assessment. His experiences include conducting management development seminars, formulating team-building programs, vocational guidance, and career path planning. Over the years, Dr. Sahl has been heavily involved in developing and installing base and incentive compensation programs for a number of organizations varying in size and nature of business. He has also conducted industry-specific compensation surveys.

Dr. Sahl's academic background is a B.S. in psychology from Albright College, an M.S. in personnel psychology from George Washington University, and a Ph.D. in industrial psychology from Colorado State University.

Dialog *from the* Workplace

QUESTION:

When talking with a client about the need for evaluating office and clerical jobs, what benefits do you set forth?

RESPONSE:

When an organization determines a need to evaluate its jobs, it is embarking on a process from which a number of benefits will be derived. First, the organization will end up with an internally equitable rank ordering of its positions. This will be based on the consistent application of the same measurement tool for measuring all jobs. This internally equitable rank ordering of jobs will get translated into a salary range for each job. These ranges will then be internally fair. This is essential for maintaining employee morale.

With this same set of data, the organization can relate its current pay practices to the marketplace and see how competitive they currently are. If a more (or less) competitive posture is desired, the salary ranges can be adjusted over time. In this manner, another benefit is realized. The organization is now neither overpaying nor underpaying its people. This results in the optimal use of payroll dollars and can reduce turnover as people recognize they are fairly paid in the market.

Typically with this approach, each position ends up with a salary range. People may be moved through this range on the basis of their performance. Hence, a third benefit surfaces. The organization can now strengthen the relationship between pay and performance.

Sometimes organizations inadvertently promote people into a "smaller" job. Once jobs have been evaluated, however, this will not occur. It now becomes a relatively straightforward process to gauge the size and reasonableness of a promotion. This, then becomes another benefit to be realized.

contract, or by government legislation or regulation. Nevertheless, within such limitations, AOMs have some responsibility in establishing standards for promotion and compensation that will attract and retain competent office support staff.

PROMOTIONS AND TERMINATIONS

In the careers of most workers, there comes a time when recognition comes for a job well done, as well as the time, for some, when separating from the company is requested.

Promotions

Successful promotion plans are definite, systematic, fair, and followed uniformly. A promotion plan must have the confidence of the employees. To provide for promotions based upon objective data and not solely upon personal opinion and assessment, the human resources department should maintain a database of all personnel. Commonly, we find that promotions are granted as rewards for successful work done in a previous position.

Terminations

No manager likes the unpleasant task of terminating a worker, but the reality is that it happens every day in organizations. Workers have a one-in-three chance of getting fired sometime during their working lives. The good news is, according to the survey, a "pink slip" does not carry with it the shame it once did. In many cases, employee termination has little or nothing to do with a person's competence or ability to do the job, but often reflects the need to reduce personnel across the board. As a result, employers today are less likely to hold such "firings" against job candidates.

Outcomes of Terminations. Regardless of the reasons or circumstances surrounding the dismissal, when an employee is released involuntarily from his or her job, the psychological bond is broken between employee and employer. What usually results is the employee's feeling a loss of control, loss of security, and loss of loyalty. If left unchecked, these feelings can manifest into increased stresses and distrust.

Moreover, when an employee is terminated, the employer and remaining staff are affected as well. Terminations have a ripple effect on those who stay. For example, those who stay may feel that the psychological bond is no longer valid

When terminating an employee, a manager should be sensitive, yet convey the message clearly. © *EyeWire*

with the organization, their loyalty is shaken, and their security is eroded. Typical reactions of those who stay may manifest as anger, distrust, guilt, relief, grief, and survivor shock.

More than 24,000 wrongful termination lawsuits were filed in federal court in 1997, up 77 percent from 1993. Short-staffed federal judges say wrongful termination cases are the biggest source of new litigation. Judges still throw out many wrongful termination lawsuits. But, when taken before juries, they are finding for the workers more than half the time. The threat of being sued, coupled with the fact that it is getting more difficult to fire workers, is driving many companies to hire workers from temporary services or to outsource entire departments.[1]

What should you as a manager do to allay these effects? Some suggestions are to increase communication with the remaining employees by being visible, providing consistent information, and soliciting employee concerns.

Exit Interviews. Because organizations lose money when employees who have been trained leave, they often conduct an exit interview and complete an exit interview form on each employee's last day of work. The purpose of an **exit interview** is to obtain information from departing employees concerning their experiences with various aspects of their employment. Management should see this as a means of evaluating its policies and procedures and not as a threat. Additionally, exit interviews are excellent ways to try to prevent important company business from disappearing along with an employee who is leaving. The mood should always be positive, but any avenues that might convey

information should be cut off early once termination of the employee has been announced.[2]

All exit interview data are prepared in statistical and/or summary form so the respondents are not linked to the responses. Furthermore, this confidential information does not become a part of the personnel file and is not seen by the employee's former manager. An example of an employee exit interview questionnaire is shown in Figure 17.1.

EMPLOYEE COMPENSATION AND BENEFITS

For the employee, salary and benefits are tangible rewards for services rendered. For the employer, salary and benefits are the single greatest expense in the budget. Therefore, it is essential that the company have a sound compensation program to motivate employees, yet keep labor costs at an acceptable level.

Compensation Legislation

As with other human resources issues, an AOM should understand the legal basis for compensation activity in his or her company. The two principal laws governing compensation activities are the Fair Labor Standards Act of 1938 (and its amendments) and the Equal Pay Act of 1963.

Fair Labor Standards Act. The **Fair Labor Standards Act (FLSA)**, passed in 1938, is the major law affecting compensation administration. Over the years, the FLSA has been amended several times in order to raise the minimum wage rates and expand on the types of employees covered. Four issues stemming from the FLSA are important for any manager to know:

1. The three major components of the FLSA are to (a) establish a minimum wage, (b) encourage limits on the number of weekly hours employees work through overtime provisions, and (c) discourage oppressive use of child labor.

2. The Wage and Hour Division of the U.S. Department of Labor enforces compliance with the provisions of the FLSA. Companies must maintain accurate employee time records for three years. Penalties for violations can include awards of back pay for affected current and former employees for up to two years.

3. The FLSA classifies employees as exempt or nonexempt. **Exempt employees** are not paid overtime and usually are classified as being in professional or administrative positions. An administrative office manager is an exempt employee. **Nonexempt employees** are paid overtime under the FLSA and are usually paid an hourly wage. There are, however, salaried-nonexempt positions like secretarial or clerical that fall under FLSA overtime provisions.

4. **Compensatory time off** ("comp time") is sometimes given in lieu of payment for time worked. In the private sector, comp time must be given at a rate of one-and-one-half times the hours worked over a forty-hour week.

Equal Pay Act of 1963. A second important piece of compensation legislation, already mentioned in Chapter 9, was passed as a major amendment to the FLSA. This amendment is called the Equal Pay Act of 1963 and is commonly referred to as the "equal pay for equal work" law. Except for differences that are justified on the basis of better performance, longer service, and quantity or quality of work, similar pay must be given for jobs requiring equal skills, equal effort, equal responsibilities, and similar working conditions.

Wage and Salary Administration

Appropriate compensation plays several vital roles in organizations. A good compensation plan (1) attracts capable employees, (2) motivates employees to perform effectively, and (3) helps retain capable employees. Part of the task in wage and salary administration is to determine what the average salaries or wages are for different types of positions.

Recognizing that jobs have different meanings to employers and employees, the goal of any compensation policy is to understand and reflect these differences equitably for both sides. Companies need to understand the politics and culture of an organization before a well-designed, useful compensation program can be implemented. A constant monitoring of the market to stay competitive is also necessary.[3]

The first step in developing a salary compensation policy is to gather and analyze external and internal data. This process is sometimes referred to as conducting a **wage survey.** If it is not feasible for an organization to conduct its own survey, an employer may use published wage surveys from sources such as trade associations and the U.S. Department of Labor.

Regardless of the source of the wage survey, the survey results must reflect several external and internal economic conditions. The external

Figure 17-1

Employee Exit
Interview
Questionnaire

INTERNATIONAL BUSINESS SERVICES

EMPLOYEE EXIT QUESTIONNAIRE

The following questionnaire was developed to obtain information from departing employees concerning their experiences with various aspects of employment. This questionnaire will assist IBS in evaluating its policies and procedures.

• This questionnaire will not become part of your personnel file and will not be seen by your former supervisor.

• The answers you give will be distributed only in statistical and/or summary form. Your answers will in no way affect your reemployment possibilities with International Business Services.

GENERAL INFORMATION

1. Your current position and department at IBS
    Position: _____
    Department: _____

2. Date hired into permanent position: _____

3. Separation Date: _____

4. Gender: ☐ Male   ☐ Female

5. Ethnicity (please check):
    ☐ African American   ☐ Asian/P. Islander   ☐ Native American
    ☐ Hispanic   ☐ White   ☐ Alaskan Native   ☐ Other

6. Job Classification (please check):
    ☐ Professional   ☐ Administrative

7. Is your separation from International Business Services (please check):
    ☐ Voluntary
    ☐ Other (Layoff, etc.)

REASON FOR LEAVING

Please use the following scale when answering these questions:

Strongly Agree	Agree	Neutral	Disagree Strongly	Disagree	Not Applicable
1	2	3	4	5	NA

My leaving IBS is due to the following reasons: (circle your response)

1. I am leaving the Phoenix area for another job.   1 2 3 4 5 NA
2. Family circumstances/health reasons.   1 2 3 4 5 NA
3. I have another job in Phoenix.   1 2 3 4 5 NA
4. Spouse is relocating to different area.   1 2 3 4 5 NA
5. I am going to return to school.   1 2 3 4 5 NA
6. Maternity/paternity concerns.   1 2 3 4 5 NA
7. Retirement/leaving job market.   1 2 3 4 5 NA
8. I have been generally dissatisfied in my job.   1 2 3 4 5 NA
9. Salary is not adequate/acceptable.   1 2 3 4 5 NA
10. Unsupportive/hostile work environment.   1 2 3 4 5 NA
11. What was/were your major reason(s) for leaving IBS?

economic factors are the local supply and demand of qualified labor, the going wage rates for the area, and cost of living factors. The internal factors that influence wage rates include the worth of the job to the company, the employee's worth (the education and years of experience an employee brings to the company), and the company's ability to pay.

Relative to gender, the latest government estimates indicate women closed the pay gap

Figure 17–1

Employee Exit
Interview
Questionnaire
(Concluded)

JOB SATISFACTION

Overall, I have been satisfied with . . . (circle your response)

1. the orientation/training.   1 2 3 4 5 NA
2. the physical condition of my work area. 1 2 3 4 5 NA
3. the work environment.   1 2 3 4 5 NA
4. the safety of my work surroundings.   1 2 3 4 5 NA
5. the support for a culturally diverse environment. 1 2 3 4 5 NA
6. my yearly salary.   1 2 3 4 5 NA
7. the benefit package.   1 2 3 4 5 NA
8. my career development at IBS.   1 2 3 4 5 NA
9. the additional training opportunities I received. 1 2 3 4 5 NA
10. co-worker relationships.   1 2 3 4 5 NA
11. the ease and effectiveness of IBS procedures. 1 2 3 4 5 NA
12. my ability to have input.   1 2 3 4 5 NA

WORK ENVIRONMENT

1. During your employment with IBS, do you believe that you have ever been sexually harassed?
   ☐ YES   ☐ NO   ☐ Not Sure
2. During your employment with IBS, do you believe that you have ever been discriminated against?
   ☐ YES   ☐ NO   ☐ Not Sure
3. If you answered "yes" to either question 1 or 2, did you report it? (if "no" skip to the next part.)
   ☐ YES   ☐ NO   ☐ Not Sure
4. Do you feel satisfied with how your issues were resolved?
   ☐ YES   ☐ NO   ☐ Not Sure

If "no" or "not sure," please explain:_____

PERFORMANCE APPRAISAL SYSTEM

1. Did you receive timely evaluations?   ☐ Yes   ☐ No
2. Did you believe your evaluations were fair? ☐ Yes   ☐ No
3. Did you believe your evaluations were helpful? ☐ Yes   ☐ No

UPON COMPLETION, PLEASE RETURN THIS FORM
TO HUMAN RESOURCES AND
SCHEDULE AN APPOINTMENT TO MEET WITH THE DIRECTOR

---

by three cents on the dollar between 1995 and 1996, but still trail men by 26 cents. Although many companies have successful programs to achieve pay equity among genders, most do not.[4]

Total Compensation Package

Although financial compensation is still important in fostering commitment and encouraging good performance, companies can further improve employee satisfaction and loyalty by making their employees feel they are needed, valued, and appreciated. Employers are assured of loyalty from their employees if they offer benefits that go beyond the usual monetary rewards. As Rosabeth Moss Kanter, the famous author and social scientist, once said: "Compensation is a right. Recognition is a gift." Employees are demanding to know that their hard work means something. If it doesn't mean something within organizations, people will find another employer with whom their work does mean something beyond a paycheck.[5]

An employee's **total compensation package** includes direct compensation and indirect compensation. **Direct compensation** is an employee's base pay as well as any incentive pay programs. **Indirect compensation** includes the whole array of benefits, some of which are required by law and others which are voluntary benefits offered by the company.

Direct Compensation.   Direct compensation to an employee is in the form of a wage (per hour amount) or salary (per month or yearly amount). Direct compensation can also include pay in the form of incentive plans. **Incentive plans** are optional but are usually based on set criteria established by the employer.

As an example of an incentive plan, we will use merit pay. Merit pay incentives are frequently paid by organizations. They are based on established criteria or performance at an exemplary level as usually reflected in an employee's performance appraisal. As with any incentive plan, merit pay has to be administered in a fair and equitable way for it to be motivating to the employee. When administering merit pay, the AOM should:

1. develop employee confidence and trust in the performance appraisal process,

2. separate merit pay from regular pay, and, most importantly,

3. establish job-related performance criteria against which merit pay will be determined.

Table 17.1 outlines the criteria on which incentive plans, such as commissions, piece rate, bonuses, stock options, profit sharing, and gainsharing, are based.

Indirect Compensation.   Indirect compensation plans, or benefits, are financial rewards and services provided to employees in addition to their regular earnings. Although there are different ways to categorize employee benefits, we shall refer to them according to these five categories: (1) benefits required by law, (2) pay for time not worked, (3) insurance plans, (4) security and retirement plans, and (5) miscellaneous benefits and services.

Benefits Required by Law.   Federal and state governments require employers to provide benefits under these government programs:

- *Federal:* Social Security, also known as the Old Age and Survivors Insurance (OASI) Program, includes four categories of benefits to those who qualify. These benefits include old age benefits, survivor benefits, disability benefits, and medical benefits. To be eligible, a worker must have contributed taxes into the system for ten years or forty quarters (three-month periods of time).
- *State:*
  a) Unemployment compensation, also referred to as unemployment insurance,

TYPES	BASED ON
Bonuses	Established goals or criteria
Commissions	Amount of sales
Gainsharing	Improved productivity or cost savings shown
Merit raises	Established criteria and policies
Piece rate	Units produced
Profit sharing	Organizational profits distributed proportionally to pay
Stock options	Achievement of specific goals
Stock ownership	Special purchase plans or bonus distributions

Table 17.1

Incentive Plans for Employees

provides unemployed workers with benefits from a fund of payroll taxes imposed on employers. To receive benefits under the law, the unemployed worker is required to register for employment at a U.S. employment office and usually must have worked for a certain period of time at a company before becoming unemployed.

b) Workers' compensation laws protect employees and their families from permanent loss of income and high medical payments as a consequence of accidental injury, illness, or death on the job. To collect workers' compensation, it does not matter who was at fault. Workers' compensation funds are provided primarily through employer contributions to a statewide fund. In some states, the amount to be paid for a given condition is stipulated in the law; in other states, guidelines are in place and judges and/or juries determine the fair and equitable payment, if any.

Pay for Time Not Worked. Most organizations today grant their employees pay for time not worked under certain conditions. These benefits normally include holidays, vacations, sick leave, jury duty, military service, and bereavement leaves.

Ethics/Choices

Suppose you were out late one evening and wanted to sleep in on a workday. Would you call in sick just because you have unused sick leave available? Why or why not?

Insurance Plans. Of all the benefit plans, this category is currently the most volatile. Because health-care costs rise so dramatically each year, some employers are now taking steps to limit these payments or require the employee to carry a higher percentage of the costs. Among the popular company-sponsored insurance plans are group life insurance, health-care insurance (medical and hospital), vision-care insurance, and dental insurance.

Security and Retirement Plans.

For many retirees, the pension, 401(K) accounts, and health-care benefits provided by their former employers are the core of their retirement security—both financial and emotional. **Pension plans** are retirement benefits established and funded by employers and employees. Though the government does not require employers to provide these plans, they cover about half of U.S. workers. Very controversial among organizations that choose to provide them, retiree health benefits are currently available to some employees. It may not last, however. As health-care costs rise dramatically, this benefit is in jeopardy.

Work/Life Benefits and Services.

With the reality of low wages, cutbacks in health insurance and the threat of being laid off are the very things that make families' lives so stressed. People must work longer hours just to maintain their standards of living. Employers have found that even a handful of relatively inexpensive work-family benefits can play a role in eliciting greater employee participation, loyalty, and job commitment, even from those who don't use them.[6]

As a result, companies continue to explore nontraditional solutions that will help employees better integrate work and life as part of their commitment to be an employer of choice. The basis of that belief lies in the concept that when people at work are distracted with personal issues, they are less effective in their jobs.[7] Companies therefore are attempting to help employees become more focused by offering nontraditional benefits. A new study by the Families and Work Institute found that although two-thirds of employers permit flextime job arrangements, nearly 40 percent don't bother to inform workers of the work/family assistance benefit programs available.[8] Table 17.2 outlines some unique offerings of these softer benefits to employees.

In addition to standard benefits, such as life insurance and medical coverage, employers are

Integrating work and life is a critical need for many workers today.
© EyeWire

BENEFIT	% IN 1994	% IN 1997	2000 PROJECTED
Alternative work arrangements	35	44	57
Long-term care insurance	10	18	46
Group financial planning	2	9	29
Prepaid legal services	4	7	21
Group auto insurance	8	14	35
Group homeowners insurance	NA	12	31

Source: Hewitt Associates, "What About Benefits?" Time, November 9, 1998, p. 122.

Table 17.2

"Softer"/Family-Friendly, Work/Life Employee Benefits

providing unconventional perks, including tickets to cultural events and free or reduced health club memberships. Moreover, companies are also helping employees cope with work and family demands by offering counseling, educational information, and referral assistance. You will see companies offer alternative work schedules in the form of telecommuting, flexible work hours, and job sharing to ensure the high quality of employees' work and professional lives. These benefits result in a win-win situation. Employees enjoy the comfort offered by these nontraditional provisions while employers benefit from lowered costs, loyal employees, and improved relationships.[9]

With so many benefit options available and the dramatic rise in the cost of health care, the dollars allocated to company benefits are stretched to capacity. For that reason, many employers are using a method of providing employees with flexible benefit packages called a **cafeteria benefit plan.**

Under the cafeteria plan, all employees receive a statement of the total dollar amount of benefits they are entitled to, along with the amount earmarked for legally required benefits. Each employee then tells the employer how to allocate the balance among the programs available. The major advantage of this benefit allocation approach is that benefit packages are better tailored to individual needs. Table 17.3 outlines the relationships among the total compensation packages employers can offer.

LABOR UNIONS

Labor unions are associations of employees formed to represent workforce concerns and interests during negotiations with management. In the past, workers have joined unions for the following reasons: higher pay, shorter hours of work, improved working conditions—both physical and psychological—and improved security. Although those reasons are still the central

DIRECT COMPENSATION	INDIRECT COMPENSATION
Base Pay: Wages and salaries	**Pay for Time Not Worked:** Vacations, breaks, holidays, sick pay, jury duty, and military duty
Incentives: Bonuses, commissions, gainsharing, merit raises, piece rate, profit sharing, stock options, and stock ownership	**Insurance Plans:** Medical, hospital, dental, life, and surgical
	Security Plans: Pension, social security, disability insurance
	Employee Services: Educational assistance, recreational programs, food services

Table 17.3

Total Employee
Compensation

motivators to joining the union, over the years membership has shifted downward in traditional occupations.

However, according to an article in the June 1998 *HR Focus* magazine, labor unions are employing aggressive and innovative organizing tactics to regain their political and economic clout. Backed by the AFL-CIO's commitment to spend $90 million on recruiting, labor has developed a coherent strategy to attract members. They are targeting industries that were considered low priority in the past, including professional groups and customer service operations. Labor is also employing full-time organizers, organizing on the Internet, and launching corporate campaigns.[10]

Union Membership and Influence

More than one-third of all American workers belonged to unions in 1950. By 1997, less than 15 percent of workers (only 10 percent of nongovernment workers) were union members. A recent AFL-CIO poll found that 44 percent of the general public employed in nonsupervisory jobs said they would vote to form a union at their workplaces.[11]

The administrative manager needs to know how to function in unionized organizations. Representation of workers by unions takes two forms. First, unions represent employees. They negotiate contracts with employers covering the workers they represent. The union contract specifies wages, benefits, work rules, and other workplace procedures. Second, within the contractual framework negotiated, unions establish a formalized grievance procedure. This procedure provides the mechanism whereby employee and union grievances can be aired and adjudicated according to prescribed and agreed upon steps.

Union Versus Employer Power

Unions are able to influence management decisions through the bargaining power they possess. At the core of this power are these forms of influence:

1. *Picket.* Unions can enlist public support by preventing customers, nonunion employees, and carriers from entering the premises.

2. *Strike.* Unions can impose significant costs on the enterprise by forcing the employer to cease operations.

3. *Boycott products.* Unions can discourage members and the public from patronizing the employer.

An employer's power in a union organization comes from the following actions:

1. *Continue operations.* Hire replacements for strikers and encourage workers to return to work.

2. *Lock out workers.* Counteract union slowdown or vandalism.

3. *Subcontract work.* Force the union to give up the strike and continue to service customers with a substitute source of labor.

Thus, in a unionized company the ability to inflict costs operates in both directions. Although adversarial relations are still the rule, there is growing attention to labor-management strategies that emphasize mutuality of interests, cooperation, and "win-win" bargaining, whenever possible.

Employees are less likely to want a third party's help if steps are taken to improve workplace policies and communication mechanisms.

Four elements of any proactive union-avoidance strategy employers can follow are as follows:

1. *An open-door complaint procedure.* Most employees join unions to feel a sense of empowerment and to have a voice in the workplace. Providing a mechanism for voicing complaints and asking work-related questions satisfies this need. Without this channel, undiscovered problems such as arbitrary treatment or unfair favoritism by a supervisor will fester, ruining morale and driving off good employees.

2. *Enhanced communication.* Whether through employee meetings (formal or informal), newsletters, memos from management, or employee attitude surveys, employers must focus on improving two-way communications. Employees want to be heard, provide input, and receive timely information (both good and bad) about their workplace and issues of concern.

3. *A personnel policies and procedures audit.* Unions frequently use various inconsistent employer policies as rallying cries to turn employee interest toward unions. Thwart such efforts with an internal audit.

4. *Management training programs.* As legal agents of the employer, supervisors can bind the employer through their actions; they also can be the source of the problems leading to organizing efforts. Train managers on such topics as recognizing employee individual rights, improving employee performance, documenting misconduct, and imposing fair discipline.[12]

ORGANIZATIONAL POLICIES AND PROCEDURES

As a manager, one of your responsibilities will be to assist in administering, interpreting, and updating organizational policies and procedures. These policies can be imposed externally through laws, for instance, or created by the organization.

If policies and procedures were not in place, organizations would not function smoothly. A **policy** is a written guideline about workplace issues. Most managers agree that policies are one of the best places to find answers to an employee's concern.

A procedure, already discussed in an earlier chapter, is a routine method of handling activities and is more specific than a policy. Procedures outline the steps to be performed when taking a particular course of action. For example, an organization may have a grievance policy, and an integral part of that policy may be a procedure outlining the sequential steps to be taken by all affected parties to resolve the grievance.

An effective way to ensure that all employees understand policies and procedures is to issue each worker an employee handbook. This handbook gives employees a reference to research specific questions they may have. It is distributed as part of the employee orientation process. With company intranets, many organizations are posting their policies on their computer servers for easy and confidential access to employees. Table 17.4 describes policies and how organizations should set policies in motion and monitor their appropriateness.

Management Tip

Managers interpret policies. It is, therefore, good advice to read and review organizational policies and to ask questions of the human resources department if sections of policies are unclear or hard for you to interpret.

POLICIES SHOULD

1. Cover only areas where employees and managers need guidance.

2. Be communicated by management to employees through training, orientation programs, and the employee handbook.

3. Be reviewed and updated on a continuous basis with any changes communicated to employees.

4. Be written as concisely and to the point as possible.

Table 17.4

Communicating Organizational Policies

Message *for* AOMs

No one offers his or her services to an organization for free. Recognition, compensation, and rewards have to do with understanding how the organization values the contributions of employees with specialized skills who help the organization achieve its mission and purpose in the marketplace.

Administrative office managers are positioned well in the organization to show office support staff that rewards and recognition go beyond compensation. They, in fact, indicate the special value the organization places on specific behaviors.

Labor unions are a permanent part of our free-enterprise economy. A union, just like any other institution, has the potential for either advancing or interfering with the common efforts of an organization. Thus, it is in management's self-interest to develop a union-management climate that is conducive to constructive relationships.

1 Terminations have a ripple effect on those who stay in that they may feel that the psychological bond is no longer valid with the organization, their loyalty is shaken, and their security is eroded.

2 Exempt workers are not paid overtime and are usually paid a salary; nonexempt workers are paid overtime and usually an hourly wage.

3 Indirect compensation consists of the following categories: benefits required by law,

pay for time not worked, insurance, and security and retirement plans.

4 Unions can picket, strike, or boycott products; employers can continue operations, lock out workers, or subcontract work.

5 A procedure is an outline of the steps necessary to carrying out a particular course of action within a policy.

summary chapter 17

QUESTIONS FOR CRITICAL THINKING

1. In what ways are exit interviews beneficial to an organization?

2. What is the purpose of a sound compensation program?

3. Argue for the advantages of setting up a flexible cafeteria benefit plan.

4. What factors have contributed to a significant drop in union membership during the past thirty years?

5. What are some means of disseminating information to workers about company policies?

Case Study 17-1: Clinger's Wage Debate

Management and employees at Clinger's Clothing Store are battling over increasing employee wage rates. Management's position is that its current employee wage structure complies with governmental factors like FLSA, equal pay legislation, comparable wage rates, and market conditions. However, management has indicated to employees that business has not been good this past year and that "some jobs are in jeopardy." In general, management would like for the employees to back off on their demands.

The employees have selected a spokesperson, Ron Wiggle, who is representing them to management. He has expressed to management that it's the employees' understanding that the company bought certain executives new cars this year and that most have gotten new furniture. Further, the rumor mill has it that executives received a 10- to 20-percent pay raise this year, and employees want to know if that is true.

Management says that it can afford to increase wages only if greater profit is made. It is management's feeling that the productivity of employees is decreasing—perhaps intentionally—due to their discontent.

Discussion Questions

1. What is the general issue between management and workers in this pay conflict?

2. If you were management, what steps would you take to resolve the stalemate?

3. If you were Ron Wiggle, what would you recommend as the next step for the employees to take?

Case Study 17-2: Best Friend Gets Terminated from Her Job

You have just learned from your boss that one of your workers and very best friend, Rita Flick, must be laid off as part of your firm's downsizing, which resulted from a takeover by a Japanese holding company. Flick has been with your firm for more than 20 years, and during this time, she has become like a sister to you.

Discussion Question

Is there a kind way to terminate Flick's services?

Case Study 17-3: Internet Research Activity

Assume that you are doing a report on *current trends in union membership and union actions.* Use the Internet to research information needed to answer the following questions. Key your responses.

1. Which Web search engine did you use?

2. Write down three of the URL addresses that you accessed during your search.

3. As a result of your search, list three items of current information you might use in your report.

Endnotes

[1]Del Jones, "Fired Workers Fight Back . . . and Win," *USA Today,* April 2, 1998, pp. 1B–2B.

[2]Tonia L. Shakespeare, "In Strictest Confidence: Keeping a Lock on Company Secrets When an Employee Bolts," *Black Enterprise,* May 1996, p. 64.

[3]Rochelle Garner, "How Much Money Does It Take to Keep Valuable IS Staff from Jumping Ship?" *Computerworld,* August 31, 1998, p. 50.

[4]Brian Tumulty, "Women's Wages Still Lower Than Men's by 26 Cents," *Gannett News Service,* April 2, 1998, n.p.

[5]Jennifer Laabs, "Satisfy Them with More Than Money," *Workforce,* November 1998, p. NA.

[6]Jane Kiser, "Behind the Scenes at a 'Family-Friendly' Workplace," *Dollars & Sense,* January–February 1998, p. 20.

[7]Ann Szostak, "Fleet Financial Tests Work/Life," *HR Focus,* November 1998, p. S14.

[8]Daniel Eisenbert, "Family Secrets at Work," *Time,* July 27, 1998, p. 66.

[9]JoAnn Davy, "Just Show Me the Benefits," *Managing Office Technology,* July–August 1998, p. 12.

[10]Scott D. Rechtschaffen, "The New Strategy of Union Organizing," *HR Focus,* June 1998, p. 3.

[11]Rebecca Piirto Heath, "The New Working Class," *American Demographics,* 1998, p. NA.

[12]Scott D. Rechtschaffen, "The New Strategy of Union Organizing," *HR Focus,* June 1998, p. 4.

Health-Related and Other Workplace Issues

chapter 18

> " There is a time in the life of every problem when it is big enough to see, yet small enough to solve.
>
> —Mike Leavitt "

objectives

After completing this chapter, you will be able to:

1. Identify three health-related issues that are present in American workplaces.

2. Distinguish between the behaviors of a workaholic and a hard worker.

3. Describe how AIDS is affecting the workplace.

4. Discuss current thinking relative to office parties and office liaisons.

5. Describe the value of office manuals.

6. List some ways to use five-minute wasted moments productively that will increase your effectiveness and, in the end, save you time.

Health-related and other workplace issues affect worker productivity as well as the manner in which AOMs perform their tasks. Chapter 18 deals with these issues.

HEALTH-RELATED WORK ISSUES

Health-related work issues impact a manager's performance. These issues include dealing with problems of substance abuse, managing a workaholic, and managing an employee who has AIDS.

Problems of Substance Abuse

A significant and costly challenge has emerged in recent decades, one that is taking an inordinate amount of managerial time: the problems of alcoholism and drug abuse. The alcohol problem is costly to industry and society in

William P. Englesbe

Vice President
Corporate Purchasing and
Environmental Affairs
Wheaton Industries Inc.
Millville, New Jersey

Wheaton Industries is a $500 million worldwide manufacturer of glass, plastic, rubber, and aluminum seal packaging. It has 4,000 employees and is a privately owned company.

William P. Englesbe received his B.S. in finance from the Wharton School, University of Pennsylvania. Prior to assuming his post with Wheaton, Mr. Englesbe served as the director of corporate purchasing for The West Company, Phoenixville, Pennsylvania, and as senior purchasing agent for Rohm & Haas Company, Philadelphia.

Dialog *from the* Workplace

QUESTION:

What role do you, as vice president of corporate purchasing and environmental affairs, play in your company's program of budgetary control?

RESPONSE:

Purchasing has three business areas of responsibility where budgets are useful tools in the decision-making process. These areas are (1) raw materials and components, (2) capital expenditures, and (3) manufacturing, repairs, and operational (MRO) supplies. The nature of the enterprise (manufacturing, distribution, service, etc.) influences the degree of sophistication required in each budget area. For our purposes here, we shall examine the latter two areas—capital expenditures and MRO supplies.

Capital Expenditures. The decision to spend capital funds is made by senior management after input from various groups within the organization. Sales, marketing, engineering, research and development, accounting, finance, and purchasing should all contribute to capital expansion decisions.

Purchasing is the primary source for creating estimated expenditures for any capital project. Once the project is begun, the actual costs will be compared to the estimated costs because management wants to know how well, or how poorly, the project compares to its stated goals. The accounting department is responsible for providing these comparative data; however, it is in purchasing's best interest to provide accurate data during the early budget process. The true test of these data will come when a capital project is approved and purchasing must then provide the labor, equipment, machinery and materials at prices comparable to their estimates.

MRO Supplies. Budgeting for MRO and supply items can be as simple or sophisticated as a company wants. Many organizations, especially manufacturing or assembly-type operations, budget these costs as a factor of labor hours, machine hours, or some other easily reportable component of the level of business activity.

Organizations that operate centralized storerooms produce annual budgets for the items they inventory and for items that might not warrant inventorying, but which are purchased through the storeroom's purchasing programs.

Annually, purchasing publishes a storeroom components budgeted costs list for distribution to the departments drawing from the storeroom. Each operating department draws on this information to create its annual operating budget.

Purchasing must routinely compare its actual costs to its budgeted costs to identify changes as they occur. These data are distributed regularly to the storeroom's customers.

Budgets are snapshots of estimates of the future. They should be used for comparisons to actual events and should evoke legitimate questions and answers when significant differences occur.

---

terms of lost work time, health and medical care expenses, property damage, wage losses, and other costs associated with traffic accidents.

A 1998 report from the Chamber of Commerce estimates that workplace drug and alcohol abuse cost U.S. businesses more than $100 billion per year. However, less than 5 percent of U.S. businesses have written policies on substance abuse.[1] Drug abuse is pervasive throughout society, from the inner-city ghettos to the wealthy suburbs. In the workplace, drug abuse includes legal drugs, such as barbiturates and tranquilizers, and illegal drugs, such as heroin and crack cocaine.

The Drug-Free Workplace Act of 1988 was passed to ensure that employers who have contracts with the U.S. government maintain a drug-free environment for their workers. Failure to do so can lead to contract termination. To be in compliance with this legislation, employers must do the following:

1. Inform employees of drug-free requirements.

2. Outline actions to be taken for violations.

Ethics/Choices

Suppose you work with another person as part of a sales team and, periodically during the workweek, you smell alcohol on his breath. He is a great guy and everyone likes him. Do you say anything to your sales manager?

3. Establish awareness programs and supervisory training.

Workaholics Versus Hard Workers

Not everyone who puts in long hours is addicted to work. Some people are inspired and energized by what they do for a living, and their sense of well-being and fulfillment is proof that they are not engaging in self-destructive activity. But for others, the diagnosis may be quite different.

To tell which side you are on, these six signs may indicate that

Management Tip

Good habits are hard to form but easy to live with; bad habits are easy to form but hard to live with.

work has become an unhealthy obsession for you: no play, trying too hard, physical symptoms, a one-track life, a one-track mind, and martyrdom. Table 18.1 explains how these workaholic behavior patterns are manifested.

Regardless of whether you are a workaholic or hard worker, a new business travel trend is emerging that could fit the bill for either. A Seattle-based company called Laptop Lane is opening private, fully equipped office spaces in airports that travelers may rent for less than $10 per half-hour. Currently available in Cincinnati and the Seattle–Tacoma airports, the offices have all the high-tech necessities of a well-equipped business office, including a T-1 line to the Internet. You can receive e-mail, participate in a conference call, get a fax, and surf the Net all at the same time. In addition, each location is staffed with a real-life **"cyber-concierge."**[2] Business work habits propel trends. As more and more businesspeople work in other-than-traditional offices, the efforts to provide assistance will continue to emerge.

AIDS Concerns

AIDS (acquired immune deficiency syndrome) is an issue that is problematic for managers and organizations. The concerns are twofold. First, managers are concerned with the eventual decline in productivity and attendance brought on by the inevitable diseases that can afflict an employee with AIDS. Second, the fear and panic in the workplace brought on by misunderstanding and misinformation can cause colleagues' productivity to change.

1. *No play.* When a workaholic isn't working, he or she feels itchy and restless, craving work as if it were an addictive drug.

2. *Trying too hard.* Nothing you produce at the office seems good enough—so you compulsively revise and polish each memo, letter, and presentation.

3. *Physical symptoms.* You feel fatigued but find it impossible to relax. Frequent headaches, stomach aches, back pains, and even ulcers may plague you, as well as fitful sleeping.

4. *One-track life.* You don't have much of a social or love life, only a work life.

5. *One-track mind.* Your single-minded dedication to work is causing interpersonal problems. Families resent the time spent on work, and co-workers are upset with your unreasonable demands and incessant expectations.

6. *Martyrdom.* You view work as torture and yourself as a martyr.

Table 18.1

Warning Signs of a Workaholic

Source: Adapted from Denise Topolnicki, "Workaholics: Are You One?" Psychology Today, *July–August 1989, p. 25.*

Great controversy surrounds what companies should do about AIDS-related issues. Should they require AIDS testing as a condition of employment? If an employee admits to being infected with AIDS, should the company retain him or her? Or should the company instead continue to pay the employee's full salary and medical and retirement benefits on the stipulation that he or she not return to work? There are no easy answers; companies are struggling to write policies dealing with AIDS.

For those companies having no formal policy for dealing with AIDS, the AOM needs to develop guidelines for supervisors to ensure that consistent treatment is provided for all HIV-infected employees and those with AIDS. These guidelines should cover topics such as:

1. The need to protect the privacy and confidentiality of infected workers who wish to remain on the job as long as they are able. The workers should be guaranteed that they will not be isolated from others.

2. How to allay the fears and anxieties of employees who believe that the disease can be transmitted by casual social or professional contact.

3. How to prepare employees for working with co-workers who have contracted HIV as well as those with full-blown AIDS.

4. The need for an ongoing educational program by means of brochures, pamphlets, newsletters, meetings, and so on, to convey current information.

5. Services provided by the company's employees assistance program—professional counseling and support for employees with AIDS, for those being tested for AIDS, and for those groups subject to high risk of HIV infection.

6. Cost-containment measures, such as case management, that deal with AIDS-related medical care. Case management involves the close monitoring and evaluation of a patient's care.

OTHER WORKPLACE ISSUES

Other workplace issues that require a manager's ability to discern the proper approach to take involve nepotism, organizational concerns about office parties, and office romances. The understanding and use of office manuals and other time-savers can help managers and employees become more efficient in these time-strapped days.

Nepotism

Nepotism is the practice of allowing relatives to work for the same employer. Most employers have policies that restrict or prohibit this practice. At issue is the potential collusion or conflicts that could occur if spouses, brothers, sisters, mothers, fathers, sons, and daughters work directly for a relative. However, continuity of the family company is normally the justification for nepotism. Totally unacceptable to most is the practice of blind, untrained, irresponsible, immature nepotism. On the other hand, what is acceptable is planned, trained, and responsible nepotism.

The accepted wisdom is that nepotism has more negatives than positives. Business owners and their advisers have often feared that non-family employees would resent and possibly treat unkindly family members brought into the business or would see the family members as roadblocks to their own career success. They also feared that some family members themselves might be incompetent or lazy, yet have an attitude of entitlement.[3]

Company policy and practice vary greatly with regard to the employment of married couples. In some offices, the employment of husband and wife makes for a close-knit, harmonious working group, and the recruitment of couples is encouraged. In other offices, the employment of a married couple may cause personality conflicts, especially when both the husband and wife work in the same department. In these firms, office supervisors cite potential morale problems (jealousy; forced competition; absenteeism; difficulties in scheduling for holidays, vacations, and deaths in the family; and conflicts of interest) in that the couples may not be able to separate their personal and professional lives.

Office Parties

There is an art to holding a successful office Christmas party. And there's literature, too—hundreds of court cases that explore the various pathways to employer liability. Under the heading of sexual harassment claims alone (skipping past assaults, illnesses, and accidents), there are

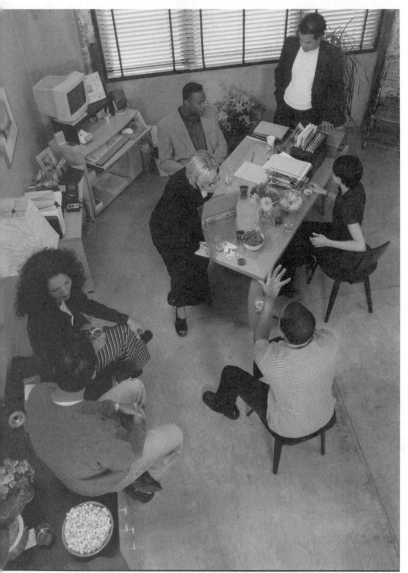

Do office parties improve morale or create problems in companies?
© *PhotoDisc, Inc.*

volumes of litigation devoted to inappropriate entertainment, provocative gifts, and lewd table decorations.

The institution of the holiday or promotion party has undergone profound changes lately. Many companies are turning their parties into family occasions that take place around lunchtime, or they have them moved off the premises to a commercial establishment where beverages are dispensed by professional bartenders.[4] Many office parties ban alcoholic drinking due in part to management's concern about drunk driving and being held liable. There is also a self-serving fear that a few glasses of wine could dissolve the sense of restraint that keeps employees from expressing their true feelings about their jobs.

Most people find it difficult to make merry with the same people they have been working with all year. But many people feel office parties improve morale and, indeed, there are businesses where the workers genuinely look forward to socializing after hours. Instead of having a big party, some companies are doing other activities to improve morale and promote team spirit. Some examples are helping to serve food at or renovating a homeless shelter.

Office Liaisons

Business colleagues share interests and values, goals and fears, triumphs and setbacks, and, of course, time—lots of time. Given all this, it is not surprising that many women and men find the prospect of an office romance too exciting to resist. In a recent article in *HR Focus,* it was estimated that about 80 percent of all workers have been involved or have seen others become involved in office romance during their years of employment. Romantic relationships in the workplace have both good and bad consequences.

On the positive side, they can boost employee morale, improve attitudes, minimize personality conflicts, and improve teamwork. On the negative side, workplace romance can give rise to sexual harassment complaints, particularly when a romantic relationship between a supervisor and a subordinate goes awry. Companies can avoid the adverse effects of office romance by implementing a written policy.[5]

Policies Against Office Romances. Some companies have policies regarding consensual amorous relationships at work. This policy prohibits any romantic relationship involving a supervisor and employee where the supervisor has direct authority, influence, or responsibility with respect to that employee. Other companies anticipate and tolerate romantic relationships until they disrupt work.

Should a relationship develop, the policy states that the supervisor will inform his or her immediate supervisor promptly so those steps can be taken to remove the relationship of authority for all purposes. Some policies state that if this consensual relationship is not discontinued, the supervisor will be subject to disciplinary action, which may include termination.

Despite the rising prevalence of office relationships, co-workers generally continue to find such pairings problematic. What is more, women continue to be judged more negatively than men in such situations. Most would conclude that the negative impact of office relationships far outweighs the positive effects.

A good office romance policy should:

- Recognize that office relationships exist.
- Establish a mechanism whereby relationships and problems are to be reported confidentially.
- Employ mediation to solve relationship problems but still reserve the use of warnings and extreme discipline measures.
- Separate romance from sexual harassment but retain the discipline measures for unreasonable or serious noncompliance.
- Rely on seminars to counsel workers on the pluses and minuses of workplace romances, including the company's climate and its procedures.
- Create a general environment of trust and support for employees.[6]

Risks and Legalities. What makes office romance so difficult is the fact that it inevitably affects the work of both parties involved. For example, if the couple has an argument on the way to the office that morning, will this argument continue through their work performance that day?

Let us look at the legalities of this dilemma and examine the reasons companies establish policies against office romances. Discrimination based on marital status is unlawful today in most states; however, even though employers are not allowed to prevent married couples or significant others from working for the same company or even within the same department, employers are allowed to prevent such couples from working for each other (i.e., in a "reporting to" supervisory situation). This policy is to protect employees and the company itself from

financial risk. Here is an example of the potential risks involved for a boss, a secretary, and the company:

1. **Personal risk to the boss.** If the relationship fails, the secretary could claim, under federal guidelines of sexual harassment, that the boss coerced the secretary into the relationship (e.g., with promises of a salary increase).

2. **Risk to the secretary.** When in control of performance reviews, salary increases, and promotions, the boss may not disclose information about promotional opportunities for fear of losing the relationship.

3. **Risk to the company.** Another employee could have a basis for a claim against the company, stating that the secretary involved was receiving preferential treatment in the form of better bonuses or additional benefits, even if it were untrue, because of their relationship.[7]

Crisis Control. If an office romance should happen to you, you may, at some point, need to manage a breakup. If the romance turns sour—or just begins to curdle—think seriously about cutting your losses early. Break up while you can still be friends or, at the least, colleagues. You may consider seeking professional help either to mend the relationship or to end it with both egos intact.

Although dozens of ultimately happy unions begin in business settings, the bottom line is that mixing love and work is risky business. Office liaisons will not stop. But the question becomes, is the payoff worth the risk? In the end, that is a personal decision.

Office Manuals and Other Time-Savers

Establishing sound administrative systems is essential in organizations. Two suggestions are to create and use office manuals and to employ time-saving practices.

Office Manuals. An office manual is a valuable, time-saving tool for any office. **Office manuals** include procedures that specify a standard way for dealing with recurring situations or activities so that they will be handled uniformly throughout an organization.

Examples of typical office procedures include formats for correspondence and reports, how to handle incoming mail, how to open files, and how to answer the telephone. The list is endless. The advantages of office manuals are many. For instance, a manual can provide written information when training new employees, reduce the problem of repetitive training, and serve as an invaluable reference book.

Other Time-Savers. Every minute of your life is precious and never to be recalled. In business, if time is money, you need to look for strategies that will help you beat the clock and save a few moments.

Getting Away from Meetings. Protecting your time by mastering the quick getaway from formal meetings or informal office "huddles" is a subtle art that can save your day. Here are some techniques that have worked for AOMs:

1. Ask to be excused and leave. This is direct and effective.

2. Ask if your presence is still needed. Say, "Excuse me. It seems as if we have finished with the part of this discussion that involves me. If so, I would like to leave."

3. Set a mental time limit. This can help when you participate in meetings or informal discussions.

4. Have an exit line ready: "That's it then. I'll let you know how things go in my area." Smile and leave.

5. Work from an unobtrusive spot. Sit at the back of the room or stand at the edge of the group where you can slip away unnoticed when the discussion loses its value for you.[8]

Undoing Desk Clutter. The average worker has 36 hours' worth of work on his or her desk and wastes 3 hours a week just searching for things, according to Priority Management Systems in Washington. Here are some tips to follow when undoing desk clutter:

An up-to-date office manual or employee handbook is an invaluable reference for all office professionals. © *Tony Freeman/PhotoEdit*

1. Remember that nothing on a messy desk is sacred—except photos to remind you that you have another life.

2. Create three general categories—mail and correspondence, work in progress, and reading—in a file system close to your desk.

3. Designate a file for "to do" material and write—on one calendar—the day you will do it. People who use multiple calendars miss several appointments at once.[9]

Using Small Amounts of Time Well. Those five-minute intervals of time-wasters come while you are waiting for an appointment, or a revised document, or the copy machine, or while you are stuck on hold. The problem is that if you have 12 five-minute delays, you have wasted an hour. Here are some suggestions to increase the value of those wasted moments:

1. *Complete simple chores.* Write thank-you notes, pay bills, write checks, balance your checkbook.

2. *Handle routine office maintenance.* Fill that laser printer tray, file old papers, eliminate clutter. You will become more efficient as you become more organized.

3. *Review your weekly schedule.* What is going to happen tomorrow? Here is your chance to jot a quick note for an upcoming meeting or gather information to improve your presentation.

4. *Delegate.* What tasks can an assistant or colleague do? Take a moment to clear your desk of tasks that can help others improve their skills.

5. *Call people back.* You probably have phone calls that have not been returned because they were not urgent. Show your courtesy by returning all calls—even if you only have to deliver a polite "no thanks" to a salesperson.

6. *Proofread.* Why take a chance on a typo in a memo with your name on it? While a word processing spell checker can catch many errors, it will not find errors in usage or words that sound the same (to, too, two).

7. *Run errands.* Create a circular road map for the errands you must run. Make sure you do not backtrack while driving.

8. *Gather all your notes and other paper reminders in one place.* Create a single "to do" list and then number the items in terms of priority.

9. *Automate your software functions to create time-savers.* Use software wizards and templates for creating standard documents. Also, record and use macros that address envelopes, print documents, dial your on-line service, upload and download mail, and so forth.

10. *Create templates for work that you have to do repetitively.* For instance, if you write many proposals, create a master form that includes the material that never changes, like your company's background, mission, and philosophy. Leave blank spots for the client's name and other variable information.

Major Time-Wasters. Dr. Jan Yager, writing *Woman's Own,* says these are five major time-wasters:

- Spreading yourself too thin by trying to do too many things at once. *Suggestion:* You must set priorities for each day and, if necessary, each hour. Get the most important things done first.
- Being afraid to delegate. *Suggestion:* Convince yourself that it's not necessary to do everything yourself.
- Not wanting to say "no" to requests. *Suggestion:* You can't say "yes" to everything without spreading yourself too thin. Decide what you must do—and want to do—and say "no" to all other requests.

- Being a slave to the phone. *Suggestions:* Have others screen your calls. Schedule a telephone hour to return all calls.
- Procrastinating. *Suggestions:* Get unpleasant chores done first—if they are important. Divide large tasks into smaller ones. Reward yourself when you accomplish something.[10]

Time is more than money. It is the stuff of life itself. If you fill dead moments with simple tasks, you will avoid boredom and be regarded by others as a more efficient person and manager.[11]

Message *for* AOMs

Companies can avoid the adverse effects of several health-related and other workplace issues by writing policy and sending the message that management is here to help, rather than to "getcha." None of the issues discussed in Chapter 18 are easy ones for managers, but all will inevitably surface in any AOM's career.

Proceed with employees carefully by first showing you care and then picking the right moment to offer assistance. Make sure the person hasn't just been shaken by some incident.

Avoid giving the impression that you are more concerned with seeing your recommendations put into practice than in helping the other person. In addition, show how the person will benefit from taking the actions you suggest.

1 Three health-related issues present in the American workplace today are drug and alcohol addiction, AIDS, and the increase of workaholics.

2 A workaholic is different from the hard worker in that, for the workaholic, there are signs which are obvious: no play, trying too hard, physical symptoms, a one-track life, a one-track mind, and martyrdom.

3 AIDS has affected the workplace because it forces a reckoning with the decline in productivity and attendance of workers, as well as the fear and panic in the workplace brought on by colleagues' concerns.

4 Though management may see improvement in employee morale from sponsoring parties, many companies are banning alcoholic drinks and/or are having families attend parties.

5 Office manuals ensure that recurring situations or activities will be handled uniformly throughout an organization.

6 Some time-saving ways to use short spans of time are to write thank-you notes, pay bills, run errands in a circular pattern, or create a single "to do" list and then number items in terms of priority.

QUESTIONS FOR CRITICAL THINKING

1. In your opinion, is there reason to believe that work has become an unhealthy obsession for many American workers?

2. If you were related to someone who wanted you to go to work for him or her, would you? Why or why not?

3. Why are office romances so prevalent in business?

4. If you wanted to promote an office "get together" to promote esprit de corps, what activities come to mind?

5. If you had three five-minute intervals of "do nothing" time, how would you use those fifteen minutes more wisely than you do now?

Case Study 18-1: A Co-Worker Has AIDS

Stuart Duffy and Craig Bunting have worked side by side for the past seven years in the computer center. Over the years the two have shared very intimate details of their personal lives with each other. This morning, Duffy comes to see you, the manager of the center, and says:

"Craig told me this morning he just saw his doctor, who diagnosed his illness as AIDS. Although we are very close, I can no longer work alongside Craig. I have my wife and children at home—and myself—to think about. You are going to have to do something—maybe move Craig to an office by himself. What's going to happen when the rest of our group finds out about Craig's problem?"

You thank Duffy for talking with you and state that after you meet with Bunting you will follow through.

Discussion Question

In view of this announcement about AIDS in your company—the first case—what steps should you take at this time?

Case Study 18-2: Christmas Party This Year?

Ms. Saikley, AOM at International Business Services, is wondering whether to vote to have a Christmas office party this year. She has just spoken with the sales manager, who told her about an incident that happened at another company last holiday season. It seems that the other organization decided to have an "employees' only" office party on Friday night from 5–8 P.M. at a local restaurant downtown.

Two weeks later, the wife of one of the workers burst into the office area and began shouting accusations at an office worker who she thought was having an affair with her husband. It was embarrassing to everyone in the organization, and most agreed it was unnecessary.

Discussion Questions

1. If you were the AOM of that organization, how would you have reacted to the situation just described? The office worker would have reported to you, and you were the first manager on the scene.

2. Should a policy be written covering office parties? If so, what would be your input to this policy?

Case Study 18-3: Internet Research Activity

Assume you are doing a report on *substance abuse in the workplace.* Use the Internet to research information needed to answer the following questions. Key your responses.

1. Which Web search engine did you use?

2. Write down three of the URL addresses that you accessed during your search.

3. As a result of your search, list three items of current information you might use in your report.

Endnotes

[1]Steve Bates, "House Passes Bill to Curb Workplace Substance Abuse," *Nation's Business,* August 1998, p. 8.

[2]Lynn Woods, "Just the Place for Terminal Workaholics," *Kiplinger's Personal Finance Magazine,* December 1998, p. 30.

[3]Sharon Nelton, "The Bright Side of Nepotism," *Nation's Business,* May 1998, p. 72.

[4]"Why Corporate America Fears Mistletoe," *U.S. News and World Report,* December 14, 1998, p. 51.

[5]Stephanie Overman, "When Labor Leads to Love," *HR Focus,* November 1998, p. 3.

[6]Ibid.

[7]Nan DeMars, "Office Ethics: Office Romance," *The Secretary,* October 1994, p. 27.

[8]"Time-Savers: Getting Away," *The Office Professional,* Sample Issue, 1994, p. 5. Reprinted from *The Office Professional* with permission from Professional Training Associates, Inc., 210 Commerce Blvd., Round Rock, Texas 78664-2189, 1-800-424-2112. Annual subscription rate is $48.

[9]Robert A. Mamis, "Undo Desk Clutter," *Inc.,* March 1993, p. 40.

[10]Dr. Jan Yager, *Woman's Own,* Harris Publications Inc., 1115 Broadway, New York, NY 10010.

[11]Daniel Janal, "Killing Time Is Killing You," *Computer,* October 1992, p. 23.

Office Design, Space, Health and Safety Issues

chapter 19

> There is no security on this earth; there is only opportunity.
>
> —*Douglas MacArthur*

objectives

After completing this chapter, you will be able to:

1. List the independent systems in an office environment that affect office design and layout.

2. Discuss three trends in office designs.

3. Define ergonomics and describe its importance to the workplace.

4. List four primary sources of the most frequent health problems in the office.

5. Describe some examples of office hazards.

6. Identify physical threats to employee safety in the workplace.

7. List examples of office recycling activities.

Offices that are designed with an eye toward managing the efficient flow of work and maximizing the use of office space impact office productivity and ultimately the profitability of the organization.

OFFICE DESIGN AND WORKFLOW

Although each organization has its own personality which adds character to the office environment, consider these basics of design and workflow that need to be in place first.

Office Design and Layout

Office design encompasses many trends, which change as business theories change. For example, office spaces are designed in some cases to encourage teamwork; in others, to reinforce new corporate values with less status-laden private offices. Primarily, however, interior

Neal E. Jones, AIA

President
Jones Studio, Inc.
Phoenix, Arizona

As president of Jones Studio, Inc., Mr. Jones has 20-years' experience in the design, production, and project management of various project types. In addition to handling all the administrative and marketing affairs of the firm, he is also responsible for directing the project team in the overall design and management of each project. Mr. Jones deals with the individual client on matters pertaining to overall project objectives, planning the delivery of services, and monitoring the results as they relate to fulfilling the client's needs in a consistent way. In addition, he assists in the coordination of appropriate staffing, monitoring and approving contract amounts and time commitments, and overall project control.

Neal E. Jones received a B.S. in architectural studies from Oklahoma State University and double Masters' degrees in architecture as well as business administration from the University of Illinois.

QUESTION:

What do you see as architectural trends in office design and use of office space?

Dialog *from the* Workplace

RESPONSE:

Overall, I would have to say, "Good design sells." By that I mean that by paying a little bit more for design excellence in an office environment, the payback is exponential in terms of increased worker productivity, less absenteeism, less office-environ sickness, and less worker turnover. People are happy to come to work because it is a cool place to work. It's fun to go to the office because the owners have created a stimulating environment.

Though it is easy to go with the flow of what everyone is doing, there are some comments I feel students should be aware of relative to important design issues.

- Although modular furniture is popular, it is a fact that having your office furniture custom designed and built is more economical. Furthermore, it maximizes the use of office space because it utilizes every square inch of space to its highest and best use. In other words, if your office is 12'-3½" x 10'-8⅜", your desk shelving, etc., will be custom built to utilize these exact measurements. With modular furniture, you might only be able to get a 12' x 10'-6" module, thus leaving "gaps" at the wall, which can look (and feel) ridiculous and wasteful.

- Office lighting is moving more and more toward task lighting at the work surface in lieu of being totally dependent on overhead general illumination. Great strides have been made in the last few years with the emergence of "lighting designers." These folks specialize in lighting. One should not be dependent on the electrical engineer to develop a lighting design for your office. More times than not, electrical engineers are not trained in lighting design and don't keep up with the current trends and product development.

- Operable windows to let fresh air in. This is done in Europe all the time. America is just discovering this concept. A possible downside of this trend is it can play havoc with the balance of the heating and air conditioning systems if not properly designed and taken into account during the initial stages of design.
- Natural daylight is recommended. It is a fact that natural daylight improves worker productivity and promotes less sickness, resulting in lower absenteeism of workers. In my opinion, natural daylight is the single most important issue with the design of office space. It cannot and should not be overlooked, no matter what anyone else tries to tell you!

designers attempt to make space totally adaptable so that corporations can change work patterns as quickly and as often as they need in order to survive and prosper in fast-changing economies.[1]

Effective office design and layout are based on the interrelationships among equipment, workflow, and employees. In general, **office layout** is described as the arrangement of facilities and workstations. If space planning is inadequate, results such as reduced employee productivity, increased absenteeism, increased turnover, decreased physical comfort, and decreased employee morale will probably surface.

Today, many companies provide employees with different workspace options. A design, for example, might include drop-in offices, conference rooms, and project rooms—all equipped with phones, computers, or whatever equipment the employees need. Individual tasks could be handled in the drop-in offices, while teams would use the project rooms for long-term jobs. Conventional wisdom, therefore, dictates that both individuals and teams have access to work areas that vary in size and set-up to meet different concentration needs. Company management must consider the need for a balance of spaces to work in and realize that no single design can be all things to all workers.[2]

Planning Layout. An office environment is made up of several interdependent systems: people, floor plans, furniture, equipment, lighting, air quality, and acoustics. These interdependent systems are constantly changing, and for that reason offices should be designed with the ability to adapt to changing needs. When planning layout, the AOM should keep these ideas in mind:

1. Become aware of the mandatory layout stipulations dictated by the Americans with Disabilities Act and design office space in keeping with the law. For example, aisles should be sufficiently wide to accommodate the rapid, efficient movement of *all* current and future employees.

2. Consider communication relationships between individuals when planning layout, and locate individuals or work groups performing similar or related duties near each other.

3. Position individuals or work groups with frequent public contact near the entrance to the premises; conversely, those individuals whose tasks require considerable concentration should be placed in a low-traffic, quiet area of the building.

4. Give high priority to safety and health considerations when planning layout.

5. Plan space so that everything in the office has a purpose. Ruthlessly eliminate—sell, trade, throw away, or even put in storage—all unnecessary items. Then reorganize the rest.[3]

Management Tip

You can tell you have a problem desk when co-workers put messages on your chair because they know that is the only place you will notice them. Moreover, that mess may not be your problem alone. It is likely that some of the buried items are preventing your co-workers from doing their jobs until you get yours done.

Design Issues. In designing an office, specific questions need to be asked regarding lighting, décor, noise, and air control.

1. What are some characteristics and types of lighting systems appropriate for the office space?

2. What are the most desirable color schemes for floors and wall coverings?

3. How can office noise be controlled through proper construction and sound-absorbing materials?

4. What are some air concerns that must be considered relative to temperature, humidity, ventilation, and cleanliness?

Table 19.1 offers some tips when solving design issues.

Use of Office Space

With real estate representing on average 25 percent of the assets of a large company, management is closely scrutinizing this investment and considering alternative methods to reduce costs and save space. These economic changes have fueled the drive toward greater space efficiency in the workplace.[4]

Three different approaches are generally taken to use office space effectively. They are open plan areas, private offices, or a blend of the two called the hybrid approach.

Open Plan Using Modular Design. The **open plan** is designed to foster the free flow of information and is characterized by the lack of interior walls and the freestanding placement of desks, partitions, and other office furnishings. The main attraction of open plan areas is flexibility because of its efficiency when teamed with modular design. The downside is noise and inability to focus on work.

In an earlier chapter, we addressed the dramatic change in the workplace with regard to "absent employees" and an increase in personnel on the move. For these reasons, organizations are turning to modular furniture that can be easily reconfigured to fit new space and that encourages communication and sharing as primary functions of employees. **Modular design** refers to the design of office furniture that facilitates the use of different components and variations in the way those components are arranged. A modular unit is custom fit and may

OFFICE SPACE SYSTEMS	KEY CONCERNS	POSSIBLE SOLUTIONS
Office Lighting	Glare Proper lighting systems	▪ Adjust most office work areas for task illumination to 100 to 150 foot-candles. ▪ Avoid overhead lighting that reflects on computer screens or off-white paper. ▪ Use adjustable window coverings. ▪ Use task lamps with at least two levels of adjustment to supplement overhead lighting.
Color	Color provides aesthetic value Color provides functional value	▪ Light colors make a small room look larger. ▪ Low ceilings appear higher by painting them a lighter color than the walls. ▪ In general, floors should be darker than walls and the walls should be darker than the ceiling. ▪ Cool colors (blue, green, violet) create calm and retiring moods; in contrast, warm colors (red, orange, yellow) create warm and cheerful moods.
Noise	Hazards to the ears Annoyance to workers of loud sounds	▪ Adjust the noise level in the average office to around 55 decibels (equivalent to average conversation at home with music in the background). ▪ Control sound problems with acoustical ceiling tile, panels with sound-absorbing materials, carpeting, and window coverings.
Air Control	Temperature control Air quality	▪ Establish uniform levels of cooling, heating, and ventilation. ▪ Redirect excess heat away from the worker and recycle into the building heating, ventilating, and air conditioning system. ▪ Add humidity into the air through humidifiers if static electricity is a problem.

Table 19.1

Office Lighting, Color/Décor, Noise, and Air Control

consist of such components as a desk or working space, storage space, file space, and shelf space.

Several office furniture manufacturers offer circular workstations, or pods, which can reduce the amount of office space required by as much as 40 percent. For example, a penta-pod has five workstations that can be individually fitted to provide functional as well as aesthetic requirements. Employees in this type of work area can easily share records, equipment, and information.

To offset the loss of privacy, the open plan design frequently incorporates conference rooms for confidential meetings or for working when deep concentration is required. In addition, soundproofing and privacy are achieved with padded separation panels.

Private Office. The private office will probably always exist in most organizations, although in decreasing fashion. Several reasons frequently cited for doing away with private offices are difficulty in supervising employees and communicating with others and problems in making layout changes as organizations reconfigure their needs.

Hybrid-Space Approach. A hybrid approach encompasses both open and closed spaces with convertibility that is easy and economical. For example, through the use of floor-to-ceiling panels, private offices are created in an instant and can be moved into other arrangements. In reality, most organizations design office space using this combination approach.

Manual and Automated Workflow

What organizations desperately need is to put knowledge in the hands of the right individual at the right time. Workflow is one way to help this to occur. **Workflow** is the movement of information from person to person within an organization. Another way of describing it is as a toolset, which enables organizations to proactively analyze, compress, and automate business processes, and then to develop and manage these processes. Workflow is definitely tied to knowledge management in that **knowledge management** is the capturing, communicating, and connecting of information with information seekers.[5]

One of the first activities in workflow management is to examine how documents move and are managed. Analytically, the process begins by examining how documents, business forms, and other information wind their way

An open plan using modular furniture offers companies flexibility and future growth opportunities. © *CORBIS*.

through an organization. For an office manager, this examination clearly pinpoints bottlenecks and outdated procedures that slow things down and add to costs.

Workflow Arrangements. To accomplish efficient office workflow, various physical arrangements are used. For example, workstations in the office can be arranged in groups or clusters to facilitate communication and efficient office operations. A cluster arrangement might be in the form of a Y, an X, or a variation of a circle as shown in Figure 19.1. Regardless of the physical arrangement used, workflow should be promoted and unnecessary traffic patterns eliminated.

When planning efficient office workflow, an AOM should:

1. Analyze the interrelationships among equipment, information, and personnel in the workflow first.

2. Have work move in a circular pattern or in as straight a line as possible, and circulate workflow around major source documents. Crisscrossing and backtracking should be avoided because they are time consumers and energy wasters.

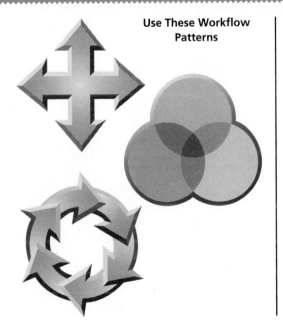

Use These Workflow Patterns

Avoid the Crisscrossing or Star Workflow Pattern

Figure 19.1

Good workflow facilitates communication and efficient office operations.

3. Take work to the employee; do not ask the employee to get up and get work to do.

On-Line Documents. Wouldn't it be nice to be able to create a document electronically, circulate it to others in your organization for comment, and then post it in a flash on the Internet or company intranet system? The advantage obviously is avoiding bottlenecks and delays while you wait for someone else to augment or reformat the document. Fortunately, vendors are developing new products to make sharing, managing, and posting to the Web in this way almost that easy. According to estimates made from a joint survey of 500 information technology managers by Information Week Research and Cap Ventures Inc., document system software seems to be growing about as fast as the Internet adds Web sites. Total spending for document system software jumped 38 percent in 1998 to $3.5 billion from $2.5 billion in 1997.[6]

One reason on-line documents are becoming so popular is because the intranet, which is an internal company network that uses Internet and Web technology, has highly successful firewalls protecting information from outside access. In other words, once a document is created from scratch on-line or scanned into an electronic or hypertext markup language (HTML) format, it can be dumped on the company intranet for internal use by employees who have been given proper access to it.

On-line document conversions range from simple to complex. Simple may refer to an individual report or manual, while complex may involve a series of libraries containing diverse, merged material. One company that uses on-line document conversion and company intranet development is Deere & Co., the world's leading producer of agricultural equipment. Essentially, Deere's intranet was built from electronic document conversion by taking existing documents, getting electronic files, and converting them to HTML format so they could be placed on Deere's intranet.

Historically, Deere's secretaries would input information into their word processors and store it on hard drives and disks. All of those files were gathered and converted. Today, Deere generates all documents on-line, which has the effect of greatly reducing internal print documents. Executives at Deere are emphatic that they view their intranet's success as an unprecedented opportunity to share the "corporate braintrust." A paradigm shift has occurred in that employees are starting to think about knowledge-sharing as part of their jobs.[7]

Workflow Automation. **Workflow automation** is a type of office software that manages workflow and on-line documents. Once the current workflow system has been analyzed and new routes laid out, workflow software is installed that conveys information instantly to the right desk and computer—whether that information is a digital image of an invoice or an e-mail query from a customer.

The trend of substituting the computer network system for a mail cart can be a great help to an AOM. It is an important step toward improving office workflow because, unfortunately, information spends most of its life moving from desk to desk or waiting in an in-basket to be acted upon or used.

For example, consider the manual steps involved in creating a simple document such as a marketing plan. First, research reports, memos, letters, and other relevant papers are gathered. Second, data are located and pulled from computer databases. Third, a first draft is written. Ensuing steps are marked by the first draft embarking on a long, twisted journey from one desk to another for review, editing, reediting, and approval. At each step, the document may wait on someone's desk or in-basket for hours or even days. As a consequence, according to consultants, gathering and transferring paper documents takes up the majority of time needed to finish typical office tasks.

Switching from paper to electronic documents, however, is only part of the solution. Unless the procedures for sharing information are revised as well, information could still be at a standstill. This is where the benefits of using workflow software surface. Workflow software makes the movement of documents automatic, eliminating the need for a human to decide who should get the information next, collapsing the travel time, and avoiding misrouting. Table 19.2 provides additional information and a further example of how workflow automation works.

Why all the sudden interest in workflow systems? In part, it is very difficult to look at improving a business process without automating its workflow. Moreover, improvements in technology make workflow automation easier and affordable for most organizations. Organizations are recognizing the ease, accuracy, and economies of scanning, storing, and moving paper documents electronically instead of manually.

Eventually, workflow management may become the backbone of many computer networks, working quietly behind the scenes to collect and move documents, fire up applications programs as needed, and do other chores as yet undefined. For now, though, companies that use workflow software are happy to have a relatively painless method for improving their productivity with lots of empty in-baskets.

An unexpected, but pleasant, benefit to workflow automation has been that simply contemplating the process appears to spark improvements. When asked to analyze and write an existing sequence of work steps, companies are forced to examine their procedures—sometimes for the first time. Because the payoffs are so obvious, experts say, workflow management is bound to become more widespread.

Office Design Trends

Major companies, such as IBM, have made significant changes away from traditional office layout and design—few private offices and even fewer amenities. At IBM, this approach reflects its mobile workforce and gives sales employees an incentive to be offsite initiating client contacts. The 600 staff members cannot come to work at the same time because there are only 220 desks. Communal facilities have been included for group activities, such as brainstorming with the aid of microcomputers and display systems.

Other companies have hotel-style check-in offices, while others have fold-down temporary desks. All the data are not in yet on the benefits of this change. There are those who believe this "unfriendly work environment" may affect staff adversely.

WORKFLOW AUTOMATION

What is workflow automation?	▪ It is both an analytical approach and a type of software.
	▪ It begins by examining how documents and business forms travel through an organization and pinpoints bottlenecks and outdated procedures that slow things down and add to costs.
	▪ It makes the movement of documents automatic, eliminating the need for a human to figure out who should get the information next, collapsing the travel times, and avoiding misrouting.

EXAMPLE: SHOWING STEPS USED TO PROCESS AN EXPENSE FORM ELECTRONICALLY

How does "workflow automation" work as It scans, stores, and moves paper documents electronically?	1. An employee fills out a "smart" expense form on a computer.
	2. The form routes itself over a computer network system to the appropriate manager for initial review. The form's arrival triggers the retrieval of the employee's files, which may also be needed by that manager.
	3. Everything checks out; however, because a payment of more than $3,000 is involved, the form automatically moves to the next level of management for special review.
	4. Upon final approval, the form sends a copy of itself to another computer, which cuts a check. Simultaneously, an electronic note is sent to remind the employee to pick up the check. The form then stores itself on an archival laser disk.

Table 19.2

Workflow Automation

Source: Adapted from John W. Verity, "Getting Work to Go with the Flow," Business Week, *June 21, 1993.*

Just as in the IBM example, futurists predict employees will increasingly divide their time between a central office, a home office, and a suburban satellite office. How will it work? One scenario is that central offices will become places where employees meet to share ideas. Even those few workers based at the central office will be more mobile, moving between different workstations as their tasks change and taking their mobile telephones with them.

This trend alone will cut the amount of wasted office space considerably. Common areas such as those for copying machines, coffee-break rooms, meetings and reception areas, which usually come second to the offices in which people spend most of the day working, will gradually become the heart of an office. This will be a natural occurrence as communication and projects completed through multi-functional teams escalate.

As a result, managers will have to abandon their long-cherished notion that a productive employee is an employee who can be seen. Appearing on time and looking busy will soon become irrelevant. Technology and new patterns of office use will make companies judge people by *what* they do, not by *where* they spend their time.

Consider the following three examples of patterns that are increasing in popularity:

1. "Nonterritorial" offices are places where workers do not have desks to call their own; instead they share desks.

2. Office "neighborhoods," for example, place the marketing, manufacturing, and design people close to each other, which makes it

easier for them to discuss ideas quickly and solve problems together.

3. "Think tank" areas are small offices equipped with a computer but no telephone. They are for the employee who just wants to be left alone to do intense, individual work.

OFFICE ERGONOMICS AND HEALTH CONCERNS

An increased concern for the health of employees is causing great interest in the area of office ergonomics. Office environmental and ergonomic factors are important to companies because they can directly affect worker productivity.

Office Ergonomics

The application of ergonomics is increasingly becoming an area of critical importance in the workplace. Ergonomics is the study of the interaction between people and their work environments. In the office, the concept embraces the idea that machines and office products should fit people, not the reverse. These products include chairs, desks, keyboards, monitors, telephones, and a grab bag of accessories, all aimed at taking the physical stress and strain out of office work.

For best results in productivity and comfort, people of different sizes and preferences require

Management Tip

Take office workers' complaints seriously. If possible, try to correct any health-related issues immediately. At the very least, you will have earned a happier worker, and you will have avoided possible litigation.

different positioning of equipment. In terms of ergonomic design, desks and chairs are the easiest items to adjust to fit a worker's needs. A company can best evaluate and satisfy its workers' ergonomic needs by fitting desks and equipment to each individual employee.

A workstation designed for the employee's size helps the employee be more productive and feel less fatigue. Figure 19.2 shows a well-designed workstation containing a microcomputer.

Employees who work in poorly lit areas, poorly designed chairs, offices with poor ventilation, and at computers are at greater risk of suffering from a variety of health problems than those who work at ergonomically sound work-

stations. Ergonomic workstations and stress-relief techniques can reduce employee injuries.

Employees who operate out of a virtual office and who do not have a fixed workplace face a number of ergonomic issues. One of these issues is the weight of the equipment that they have to carry while they work on-the-go. Selecting a briefcase with wide, padded shoulder straps can lessen this load. Still another ergonomic issue that needs to be addressed by virtual employees concerns the small screens and keyboards of laptops and notebook computers. In examining the ergonomics of these smaller computers, users should pay attention to how the equipment is designed, used, and transported, as well as how it functions.[8]

Figure 19.2

Work and comfort do go together in an ergonomically sound workstation.

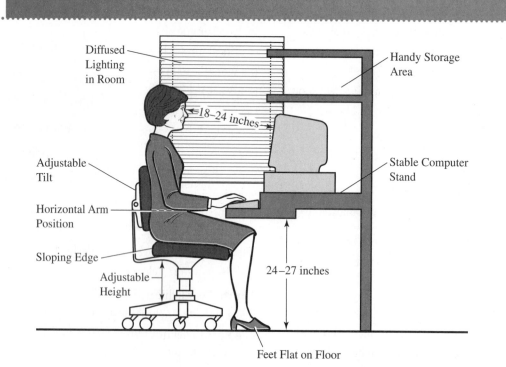

Diffused Lighting in Room

Handy Storage Area

←18–24 inches→

Adjustable Tilt

Horizontal Arm Position

Sloping Edge

Adjustable Height

Stable Computer Stand

24–27 inches

Feet Flat on Floor

Picture this typical scenario: An employee spends hours typing into a computer, with a telephone receiver crammed between his or her left ear and shoulder. By the afternoon, the lower back and the right side of the neck are throbbing. Working in an office can damage your health. Let's examine some health factors related to office work and some possible ways to minimize their effects.

Health Factors Related to Office Work

There appear to be, according to occupational health experts, four primary sources of frequent physical problems in offices: air, chairs, lights, and computers. Though these four health factors abound in offices, they can be controlled in several ways.

Air. Air quality is a growing concern because of the steadily increasing number of sealed office structures. The so-called "sick building syndrome" has been used to describe a range of complaints that encompass eye, nose, throat, and skin irritation, headache, fatigue, dizziness, difficulty in concentration, and shortness of breath. This syndrome is considered to exist in a particular building when at least 20 percent of the employees complain of similar symptoms, but the symptoms tend to disappear after employees leave the premises.

Although it is difficult to establish direct cause-and-effect relationships between office conditions and such illnesses, some serious ailments can be linked to microorganisms born in air conditioning or ventilation systems. Similarly, chemicals in carpets, drapes, and copying machines or the building materials themselves may induce physical reactions or illnesses.

One easy, yet relatively inexpensive, way to improve air quality is to add plants. Certain houseplants that require low light are especially effective in filtering certain chemicals from the air. Not only are plants used to improve air quality, they can also serve two functional purposes: as work dividers and as sound absorbers.

Chairs. Backaches and neck aches are related directly to the design and condition of the chair. In addition, musculoskeletal injuries caused by sitting in a chair for too long can be traced to poor lumbar (low back) support. What should you look for in a good chair?

1. Chairs should be adjustable to fit your body height, giving your legs good circulation (your feet should be able to rest flat on the floor with your knees bent at 90 degrees).

2. The seat and back should be contoured to the curves of your thighs and back.

3. Adjustable armrests should take some of the pressure off when you keyboard.

4. A chair should let you fidget—tilting, swiveling, and rocking as the spirit moves you.

The major problem with new chair options today is that many workers either do not know how or do not bother to make the needed adjustments. However, regardless of how the chair is designed, it is important to walk every half hour. Otherwise, you will invite fatigue and muscle stiffness.

Light. Poor lighting may lead to headaches or fatigue. Natural lighting is easiest on your eyes; but, because natural light is not always available in offices, incandescent lighting, which *almost* replicates natural daylight, is often used. One of the more common lighting problems, a desktop in shadow, can be taken care of easily with a desk lamp. The recommended intensity range for office lighting is 100 to 150 foot-candles. Eyestrain from dim lighting or harsh shadows should be corrected. Many vision problems office workers have today, however, are related to computers.

Computers. Increased use of personal computers for word processing, data entry, personal organization, and other business tasks related to using the Internet and intranets has drawn new attention to workplace ailments that can reduce employee productivity and increase a company's costs for workers' compensation. Some common ailments resulting from computer use are eyestrain and repetitive strain injury (RSI).

Eyestrain. How do computers cause eyestrain? It is not that monitors emit rays that are harmful to the eyes; rather, staring at small letters and numerals on a screen for hours on end can create visual fatigue. This is also caused by the glare of an overbright or badly placed light that reflects off a computer screen.

For any computer operator, a regular eye examination is important. In addition, a number of eye specialists recommend following the 20-20 rule: Keep your face at least 20 inches from the screen and pause every 20 minutes to look around the room. In addition, exercising the eyes can help reduce eyestrain. Proper eye-care is essential; poor work habits and inadequate lighting cause many cases of fatigue, headaches, and eyestrain.[9]

Repetitive Strain Injury. Tingling in fingers, pain in hands or wrists that doesn't disappear if you rest for 24 to 48 hours, loss of dexterity, muscle fatigue, loss of gripping strength, a sudden inability to perform normal tasks such as washing your hair or opening a jar—any of these complaints could be a symptom of repetitive strain injury.[10] Though workers have been typing for decades, it is believed that, since computer keyboards are larger than those of typewriters and lack the built-in pause provided by carriage returns, RSI is becoming more common among office workers. Pain in the neck, back, shoulders, arms, wrists, and legs can be thwarted by taking regular full-body stretches away from the computer workstation or desk.

Workers often forget how long they have been sitting in one position. As a result, some muscles may tighten and connective tissue may strain. The idea is that shifting the body or changing its relation to the screen and keyboard will help. Repetitive strain injuries, such as carpal tunnel syndrome and tendinitis, are caused from poor keyboarding position, such as elevated elbows, bent wrists, and excessive pounding of the keyboard. Here are some exercises that will help to reduce strain on the carpal tunnel area:

- Rest your forearm on the edge of the desk, palm down. Grasp the fingers of the resting hand and gently bend your wrist back for 5 seconds. Repeat with the other hand.
- Gently press your hand against the table and stretch your wrist and fingers for 5 seconds. Repeat with the other hand.
- Tightly clench both hands and release, fanning and stretching your fingers out.

- Sit upright in your chair with your feet flat on the floor. Lower your head and slowly roll your body as far as you can toward your knees. Hold this position for 20 seconds. Push yourself up with your leg muscles. Repeat three times.
- Keep a squeeze toy by your desk, or some Silly Putty or Play-Doh to give your hands a little workout once in a while.[11]

Preventing Computer Injuries

In *ZAP! How Your Computer Can Hurt You—And What You Can Do About It,* author Don Sellers offers these suggestions to avoid computer-related injuries:

1. Correct ergonomic problems promptly. The longer stresses continue, the more difficult the damage is to repair.

2. Minimize the strain. If possible, intersperse computer work with other tasks. Type with less force.

3. Move. Every 50 minutes or so, get up. Walk down the hall. Move your hands, wrists, and arms. Bend and stretch. Rotate your shoulders. Turn your head.

4. Rest your eyes periodically. Take a 15-minute rest break every two hours for moderately demanding computer work. During the break, make phone calls, file, or do pencil-and-paper planning.

5. Invest in special computer glasses designed for computer use. Make the design correct for the distance and angle at which you view the monitor.

6. Balance the lighting. When you look at your computer screen, there should be no hot spots of bright light around it.

7. Position your monitor 18 to 24 inches from your eyes. Adjust the angle to eliminate reflections and clean the screen regularly.

8. Sit in a chair that fits you. Have a co-worker check your posture when you are sitting at your computer.

9. Adjust the surface on which the keyboard sits so that your wrists are not forced into unnatural positions—bent up or down.

10. Work defensively. Sit directly in front of your keyboard.[12]

Table 19.3 summarizes the four major health risks, as well as their symptoms if each is not controlled.

OFFICE HAZARDS

Small businesses need to plan for managerial crises as much as large corporations do. These crises can be accidental, criminal, or legal in nature and require a way to coordinate employees and to communicate with the public effectively.

Handling Crisis Situations

In this age of heightened consumer awareness and

> **Management Tip**
>
> *The first action to take if someone is injured is to call for professional help. While you wait for emergency personnel to arrive, you can begin administering first aid. Take time now to learn CPR. Your ability to respond may make a life-saving difference to an injured co-worker.*

FACTOR	RISK	SYMPTOMS, IF NOT CONTROLLED
Air	"Sick building syndrome"	▪ Eye, nose, throat, and skin irritation ▪ Headache, fatigue, dizziness, shortness of breath
Chairs	Musculoskeletal injuries (due to the design and condition of the chair)	▪ Backaches and neck aches
Lights	Poor lighting	▪ Eyestrain from dim lighting, glares, or shadows that often results in headaches or feelings of fatigue
Computers	Eyestrain (from staring at small letters on a screen) Repetitive stress injury (from poor position at the keyboard and lack of frequent bodily movement)	▪ Visual fatigue ▪ Pain in the neck, back, shoulders, arms, wrists ▪ Carpal tunnel syndrome ▪ Tendinitis

Table 19.3

Major Office
Health Risks

rapid news dissemination, preparing to manage crises and respond under fire can help mitigate the effects of almost every kind of problem—ranging from allegations of defective products to workplace accidents.

Why plan ahead? Every decision you can make *before* a crisis is usually more rational than those made in the middle of one. If you have prepared for the crisis, decisions will be more rational and better received, and the crisis will be of shorter duration.

Accidents in the Office

Many people think of work accidents as happening only in factories or at construction sites. However, accidents also happen in the office. Accidents occur most often when workers are tired, overstressed, or impatient and try to take shortcuts. Most job-related accidents are preventable but require all workers to play a key, proactive role in creating safe workplaces. Some examples of typical office hazards and their consequences are:

1. opening more than one file drawer at a time, causing the cabinet to fall over;

2. leaving a handbag or briefcase on the floor, causing someone to trip;

3. standing on a chair that moves, causing someone to fall;

4. stooping and lifting improperly, causing back injuries;

5. tripping over exposed cords; and

6. having insufficient electrical voltage for all the equipment, causing a power shortage or fire.

For the AOM, the key to providing a safe workplace and reducing on-the-job injuries and accidents is to recognize hazardous conditions and take steps *immediately* to correct them. One effective technique is to use an end-of-the-day safety checklist that might include the following questions. Coffeepots off? Hot plates off? Printers off? Copy Machines off? Lights off?

OFFICE SAFETY

Threats to employee safety in the workplace are increasing in frequency and severity and, contrary to most thinking, are not limited to big cities or high-profile companies. Daily news reports reaffirm that holdups, homicides, hostage taking, rape, and other acts of violence are being committed every day where people work.

Many people, even those who take every precaution to safeguard their lives and property at home, take their personal safety at work for

In what ways does this office setting invite safety concerns?
© *PhotoDisc, Inc.*

granted. It is natural to be complacent while you're working: You are focused on accomplishing the tasks of the day and assume your employer will see to your protection. But your safety is something you cannot afford to take for granted. As an AOM, you can protect yourself and your co-workers by being prepared for office theft, workplace violence, and office rapes.

Office Theft

Office thefts can range from someone absconding with the corporate credit cards to a major break-in involving your company's equipment, cash, and other assets. Here are a few ways to thwart would-be burglars.

1. Limit access. Put a barrier, such as a counter or half door, between the workspace and the public area.

2. Do not keep a lot of cash or valuables on the premises. Consider electronic surveillance or on-site security.

3. Lock the door after dark, even if your company is still open for business. Install a bell or buzzer system to alert you to incoming visits.

4. Cancel immediately any company-issued access or credit cards of terminated employees. Also change the locks—especially if keys have not been collected.

5. Identify with an engraved number portable equipment such as calculators, computers, and radios.

6. Maintain well-lighted premises.

7. Keep an eye on your wallet or purse. Keep it out of sight and locked in your drawer, a closet, or a nearby file cabinet.[13]

Workplace Violence

Increased stress, easy access to handguns, the dehumanization of the worker—experts cite all these as reasons for growing violence in the American workplace.[14] The loss of life in workplace violence is mercifully rare, but the impact of violence of any kind can be tremendous. A certain level of civility and cooperation is fundamental to the operation of any business; shatter that level through an act of violence, and the effect can be devastating. Because violence is so destructive, businesses should try to head it off and not look for ways to deal with it *after* it occurs.

Although many acts of workplace violence appear completely random, violence experts agree there are actually many things companies can do to prevent violent outbreaks from occurring. Here are some of their suggestions for combating violence:

- Screen potential employees thoroughly. If you don't have the resources on staff to do so, then hire outside services to conduct criminal background checks for a nominal cost.
- Implement a zero-tolerance policy with harsh repercussions for violent or threatening behavior at the workplace.
- Report all threats of violence to the police. Certain circumstances may even warrant the temporary use of a security firm.
- Create a workplace culture that encourages mutual respect and open communication. Conduct training for employees and supervisors that covers conflict resolution, how to report and handle complaints of unfair treatment, and how to recognize signs of a potentially violent employee.
- Provide job counseling for terminated employees. Termination is a traumatic

change and counseling can help these individuals cope.

- Address workplace security as part of an overall plan that includes building access, use of access cards, visitor controls, emergency procedures, monitoring systems and security guards. Give particular attention to night-shift workers.[15]

Office Rapes

According to Linda Fairstein's book *Sexual Violence: Twenty Years as a Sex Crimes Prosecutor,* two in ten stranger rapes handled by her office occur at work or en route to or from work. In addition, one in ten acquaintance-rape cases is work related. The most common scenarios involve business trips, office parties, and out-of-the-office meetings.[16]

Some advice for AOMs and working women is to look for security risks. For example, look for unlocked bathrooms, lack of night security, unoccupied floors, and unlit parking lots, and ask the boss to correct these risks immediately. Remember that if security risks were brought to the attention of management and they were ignored, employers can be held liable for stranger rapes.

Although most companies are very conscious of liability and risk management and their associated costs, not all of them have a formal security program. Things happen so fast during a crisis you do not have time to think. That is why it is important to plan ahead for emergencies and train employees to follow prescribed company procedures. For example, banks have trained their employees in the procedures to follow in the event of a robbery.

This knowledge has saved countless lives over the years.

When faced with danger at your desk, a cool head and common sense greatly increase your chances of survival. You can protect yourself and your co-workers by being prepared.

OFFICE RECYCLING

The three R's—recycling, reusing, and reducing—apply to a lot more than copy paper and aluminum cans from the vending machine. Office recycling has gone from a feel-good issue to a bottom-line issue. If you minimize waste and maximize resources efficiency, you cannot help but improve profitability.

Recycle

Today, offices use items that could not be recycled a few years ago. For example, consider toner cartridges for laser printers and copiers. Even in this electronic age, paper copiers are a must, so most offices go through boxloads of cartridges, which cost upwards of $100 each.

By replacing the inside works, you can save up to 30 percent over the cost of new cartridges. Consider these other recycling ideas:

1. Buy pens with replaceable cartridges and mechanical pencils that can be refilled instead of disposable items.

2. Buy white legal pads over the traditional yellow ones, because colored paper requires bleaching, which raises the cost of producing recycled products.

3. Use only paper that has been recycled and is recyclable.

4. Donate computer printouts and other paper to a nursery or elementary school so they can be used for painting, drawing, and scribbling.

In addition, AOMs should consider recycling obsolete computers, telephones, or other equipment no longer needed. Organizations exist that will match your out-of-date equipment with a charity or nonprofit group that needs it.

Reuse

Large-corporation downsizing has fueled an expanding market in recycled office furnishings. As a result, value-conscious administrative office managers are only too happy to absorb the deluge of preowned desks, chairs, tables, and panels that, sold scuffed and bruised "as-is," offer savings of as much as 80 percent off the manufacturer's list price. Even after they are given "like new" upholstery and veneer, used work surfaces and chairs will save as much as 74 percent over purchasing new ones.[17]

Reduce

It is human nature to continue using items at the same level, rather than reducing their use. Examples abound, but reduction methods used at some organizations include:

- duplexing (producing two-sided) copies instead of running single sheets,

- saving used, one-sided paper copies and making note pads

- using transparency overheads instead of multipage copies of handouts at meetings,

- routing messages on e-mail instead of memos,

- posting reminders to turn off lights or equipment when not in use or installing occupancy sensors in the lunchroom, restrooms, or other lower traffic locations where employees might forget to turn off the lights when they leave,

- cutting down on packaging by ordering office supplies and materials in bulk,

- investing in energy-saving lightbulbs and lighting equipment,

- using all of the paper as possible. For example, limit the use of wide margins, double-spacing, and large print on letters and memos.

- hanging a bulletin board in a prominent location; instead of sending a memo to everyone, post important notices on the board, and

- encouraging people to commute together by sponsoring a rideshare program.

Message *for* AOMs

Perhaps the most control an employer can exercise over health costs is control over the employee's work environment. Making an office environment human-friendly is easier to do when utilizing the advice and suggestions in this chapter. In the office, as in other areas of our lives, little things can and do mean a lot. The results of planning ahead generally pay off in a substantial way over time.

Taking precautions to prevent office-related problems as they occur need not be complex or expensive. In relation to the workstation environment, for example, just simply looking at how a person is using the workstation will probably tell you if he or she is comfortable.

1 An office environment is made up of several interdependent systems: people, floor plans, furniture, equipment, lighting, air quality, and acoustics.

2 "Nonterritorial" offices are places where workers do not have desks to call their own; instead, they share desks. Office "neighborhoods," for example, place the marketing, manufacturing, and design people close to each other, which makes it easier for them to discuss ideas quickly and solve problems together. "Think tank" areas are small offices equipped with a computer, but no telephone, and are for the employee who just wants to be left alone to do intense, individual work.

3 Ergonomics is the study of the interaction between people and their work environments. In the office, the concept embraces the idea that machines and office products should fit people, not the reverse.

4 Four primary sources of frequent physical problems in offices are air, chairs, lights, and computers.

5 Some examples of office hazards are opening more than one file drawer at a time, causing the cabinet to fall over; leaving a handbag or briefcase on the floor, causing someone to trip; and standing on a chair that moves, causing someone to fall.

6 Some physical threats to employee safety in the workplace are holdups, homicides, hostage taking, and rape.

7 Some examples of office recycling activities are using only paper that has been recycled and is recyclable; donating computer printouts and other paper to a nursery or elementary school so they can be used for painting, drawing, and scribbling; and recycling obsolete computers, telephones, or other equipment no longer needed.

QUESTIONS FOR CRITICAL THINKING

1. In your opinion, what are the three most important design and layout issues when creating a pleasant office environment?

2. Why are so many offices using an open plan area design?

3. To enhance effective office workflow, describe ways in which workstations can be arranged.

4. What are the advantages of on-line documents to an organization?

5. Which future trend in office design do you feel is most likely to occur?

6. Why is ergonomics important in today's workplace?

7. Rank the four primary sources of frequent physical problems in the office according to their seriousness for the office worker.

8. If you know people who suffer from carpal tunnel syndrome or tendinitis, describe their causes or symptoms.

9. Describe at least two examples of office hazards that can easily be avoided.

10. In your opinion, have office workers become supportive of recycling activities because of financial reasons or because of environmental awareness? Explain.

Case Study 19-1: Desk Clutter

Mr. Jerry Odell, senior manager at Odell Legal Corporation, has recently announced a new policy. The policy states that there will be no appearance of cluttered desks at the end of the day in the law firm. When asked about the change, Mr. Odell said the idea came from a time-and-stress management seminar he attended two weeks ago. The new idea was that the average worker has 36 hours' worth of work on his or her desk and wastes three hours a week just searching for things. In addition, whether employees are conscious of it or not, a cluttered desk is a stress-provoking symbol of failure when a person scans his or her desk at the end of every day and sees it as cluttered as much or more as it was that morning. If you worked in this firm, would you willingly buy into this new policy?

Discussion Questions

1. Do you feel a cluttered desk is a problem in many offices today?

2. What factors in the typical office environment contribute to cluttered desks.

3. What are some suggestions you could recommend to lessen clutter on desks and address this problem?

Case Study 19-2: Domestic Violence on the Job

Margie Psalmonds, administrative office manager at Glendale Insurance Company, notices that Sylvia, an office worker, has been looking toward the front door and acting jumpy since arriving at work an hour ago. It appears also that Sylvia is not focused on getting her work done.

Margie approaches Sylvia and asks if she can meet with her for a moment in the conference room. After closing the door, Margie asked if Sylvia was all right. Sylvia said that she was really scared. She had separated from her husband last night after a violent argument and is afraid he will come to see her on the job today. She said that he threatened her last night, saying that if she left him, she'd be sorry.

Discussion Questions

1. In your opinion, is there reason for a safety concern on the AOM's part? If so, why?

2. What are the initial steps an AOM should take in this situation? Be as specific as you can.

Case Study 19-3: Internet Research Activity

Assume you are doing a report on *on-line documents*. Use the Internet to research information needed to answer the following questions. Key your responses.

1. Which Web search engine did you use?

2. Write down three of the URL addresses that you accessed during your search.

3. As a result of your search, list three items of current information you might use in your report.

Endnotes

[1]Judith Davidson, "The Changing Office," *Interior Design*, May 1997, p. 87.

[2]Phyl Smith and Lynn Kearny, "Too Much Togetherness: Is Your Office Design Hurting Productivity?" *Managing Office Technology*, September 1998, p. 27.

[3]Barbara Stein, "Squeezing into a Small Space," *Home Office Computing*, September 1993, p. 29.

[4]Teresita Deupi, "Designing for the New Century: Making the Office More Powerful," *Managing Office Technology*, April 1997, p. 24.

[5]John Dykeman, "The Road Ahead for Workflow: The Future of Managing the Information Process," *Managing Office Technology*, April 1998, pp. 29–30.

[6]John Eckhouse, "More Document Flexibility," *Information Week*, August 3, 1998, p. 2.

[7]Kenneth W. Volgman, "Instant Information Access: Redefining the Workplace," *IIE Solutions*, July 1998, pp. 37–38.

[8]Gregg Labar, "Ergonomics for the Virtual Office," *Managing Office Technology*, October 1997, p. 23.

[9]Doug Fine, "Hands-On Guide to No-Pain Computing," *PC World*, June 1996, p. 151.

[10]Don Sellers, "Finding a Computer-Savvy Doctor," *Macworld*, June 1996, p. 166.

[11]Ibid., p. 153.

[12]Don Sellers, *ZAP! How Your Computer Can Hurt You— And What You Can Do About It* (Peachpit Press: Berkeley, CA, 1994).

[13]Kim Toner, "Dealing with Workplace Dangers," *The Secretary*, June–July 1994, p. 13.

[14]Jesse Leavenworth and Liz Halloran, "Stress, Access to Guns Blamed for Rise in Violence," *Hartford Courant*, March 7, 1998, p. A7.

[15]Shari Caudron, "Tips to Combat Workplace Violence," *Workforce*, August 1998, p. 47.

[16]Marua Sheehy, "Linda Fairstein: Fighting the Rise of Office Rapes," *Working Woman*, October 1993, p. 13.

[17]Karen E. Carney, "The Business's Yard Sale," *Inc.*, July 1994, p. 102.

Other Office Systems: Records, Copying, Telephone, Mail, and Accounting

chapter 20

> It's amazing what ordinary people can do if they set out without preconceived notions.
>
> —Charles Kettering

objectives

After completing this chapter, you will be able to:

1. **List major office systems used in organizations in addition to computer systems.**

2. **List the four major classifications for records in a records management system.**

3. **Explain the differences between microfiche and microfilm as options for paper filing and storage.**

4. **Discuss the advantages of a centralized copy center as compared to decentralized copier locations.**

5. **List some special features that can be added to a phone system.**

6. **Identify benefits of voice mail to the organization and its customers.**

7. **List typical services available from the U.S. Postal Service.**

8. **Describe the importance to organizations of preparing financial statements on a regular basis.**

Corporate America is faced with a problem unlike anything it has experienced since the Great Depression—a customer crisis. This stems from the fact that we are a better educated and more affluent, discerning, and demanding society in terms of product quality and service responsiveness. Traditional allegiance to a brand, an institution, or even a party line is history. Whether a customer remains loyal could depend on how efficient office systems (other than computers) are managed to serve customer needs in a superior manner. These other office systems include records management, reprographics (copier), telephone, mail, and accounting systems.

RECORDS AND MICROIMAGE SYSTEMS

Protecting records is one of the most important tasks for any organization. References to business records are in the news media virtually every

Elizabeth A. Regan, Ph.D.

Systems Consultant
Information Systems
Development Division
Mass. Mutual Life Insurance
Company
Springfield, Massachusetts

As a consultant at Mass. Mutual Life Insurance Company, Elizabeth A. Regan currently has responsibility for implementing a major strategic effort for the company's insurance and financial management line of business. This multiyear project involves significant business cultural changes in the company's insurance agency distribution system as well as reengineering in the home office. Dr. Regan has served as president of the Office Systems Research Association (OSRA).

QUESTION:

A classic problem for records management is helping people "put their finger on the right information at the right time." How are information systems helping the insurance industry address this problem, and what effect are these efforts having on records management?

To a large extent, paper files have become a major bottleneck in restructuring business processes. Dependency on paper forces many tasks to be done in a linear, step-by-step sequence, as the paper file is passed from one workstation to another. If all the information were on-line, many

Dialog *from the* Workplace

RESPONSE:

In a world where change has become a constant, employees are continually barraged with communications but often have trouble finding the information they need to get the job done. Existing procedures for documenting, learning, and managing business information are no longer meeting the demand.

The emphasis today is on integrated solutions that support business processes rather than isolated functional solutions. I think we'll see more of a trend in that direction. The emphasis on systems support is on active records rather than archival records; however, steps taken to put information on-line will eventually have an impact on all records management. Just the fact that the information is available on-line, whether or not it is also available on paper, has many implications.

steps in the process could be handled simultaneously. Two new tools for addressing these issues are image systems and workflow processing software. Although image systems have not won wide acceptance as a records management tool in the past, I think the opportunities they offer, when coupled with workflow software, to restructure business processes will win widespread application.

Getting rid of paper is an issue of getting users to accept electronic media as a delivery platform for information. In order to induce people to give up their paper, on-line systems must be flexible, accessible, and easy to use. They must deliver real benefits that are immediately apparent to the user. If they do, little arm-twisting will be necessary.

day. Corporations find themselves defending in the press or explaining in court statements made in documents written many years ago. The irony is that establishing a corporate records management program could prevent most of these oft-publicized problems.

These realities make it imperative to have a program that addresses records retention, inactive record storage, and active record management. Whether you are managing files for your department or the entire organization, these guidelines can help establish a plan and secure staff support.

The longer an organization remains in business, the greater the accumulation of records. As a result, the amount of misfiled paperwork increases, old records cannot be located, and pieces of a file may become scattered among several locations and eventually misplaced or lost.

In an organization, **records management** deals with the control, retention, and security of records and files. The pace of business today demands that information be made available in a matter of seconds, rather than hours. This demand requires that organizations develop effective records management guidelines which provide safeguards to protect organizations from the loss of records vital to the operation of the business.

Often companies keep records longer than necessary because employees do not know what they must keep and what they can safely throw away. A records retention schedule resolves that situation because it is a listing of all the organization's records categories, specifying the time period that each should be retained.[1]

Records Management Guidelines

Figure 20.1 illustrates the consequence of a poor records management system. Improper records maintenance and destruction can create severe legal problems for a business.

Can some records management systems give you this feeling?

HELP!!

RECORDS   RECORDS

Figure 20.1

Records are of no use to anyone in the organization unless they are accessible and managed well.

Organizations must establish procedures to follow and guidelines to keep in mind when making decisions, such as which records should be kept, which are obsolete, and which should be destroyed. The costs associated with records maintenance include filing and retrieval time, equipment and supplies for housing records, in-house storage space, and out-of-house storage of old or inactive records.

The time necessary to file or retrieve a record increases in proportion to the growth of records. Many companies either keep records forever or, because of high costs and lack of space, indiscriminately destroy old ones. At best, maintenance decisions often are based on educated guesses or the mythological "seven-year rule."

When an organization sets up a solid, well-managed records system, specific guidelines should be clearly established for legal as well as efficiency purposes. Table 20.1 describes what

an office manager must develop and plan for when setting up an effective records management system.

One of the most important skills in records management is classifying documents and records correctly. Generally, the four classifications used are records that are vital, important, useful, and nonessential. Table 20.2 shows the four classifications of records, their retention time, and also some examples of each type of office record.

Microimage Technology and Trends

The infiltration of electronic computers, magnetic tape, and disk storage in the workplace has not replaced paper documents or the need for an effective way to store them. Recent technology provides companies with many options for paper storage, including micrographic and imaging systems.

AN EFFECTIVE RECORDS MANAGEMENT SYSTEM SHOULD DETAIL

1. How to locate and organize records for easy access.

2. How to identify inactive records, when to retire records to storage, and how to maintain these records in accordance with established records management procedures, as well as what the statute of limitations is for retention purposes.

3. How office personnel will be trained in the use and function of established records management procedures.

4. When and who evaluates current records programs for possible computer or microimaging applications.

5. Who is responsible for updating all records programs.

6. Who is assigned to supervise the microimaging production and retrieval systems.

Table 20.1

Records Management Guidelines

CLASSIFICATION	EXAMPLES	RECOMMENDED RETENTION TIME
Vital Records	Irreplaceable documents, such as property deeds, copyrights, leases, contracts, and other legal documents	Kept permanently
Important Records	Documents that contribute to the smooth operation of the business but can usually be replaced, such as financial documents, inventory, and tax records	Kept for a longer period of time but are eventually destroyed
Useful Records	Documents reflective of everyday business operations, such as correspondence and reports	Kept based on state statutes of limitations
Nonessential Records	Documents such as internal memos and correspondence	Can be destroyed when their purpose is accomplished

Table 20.2

Guide to Classifying Documents

Adapted from "For the Record" by Elizabeth H. Stanford, The Secretary, *August/September 1994.*

Microimage Technology. Microimage technology takes the form of both microfilm and microfiche. **Microfilm,** which generally comes as a 35-mm or 16-mm roll of film, is a proven archival medium for long-term storage with low equipment costs and comparatively fast retrieval. This medium is used extensively for storage of newspapers and other full-text documents. After processing, the original paper records can be destroyed or recycled.

Microfiche, on the other hand, consists of index-card-sized film that can be read on a variety of microfiche readers or printed out in the form of paper enlargements, usually 8 ½" × 11". Microfiche is also easy to copy and mail in a regular envelope. Reader-printers, which are operated manually or electrically, are fairly inexpensive, easy to use, and constantly undergoing improvement to provide users with cost-effective access to data stored on either microfiche or microfilm. These technologies are well developed and are used to record both text and numbers in an inexpensive and durable format. Companies that use micrographic technology decrease storage space, reduce retrieval time, and eliminate file duplication.

Micrographics can be linked to computers in different ways to improve both input and output speed. For example, **computer output microfilm (COM),** which has been around for

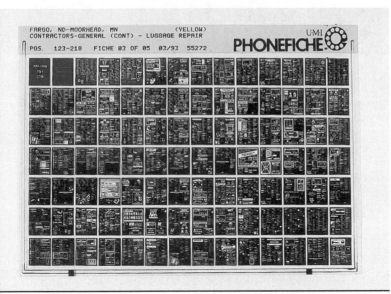

An example of microfiche.   © *Jeff Greenberg/MRp*

on compact disk is that it allows more data to be stored in less space. For instance, images are transferable between microfilm and disk. Data is first stored on optical disks for 30 to 90 days—the period of highest use—and then the data is archived to microfilm. As a result, the disks can then be reused.

Imaging systems offer many benefits to the businessperson. They offer the dependability of micrographics and the sophistication and state-of-the-art technology of optical disks. Companies see integrated micrographics and optical disk systems as the best way to accomplish automated data entry, networking, high-capacity storage, and laser printer output.

REPROGRAPHIC (COPIER) SYSTEMS

Office copier systems can be set up either as a centralized copy center where copier specialists perform all copying or as several decentralized copiers available to employees on an "on-demand" basis.

Centralized Copying

Centralized copy centers can save organizations money by limiting the number of individual copiers needed and by reducing per-copy costs. Upfront costs may be high due to the cost of machines designed to handle high-volume photocopying, but the benefits of centralized copying are many. Besides cost issues, advantages include increased security via access codes and the opportunity to review printing statistics for a specific department or organization. Issues to consider when installing a centralized copy center include convenience, storage and workspace

many years, transfers computer data directly to microfilm through automated conversion of digital information. COM records can operate either on-line or off-line. Currently, the majority of reports output from computers are printed on paper. Yet, COM is a faster and less expensive medium than paper.

Still another microimage technology is integrating microfilm recorders with computers, laser printers, and digital scanners. Paper documents can then be transformed into computer-generated and computer-stored images. Such imaging systems are beneficial to companies that require high-capacity storage, networking, and laser printer output.

Imaging Systems. Advances in records management technology, such as intelligent character recognition and optical storage on compact disks, promise to make the maintenance of data more efficient. The advantage of optical storage requirements, and location. A user evaluation of the copy center's effectiveness should be conducted by the AOM on a regular basis.

Decentralized Copying

In a decentralized reprographics environment, copiers are strategically and conveniently located throughout a company. As copies become less expensive and equipment more sophisticated, many offices are choosing to purchase additional individual copiers. Employees do not have to walk far to reach the machines, and they can make copies whenever they need them.

This kind of "on-demand" system works well in small offices where the volume of copies does not justify a centralized system. The biggest advantage of the decentralized approach is convenience, and the major disadvantage is lack of control.

Copier Controls

Regardless of whether a copier system is centralized or decentralized, the use of copier controls is growing as companies strive to keep costs down and reduce waste. It is estimated that more than 600 billion copies are made annually, and 25 percent of these copies are unnecessary. By using copier controls, a company can discern if any machines are being used too little or too much.[2]

Several methods of copier control have been developed to help eliminate copier abuse and misuse. One method is to assign numbers to users so that every time an employee uses the copier, a preassigned number is entered that serves to track usage. Another method is to ask employees to use a magnetic-stripe card, much

Office copier systems can be either centralized or decentralized.
© *PhotoDisc, Inc.*

like a credit card, that will authorize use and activate the copier.

A new monitoring technique is to collect information about all copier activity through telecommunications technology. A phone line, PC, modem, and software now permit a central computer terminal to generate reports of all copier activity within a company. In that way, costs per copy are attributed to specific users or departments. Popular copier features are described in Table 20.3.

What can businesses expect of future reprographic systems? The role of photocopiers is becoming increasingly important with, for example, the advent of the use of digital technology for document imaging. Document imaging is performed with a personal computer that is linked to a copier, a scanner, or fax machine.

FEATURE	EXAMPLES OF FUNCTIONS
Copy size	Can accommodate from 5½" × 8½" to 11" × 17"
Originals	Can be sheets, books, 3-D objects
Speed	Can run from 23 to 80+ copies per minute
Collating and stapling	Can copy in an assembled fashion and staple top-left corner of set, if desired
Duplexing	Can copy front-to-back copies
Reducing and magnifying	Can adjust copy in increments of size
Other	Front-loading paper drawers, image shift, book copy, automatic paper selection, automatic magnification selection, auto tray switching, large capacity cassette tray, dual original copying, 20+ bin sorter, color units, energy save, help screens, and multiple copy countdown system

Table 20.3

Features of Copier Systems

With this set-up, the user can first scan or create a document and then send it to a copier. Additional advances in copier technology include improved copy quality, reliability, and affordability. Many businesses have been hesitant to pay the high price for a color copier, but as new software programs and color printers are made available, demand for color copiers will increase.

Reprographic Technology and Trends

There is a growing market for digital copiers, according to the market research firm Dataquest. It reported that sales of digital copiers tripled from 1996 to 1997. **Digital copiers** scan documents, convert them into computer files, and then print copies from those files. Although they can cost in excess of 15 percent more than analog units and generally take longer to produce a first copy, digital copiers reproduce images better and are far more versatile. Many models can be outfitted with modules that transform them into printers, scanners, or fax machines, making it possible for a square-footage-strapped business to substitute one piece of equipment for many.[3]

TELEPHONE SYSTEMS

The telephone is perhaps *the* most important piece of business equipment. Businesses use telephones to make first impressions, sell products, provide customer service, and negotiate contracts. The telephone can be a painful interruption to the business at hand, or it can be a vital tool for getting things done. The difference, of course, is determined by how you use it. When properly used, communications tools that make an organization's telephone system more efficient greatly improve customer service.

Organizations can elect to install either a private branch exchange (PBX) or a Centrex telephone system. The private branch exchange system is one in which all calls are answered by an operator or receptionist and then transferred to the person requested. The Centrex system, in contrast, is one in which individuals can directly answer calls. Which system is selected depends on the organization's need for immediate and direct interaction with customers, as well as employees' preferences with respect to how they work best.

Telephone Services and Features

Depending on your needs, a wide range of services and features can be added and adapted to an existing business phone system. These optional calling services include

1. Call waiting

2. Caller ID

3. Call-waiting ID

4. Voice messaging Service

5. Call forwarding

6. Call rejection

7. Call trace

8. Continuous redial

9. Last-call return

10. Priority call

11. Selective call forwarding

12. Speed calling

13. Caller ID blocking options

14. Three-way calling

> **Management Tip**
>
> *To stay current on telecommunication technology, skim the front pages of the phone book each year to find out which offerings have been added to those of last year or modified and improved in some way.*

Table 20.4 provides a brief explanation of several optional calling services.

Conference Calling

The administrative office manager with an eye to productivity knows that conference calling is the high-tech ticket to the essential real-time meeting of multiple minds. Business conference calling makes sense because it eliminates travel and inconvenience for everyone.

There are some things you can do to ensure smooth and effective conference calls:

1. Check out your speakerphone with the operator. Many sound problems are caused by a poor-quality speakerphone.

2. Choose a telephone with no external interruptions such as call waiting.

3. Establish a meeting agenda before the conference to keep the meeting running smoothly.

TELEPHONE SYSTEMS	
PBX	Operator-Assisted Calls
Centrex	Individual Answers Own Calls
Business Services:	1. *Automatic callback.* When you call a busy number, the automatic callback feature "remembers" the number and dials it for you automatically after you hang up.
	2. *Call forwarding—busy line—don't answer.* If your line is busy or if you don't answer after so many rings, this feature reroutes calls to a designated answering station.
	3. *Call waiting.* This feature allows the caller to reach you even when your line is busy. A gentle signal alerts you to an incoming call while you are talking.
	4. *Distinctive ring.* This ring signals the source of an incoming call. One ring means it is an inside call; two rings mean it is an outside call.
	5. *Speed calling.* Speed calling saves time and avoids wrong numbers by dialing frequently called numbers with a fast one- or two-digit code that you have programmed into the phone system.
	6. *Wide-area telecommunications service.* The WATS feature is a service that allows companies to cut costs if they make frequent long-distance calls within a geographic area.
	7. *800/888 service.* This service is free to callers. Long-distance charges for calls are paid at a volume discount rate by the company you are calling.
	8. *Intercom.* An intercom is essentially a fast connection to a telephone within the company.
	9. *Caller ID.* Caller ID shows you the name and number of the person who is calling and keeps a log of recent calls.
	10. *Anonymous Call Rejection.* This feature blocks anonymous or private phone calls unless the calling party reveals his phone number.

Table 20.4

Telephone
Systems and
Business Services

4. Help conference participants value meeting etiquette by

- being prepared with the information needed for the call,

- keeping paper shuffling and extraneous conversation to a minimum, and

- using the mute button on the speakerphone when not talking.

Voice Mail

At a time when qualified, skilled employees are harder than ever to find, eliminating the need to hire extra telephone receptionists to handle routine calls—from vendors, employees, and/or salespeople—makes good economic sense. **Voice mail** is a computerized telephone system that allows callers to leave messages. This technology permits a higher volume of phone traffic to be handled quickly, without having to add extra employees to the payroll. An automated phone system relieves the constant pressure and wear on an already busy staff, while virtually eliminating inaccurate messages.

Benefits of Voice Mail. Some experts say that voice mail is the most important piece of office automation since the copier. Estimates are that voice mail technology has cut callbacks in half. Users also cite reliability and convenience as key factors in switching to voice mail. In other words, voice mail makes every call count.

Supporters of voice mail say a well-designed voice mail system cuts down on missed phone calls, eliminates long waits on hold, delivers clear messages, and ends infuriating bouts of "telephone tag." In addition, modern systems can field routine calls quickly and automatically, which frees operators for those calls that require a personal response.

These new telecommunications marvels include automated attendant, sophisticated messaging services, and call processing—all available through the wonder of computer chips. These features enable phone systems to keep the often tangled web of business communications aligned and functioning smoothly.

Deciding to Install Voice Mail. Consultants advise that if you answer "yes" to two or more of the following questions, you probably should consider installing voice mail:

1. Do you spend a lot of time providing the same information to many callers?

2. Are most of your callers in different time zones?

3. Do you want to add services but lack the personnel to handle the phones?

4. Do callers complain that they frequently get busy signals?

5. Could your customers order your product or service after hearing an informational message without speaking to you personally?

6. Do you often work on a number of projects at the same time?[4]

Table 20.5 provides information on different voice mail systems and how they can be acquired.

For small businesses or home-based workers, usually using a service offered by the local phone company or outside service bureau is probably the simplest, most effective, and least expensive, at least in the short run. You pay anywhere from $5 to $20 a month for voice messaging and answering options, depending on the number of mailboxes and other options you require. Typically, a voice messaging system works this way. When you pick up your phone, a beeping tone notifies you that you have a message waiting, which you retrieve by dialing a special number. Another advantage of this option is you can also pick up messages from any other touch-tone phone by dialing a special message number assigned to your account.

What Can Voice Mail Systems Do for the Business Office?

Voice mail systems can answer and route calls, direct inquiries, record messages, provide information, and take sales orders.

What Types of Voice Mail Systems Are Available to a Business?

1. You can buy and install a voice mail board in your computer. The voice mail software runs in the background while you work in another program. You record a greeting or series of greetings and callers leave voice messages stored on your disk. You receive an on-screen notification that you have a message. One possible drawback to voice mail is that you have to leave the computer on to keep voice mail active. The main advantage of voice mail boards is their low cost. They start at around $200.

2. You can purchase a stand-alone system. This stand-alone system includes its own computer. All you do is plug it into your power and phone lines, record your outgoing messages, and you are in business. However, the stand-alone voice mail systems are expensive, starting at around $3,000, so they make the most sense for a large business with several phone lines and many workers.

3. You can use a service offered by your local telephone company or an outside service bureau.

Table 20.5

Voice Mail
Systems

Concerns About Voice Mail. It is true that among the more frustrating technological developments of recent years are the automated phone-answering systems that imprison callers in loops, sentencing them to listen to endless recorded messages. Often, potential customers are left yearning for a human voice or just to go back to the previous menu.

According to Donald Van Doren, president of Vanguard Communications Corporation in New Jersey, the way to avoid trapping your callers has more to do with *how* you set up your system than with *which* system you choose. He makes these suggestions:

1. Decide whose phones should and should not be answered by voice mail. For instance, people should answer lines directed to receptionists, customer service representatives, and top managers.

2. Make sure callers get clear instructions on how to reach a "live" person again after they have been routed to individual voice mailboxes. Keep recorded instructions brief.

3. Change your outgoing message whenever you plan to be out of the office or tied up in meetings. Ideally, you should change your message every day.[5]

MAILING SYSTEMS

The mailroom technology field is one of the fastest growing, thanks in part to new software applications and in part to the impetus provided by the 1996 Mail Classification Reform, the most sweeping changes in mail in the last century. What will the reform do? Mailers can reduce their postage to 26 cents or less by conforming with the United States Postal Service address quality standards, printing the delivery point bar code, mailing in quantities of 500 or more pieces in trays, and performing minimal sorting.[6]

Most businesses rely heavily on communicating with their customers and clients. Efficient mail systems are designed and set up in organizations to ensure cost effectiveness and efficiency, thereby delivering better service to customers.

For that reason, AOMs need to advise others in the organization about how to get the maximum benefits from mail services. Workers, for example, need to know what postal and delivery services are available and the procedures to follow when processing and routing incoming and outgoing mail.

Mail Services

Although fax machines are cost-effective and quick when used to send information, the U.S. Postal Service offers several delivery services to corporate customers that can be more effective than other methods. These types of services include special delivery, certificates of mailing, certified mail, collect on delivery, return receipts, insurance, registered mail, express overnight, 2- to 3-day delivery, and many forms of international mail service. In addition, you can use commercial delivery services such as Federal Express, United Parcel Service, or a variety of air delivery services.

Advanced Mail Equipment

Inserting machines, sorting equipment, and other forms of document processing technology can help companies manage their mail more effectively. Mail sorting automation can generate financial and labor savings and improve communications management. Companies benefit from postal discounts, improved accuracy of mailings, and a more integrated messaging process.

A number of factors need to be considered when purchasing document-processing equipment. After considering the strategies and objectives of the organization, attention should be paid to details such as systems compatibility, floor space, environmental requirements, staffing and scheduling, and operator skill level. Today, the more automated the mail, the greater the postal and labor savings. Along with savings, automation brings increased productivity and improved control over the messaging process.[7]

Mail Procedures

The U.S. Post Office provides postal business centers in each state to help speed mail processing. If clients complain that it takes forever to get company mail, the postal business center will, upon request, review your company's mail-room procedures and suggest ways to save money. A typical scenario might be a letter impeccably written and typed, but improperly addressed. This letter could wander through the recipient's office building for days.

For companies to process mail accurately and efficiently, each employee should be trained in the process of incoming and outgoing mail procedures. As a reminder to AOMs, the typical procedures for processing incoming and outgoing mail are reviewed in Table 20.6.

Incoming Mail	1. Sort the mail.
	2. Open the mail.
	3. Date and time stamp the mail.
	4. Read and annotate the mail.
	5. Prioritize and arrange the mail.
	6. Perform other activities such as attaching related material, using action-requested slips, saving advertisements and circulars (junk mail), and keeping a mail register.
	7. Distribute the mail.
Outgoing Mail	1. Assemble the mail in proper order if there is more than one page.
	2. Make sure the letter has been signed.
	3. Check that any enclosures have been included with the letter.
	4. Verify that the address on the letter and the address on the envelope are the same.
	5. Select the appropriate mail classification from among first class, second class, third class, fourth class, or express mail.

Table 20.6
Basic Procedures for Processing Incoming and Outgoing Mail

ACCOUNTING SYSTEMS

Business organizations of all types must keep financial records and establish accounting systems either electronically through the use of computers or manually with paper. One reason the government requires businesses to keep records is that certain information must be reported to the Internal Revenue Service on a periodic basis. Another reason is that accurate records are the basis for sound business decisions.

Businesses thrive, in part, as a result of maintaining accurate, up-to-date records in usable form. This is because competition in business rewards maximum efficiency. Inaccurate accounting records can contribute to business failure and bankruptcy. As business owners and managers strive for economic success, sound decisions and plans require the use of complete and accurately prepared accounting cycle information.

Accounting Cycle

The **accounting cycle** involves recording, classifying, and summarizing financial information for owners, managers, and other interested parties. Summaries of financial information are reported for a specific period of time in the form of financial statements.

Financial Statements

Financial statements permit owners, managers, and accountants to analyze business activities and interpret their effectiveness. Analyzing financial statements provides answers to questions such as "How do sales and profits from this year compare with sales and profits from the last two years?" or "What was our cash flow this month?"

All businesses should prepare financial statements on a regular basis so that any changes or trends can be noted immediately. Although office managers do not prepare financial statements per se, they should understand their importance and be able to interpret critical data from them that indicate trends or changes affecting office administration. In organizations, usually the accounting department or business office is available to assist in these financial areas. The two most common financial statements used to answer these types of questions or track records are the balance sheet and the income statement.

Balance Sheet. The **balance sheet** shows the financial condition of a business at a particular time—for example, on December 31 or June 30. In reality, the details of a company's financial condition change constantly. Every day, a company pays bills and receives payments. Every day, some inventory is used and must be replaced. All balance sheets, however, must satisfy this basic accounting equation:

$$\text{Assets} = \text{Liabilities} + \text{Capital.}$$

Figure 20.2 shows an example of a simple balance sheet.

Income Statement. An **income statement** is a summary of all income and expenses for a certain time period, such as a month or year. It is probably the most frequently studied of all financial statements. Owners study an income statement to determine how much profit they are making. Bankers study income statements to decide whether to approve a business loan.

INTERNATIONAL BUSINESS SERVICES
BALANCE SHEET
9/30/—

ASSETS

Cash	$141,211	
Petty Cash	500	
Supplies—Office	2,737	
Total Assets		**$144,448**

LIABILITIES

Phoenix Office Supply	$ 1,118	

CAPITAL

Patricia Gibson, Capital	143,330	
Total Liabilities and Capital		**$144,448**

Unlike a balance sheet, which represents a stationary financial picture, an income statement reflects a business's profitability over a given time period. The accounting formula for income statements is as follows:

Net Income = Revenue − Expenses.

An example of a simple income statement is represented in Figure 20.3.

INTERNATIONAL BUSINESS SERVICES
INCOME STATEMENT
FOR PERIOD ENDED 9/30/—

REVENUE

Computer Consulting Fees	$72,375	
Human Resources Consulting Fees	26,090	
Total Revenue		**$98,465**

EXPENSES

Advertising Expense	$ 585	
Rent Expense	1,200	
Utilities Expense	265	
Supplies Expense—Office	295	
Salaries	71,600	
Total Expenses		73,945

NET INCOME | | | **$24,520**

Message *for* AOMs

"

As we enter the twenty-first century, the pace of change seems faster and faster. The one thing we know is that tomorrow's business will be very different from today's business. However, some things do not or should not change, even as we get more technologically advanced. Customers still expect their needs to be met by office staff in a timely, consistent fashion.

In other words, customers have grown to expect a company they do business with to serve them in an exemplary fashion.

An AOM needs to stay on top of the office systems on a daily basis. There is no doubt technology will make these systems easier to handle by office staff; however, office workers are critical to the efficiency of the systems and the direct link to customers.

1 In addition to the computer, other major office systems include records management, reprographics (copier), telephone, mail, and accounting systems.

2 The four classifications for records are vital, important, useful, and nonessential.

3 Microfilm, which generally comes as a 35-mm or 16-mm roll of film, is a proven archival medium for long-term storage with low equipment costs and comparatively fast retrieval. Microfiche, on the other hand, consists of index-card-sized film that can be read on a broad variety of microfiche readers or printed out in the form of paper enlargements, usually 8 ½" × 11".

4 An office copier system can be set up either as a centralized copy center where copier specialists perform all copying for employees or as several decentralized copiers available to any employee on an "on-demand" basis.

5 Special features that can be added to a phone system include call-waiting, caller ID, call-waiting ID, voice messaging service, call forwarding, call rejection, call trace, continuous redial, last-call return, priority call, selective call forwarding, speed calling, caller ID blocking options, and three-way calling.

6 Supporters of voice mail say a well-designed voice mail system cuts down on missed phone calls, eliminates long waits on hold, delivers clear messages, and ends infuriating bouts of "telephone tag."

7 Typical U.S. Postal services include special delivery, certificates of mailing, certified mail, collect on delivery, return receipts, insurance, registered mail, express overnight, 2- to 3-day delivery, and many forms of international mail.

8 All businesses should prepare financial statements on a regular basis so that any changes or trends can be noted immediately and decisions can be more accurate.

QUESTIONS FOR CRITICAL THINKING

1. Of the fourteen optional features mentioned in the chapter, recommend four special features that can be added and adapted to an organization's telephone system that you feel best serve the customers' needs.

2. What are the advantages to the customer or business of a well-designed voice mail system?

3. In your opinion, are the services that the U.S. Postal Service offers unique when compared to other commercial mail delivery services? Explain.

4. What are the major advantages and disadvantages of the decentralized copier approach?

5. Based on your experience as a student, have previous schools you've attended had good records management systems? Briefly describe your experiences.

6. How is the purpose of a balance sheet different from the purpose of an income statement?

Case Study 20-1: The Displaced Receptionist

A new chief executive officer (CEO) has just been brought in to run Accessories Unlimited, a well-established company with more than 200 employees. Mr. Casey Donoho, the new CEO, is so different from Mr. Ray Garcia (the former CEO) in his approach to innovative systems that it has many employees just a little bit nervous.

For example, Mr. Donoho wants to change Hilda's job. Hilda has been the only receptionist at the company for more than 15 years. Mr. Donoho says that within 3 weeks Accessories Unlimited will have a fully automated voice mail system installed, and Hilda will become a part of the new customer service team. (No one knows what that is yet.) Mr. Donoho also informed staff that customer service training will start next month. There is also a rumor that some managers may go back into their old positions. For now, morale is very low at Accessories Unlimited.

Discussion Questions

1. If you were an employee at Accessories Unlimited, how would you feel right about now?

2. Is there cause for alarm in the organization, or is this a natural development as companies become more competitive in a world-class economy? Discuss your ideas.

3. If you were to advise your closest friends at work on what their response to this new CEO should be, what would you say?

Case Study 20-2: A Real Hodgepodge Record System

Reynolds Steelcase Products in Tallahassee, Florida, has been manufacturing filing cabinets and other products for 20 years. It has 35 employees and enjoys $2 million in sales annually. Recently, however, it has become apparent that there is a problem in their current computerized and manual record-keeping procedures.

The departments—sales, accounting, production, and shipping—realize they are making frequent errors because of information they cannot find and are wasting time and supplies having to redo a form or other documents in the course of each day's work.

Discussion Questions

1. What effect would the following suggestions have on providing a solution to the problems Reynolds Steelcase Products is facing?

   - Install a computer network with terminals in each department.
   - Assign a person to be responsible for records management throughout the company.

2. Which of the two suggestions would you implement first and why?

Case Study 20-3: Internet Research Activity

Assume you are doing an oral report on *trends in office copier systems.* Access the home pages of Xerox and Canon copiers and describe the most recent copier systems for each company. Include, for example, the major features, speed, cost, and ordering procedure. As a result of your research, list three items of current information you might use in your report about each company's most recent copier products.

Endnotes

[1]Susan Z. Diamond, "A Precious Resource," *The Secretary,* January 1997, pp. 9–10.

[2]Rick Friedman, "Copier Controls Cut Costs," *The Office,* January 1993, p. 66.

[3]Mie-Yun Lee, "Clear As Day," *Inc., Tech 1998,* August 1998, p. 114.

[4]June Langhoff, "Is it Time to Junk Your Answering Machine?" *Home Office Computing,* February 1993, p. 44.

[5]Sarah Glazer, "Before and After," *Inc.,* June 1994, p. 78.

[6]"Mailroom Automation Is Today's Necessity," *Managing Office Technology,* August 1996, p. 31.

[7]Carro Ford, "Advanced Mail Equipment Pushes the Envelope," *Managing Office Technology,* September 1997, p. 48.

glossary

Accountability: The process that involves judging the extent to which employees fulfill their responsibilities.

Accounting Cycle: The process of recording, classifying, and summarizing financial information for owners, managers, and other interested parties.

Active Listening: A restatement of the sender's total communication to include both thoughts and feelings.

Alternative Work Systems: Nontraditional working arrangements that include office sharing, job sharing, flextime, and telecommuting.

Americans with Disabilities Act (ADA): Legislation that provides people with physical or mental disabilities legal recourse to redress disability discrimination.

Authority: The right to do something, to tell someone else to do it, or to make decisions that affect the reaching of organizational objectives.

b

Balance Sheet: A financial statement that shows the financial condition of a business at a particular time.

Biometrics Devices: The use of a device that authenticates a person requesting access by verifying personal characteristics such as fingerprints, signature, and retinal (eye) and voice patterns.

Broadbanding: The technique to organize employees into a few broad job categories, rather than the dozens of titles used in traditional systems.

Buddy System: The practice in some organizations that matches a new employee with an experienced employee who maintains close contact with the new employee and lends support by answering routine questions.

Budgets: Statements of planned revenues and expenditures which are organized by category and period of time.

Burnout: A stress-related affliction resulting when people invest most of their time and energy in a particular activity.

Cafeteria Benefit Plan: A flexible benefits package whereby employees select which benefits they want to receive up to a certain dollar amount and are able to tailor a plan to their needs.

Call Center: An umbrella term that refers to customer information centers, help desks, reservation centers, or customer-service centers.

Centralized Authority: The concentration of power and authority is near the top of an organization or similar functions are carried out in one place.

Certified Professional Secretary (CPS): The rating that is awarded to those who pass a one-day, three-part examination and have a specific number of years of experience in the administrative support/secretarial profession.

Chain of Command: The means of showing the authority-responsibility relationships that link superiors and subordinates throughout the entire organization.

Collaborative Screen Sharing: A communication method that uses a simple audio hookup to link conversations and computer screens to view and manipulate the same page layout or diagram.

Communication: The exchange of messages, which can be verbal, using spoken or written words; or non-verbal, using symbols, gestures, expressions, and body language.

Compact Disk Read-Only Memory (CD-ROM): A prerecorded optical disk that can store in excess of 300,000 pages of information.

Comparable Worth: An employment concept which implies that jobs with comparable levels of knowledge, skill, and ability should be paid similarly even if actual duties differ significantly.

Compensatory Time Off: A method of allowing employees to take time off in lieu of payment for time worked.

Compressed Workweek: An alternative workstyle that condenses the hours worked each week into fewer days.

Computer: An electronic device operating under the control of instructions stored in its memory.

Computer Monitoring: The use of computers to observe, record, and review an individual's use of the computer, including communications such as e-mail, keyboard activity, and Internet sites visited.

Computer Network: The linking together of central processing units and terminals via a communication system that allows users at different locations to share files, devices, and programs.

Computer Output Microfilm (COM): The medium that accepts computer data directly to microfilm through automated conversion of digital information.

Computer System: A group of computer devices that are connected, coordinated, and linked in such a way that they work as one to complete a task.

Connectivity: A concept that gives equal support to members of a work group by efficiently moving electronic information from point A to point B.

Continuous Improvement Process (CIP): An ongoing, continuous commitment to prevention of problems by focusing on the process.

Controlling: The management function of devising ways and means of ensuring that planned performance throughout the process is actually achieved.

Cookie: A small file that a Web server stores on your computer that contains data about you, such as your user name or viewing preferences.

Core Competencies: The root business a company is in and the primary functions of that business.

Corporate Culture: A set of behaviors or qualities that is valued in an organization not because competition forces all companies to value them but simply because that's the way things are.

Corporate Universities: A concept for organized learning that is designed to perpetuate the organization by providing all training and education at a given company.

Cross-Functional Teams: A group of workers from different areas in an organization who work together in a way that makes them aware of changes that may affect their individual jobs.

Cultural Diversity: Human qualities that are different from our own and outside the groups to which we belong.

Customer: An individual inside or outside an organization who depends on the output of an organization's efforts.

Cyberconcierge: A person who helps travelers in certain airports receive e-mail, participate in a conference call, get a fax, or surf the Net.

Database Management: Software that computerizes and manages record-keeping and information tasks by storing, organizing, and retrieving information more efficiently than by using paper file folders.

Decentralized Authority: The concentration of power and authority is dispersed to successively lower levels of the organization.

Decision Making: The process of choosing between two or more alternative courses of action.

Defensive Reaction: A way of thinking that cushions the blow resulting from an immediate inability to overcome an obstacle or barrier that has been placed in a person's path.

Delegation: The process by which managers distribute and entrust activities and related authority to subordinates in the organization.

Desktop Publishing (DTP):   Software that uses a computer to assemble words and illustrations on pages and to print those pages on a high-quality printer.

Digital Cameras: Devices that capture images with sensors and computer memories rather than with traditional film.

Digital Copiers: A unit that scans documents, converts them into computer files, and then prints copies from those files.

Direct Compensation: An employee's base pay as well as any incentive pay programs.

Downward Communication: The manner in which communication follows the organization's formal chain of command from top to bottom.

e

Effectiveness: The ability to get the "right things" accomplished by selecting the most suitable goals and the proper steps, people, and physical resources to achieve them.

Efficiency: The ability to "get things right" in a reasonable and timely manner with a minimum expenditure of resources.

Electronic Commerce (e-commerce):   A means for Internet users to perform such activities as shopping, investing, and banking that uses either electronic money or electronic data interchange.

Electronic Data Interchange (EDI):   The transmission of business documents or data over communications media.

Electronic Mail (e-mail):   The process of delivering mail by electronic signals over telecommunication lines using a personal computer or desktop terminal.

Electronic Money (e-money):   A means of paying for goods and services over the Internet.

Employee Selection: The process of choosing individuals who have relevant qualifications to fill jobs in an organization.

Employment Application Form: A document that is the basis for screening minimum qualifications; becomes the basis for any subsequent interview.

Employment Recruitment: The process of generating a pool of qualified applicants for organizational job vacancies.

Empowerment: The process of giving employees closest to the customer the authority and tools needed to make more decisions.

Equal Employment Opportunity Act: Federal legislation that forbids discrimination on the basis of race, sex, religion, or national origin.

Equal Employment Opportunity Commission (EEOC):   Federal agency that handles complaints relative to race, sex, color, religion, and national origin plus age and disability discrimination and compensation charges.

Equal Pay Act of 1963:   Federal legislation that provides equal pay for equal work, regardless of sex.

Ergonomics: A concept that furniture, equipment, and office products should fit people, not the reverse.

Ethics: The systematic thinking about the moral consequences of decisions.

Exempt Employees: Workers who are not paid overtime and usually are classified as either professional or administrative.

Exit Interview: The process of obtaining information from departing employees concerning their experiences with various aspects of their employment.

f

Facsimile (fax): A machine that translates copies of text or graphics documents into electronic signals, which are then transmitted over telephone lines or by satellite.

Fair Labor Standards Act (FLSA): The major law affecting compensation administration in organizations.

Feedback: The verbal and nonverbal responses that the receiver gives by further communicating with the original sender or another person.

File Server: A computer device and part of the LAN that allows for sharing of peripheral devices such as printers and hard-disk storage units.

Filtering: The tendency for a message to be watered down or halted completely at some point during transmission.

Firewall: A general term that refers to both hardware and software used to restrict access to data on a network.

Formal groups: A type of grouping in organizations that is deliberately formed and created by management for the purpose of attaining organizational goals and objectives.

Gigabyte (GB): A measure of computer storage capacity that is equal to approximately one billion bytes.

Grapevine: The transmission of information by word of mouth without regard for organizational levels.

Graphics Software: An application software package used to present numerical data clearly and quickly in visual form on a computer.

Group: Two or more people who personally interact with each other in order to achieve a common goal.

Groupthink: The tendency of highly cohesive groups to lose their critical evaluative abilities and, out of a desire for unanimity, overlook realistic, meaningful alternatives as attitudes are formed and decisions are made.

Groupware: Collaborative software that combines with electronic technology and group processes to support teams and organizations as they work together on projects and share information over a network.

h

Hacking: An illegal activity of gaining unauthorized access to another computer.

Hard Disks: Nonvolatile storage devices; a permanent part of a hard disk drive encased within the system unit.

Hidden Agendas: The composition of attitudes and feelings that an individual brings to the group.

Horizontal Organizations: The trend in organizations to manage "across" in a more flat manner rather than "up and down" in a top-heavy hierarchy.

Hostile Work Environment: A type of sexual harassment where supervisors or co-workers do things to make the work atmosphere more difficult for people based on their gender.

Human Resource Management: The functional area in organizations that develops plans and practices that facilitate realizing the full potential of workers and using that potential to pursue the organization's quality and performance objectives.

i

Incentive Plans: Optional compensation plans, usually based on set criteria, which reward an employee for efforts beyond normal performance expectations.

Income Statement: A financial statement that summarizes all income and expenses for a certain period of time.

Incremental Budgeting: The budgeting method of adding a given percentage of increase (the increment) to the budgeted amounts of the preceding period to arrive at new figures.

Indirect Compensation: The whole array of benefits employees are entitled to, including those required by law and others that are voluntary benefits offered by the company.

Informal Groups: A type of grouping in organizations that arises spontaneously throughout all levels of the company and evolves out of employees' needs for social interaction, friendship, communication, and status.

Information: Data that has been processed and is useful in decision making.

Information Technology (IT): The study, design, development, implementation, support, and management of computer-based information systems—particularly software applications and computer hardware. Also technology that combines computing with telecommunications and networking to produce usable information.

Information Technology (IT) Department: The departmental area in organizations that has overall responsibility for the manner in which networked computers, information technology equipment, and software are used throughout the organization.

Injunction: A court order requiring a person or corporation to do or to refrain from doing a particular act.

Integration: A conflict management technique that includes bringing the conflicting parties together to discuss the issues face-to-face.

Internet: An international "network of networks" comprised of government, academic, and business-related networks that allows people at diverse locations around the world to communicate through electronic mail, to transfer files back and forth, and to log on to remote computer facilities.

Intranets: The internal networks of particular company data that use Internet and Web technology.

Job Analysis: The process of collecting and organizing information about jobs performed in the organization.

Job Description: A written definition that describes the tasks, duties, and responsibilities of a particular job.

Job Sharing: The alternative workstyle that allows two people to share the duties—and prorate the salaries and benefits—of one full-time position.

Job Specification: A written description that clarifies the knowledge, degree, skills, and abilities a worker needs in order to do the job competently.

Just-in-Time Hiring: A hiring practice that allows workers who are equipped with many different abilities to have an improved chance of finding employment through temporary work situations in various company settings.

Knowledge Management: The capturing, communicating, and connecting of information with information seekers.

Labor Unions: Associations of employees formed to represent workforce concerns and interests during negotiations with management.

Lateral Communication: The communication that occurs between departments or functional units, usually as a coordinating or problem-solving effort.

Leading: The management function of motivating individuals and influencing group activities to accomplish objectives.

Learning Organization: The concept that training in organizations is central to actual work.

Lifelong Learning: A concept that stresses the importance of continuous learning to upgrade skills, attitudes, and ideas.

Local-Area Network (LAN): A computer and communications network that covers a limited geographical area, allows every node to communicate with every other node, and does not require a central node or processor.

Lose-Lose Negotiating Style: A negotiating style that is created when one party attempts to win at the expense of the other.

Mainframes: A very fast, powerful, and multiuser computer system that is also freestanding and larger than most minicomputers and which requires special wiring and environmental controls to operate efficiently.

Management: The process of administering and coordinating resources in an effort to achieve the goals of the organization.

Management Information System: An integrated computer system that provides information and aids in decision making in organizations.

Mentor: An adviser, teacher, sounding board, cheerleader, and critic with whom a worker can freely talk through problems, analyze mistakes, and celebrate successes.

Microcomputer: The computer system that is the smallest in size, has the least amount of memory capacity, is slower, and costs the least compared to the other computer systems. Also known as a PC or personal computer.

Microfiche: A medium consisting of index-card-sized film that can be read on a broad variety of microfiche readers or printed out on paper.

Microfilm: An archival medium which generally comes as a 35-mm or 16-mm roll of film that is used for long-term storage and has low equipment costs and comparatively fast retrieval.

Minicomputers: Computers that are larger than desktop microcomputers and servers and are popular for multiuser applications.

Modem: A device used to link a computer to telephone lines, so that communicating with other computers is possible.

Modular Design: The design of office furniture that facilitates the use of different components and variations in the way those components are arranged.

Modular Furniture: A collection of integrated, interdependent furniture components that can be quickly and easily assembled, disassembled, and rearranged to meet employee and department needs.

Monitor: A device that resembles a television set and displays output on a screen.

Mouse: A device used for moving the cursor-like insertion point around the text and for pointing.

Multiskilling: The informal training concept that requires team members to learn every job on the team in order to cover for each other and to respond quickly when conditions change.

Nepotism: The practice of allowing relatives to work for the same employer.

Network Operating System (NOS): A special control program that resides in a file server within a LAN system.

Node: A station, terminal, computer, or other device in a computer network.

Nonexempt Employees: Workers who work overtime and are usually paid an hourly wage.

Norm: A generally agreed-upon standard of behavior that every member of the group is expected to follow.

Notebook Computers: General-purpose computers that are small enough to be carried in a briefcase and can run most application software packages.

Objectives: The end result, the goals or targets that an organization, department, or individual seeks to attain.

Office Layout: The arrangement of facilities and workstations in an organization.

Office Manuals: An office tool that includes procedures that specify a standard way for dealing with recurring situations or activities so that they will be handled uniformly throughout an organization.

Open plan: An office layout designed to foster the free flow of information, characterized by the lack of interior walls and the freestanding placement of desks, partitions, and other office furnishings.

Organizing: The multifaceted management function that gets things done.

Orientation: The activity that specifically prepares employees for working in a particular organization and working environment.

Outsourcing: A management strategy by which an organization utilizes specialized, efficient service providers to perform major, noncore functions.

P

Paradigm: A set of assumptions or a frame of reference.

Paradigm Shift: A fundamental change in the assumptions that are made about a certain body of knowledge.

Pension Plans: The retirement benefits established and funded by employers and employees.

Performance Appraisal: The evaluation and constructive criticism of an employee's work.

Peripherals: Hardware devices that are optional to the operation of the basic computer unit.

Permatemps: The type of employee who is a long-term temporary employee because of corporate downsizing and high-tech labor shortages in organizations.

Personal Power: An informal authority manifested by the extent to which followers are willing to follow a leader.

Personality Disorders: The defensive reactions and abnormal behaviors motivated by a person's need to survive.

Pilferage: The taking (theft) of items or services without permission.

Planning: The management function of choosing or generating organizational objectives and then determining the courses of action needed to achieve those objectives.

Policy: A written guideline about workplace issues.

Portable Skills: The skills that allow persons to transfer what they already know to slightly new situations.

Portfolio: A collection of items that document and chronicle a worker's accomplishments.

Position Approval Form: A document used to identify the position title, related classification, and essential functions of the position and the duties, experience, education, and training needed to perform the duties.

Position Power: The formal authority granted by the organization giving employees permission to tell others what to do.

Prevention: The concept that problems can be resolved before they occur by doing the job right the first time.

Previewing: The process of scanning a document, looking for main points, and discovering how the material is organized.

Principles: Broad, general statements that are considered to be true and that accurately reflect real-world conditions in all walks of life.

Procedure: A written, step-by-step standardized pattern of behavior that is followed when completing a specific task or activity.

q

Quality: The extent to which the customers or users believe the product or service meets, or preferably surpasses, their needs and expectations.

r

Random-Access Memory (RAM): Memory chips that reside in the system unit where program and document instructions are stored while the user is working on them. Also called main memory or primary storage.

Read-Only Memory (ROM): Chips that are used for the permanent storage of certain instructions inside the computer system unit.

Ready-to-Assemble (RTA) Products: Pieces of furniture the consumer or home office worker puts together at home.

Reasonable Accommodation: A modification or an adjustment to a job or the work environment that will enable a qualified applicant or employee with a disability to perform essential job functions.

Records Management: The organizational function that deals with the control, retention, and security of records and files.

Reengineering: A name for the stem-to-stern redesign of the way a company works, from its organizational structure to its corporate culture.

Reframing: The process of looking for evidence of a more positive, less catastrophic, view of some change.

Responsibility: The obligation that is created when an employee accepts a manager's delegation of authority.

s

Scanner: An input device that acts like a miniature photocopy machine connected to a computer that copies graphic images and typewritten pages into the computer's memory.

Serious Health Condition: One requiring inpatient, hospital, hospice, or residential medical care by a physician and one that prevents a person from going about his or her regular activities for three or more consecutive days.

Server Computers: Computer system designed to support a computer network that allows all employees to share files, application software, hardware, and other network resources.

Sexual Harassment: Unwelcome sexual advances, requests for sexual favors, and other verbal or physical conduct of a sexual nature that creates an intimidating, offensive, or hostile work environment.

Shredders: Devices that provide document security in the office by destroying sensitive paper material while at the same time helping the environment.

Software: A group of instructions executed by the computer. Also known as a program.

Span of Control: A management principle that describes the number of employees who are directly supervised by one person.

Specialist: A person who masters or becomes expert at doing a certain type of work.

Spreadsheets: Software that serves as a financial planning tool that performs mathematical calculations in organizations.

Strategic Planning Process: An activity that defines an organization's mission, sets its objectives, and develops strategies that will enable it to operate successfully in its internal and external environment.

Stress: Any external stimulus that produces wear and tear on a person's psychological or physical well-being.

Supercomputers: The largest, fastest, and most expensive computer system available, used mainly for scientific applications requiring great speed and enormous memory capacity.

System: A group of parts that are interrelated in a manner that forms a unified whole and works together to attain a definite objective.

Technojargon: A trendy expression of technical terms.

Technology: An aid to make a task easier by using equipment and procedures to create, process, and output information.

Telecommunications: The transfer of data from one place to another over communication lines or channels; includes the communication of all forms of information, including voice and video.

Telecommuting: An alternative workstyle that allows workers to perform their work at home connected to office database and information systems through telecommunications equipment and connected computers.

Teleconferencing: A phone conferencing technology that allows for audio-only conferences and permits in excess of sixty people to call in at once.

Terabyte (TB): A measure of computer storage capacity that is equal to approximately one trillion bytes.

Theory: The general framework that explains the basic relationships among sets of principles.

Theory X: The view in worker behavior that assumes people generally dislike work, lack ambition, and work primarily because they have to get money to live.

Theory Y: The view in worker behavior that assumes people generally see work as natural as rest or play and that workers will accept responsibility when self-direction and self-control can be used to pursue valued objectives.

Theory Z: The view in organizations that emphasizes long-range planning, consensus decision making, and strong mutual worker-employer loyalty to achieve increased productivity.

Total Compensation Package: A method of describing both direct compensation and indirect compensation that an employee may receive.

Total Quality Management (TQM): A philosophy of management that applies quality principles to everything that a company does.

Training: Specific preparation to carry out the tasks and functions of a particular job.

Train-the-Trainer Workshops: Training situations specifically designed to support in-house training needs that teach peer experts interactive and instructional skills.

Transactional Employment: The work environment where employees continuously develop their skills to allow them to constantly jump from one employer to another.

Unity of Command: A management principle which states that each employee should receive orders from, and be responsible to, only one supervisor.

Upward Communication: The feedback of data or information from lower levels in the organization to upper management levels.

Value-Driven Companies: Organizations that find ways to link their daily operations to social and environmental concerns, as well as to integrate employee and community well-being into their decision making.

Videoconferencing: A long-distance communication option that provides two-way audio, two-way video and two-way document exchange.

Virtual Assistants: Working arrangement that allows office support workers to perform administrative tasks in their own homes.

Virtual Organizations: Collaborative networks that make it possible to draw on vital resources as needed in organizations, regardless of where they are located physically and regardless of who owns them—supplier or customer.

Virtual Workers: People who work at home or away from the workplace and have their own computers and data communication devices.

Voice Mail: A computerized telephone system that allows callers to leave messages.

Wage Survey: A process used in developing a salary compensation policy where compensation data is gathered external and internal to the organization and then analyzed.

Win-Lose Negotiating Style: A negotiating style that assumes one side will win by achieving its goals and the other side will lose.

Win-Win Negotiating Style: A negotiating style that assumes a solution can be reached that will satisfy the needs of all parties.

Word Processing: Software that allows you to create, edit, format, print, and save documents.

Workflow: The movement of information from person to person within an organization.

Workflow Automation: A type of office software that manages workflow and on-line documents.

Workplace Literacy: The aspect of functional literacy that is related to employability and skill requirements for particular jobs.

World Wide Web (WWW):   A worldwide collection of electronic documents called web home pages that have built-in links to other related documents.

Z

Zero-Base Budgeting: A resource-allocation method that requires budget makers to examine every expenditure anew each budget period and to justify the expenditure in light of current needs and developments.

index